Machine Learning

This book introduces machine learning for readers with some background in basic linear algebra, statistics, probability, and programming. In a coherent statistical framework, it covers a selection of supervised machine learning methods, from the most fundamental (k-nearest neighbours, decision trees, and linear and logistic regression) to more advanced methods (deep neural networks, support vector machines, Gaussian processes, random forests, and boosting), plus commonly used unsupervised methods (generative modelling, k-means, PCA, autoencoders, and generative adversarial networks). Careful explanations and pseudo-code are presented for all methods. The authors maintain a focus on the fundamentals by drawing connections between methods and discussing general concepts such as loss functions, maximum likelihood, the bias-variance decomposition, ensemble averaging, kernels, and the Bayesian approach along with generally useful tools such as regularisation, cross validation, evaluation metrics, and optimisation methods. The final chapters offer practical advice for solving real-world supervised machine learning problems and on ethical aspects of modern machine learning.

Andreas Lindholm is a machine learning research engineer at Annotell in Gothenburg, Sweden, working with data annotation and data quality questions for autonomous driving.

Niklas Wahlström is Assistant Professor at the Division of Systems and Control, Department of Information Technology, Uppsala University.

Fredrik Lindsten is Associate Professor at the Division of Statistics and Machine Learning, Department of Computer and Information Science, Linköping University.

Thomas B. Schön is Beijer Professor of Artificial Intelligence, Department of Information Technology, Uppsala University.

Machine Learning

A First Course for Engineers and Scientists

ANDREAS LINDHOLM

Annotell, Sweden

NIKLAS WAHLSTRÖM

Uppsala University, Sweden

FREDRIK LINDSTEN

Linköping University, Sweden

THOMAS B. SCHÖN

Uppsala University, Sweden

CAMBRIDGE
UNIVERSITY PRESS

University Printing House, Cambridge CB2 8BS, United Kingdom

One Liberty Plaza, 20th Floor, New York, NY 10006, USA

477 Williamstown Road, Port Melbourne, VIC 3207, Australia

314–321, 3rd Floor, Plot 3, Splendor Forum, Jasola District Centre,
New Delhi – 110025, India

103 Penang Road, #05–06/07, Visioncrest Commercial, Singapore 238467

Cambridge University Press is part of the University of Cambridge.

It furthers the University's mission by disseminating knowledge in the pursuit of
education, learning, and research at the highest international levels of excellence.

www.cambridge.org
Information on this title: www.cambridge.org/9781108843607
DOI: 10.1017/9781108919371

First published 2022

Printed in the United Kingdom by TJ Books Ltd, Padstow Cornwall

A catalogue record for this publication is available from the British Library.

Library of Congress Cataloging-in-Publication Data
Names: Lindholm, Andreas, 1989- author.
Title: Machine learning : a first course for engineers and scientists /
   Andreas Lindholm, Annotell, Niklas Wahlström, Uppsala Universitet,
   Sweden, Fredrik Lindsten, Linköping University, Thomas B. Schön,
   Uppsala Universitet, Sweden.
Description: Cambridge, UK ; New York, NY : Cambridge University Press, 2022. |
   Includes bibliographical references and index.
Identifiers: LCCN 2021030297 (print) | LCCN 2021030298 (ebook) |
   ISBN 9781108843607 (hardback) | ISBN 9781108919371 (epub)
Subjects: LCSH: Machine learning.
Classification: LCC Q325.5 .L56 2021 (print) | LCC Q325.5 (ebook) |
   DDC 006.3/1–dc23
LC record available at https://lccn.loc.gov/2021030297
LC ebook record available at https://lccn.loc.gov/2021030298

ISBN 978-1-108-84360-7 Hardback

Contents

Contents

Acknowledgements

Many people have helped us throughout the writing of this book. First of all, we want to mention David Sumpter, who, in addition to giving feedback from using the material for teaching, contributed the entire Chapter 12 on ethical aspects. We have also received valuable feedback from many students and other teacher colleagues. We are, of course, very grateful for each and every comment we have received; in particular, we want to mention David Widmann, Adrian Wills, Johannes Hendricks, Mattias Villani, Dmitrijs Kass, and Joel Oskarsson. We have also received useful feedback on the technical content of the book, including the practical insights in Chapter 11, from Agrin Hilmkil (at Peltarion), Salla Franzén and Alla Tarighati (at SEB), Lawrence Murray (at Uber), James Hensman and Alexis Boukouvalas (at Secondmind), Joel Kronander and Nand Dalal (at Nines), and Peter Lindskog and Jacob Roll (at Arriver). We also received valuable comments from Arno Solin on Chapters 8 and 9, and Joakim Lindblad on Chapter 6. Several people helped us with the figures illustrating the examples in Chapter 1, namely Antônio Ribeiro (Figure 1.1), Fredrik K. Gustafsson (Figure 1.4), and Theodoros Damoulas (Figure 1.5). Thank you all for your help!

During the writing of this book, we enjoyed financial support from AI Competence for Sweden, the Swedish Research Council (projects: 2016-04278, 2016-06079, 2017-03807, 2020-04122), the Swedish Foundation for Strategic Research (projects: ICA16-0015, RIT12-0012), the Wallenberg AI, Autonomous Systems and Software Program (WASP) funded by the Knut and Alice Wallenberg Foundation, ELLIIT, and the Kjell och Märta Beijer Foundation.

Finally, we are thankful to Lauren Cowles at Cambridge University Press for helpful advice and guidance through the publishing process and to Chris Cartwright for careful and helpful copyediting.

Notation

Symbol	Meaning

General mathematics

b	a scalar
$\mathbf{b}$	a vector
$\mathbf{B}$	a matrix
T	transpose
$\text{sign}(x)$	the sign operator; $+1$ if $x > 0$, -1 if $x < 0$
∇	del operator; ∇f is the gradient of f
$\|\mathbf{b}\|_2$	Euclidean norm of $\mathbf{b}$
$\|\mathbf{b}\|_1$	taxicab norm of $\mathbf{b}$
$p(z)$	probability density (if z is a continuous random variable) or probability mass (if z is a discrete random variable)
$p(z\|x)$	the probability density (or mass) for z conditioned on x
$\mathcal{N}(z; m, \sigma^2)$	the normal probability distribution for the random variable z with mean m and variance σ^2

The supervised learning problem

$\mathbf{x}$	input
y	output
$\mathbf{x}_\star$	test input
$y_\star$	test output
$\widehat{y}(\mathbf{x}_\star)$	a prediction of $y_\star$
ε	noise
n	number of data points in training data
$\mathcal{T}$	training data $\{\mathbf{x}_i, y_i\}_{i=1}^n$
L	loss function
J	cost function

Supervised methods

$\boldsymbol{\theta}$	parameters to be learned from training data
$g(\mathbf{x})$	model of $p(y \| \mathbf{x})$ (most classification methods)
λ	regularisation parameter
ϕ	link function (generalised linear models)
h	activation function (neural networks)

$\mathbf{W}$ weight matrix (neural networks)

$\mathbf{b}$ offset vector (neural networks)

γ learning rate

B number of members in an ensemble method

κ kernel

$\boldsymbol{\phi}$ nonlinear feature transformation (kernel methods)

d dimension of $\boldsymbol{\phi}$; number of features (kernel methods)

Evaluation of supervised methods

E error function

E_{new} new data error

E_{train} training data error

$E_{k\text{-fold}}$ estimate of E_{new} from k-fold cross validation

$E_{\text{hold-out}}$ estimate of E_{new} from hold-out validation data

1 Introduction

Machine learning is about learning, reasoning, and acting based on data. This is done by constructing computer programs that process the data, extract useful information, make predictions regarding unknown properties, and suggest actions to take or decisions to make. What turns data analysis into machine learning is that the process is automated and that the computer program is *learnt* from data. This means that generic computer programs are used, which are adapted to application-specific circumstances by automatically adjusting the settings of the program based on observed, so-called *training data*. It can therefore be said that machine learning is a way of *programming by example*. The beauty of machine learning is that it is quite arbitrary what the data represents, and we can design general methods that are useful for a wide range of practical applications in different domains. We illustrate this via a range of examples below.

The 'generic computer program' referred to above corresponds to a *mathematical model* of the data. That is, when we develop and describe different machine learning methods, we do this using the language of mathematics. The mathematical model describes a relationship between the quantities involved, or *variables*, that correspond to the observed data and the properties of interest (such as predictions, actions, etc.) Hence, the model is a compact representation of the data that, in a precise mathematical form, captures the key properties of the phenomenon we are studying. Which model to make use of is typically guided by the machine learning engineer's insights generated when looking at the available data and the practitioner's general understanding of the problem. When implementing the method in practice, this mathematical model is translated into code that can be executed on a computer. However, to understand what the computer program actually does, it is important also to understand the underlying mathematics.

As mentioned above, the model (or computer program) is learnt based on the available training data. This is accomplished by using a *learning algorithm* which is capable of automatically adjusting the settings, or *parameters*, of the model to agree with the data. In summary, the three cornerstones of machine learning are:

> 1. The data   2. The mathematical model   3. The learning algorithm.

In this introductory chapter, we will give a taste of the machine learning problem by illustrating these cornerstones with a few examples. They come from different application domains and have different properties, but nevertheless, they can all be addressed using similar techniques from machine learning. We also give some advice on how to proceed through the rest of the book and, at the end, provide references to good books on machine learning for the interested reader who wants to dig further into this topic.

1.1 Machine Learning Exemplified

Machine learning is a multifaceted subject. We gave a brief and high-level description of what it entails above, but this will become much more concrete as we proceed throughout this book and introduce specific methods and techniques for solving various machine learning problems. However, before digging into the details, we will try to give an intuitive answer to the question *'What is machine learning?'*, by discussing a few application examples of where it can (and has) been used.

We start with an example related to medicine, more precisely cardiology.

Example 1.1 Automatically diagnosing heart abnormalities

The leading cause of death globally is conditions that affect the heart and blood vessels, collectively referred to as cardiovascular diseases. Heart problems often influence the electrical activity of the heart, which can be measured using electrodes attached to the body. The electrical signals are reported in an electrocardiogram (ECG). In Figure 1.1 we show examples of (parts of) the measured signals from three different hearts. The measurements stem from a healthy heart (top), a heart suffering from atrial fibrillation (middle), and a heart suffering from right bundle branch block (bottom). Atrial fibrillation makes the heart beat without rhythm, making it hard for the heart to pump blood in a normal way. Right bundle branch block corresponds to a delay or blockage in the electrical pathways of the heart.

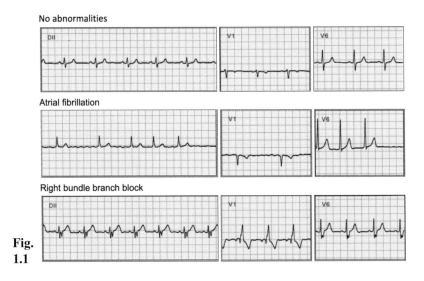

Fig. 1.1

By analysing the ECG signal, a cardiologist gains valuable information about the condition of the heart, which can be used to diagnose the patient and plan the treatment.

To improve the diagnostic accuracy, as well as to save time for the cardiologists, we can ask ourselves if this process can be automated to some extent. That is, can we construct a computer program which reads in the ECG signals, analyses the data, and returns a *prediction* regarding the normality or abnormality of the heart? Such models, capable of accurately interpreting an ECG examination in an automated fashion, will find applications globally, but the needs are most acute in low- and middle-income countries. An important reason for this is that the population in these countries often do not have easy and direct access to highly skilled cardiologists capable of accurately carrying out ECG diagnoses. Furthermore, cardiovascular diseases in these countries are linked to more than 75% of deaths.

The key challenge in building such a computer program is that it is far from obvious which computations are needed to turn the raw ECG signal into a predication about the heart condition. Even if an experienced cardiologist were to try to explain to a software developer which patterns in the data to look for, translating the cardiologist's experience into a reliable computer program would be extremely challenging.

To tackle this difficulty, the machine learning approach is to instead teach the computer program through examples. Specifically, instead of asking the cardiologist to specify a set of rules for how to classify an ECG signal as normal or abnormal, we simply ask the cardiologist (or a group of cardiologists) to *label* a large number of recorded ECG signals with labels corresponding to the the the underlying heart condition. This is a much easier (albeit possibly tedious) way for the cardiologists to communicate their experience and encode it in a way that is interpretable by a computer.

The task of the learning algorithm is then to automatically adapt the computer program so that its predictions agree with the cardiologists' labels on the labelled training data. The hope is that, if it succeeds on the training data (where we already know the answer), then it should be possible to use the predictions made the by program on previously unseen data (where we *do not* know the answer) as well.

This is the approach taken by Ribeiro et al. (2020), who developed a machine learning model for ECG prediction. In their study, the training data consists of more than 2 300 000 ECG records from almost 1 700 000 different patients from the state of Minas Gerais in Brazil. More specifically, each ECG corresponds to 12 time series (one from each of the 12 electrodes that were used in conducting the exam) of a duration between 7 to 10 seconds each, sampled at frequencies ranging from 300 Hz to 600 Hz. These ECGs can be used to provide a full evaluation of the electrical activity of the heart, and it is indeed the most commonly used test in evaluating the heart. Importantly, each ECG in the dataset also comes with a label sorting it into different classes – no abnormalities, atrial fibrillation, right bundle branch block, etc. – according to the status of the heart. Based on this data, a machine learning model is trained to automatically classify a new ECG recording without requiring a human doctor to be involved. The model used is a deep neural network, more specifically a so-called residual network, which is commonly used for images. The researchers adapted this to work for the ECG signals of relevance for this study. In Chapter 6, we introduce deep learning models and their training algorithms.

Evaluating how a model like this will perform in practice is not straightforward. The approach taken in this study was to ask three different cardiologists with experience in electrocardiography to examine and classify 827 ECG recordings from distinct patients. This dataset was then evaluated by the algorithm, two 4th year cardiology residents, two 3rd year emergency residents, and two 5th year medical students. The average performance was then compared. The result was that the algorithm achieved better or the same result when compared to the human performance on classifying six types of abnormalities.

Before we move on, let us pause and reflect on the example introduced above. In fact, many concepts that are central to machine learning can be recognised in this example.

As we mentioned above, the first cornerstone of machine learning is the data. Taking a closer look at what the data actually is, we note that it comes in different forms. First, we have the *training data* which is used to train the model. Each training data point consists of both the ECG signal, which we refer to as the *input*, and its label corresponding to the type of heart condition seen in this signal, which we refer to as the *output*. To train the model, we need access to both the inputs and the outputs, where the latter had to be manually assigned by domain experts (or possibly some auxiliary examination). Training a model from lableled data points is therefore referred to as *supervised learning*. We think of the learning as being supervised by the domain expert, and the learning objective is to obtain a computer program that can mimic the labelling done by the expert. Second, we have the (unlabelled) ECG signals that will be fed to the program when it is used 'in production'. It is important to remember that the ultimate goal of the model is to obtain accurate predictions in this second phase. We say that the predictions made by the model must *generalise beyond the training data*. How to train models that are capable of generalising, and how to evaluate to what extent they do so, is a central theoretical question studied throughout this book (see in particular Chapter 4).

We illustrate the training of the ECG prediction model in Figure 1.2. The general structure of the training procedure is, however, the same (or at least very similar) for all supervised machine learning problems.

Another key concept that we encountered in the ECG example is the notion of a *classification* problem. Classification is a supervised machine learning task which amounts to predicting a certain class, or label, for each data point. Specifically, for classification problems, there are only a finite number of possible output values. In the ECG example, the classes correspond to the type of heart condition. For instance, the classes could be 'normal' or 'abnormal', in which case we refer to it as a binary classification problem (only two possible classes). More generally, we could design a model for classifying each signal as either 'normal', or assign it to one of a predetermined set of abnormalities. We then face a (more ambitious) multi-class classification problem.

Classification is, however, not the only application of supervised machine learning that we will encounter. Specifically, we will also study another type of problem referred to as *regression problems*. Regression differs from classification in that the

Training data

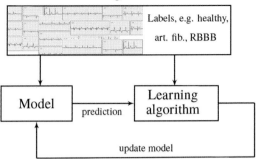

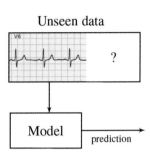

Figure 1.2 Illustrating the supervised machine learning process with training to the left and then the use of the trained model to the right. **Left:** Values for the unknown parameters of the model are set by the learning algorithm such that the model best describes the available training data. **Right:** The learned model is used on new, previously unseen data, where we hope to obtain a correct classification. It is thus essential that the model is able to generalise to new data that is not present in the training data.

output (that is, the quantity that we want the model to predict) is a numerical value. We illustrate with an example from material science.

Example 1.2 Formation energy of crystals

Much of our technological development is driven by the discovery of new materials with unique properties. Indeed, technologies such as touch screens and batteries for electric vehicles have emerged due to advances in materials science. Traditionally, materials discovery was largely done through experiments, but this is both time consuming and costly, which limited the number of new materials that could be found. Over the past few decades, computational methods have therefore played an increasingly important role. The basic idea behind computational materials science is to screen a very large number of hypothetical materials, predict various properties of interest by computational methods, and then attempt to experimentally synthesise the most promising candidates.

Crystalline solids (or, simply, crystals) are a central type of inorganic material. In a crystal, the atoms are arranged in a highly ordered microscopic structure. Hence, to understand the properties of such a material, it is not enough to know the proportion of each element in the material, but we also need to know how these elements (or atoms) are arranged into a crystal. A basic property of interest when considering a hypothetical material is therefore the *formation energy* of the crystal. The formation energy can be thought of as the energy that nature needs to spend to form the crystal from the individual elements. Nature strives to find a minimum energy configuration. Hence, if a certain crystal structure is predicted to have a formation energy that is significantly larger than alternative crystals composed of the same elements, then it is unlikely that it can be synthesised in a stable way in practice.

A classical method (going back to the 1960s) that can be used for computing the formation energy is so-called density functional theory (DFT). The DFT method, which is based on quantum mechanical modelling, paved the way for the first

---

5

breakthrough in computational materials science, enabling high throughput screening for materials discovery. That being said, the DFT method is computationally very expensive, and even with modern supercomputers, only a small fraction of all potentially interesting materials have been analysed.

To handle this limitation, there has been much recent interest in using machine learning for materials discovery, with the potential to result in a second computational revolution. By training a machine learning model to, for instance, predict the formation energy – but in a fraction of the computational time required by DFT – a much larger range of candidate materials can be investigated.

As a concrete example, Faber et al. (2016) used a machine learning method referred to as kernel ridge regression (see Chapter 8) to predict the formation energy of around 2 million so-called elpasolite crystals. The machine learning model is a computer program which takes a candidate crystal as input (essentially, a description of the positions and elemental types of the atoms in the crystal) and is asked to return a prediction of the formation energy. To train the model, 10 000 crystals were randomly selected, and their formation energies were computed using DFT. The model was then trained to predict formation energies to agree as closely as possible with the DFT output on the training set. Once trained, the model was used to predict the energy on the remaining ~99.5% of the potential elpasolites. Among these, 128 new crystal structures were found to have a favorable energy, thereby being potentially stable in nature.

Comparing the two examples discussed above, we can make a few interesting observations. As already pointed out, one difference is that the ECG model is asked to predict a certain class (say, normal or abnormal), whereas the materials discovery model is asked to predict a numerical value (the formation energy of a crystal). These are the two main types of prediction problems that we will study in this book, referred to as classification and regression, respectively. While conceptually similar, we often use slight variations of the underpinning mathematical models, depending on the problem type. It is therefore instructive to treat them separately.

Both types are supervised learning problems, though. That is, we train a predictive model to mimic the predictions made by a 'supervisor'. However, it is interesting to note that the supervision is not necessarily done by a human domain expert. Indeed, for the formation energy model, the training data was obtained by running automated (but costly) density functional theory computations. In other situations, we might obtain the output values naturally when collecting the training data. For instance, assume that you want to build a model for predicting the outcome of a soccer match based on data about the players in the two teams. This is a classification problem (the output is 'win', 'lose', or 'tie'), but the training data does not have to be manually labelled, since we get the labels directly from historical matches. Similarly, if you want to build a regression model for predicting the price of an apartment based on its size, location, condition, etc., then the output (the price) is obtained directly from historical sales.

Finally, it is worth noting that, although the examples discussed above correspond to very different application domains, the problems are quite similar from a machine learning perspective. Indeed, the general procedure outlined in Figure 1.2 is also applicable, with minor modifications, to the materials discovery problem. This generality and versatility of the machine learning methodology is one of its main strengths and beauties.

In this book, we will make use of statistics and probability theory to describe the models used for making predictions. Using probabilistic models allows us to systematically represent and cope with the *uncertainty* in the predictions. In the examples above, it is perhaps not obvious why this is needed. It could (perhaps) be argued that there is a 'correct answer' both in the ECG problem and the formation energy problem. Therefore, we might expect that the machine learning model should be able to provide a definite answer in its prediction. However, even in situations when there is a correct answer, machine learning models rely on various assumptions, and they are trained from data using computational learning algorithms. With probabilistic models, we are able to represent the uncertainty in the model's predictions, whether it originates from the data, the modelling assumptions, or the computation. Furthermore, in many applications of machine learning, the output is uncertain in itself, and there is no such thing as a definite answer. To highlight the need for probabilistic predictions, let us consider an example from sports analytics.

Example 1.3 Probability of scoring a goal in soccer

Soccer is a sport where a great deal of data has been collected on how individual players act throughout a match, how teams collaborate, how they perform over time, etc. All this data is used to better understand the game and to help players reach their full potential.

Consider the problem of predicting whether or not a shot results in a goal. To this end, we will use a rather simple model, where the prediction is based only on the player's position on the field when taking the shot. Specifically, the input is given by the distance from the goal and the angle between two lines drawn from the player's position to the goal posts; see Figure 1.3. The output corresponds to whether or not the shot results in a goal, meaning that this is a binary classification problem.

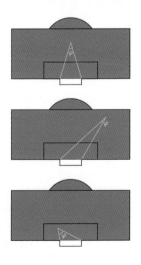
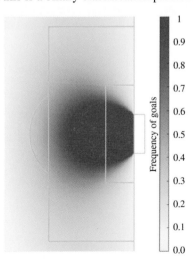

Fig. 1.3

Clearly, knowing the player's position is not enough to definitely say if the shot will be successful. Still, it is reasonable to assume that it provides *some information* about the chance of scoring a goal. Indeed, a shot close to the goal line with a large angle is intuitively more likely to result in a goal than one made from a position close to the sideline. To acknowledge this fact when constructing a machine learning model, we will not ask the model to predict the outcome of the shot but rather to predict *the probability of a goal*. This is accomplished by using a probabilistic model which is trained by maximising the total probability of the observed training data with respect to the probabilistic predictions. For instance, using a so-called *logistic regression* model (see Chapter 3) we obtain a predicted probability of scoring a goal from any position, illustrated using a heat map in the right panel in Figure 1.3.

The supervised learning problems mentioned above were categorised as either classification or regression problems, depending on the type of output. These problem categories are the most common and typical instances of supervised machine learning, and they will constitute the foundation for most methods discussed in this book. However, machine learning is in fact much more general and can be used to build complex predictive models that do not naturally fit into either the classification or the regression category. To whet the appetite for further exploration of the field of machine learning, we provide two such examples below. These examples go beyond the specific problem formulations that we explicitly study in this book, but they nevertheless build on the same core methodology.

In the first of these two examples, we illustrate a computer vision capability, namely how to classify each individual pixel of an image into a class describing the object that the pixel belongs to. This has important applications in, for example, autonomous driving and medical imaging. When compared to the earlier examples, this introduces an additional level of complexity, in that the model needs to be able to handle spatial dependencies across the image in its classifications.

Example 1.4 Pixel-wise class prediction

When it comes to machine vision, an important capability is to be able to associate each pixel in an image with a corresponding class; see Figure 1.4 for an illustration in an autonomous driving application. This is referred to as *semantic segmentation*. In autonomous driving, it is used to separate cars, road, pedestrians, etc. The output is then used as input to other algorithms, for instance for collision avoidance. When it comes to medical imaging, semantic segmentation is used, for instance, to tell apart different organs and tumors.

To train a semantic segmentation model, the training data consist of a large number of images (inputs). For each such image, there is a corresponding output image of the same size, where each pixel has been labelled by hand to belong to a certain class. The supervised machine learning problem then amounts to using this data to find a mapping that is capable of taking a new unseen image and produce a corresponding output in the form of a predicted class for each pixel. Essentially, this is a type of classification problem, but all pixels need to be classified simultaneously while respecting the spatial dependencies across the image to result in a coherent segmentation.

Fig. 1.4

The bottom part of Figure 1.4 shows the prediction generated by such an algorithm, where the aim is to classify each pixel as either car (blue), traffic sign (yellow), pavement (purple), or tree (green). The best performing solutions for this task today rely on cleverly crafted deep neural networks (see Chapter 6).

In the final example, we raise the bar even higher, since here the model needs to be able to explain dependencies not only over space, but also over time, in a so-called spatio-temporal problem. These problems are finding more and more applications as we get access to more and more data. More precisely, we look into the problem of how to build probabilistic models capable of better estimating and forecasting air pollution across time and space in a city, in this case London.

Example 1.5 Estimating air pollution levels across London

Roughly 91% of the world's population lives in places where the air quality levels are worse than those recommended by the world health organisation. Recent estimates indicate that 4.2 million people die each year from stroke, heart disease, lung cancer, and chronic respiratory diseases caused by ambient air pollution.

A natural first step in dealing with this problem is to develop technology to measure and aggregate information about the air pollution levels across time and space. Such information enables the development of machine learning models to better estimate and accurately forecast air pollution, which in turn permits suitable interventions. The work that we feature here sets out to do this for the city of London, where more than 9 000 people die early every year as a result of air pollution.

Air quality sensors are now – as opposed to the situation in the recent past – available at relatively low cost. This, combined with an increasing awareness of the problem, has caused interested companies, individuals, non-profit organisations, and community groups to contribute by setting up sensors and making the data available. More specifically, the data in this example comes from a sensor network of ground sensors providing hourly readings of NO_2 and hourly satellite data at a spatial resolution of 7 km × 7 km. The resulting supervised machine learning problem is to build a model that can deliver forecasts of the air pollution level across time and space. Since the output – pollution level – is a continuous variable, this is a type of regression problem. The particularly challenging aspect here is that the measurements are reported at different spatial resolutions and on varying timescales.

The technical challenge in this problem amounts to merging the information from many sensors of different kinds reporting their measurements on different spatial scales, sometimes referred to as a multi-sensor multi-resolution problem. Besides the problem under consideration here, problems of this kind find many different applications. The basis for the solution providing the estimates exemplified in Figure 1.5 is the Gaussian process (see Chapter 9).

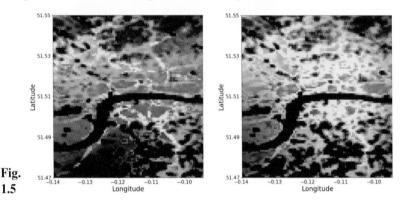

Fig. 1.5

Figure 1.5 illustrates the output from the Gaussian process model in terms of spatio-temporal estimation and forecasting of NO_2 levels in London. To the left, we have the situation on February 19, 2019 at 11:00 using observations from both ground sensors providing hourly readings of NO_2 and from satellite data. To the right, we have the situation on 19 February 2019 at 17:00 using only the satellite data.

The Gaussian process is a non-parametric and probabilistic model for nonlinear functions. Non-parametric means that it does not rely on any particular parametric functional form to be postulated. The fact that it is a probabilistic model means that it is capable of representing and manipulating uncertainty in a systematic way.

1.2 About This Book

The aim of this book is to convey the spirit of supervised machine learning, without requiring any previous experience in the field. We focus on the underlying mathematics as well as the practical aspects. This book is a textbook; it is not a reference work or a programming manual. It therefore contains only a careful (yet comprehensive) selection of supervised machine learning methods and no programming code. There are by now many well-written and well-documented code packages available, and it is our firm belief that with a good understanding of the mathematics and the inner workings of the methods, the reader will be able to make the connection between this book and his/her favorite code package in his/her favorite programming language.

We take a statistical perspective in this book, meaning that we discuss and motivate methods in terms of their statistical properties. It therefore requires some previous knowledge in statistics and probability theory, as well as calculus and linear algebra. We hope that reading the book from start to end will give the reader a good starting point for working as a machine learning engineer and/or pursuing further studies within the subject.

The book is written such that it can be read back to back. There are, however, multiple possible paths through the book that are more selective depending on the interest of the reader. Figure 1.6 illustrates the major dependencies between the chapters. In particular, the most fundamental topics are discussed in Chapters 2, 3, and 4, and we do recommend the reader to read those chapters before proceeding to the later chapters that contain technically more advanced topics (Chapters 5–9). Chapter 10 goes beyond the supervised setting of machine learning, and Chapter 11 focuses on some of the more practical aspects of designing a successful machine learning solution and has a less technical nature than the preceding chapters. Finally, Chapter 12 (written by David Sumpter) discusses certain ethical aspects of modern machine learning.

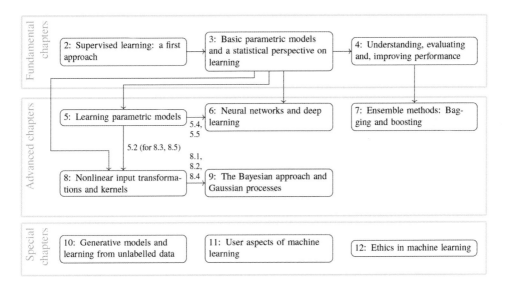

Figure 1.6 The structure of this book, illustrated by blocks (chapters) and arrows (recommended order in which to read the chapters). We do recommend everyone to read (or at least skim) the fundamental material in Chapters 2, 3, and 4 first. The path through the technically more advanced Chapters 5–9, can be chosen to match the particular interest of the reader. For Chapters 11, 10, and 12, we recommend reading the fundamental chapters first.

1.3 **Further Reading**

There are by now quite a few extensive textbooks available on the topic of machine learning, which introduce the area in different ways compared to how we do so in this book. We will only mention a few here. The book of Hastie et al. (2009) introduces the area of statistical machine learning in a mathematically solid and accessible manner. A few years later, the authors released a different version of their book (James et al. 2013), which is mathematically significantly lighter, conveying the main ideas in an even more accessible manner. These books do not venture long either into the world of Bayesian methods or the world of neural networks. However, there are several complementary books that do exactly that – see e.g. Bishop (2006) and Murphy (2021). MacKay (2003) provides a rather early account drawing interesting and useful connections to information theory. It is still very much worth looking into. The book by Shalev-Shwartz and Ben-David (2014) provides an introduction with a clear focus on the underpinning theoretical constructions, connecting very deep questions – such as 'what is learning?' and 'how can a machine learn' – with mathematics. It is a perfect book for those of our readers who would like to deepen their understanding of the theoretical background of that area. We also mention the work of Efron and Hastie (2016), where the authors take a constructive historical approach to the development of the area, covering the revolution in data analysis that emerged with computers. Contemporary introductions to the mathematics of machine learning are provided by Strang (2019) and Deisenroth et al. (2019).

For a full account of the work on automatic diagnosis of heart abnormalities, see Ribeiro et al. 2020, and for a general introduction to the use of machine learning – in particular deep learning – in medicine, we point the reader to Topol (2019). The application of kernel ridge regression to elpasolite crystals was borrowed from Faber et al. (2016). Other applications of machine learning in materials science are reviewed in the collection edited by Schütt et al. (2020). The London air pollution study was published by Hamelijnck et al. (2019), where the authors introduce interesting and useful developments of the Gaussian process model that we explain in Chapter 9. When it comes to semantic segmentation, the ground-breaking work of Long et al. (2015) has received massive interest. The two main bases for the current development in semantic segmentation are Zhao et al. (2017) and L.-C. Chen et al. (2017). A thorough introduction to the mathematics of soccer is provided in the book by David Sumpter (2016), and a starting point to recent ideas on how to assess the impact of player actions is given in Decroos et al. (2019).

2 Supervised Learning

A First Approach

In this chapter, we will introduce the supervised machine learning problem as well as two basic machine learning methods for solving it. The methods we will introduce are called k-nearest neighbours and decision trees. These two methods are relatively simple, and we will derive them on intuitive grounds. Still, these methods are useful in their own right and are therefore a good place to start. Understanding their inner workings, advantages, and shortcomings also lays a good foundation for the more advanced methods that are to come in later chapters.

2.1 Supervised Machine Learning

In supervised machine learning, we have some *training data* that contains examples of how some *input*[1] variable $\mathbf{x}$ relates to an *output*[2] variable y. By using some mathematical model or method, which we adapt to the training data, our goal is to *predict* the output y for a new, previously unseen, set of *test data* for which only $\mathbf{x}$ is known. We usually say that we *learn* (or *train*) a model from the training data, and that process involves some computations implemented on a computer.

Learning from Labelled Data

In most interesting supervised machine learning applications, the relationship between input $\mathbf{x}$ and output y is difficult to describe explicitly. It may be too cumbersome or complicated to fully unravel from application domain knowledge, or even unknown. The problem can therefore usually not be solved by writing a traditional computer program that takes $\mathbf{x}$ as input and returns y as output from a set of rules. The supervised machine learning approach is instead to learn the relationship between $\mathbf{x}$ and y from data, which contains examples of observed pairs of input and output values. In other words, supervised machine learning amounts to learning from examples.

The data used for learning is called *training data*, and it has to consist of several input–output data points (samples) $(\mathbf{x}_i, y_i)$, in total n of them. We will compactly

---

[1] The input is commonly also called feature, attribute, predictor, regressor, covariate, explanatory variable, controlled variable, and independent variable.

[2] The output is commonly also called response, regressand, label, explained variable, predicted variable, or dependent variable.

write the training data as $\mathcal{T} = \{\mathbf{x}_i, y_i\}_{i=1}^{n}$. Each data point in the training data provides a snapshot of how y depends on $\mathbf{x}$, and the goal in supervised machine learning is to squeeze as much information as possible out of $\mathcal{T}$. In this book, we will only consider problems where the individual data points are assumed to be (probabilistically) *independent*. This excludes, for example, applications in time series analysis, where it is of interest to model the correlation between $\mathbf{x}_i$ and $\mathbf{x}_{i+1}$.

The fact that the training data contains not only input values $\mathbf{x}_i$ but also output values y_i is the reason for the term 'supervised' machine learning. We may say that each input $\mathbf{x}_i$ is accompanied by a label y_i, or simply that we have *labelled data*. For some applications, it is only a matter of jointly recording $\mathbf{x}$ and y. In other applications, the output y has to be created by labelling of the training data inputs $\mathbf{x}$ by a domain expert. For instance, to construct a training dataset for the cardiovascular disease application introduced in Chapter 1, a cardiologist needs to look at all training data inputs (ECG signals) $\mathbf{x}_i$ and label them by assigning to the variable y_i to correspond to the heart condition that is seen in the signal. The entire learning process is thus 'supervised' by the domain expert.

We use a vector boldface notation $\mathbf{x}$ to denote the input, since we assume it to be a p-dimensional vector, $\mathbf{x} = [x_1 \ x_2 \ \cdots \ x_p]^\mathsf{T}$, where $^\mathsf{T}$ denotes the transpose. Each element of the input vector $\mathbf{x}$ represents some information that is considered to be relevant for the application at hand, for example the outdoor temperature or the unemployment rate. In many applications, the number of inputs p is large, or put differently, the input $\mathbf{x}$ is a high-dimensional vector. For instance, in a computer vision application where the input is a greyscale image, $\mathbf{x}$ can be all pixel values in the image, so $p = h \times w$ where h and w denote the height and width of the input image.[3] The output y, on the other hand, is often of low dimension, and throughout most of this book, we will assume that it is a scalar value. The *type* of the output value, numerical or categorical, turns out to be important and is used to distinguish between two subtypes of the supervised machine learning problems: *regression* and *classification*. We will discuss this next.

Numerical and Categorical Variables

The variables contained in our data (input as well as output) can be of two different types: *numerical* or *categorical*. A numerical variable has a natural ordering. We can say that one instance of a numerical variable is larger or smaller than another instance of the same variable. A numerical variable could, for instance, be represented by a continuous real number, but it could also be discrete, such as an integer. Categorical variables, on the other hand, are always discrete, and importantly, they lack a natural

---

[3]For image-based problems it is often more convenient to represent the input as a matrix of size $h \times w$ than as a vector of length $p = hw$, but the dimension is nevertheless the same. We will get back to this in Chapter 6 when discussing the convolutional neural network, a model structure tailored to image-type inputs.

Table 2.1 Examples of numerical and categorical variables.

Variable type	Example	Handled as
Number (continuous)	32.23 km/h, 12.50 km/h, 42.85 km/h	Numerical
Number (discrete) with natural ordering	0 children, 1 child, 2 children	Numerical
Number (discrete) without natural ordering	1 = Sweden, 2 = Denmark, 3 = Norway	Categorical
Text string	Hello, Goodbye, Welcome	Categorical

ordering. In this book we assume that any categorical variable can take only a finite number of different values. A few examples are given in Table 2.1 above.

The distinction between numerical and categorical is sometimes somewhat arbitrary. We could, for instance, argue that having no children is qualitatively different from having children, and use the categorical variable 'children: yes/no' instead of the numerical '0, 1 or 2 children'. It is therefore a decision for the machine learning engineer whether a certain variable is to be considered as numerical or categorical.

The notion of categorical vs. numerical applies to both the output variable y and to the p elements x_j of the input vector $\mathbf{x} = [x_1\ x_2\ \cdots\ x_p]^\mathsf{T}$. All p input variables do not have to be of the same type. It is perfectly fine (and common in practice) to have a mix of categorical and numerical inputs.

Classification and Regression

We distinguish between different supervised machine learning problems by the type of the output y.

> *Regression* means that the output is numerical, and *classification* means that the output is categorical.

The reason for this distinction is that the regression and classification problems have somewhat different properties, and different methods are used for solving them.

Note that the p input variables $\mathbf{x} = [x_1\ x_2\ \cdots\ x_p]^\mathsf{T}$ can be either numerical or categorical for both regression and classification problems. It is only the type of the output that determines whether a problem is a regression or a classification problem. A method for solving a classification problems is called a *classifier*.

For classification, the output is categorical and can therefore only take values in a finite set. We use M to denote the number of elements in the set of possible output values. It could, for instance, be {false, true} ($M = 2$) or {Sweden, Norway, Finland, Denmark} ($M = 4$). We will refer to these elements as *classes* or *labels*. The number of classes M is assumed to be known in the classification problem. To prepare for a concise mathematical notation, we use integers $1, 2, \ldots, M$ to denote the output classes if $M > 2$. The ordering of the integers is arbitrary and does *not* imply any ordering of the classes. When there are only $M = 2$ classes, we have the important special case of *binary* classification. In binary classification we use the labels -1 and 1 (instead of 1 and 2). Occasionally we will also use the equivalent terms *negative* and *positive* class. The only reason for using a different convention for binary classification is that it gives a more compact mathematical notation for some of the methods, and it carries no deeper meaning. Let us now have a look at a classification and a regression problem, both of which will be used throughout this book.

Example 2.1 Classifying songs

Say that we want to build a 'song categoriser' app, where the user records a song, and the app answers by reporting whether the song has the artistic style of either the Beatles, Kiss, or Bob Dylan. At the heart of this fictitious app, there has to be a mechanism that takes an audio recording as an input and returns an artist's name.

If we first collect some recordings with songs from the three groups/artists (where we know which artist is behind each song: a labelled dataset), we could use supervised machine learning to *learn* the characteristics of their different styles and therefrom *predict* the artist of the new user-provided song. In supervised machine learning terminology, the artist name (the `Beatles`, `Kiss`, or `Bob Dylan`) is the output y. In this problem, y is categorical, and we are hence facing a classification problem.

One of the important design choices for a machine learning engineer is a detailed specification of what the input $\mathbf{x}$ really is. It would in principle be possible to consider the raw audio information as input, but that would give a very high-dimensional $\mathbf{x}$ which (unless an audio-specific machine learning method is used) would most likely require an unrealistically large amount of training data in order to be successful (we will discuss this aspect in detail in Chapter 4). A better option could therefore be to define some summary statistics of audio recordings and use those so-called *features* as input $\mathbf{x}$ instead. As input features, we could, for example, use the length of the audio recording and the 'perceived energy' of the song. The length of a recording is easy to measure. Since it can differ quite a lot between different songs, we take the logarithm of the actual length (in seconds) to get values in the same range for all songs. Such feature transformations are commonly used in practice to make the input data more homogeneous.

The energy of a song[a] is a bit more tricky, and the exact definition may even be ambiguous. However, we leave that to the audio experts and re-use a piece of software that they have written for this purpose[b] without bothering too much about its inner workings. As long as this piece of software returns a number for any recording that is fed to it, and always returns the same number for the same recording, we can use it as an input to a machine learning method.

In Figure 2.1 we have plotted a dataset with 230 songs from the three artists. Each song is represented by a dot, where the horizontal axis is the logarithm of its length (measured in seconds) and the vertical axis the energy (on a scale 0–1). When we later return to this example and apply different supervised machine learning methods to it, this data will be the training data.

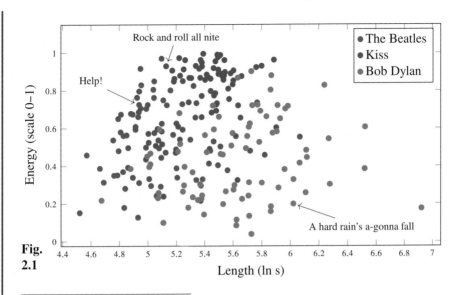

Fig. 2.1

*a*We use this term to refer to the perceived musical energy, not the signal energy in a strict sense.

*b*Specifically, we use http://api.spotify.com/ here.

Example 2.2 Car stopping distances

Ezekiel and Fox (1959) present a dataset with 62 observations of the distance needed for various cars at different initial speeds to brake to a full stop.*a* The dataset has the following two variables:
- Speed: The speed of the car when the brake signal is given.
- Distance: The distance traveled after the signal is given until the car has reached a full stop.

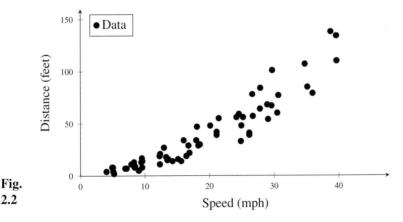

Fig. 2.2

To make a supervised machine learning problem out of this, we interpret Speed as the input variable x and Distance as the output variable y, as shown in Figure 2.2. Note that we use a non-bold symbol for the input here since it is a scalar value and not a vector of inputs in this example. Since y is numerical, this is a regression problem. We then ask ourselves what the stopping distance would be if the initial speed were, for example, 33 mph or 45 mph, respectively (two speeds at which no data has been recorded). Another way to frame this question is to ask for the *prediction* $\widehat{y}(x_\star)$ for $x_\star = 33$ and $x_\star = 45$.

---

[a]The data is somewhat dated, so the conclusions are perhaps not applicable to modern cars.

Generalising Beyond Training Data

There are two primary reasons why it can be of interest to mathematically model the input–output relationships from training data.

(i) To *reason about and explore* how input and output variables are connected. An often-encountered task in sciences such as medicine and sociology is to determine whether a correlation between a pair of variables exists or not ('does eating seafood increase life expectancy?'). Such questions can be addressed by learning a mathematical model and carefully reasoning about the likelihood that the learned relationships between input $\mathbf{x}$ and output y are due only to random effects in the data or if there appears to be some substance to the proposed relationships.

(ii) To *predict* the output value $y_\star$ for some new, previously unseen input $\mathbf{x}_\star$. By using some mathematical method which generalises the input–output examples seen in the training data, we can make a prediction $\widehat{y}(\mathbf{x}_\star)$ for a previously unseen test input $\mathbf{x}_\star$. The hat $\widehat{}$ indicates that the prediction is an estimate of the output.

These two objectives are sometimes used to roughly distinguish between classical statistics, focusing more on objective (i), and machine learning, where objective (ii) is more central. However, this is not a clear-cut distinction since predictive modelling is a topic in classical statistics too, and explainable models are also studied in machine learning. The primary focus in this book, however, is on making predictions, objective (ii) above, which is the foundation of supervised machine learning. Our overall goal is to obtain as accurate predictions $\widehat{y}(\mathbf{x}_\star)$ as possible (measured in some appropriate way) for a wide range of possible test inputs $\mathbf{x}_\star$. We say that we are interested in methods that *generalise well* beyond the training data.

A method that generalises well for the music example above would be able to correctly tell the artist of a new song which was not in the training data (assuming that the artist of the new song is one of the three that was present in the training data, of course). The ability to generalise to new data is a key concept of machine learning. It is not difficult to construct models or methods that give very accurate predictions if they are only evaluated on the training data (we will see an example in the next section). However, if the model is not able to generalise, meaning that the predictions are poor when the model is applied to new test data points, then the model is of little use in practice for making predictions. If this is the case, we say that the model is *overfitting* to the training data. We will illustrate the issue of overfitting for a specific machine learning model in the next section, and in Chapter 4 we will return to this concept using a more general and mathematical approach.

2.2 A Distance-Based Method: *k*-NN

It is now time to encounter our first actual machine learning method. We will start with the relatively simple *k*-nearest neighbours (*k*-NN) method, which can be used for both regression and classification. Remember that the setting is that we have access to training data $\{\mathbf{x}_i, y_i\}_{i=1}^n$, which consists of n data points with input $\mathbf{x}_i$ and corresponding output y_i. From this we want to construct a prediction $\widehat{y}(\mathbf{x}_\star)$ for what we believe the output $y_\star$ would be for a new $\mathbf{x}_\star$, which we have not seen previously.

The *k*-Nearest Neighbours Method

Most methods for supervised machine learning build on the intuition that *if the test data point* $\mathbf{x}_\star$ *is close to training data point* $\mathbf{x}_i$, *then the prediction* $\widehat{y}(\mathbf{x}_\star)$ *should be close to* y_i. This is a general idea, but one simple way to implement it in practice is the following: first, compute the Euclidean distance[4] between the test input and all training inputs, $\|\mathbf{x}_i - \mathbf{x}_\star\|_2$ for $i = 1, \ldots, n$; second, find the data point $\mathbf{x}_j$ with the *shortest distance* to $\mathbf{x}_\star$, and use its output as the prediction, $\widehat{y}(\mathbf{x}_\star) = y_j$.

   This simple prediction method is referred to as the 1-nearest neighbour method. It is not very complicated, but for most machine learning applications of interest it is too simplistic. In practice we can rarely say *for certain* what the output value y will be. Mathematically, we handle this by describing y as a random variable. That is, we consider the data as *noisy*, meaning that it is affected by random errors referred to as noise. From this perspective, the shortcoming of 1-nearest neighbour is that the prediction relies on only one data point from the training data, which makes it quite 'erratic' and sensitive to noisy training data.

   To improve the 1-nearest neighbour method, we can extend it to make use of the k nearest neighbours instead. Formally, we define the set $\mathcal{N}_\star = \{i : \mathbf{x}_i$ is one of the k training data points closest to $\mathbf{x}_\star\}$ and aggregate the information from the k outputs y_j for $j \in \mathcal{N}_\star$ to make the prediction. For regression problems, we take the average of all y_j for $j \in \mathcal{N}_\star$, and for classification problems, we use a majority vote.[5] We illustrate the *k*-nearest neighbours (*k*-NN) method by Example 2.3 and summarise it in Method 2.1.

---

[4]The Euclidean distance between a test point $\mathbf{x}_\star$ and a training data point $\mathbf{x}_i$ is $\|\mathbf{x}_i - \mathbf{x}_\star\|_2 = \sqrt{(x_{i1} - x_{\star 1})^2 + (x_{i2} - x_{\star 2})^2}$. Other distance functions can also be used and will be discussed in Chapter 8. Categorical input variables can be handled, as we will discuss in Chapter 3.

[5]Ties can be handled in different ways, for instance by a coin-flip, or by reporting the actual vote count to the end user, who gets to decide what to do with it.

Methods that explicitly use the training data when making predictions are referred to as *nonparametric*, and the k-NN method is one example of this. This is in contrast with *parametric* methods, where the prediction is given by some function (a model) governed by a fixed number of parameters. For parametric methods, the training data is used to *learn* the parameters in an initial training phase, but once the model has been learned, the training data can be discarded since it is not used explicitly when making predictions. We will introduce parametric modelling in Chapter 3.

Data: Training data $\{\mathbf{x}_i, y_i\}_{i=1}^{n}$ and test input $\mathbf{x}_\star$
Result: Predicted test output $\widehat{y}(\mathbf{x}_\star)$

1. Compute the distances $\|\mathbf{x}_i - \mathbf{x}_\star\|_2$ for all training data points $i = 1,\ldots,n$
2. Let $\mathcal{N}_\star = \{i : \mathbf{x}_i$ is one of the k data points closest to $\mathbf{x}_\star\}$
3. Compute the prediction $\widehat{y}(\mathbf{x}_\star)$ as

$$\widehat{y}(\mathbf{x}_\star) = \begin{cases} \text{Average}\{y_j : j \in \mathcal{N}_\star\} & \text{(Regression problems)} \\ \text{MajorityVote}\{y_j : j \in \mathcal{N}_\star\} & \text{(Classification problems)} \end{cases}$$

Method 2.1 k-nearest neighbour, k-NN

Example 2.3 Predicting colours with k-NN

We consider a synthetic binary classification problem ($M = 2$). We are given a training dataset with $n = 6$ observations of $p = 2$ input variables x_1, x_2 and one categorical output y, the colour Red or Blue,

i	x_1	x_2	y
1	−1	3	Red
2	2	1	Blue
3	−2	2	Red
4	−1	2	Blue
5	−1	0	Blue
6	1	1	Red

and we are interested in predicting the output for $\mathbf{x}_\star = [1\ \ 2]^\mathsf{T}$. For this purpose we will explore two different k-NN classifiers, one using $k = 1$ and one using $k = 3$.

First, we compute the Euclidean distance $\|\mathbf{x}_i - \mathbf{x}_\star\|_2$ between each training data point $\mathbf{x}_i$ (red and blue dots) and the test data point $\mathbf{x}_\star$ (black dot), and then sort them in ascending order.

Since the closest training data point to $\mathbf{x}_\star$ is the data point $i = 6$ (Red), this means that for k-NN with $k = 1$, we get the prediction $\widehat{y}(\mathbf{x}_\star) = $ Red. For $k = 3$, the three nearest neighbours are $i = 6$ (Red), $i = 2$ (Blue), and $i = 4$ (Blue). Taking a majority vote among these three training data points, Blue wins with 2 votes against 1, so our prediction becomes $\widehat{y}(\mathbf{x}_\star)$ = Blue. In Figure 2.3, $k = 1$ is represented by the inner circle and $k = 3$ by the outer circle.

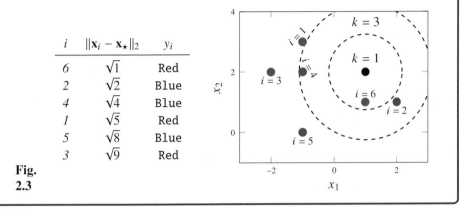

i	$\|\mathbf{x}_i - \mathbf{x}_\star\|_2$	y_i
6	$\sqrt{1}$	Red
2	$\sqrt{2}$	Blue
4	$\sqrt{4}$	Blue
1	$\sqrt{5}$	Red
5	$\sqrt{8}$	Blue
3	$\sqrt{9}$	Red

Fig. 2.3

Decision Boundaries for a Classifier

In Example 2.3 we only computed a prediction for one single test data point $\mathbf{x}_\star$. That prediction might indeed be the ultimate goal of the application, but in order to visualise and better understand a classifier, we can also study its *decision boundary*, which illustrates the prediction for all possible test inputs. We introduce the decision boundary using Example 2.4. It is a general concept for classifiers, not only k-NN, but it is only possible to visualise easily when the dimension of $\mathbf{x}$ is $p = 2$.

Example 2.4 Decision boundaries for the colour example

In Example 2.3 we computed the prediction for $\mathbf{x}_\star = [1 \ 2]^\mathsf{T}$. If we were to shift that test point by one unit to the left at $\mathbf{x}_\star^{\text{alt}} = [0 \ 2]^\mathsf{T}$, the three closest training data points would still include $i = 6$ and $i = 4$, but now $i = 2$ is exchanged for $i = 1$. For $k = 3$ this would give two votes for Red and one vote for Blue, and we would therefore predict $\widehat{y}$ = Red. In between these two test data points $\mathbf{x}_\star$ and $\mathbf{x}_\star^{\text{alt}}$, at $[0.5 \ 2]^\mathsf{T}$, it is equally far to $i = 1$ as to $i = 2$, and it is undecided if the 3-NN classifier should predict Red or Blue. (In practice this is most often not a problem, since the test data points rarely end up exactly at the decision boundary. If they do, this can be handled by a coin-flip.) For all classifiers, we always end up with points in the input space where the class prediction abruptly changes from one class to another. These points are said to be on the *decision boundary* of the classifier.

Continuing in a similar way, changing the location of the test input across the entire input space and recording the class prediction, we can compute the complete decision boundaries for Example 2.3. We plot the decision boundaries for $k = 1$ and $k = 3$ in Figure 2.4.

In Figure 2.4 the decision boundaries are the points in input space where the class prediction changes, that is, the borders between red and blue. This type of figure gives a concise summary of a classifier. However, it is only possible to draw such a plot in the simple case when the problem has a 2-dimensional input $\mathbf{x}$. As we can see, the decision boundaries of k-NN are not linear. In the terminology we will introduce later, k-NN is thereby a non-linear classifier.

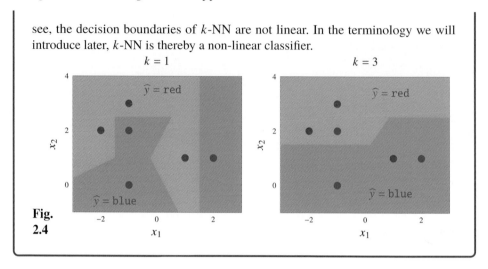

Fig. 2.4

Choosing *k*

The number of neighbours k that are considered when making a prediction with k-NN is an important choice the user has to make. Since k is not learned by k-NN itself, but is design choice left to the user, we refer to it as a *hyperparameter*. Throughout the book, we will use the term 'hyperparameter' for similar tuning parameters for other methods.

The choice of the hyperparameter k has a big impact on the predictions made by k-NN. To understand the impact of k, we study how the decision boundary changes as k changes in Figure 2.5, where k-NN is applied to the music classification Example 2.1 and the car stopping distance Example 2.2, both with $k = 1$ and $k = 20$.

With $k = 1$, all training data points will, by construction, be correctly predicted, and the model is adapted to the exact **x** and y values of the training data. In the classification problem there are, for instance, small green (Bob Dylan) regions within the red (the Beatles) area that are most likely misleading when it comes to accurately predicting the artist of a new song. In order to make good predictions, it would probably be better to instead predict red (the Beatles) for a new song in the entire middle-left region since the vast majority of training data points in that area are red. For the regression problem, $k = 1$ gives quite shaky behaviour, and also for this problem, it is intuitively clear that this does not describe an actual effect, but rather that the prediction is adapting to the noise in the data.

The drawbacks of using $k = 1$ are not specific to these two examples. In most real world problems there is a certain amount of randomness in the data, or at least insufficient information, which can be thought of as a random effect. In the music example, the $n = 230$ songs were selected from all songs ever recorded from these artists, and since we do not know how this selection was made, we may consider it random. Furthermore, and more importantly, if we want our classifier to generalise to completely new data, like new releases from the artists in our example (overlooking the obvious complication for now), then it is not reasonable to assume that the length and energy of a song will give a complete picture of the artistic styles. Hence,

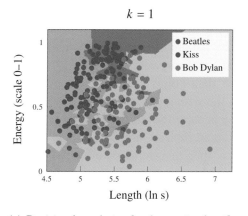

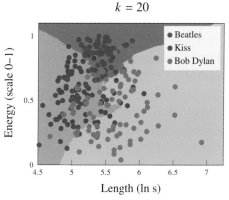

(a) Decision boundaries for the music classification problem using $k = 1$. This is a typical example of overfitting, meaning that the model has adapted too much to the training data so that it does not generalise well to new previously unseen data.

(b) The music classification problem again, now using $k = 20$. A higher value of k gives a smoother behaviour which, hopefully, predicts the artist of new songs more accurately.

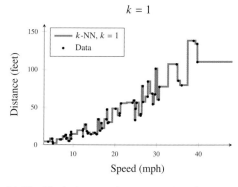

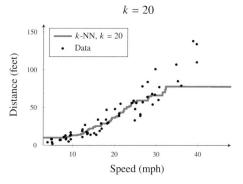

(c) The black dots are the car stopping distance data, and the blue line shows the prediction for k-NN with $k = 1$ for any x. As for the classification problem above, k-NN with $k = 1$ overfits to the training data.

(d) The car stopping distance, this time with $k = 20$. Except for the boundary effect at the right, this seems like a much more useful model which captures the interesting effects of the data and ignores the noise.

Figure 2.5 k-NN applied to the music classification Example 2.1 (a and b) and the car stopping distance Example 2.2 (c and d). For both problems k-NN is applied with $k = 1$ and $k = 20$.

even with the best possible model, there is some ambiguity about which artist has recorded a song if we only look at these two input variables. This ambiguity is modelled as random noise. Also for the car stopping distance, there appear to be a certain amount of random effects, not only in x but also in y. By using $k = 1$ and thereby adapting very closely to the training data, the predictions will depend not only on the interesting patterns in the problem but also on the (more or less) random effects that have shaped the training data. Typically we are not interested in capturing these effects, and we refer to this as *overfitting*.

With the k-NN classifier, we can mitigate overfitting by increasing the region of the neighbourhood used to compute the prediction, that is, increasing the hyperparameter k. With, for example, $k = 20$, the predictions are no longer based only on the closest neighbour but are instead a majority vote among the 20 closest neighbours. As a consequence, all training data points are no longer perfectly classified, but some of the songs end up in the wrong region in Figure 2.5b. The predictions are, however, less adapted to the peculiarities of the training data and thereby less overfitted, and Figure 2.5b and d are indeed less 'noisy' than Figure 2.5a and c. However, if we make k too large, then the averaging effect will wash out all interesting patterns in the data as well. Indeed, for sufficiently large k the neihbourhood will include all training data points, and the model will reduce to predicting the mean of the data for any input.

Selecting k is thus a trade-off between flexibility and rigidity. Since selecting k either too big or too small will lead to a meaningless classifiers, there must exist a sweet spot for some moderate k (possibly 20, but it could be less or more) where the classifier generalises the best. Unfortunately, there is no general answer to the k for which this happens, and this is different for different problems. In the music classification problem, it seems reasonable that $k = 20$ will predict new test data points better than $k = 1$, but there might very well be an even better choice of k. For the car stopping problem, the behaviour is also more reasonable for $k = 20$ than $k = 1$, except for the boundary effect for large x, where k-NN is unable to capture the trend in the data as x increases (simply because the 20 nearest neighbours are the same for all test points $x_\star$ around and above 35). A systematic way of choosing a good value for k is to use cross-validation, which we will discuss in Chapter 4.

> **Time to reflect 2.1** *The prediction $\widehat{y}(x_\star)$ obtained using the k-NN method is a piecewise constant function of the input $x_\star$. For a classification problem, this is natural, since the output is categorical (see, for example, Figure 2.5 where the coloured regions correspond to areas of the input space where the prediction is constant according to the colour of that region). However, k-NN will also have piecewise constant predictions for regression problems. Why?*

Input Normalisation

A final important practical aspect when using k-NN is the importance of normalisation of the input data. Imagine a training dataset with $p = 2$ input variables $\mathbf{x} = [x_1 \ x_2]^\mathsf{T}$ where all values of x_1 are in the range $[100, \ 1100]$ and the values for x_2 are in the much smaller range $[0, \ 1]$. It could, for example, be that x_1 and x_2 are measured in different units. The Euclidean distance between a test point $\mathbf{x}_\star$ and a training data point $\mathbf{x}_i$ is $\|\mathbf{x}_i - \mathbf{x}_\star\|_2 = \sqrt{(x_{i1} - x_{\star 1})^2 + (x_{i2} - x_{\star 2})^2}$. This expression will typically be dominated by the first term $(x_{i1} - x_{\star 1})^2$, whereas the second term $(x_{i2} - x_{\star 2})^2$ tends to have a much smaller effect, simply due to the different magnitude of x_1 and x_2. That is, the different ranges lead to x_1 being considered much more important than x_2 by k-NN.

To avoid this undesired effect, we can re-scale the input variables. One option, in the mentioned example, could be to subtract 100 from x_1 and thereafter divide it by 1 000 and create $x_{i1}^{\text{new}} = \frac{x_{i1}-100}{1\,000}$ such that x_1^{new} and x_2 both are in the range [0, 1]. More generally, this normalisation procedure for the input data can be written as

$$x_{ij}^{\text{new}} = \frac{x_{ij} - \min_\ell(x_{\ell j})}{\max_\ell(x_{\ell j}) - \min_\ell(x_{\ell j})}, \qquad \text{for all } j = 1,\ldots,p, \quad i = 1,\ldots,n. \quad (2.1)$$

Another common normalisation approach (sometimes called standardising) is by using the mean and standard deviation in the training data:

$$x_{ij}^{\text{new}} = \frac{x_{ij} - \bar{x}_j}{\sigma_j}, \qquad \forall j = 1,\ldots,p, \quad i = 1,\ldots,n, \quad (2.2)$$

where $\bar{x}_j$ and σ_j are the mean and standard deviation for each input variable, respectively.

It is crucial for k-NN to apply some type of input normalisation (as was indeed done in Figure 2.5), but it is a good practice to apply this also when using other methods, for numerical stability if nothing else. It is, however, important to compute the scaling factors ($\min_\ell(x_{\ell j})$, $\bar{x}_j$, etc.) using training data only and to also apply that scaling to future test data points. Failing to do this, for example by performing normalisation before setting test data aside (which we will discuss more in Chapter 4), might lead to wrong conclusions on how well the method will perform in predicting future (not yet seen) data points.

2.3 A Rule-Based Method: Decision Trees

The k-NN method results in a prediction $\widehat{y}(\mathbf{x}_\star)$ that is a piecewise constant function of the input $\mathbf{x}_\star$. That is, the method partitions the input space into disjoint regions, and each region is associated with a certain (constant) prediction. For k-NN, these regions are given implicitly by the k-neighbourhood of each possible test input. An alternative approach, that we will study in this section, is to come up with a set of *rules* that defines the regions explicitly. For instance, considering the music data in Example 2.1, a simple set of high-level rules for constructing a classifier would be: inputs to the right in Figure 2.1 are classified as green (Bob Dylan), in the left as red (The Beatles), and in the upper part as blue (Kiss). We will now see how such rules can be learned systematically from the training data.

The rule-based models that we consider here are referred to as *decision trees*. The reason is that the rules used to define the model can be organised in a graph structure referred to as a binary tree. The decision tree effectively divides the input space into multiple disjoint regions, and in each region, a constant value is used for the prediction $\widehat{y}(\mathbf{x}_\star)$. We illustrate this with an example.

Example 2.5 Predicting colours with a decision tree

We consider a classification problem with two numerical input variables $\mathbf{x} = [x_1 \; x_2]^\mathsf{T}$ and one categorical output y, the colour Red or Blue. For now, we do not consider any training data or how to actually learn the tree but only how an already existing decision tree can be used to predict $\widehat{y}(\mathbf{x}_\star)$.

The rules defining the model are organised in the graph in Figure 2.6, which is referred to as a binary tree. To use this tree to predict a label for the test input $\mathbf{x}_\star = [x_{\star 1} \; x_{\star 2}]^\mathsf{T}$, we start at the top, referred to as the *root node* of the tree (in the metaphor, the tree is growing upside down, with the root at the top and the leaves at the bottom). If the condition stated at the root is true, that is, if $x_{\star 2} < 3.0$, then we proceed down the left *branch*, otherwise along the right *branch*. If we reach a new *internal node* of the tree, we check the rule associated with that node and pick the left or the right branch accordingly. We continue and work our way down until we reach the end of a branch, called a *leaf node*. Each such final node corresponds to a constant prediction $\widehat{y}_m$, in this case one of the two classes Red or Blue.

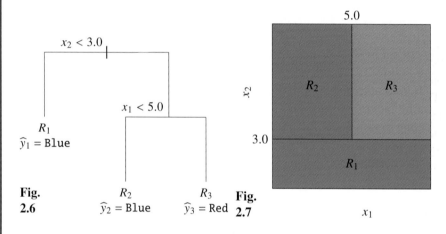

Fig. 2.6

Fig. 2.7

A classification tree. At each internal node, a rule of the form $x_j < s_k$ indicates the left branch coming from that split, and the right branch then consequently corresponds to $x_j \geq s_k$. This tree has two internal nodes (including the root) and three leaf nodes.

A region partition, where each region corresponds to a leaf node in the tree. Each border between regions corresponds to a split in the tree. Each region is coloured with the prediction corresponding to that region, and the boundary between red and blue is therefore the decision boundary.

The decision tree partitions the input space into axis-aligned 'boxes', as shown in Figure 2.7. By increasing the depth of the tree (the number of steps from the root to the leaves), the partitioning can be made finer and finer and thereby describes more complicated functions of the input variable.

Pseudo-code for predicting a test input with the tree in Figure 2.6 would look like:

```
if x_2 < 3.0 then
        return Blue
else
        if x_1 < 5.0 then
```

```
                return Blue
          else
                return Red
          end
    end
```

As an example, if we have $\mathbf{x}_\star = [2.5 \ 3.5]^\mathsf{T}$, in the first split we would take the right branch since $x_{\star 2} = 3.5 \geq 3.0$, and in the second split we would take the left branch since $x_{\star 1} = 2.5 < 5.0$. The prediction for this test point would be $\widehat{y}(\mathbf{x}_\star) = $ Blue.

To set the terminology, the endpoint of each branch R_1, R_2, and R_3 in Example 2.5 are called *leaf nodes*, and the internal splits, $x_2 < 3.0$ and $x_1 < 5.0$, are known as *internal nodes*. The lines that connect the nodes are referred to as *branches*. The tree is referred to as *binary* since each internal node splits into exactly two branches.

With more than two input variables, it is difficult to illustrate the partitioning of the input space into regions (Figure 2.7), but the tree representation can still be used in the very same way. Each internal node corresponds to a rule where one of the p input variables x_j, $j = 1, \ldots, p$, is compared to a threshold s. If $x_j < s$, we continue along the left branch, and if $x_j \geq s$, we continue along the right branch.

The constant predictions that we associate with the leaf nodes can be either categorical (as in Example 2.5 above) or numerical. Decision trees can thus be used to address both classification and regression problems.

Example 2.5 illustrated how a decision tree can be used to make a prediction. We will now turn to the question of how a tree can be learned from training data.

Learning a Regression Tree

We will start by discussing how to learn (or, equivalently, train) a decision tree for a regression problem. The classification problem is conceptually similar and will be explained later.

As mentioned above, the prediction $\widehat{y}(\mathbf{x}_\star)$ from a regression tree is a piecewise constant function of the input $\mathbf{x}_\star$. We can write this mathematically as,

$$\widehat{y}(\mathbf{x}_\star) = \sum_{\ell=1}^{L} \widehat{y}_\ell \mathbb{I}\{\mathbf{x}_\star \in R_\ell\}, \tag{2.3}$$

where L is the total number of regions (leaf nodes) in the tree, R_ℓ is the ℓth region, and $\widehat{y}_\ell$ is the constant prediction for the ℓth region. Note that in the regression setting, $\widehat{y}_\ell$ is a numerical variable, and we will consider it to be a real number for simplicity. In the equation above, we have used the indicator function, $\mathbb{I}\{\mathbf{x} \in R_\ell\} = 1$ if $\mathbf{x} \in R_\ell$ and $\mathbb{I}\{\mathbf{x} \in R_\ell\} = 0$ otherwise.

Learning the tree from data corresponds to finding suitable values for the parameters defining the function (2.3), namely the regions R_ℓ and the constant predictions $\widehat{y}_\ell$, $\ell = 1, \ldots, L$, as well as the total size of the tree L. If we start by assuming that the shape of the tree, the partition $(L, \{R_\ell\}_{\ell=1}^{L})$, is known, then we can compute the constants $\{\widehat{y}_\ell\}_{\ell=1}^{L}$ in a natural way, simply as the average of the training data points falling in each region:

$$\boxed{\widehat{y}_\ell = \text{Average}\{y_i : \mathbf{x}_i \in R_\ell\}.}$$

It remains to find the shape of the tree, the regions R_ℓ, which requires a bit more work. The basic idea is, of course, to select the regions so that the tree fits the training data. This means that the output predictions from the tree should match the output values in the training data. Unfortunately, even when restricting ourselves to seemingly simple regions such as the 'boxes' obtained from a decision tree, finding the tree (a collection of splitting rules) that optimally partitions the input space to fit the training data as well as possible turns out to be computationally infeasible. The problem is that there is a combinatorial explosion in the number of ways in which we can partition the input space. Searching through all possible binary trees is not possible in practice unless the tree size is so small that it is not of practical use.

To handle this situation, we use a heuristic algorithm known as *recursive binary splitting* for learning the tree. The word recursive means that we will determine the splitting rules one after the other, starting with the first split at the root and then building the tree from top to bottom. The algorithm is *greedy*, in the sense that the tree is constructed one split at a time, without having the complete tree 'in mind'. That is, when determining the splitting rule at the root node, the objective is to obtain a model that explains the training data as well as possible after a single split, without taking into consideration that additional splits may be added before arriving at the final model. When we have decided on the first split of the input space (corresponding to the root node of the tree), this split is kept fixed, and we continue in a similar way for the two resulting half-spaces (corresponding to the two branches of the tree), etc.

To see in detail how one step of this algorithm works, consider the situation when we are about to do our very first split at the root of the tree. Hence, we want to select one of the p input variables $x_1, \ldots, x_p$ and a corresponding cutpoint s which divide the input space into two half-spaces,

$$R_1(j, s) = \{\mathbf{x} \mid x_j < s\} \qquad \text{and} \qquad R_2(j, s) = \{\mathbf{x} \mid x_j \geq s\}. \tag{2.4}$$

Note that the regions depend on the index j of the splitting variable as well as the value of the cutpoint s, which is why we write them as functions of j and s. This is the case also for the predictions associated with the two regions,

$$\widehat{y}_1(j, s) = \text{Average}\{y_i : \mathbf{x}_i \in R_1(j, s)\} \quad \text{and} \quad \widehat{y}_2(j, s) = \text{Average}\{y_i : \mathbf{x}_i \in R_2(j, s)\},$$

since the averages in these expressions range over different data points depending on the regions.

For each training data point $(\mathbf{x}_i, y_i)$, we can compute a prediction error by first determining which region the data point falls in and then computing the difference between y_i and the constant prediction associated with that region. Doing this for all training data points, the sum of squared errors can be written as

$$\sum_{i: \mathbf{x}_i \in R_1(j,s)} (y_i - \widehat{y}_1(j,s))^2 + \sum_{i: \mathbf{x}_i \in R_2(j,s)} (y_i - \widehat{y}_2(j,s))^2 . \tag{2.5}$$

The square is added to ensure that the expression above is non-negative and that both positive and negative errors are counted equally. The squared error is a common *loss function* used for measuring the closeness of a prediction to the training data, but other loss functions can also be used. We will discuss the choice of loss function in more detail in later chapters.

To find the optimal split, we select the values for j and s that minimise the squared error (2.5). This minimisation problem can be solved easily by looping through all possible values for $j = 1, \ldots, p$. For each j, we can scan through the finite number of possible splits and pick the pair (j, s) for which the expression above is minimised. As pointed out above, when we have found the optimal split at the root node, this splitting rule is fixed. We then continue in the same way for the left and right branches independently. Each branch (corresponding to a half-space) is split again by minimising the squared prediction error over all training data points following that branch.

In principle, we can continue in this way until there is only a single training data point in each of the regions – that is, until $L = n$. Such a fully grown tree will result in predictions that exactly match the training data points, and the resulting model is quite similar to k-NN with $k = 1$. As pointed out above, this will typically result in too erratic a model that has overfitted to (possibly noisy) training data. To mitigate this issue, it is common to stop the growth of the tree at an earlier stage using some stopping criterion, for instance by deciding on L beforehand, limiting the maximum depth (number of splits in any branch), or adding a constraint on the minimum number of training data points associated with each leaf node. Forcing the model to have more training data points in each leaf will result in an averaging effect, similar to increasing the value of k in the k-NN method. Using such a stopping criterion means that the value of L is not set manually but is determined adaptively based on the result of the learning procedure.

A high-level summary of the method is given in Method 2.2. Note that the learning in Method 2.2 includes a recursive call, where in each recursion we grow one branch of the tree one step further.

Classification Trees

Trees can also be used for classification. We use the same procedure of recursive binary splitting but with two main differences. Firstly, we use a majority vote instead of an average to compute the prediction associated with each region:

$$\widehat{y}_\ell = \text{Majority Vote}\{y_i : \mathbf{x}_i \in R_\ell\}.$$

Learn a decision tree using recursive binary splitting

Data: Training data $\mathcal{T} = \{\mathbf{x}_i, y_i\}_{i=1}^n$

Result: Decision tree with regions $R_1, \ldots, R_L$ and corresponding predictions $\widehat{y}_1, \ldots, \widehat{y}_L$

1 Let R denote the whole input space

2 Compute the regions $(R_1, \ldots, R_L) = \mathtt{Split}(R, \mathcal{T})$

3 Compute the predictions $\widehat{y}_\ell$ for $\ell = 1, \ldots, L$ as

$$\widehat{y}_\ell = \begin{cases} \text{Average}\{y_i : \mathbf{x}_i \in R_\ell\} & \text{(Regression problems)} \\ \text{Majority Vote}\{y_i : \mathbf{x}_i \in R_\ell\} & \text{(Classification problems)} \end{cases}$$

4 **Function** $\mathtt{Split}(R, \mathcal{T})$:

5   **if** *stopping criterion fulfilled* **then**

6   **return** R

7   **else**

8   Go through all possible splits $x_j < s$ for all input variables $j = 1, \ldots, p$.

9   Pick the pair (j, s) that minimises (2.5)/(2.6) for regression/classification problems.

10   Split region R into R_1 and R_2 according to (2.4).

11   Split data $\mathcal{T}$ into $\mathcal{T}_1$ and $\mathcal{T}_2$ accordingly.

12   **return** $\mathtt{Split}(R_1, \mathcal{T}_1)$, $\mathtt{Split}(R_2, \mathcal{T}_2)$

13   **end**

14 **end**

Predict from a decision tree

Data: Decision tree with regions $R_1, \ldots, R_L$, training data $\mathcal{T} = \{\mathbf{x}_i, y_i\}_{i=1}^n$, test data point $\mathbf{x}_\star$

Result: Predicted test output $\widehat{y}(\mathbf{x}_\star)$

1 Find the region R_ℓ which $\mathbf{x}_\star$ belongs to.

2 Return the prediction $\widehat{y}(\mathbf{x}_\star) = \widehat{y}_\ell$.

Method 2.2 Decision trees

Secondly, when learning the tree, we need a different splitting criterion than the squared prediction error to take into account the fact that the output is categorical. To define these criteria, note first that the split at any internal node is computed by solving an optimisation problem of the form

$$\min_{j,s} n_1 Q_1 + n_2 Q_2, \tag{2.6}$$

where n_1 and n_2 denote the number of training data points in the left and right nodes of the current split, respectively, and Q_1 and Q_2 are the costs (derived form the prediction errors) associated with these two nodes. The variables j and s denote the index of the splitting variable and the cutpoint as before. All of the terms n_1, n_2, Q_1, and Q_2 depend on these variables, but we have dropped the explicit dependence from the notation for brevity. Comparing (2.6) with (2.5), we see that we recover the regression case if Q_ℓ corresponds to the mean-squared error in node ℓ.

To generalise this to the classification case, we still solve the optimisation problem (2.6) to compute the split, but choose Q_ℓ in a different way which respects the categorical nature of a classification problem. To this end, we first introduce

$$\widehat{\pi}_{\ell m} = \frac{1}{n_\ell} \sum_{i:\mathbf{x}_i \in R_\ell} \mathbb{I}\{y_i = m\}$$

to be the proportion of training observations in the ℓth region that belong to the mth class. We can then define the *splitting criterion*, Q_ℓ, based on these class proportions. One simple alternative is the *misclassification rate*

$$Q_\ell = 1 - \max_m \widehat{\pi}_{\ell m}, \tag{2.7a}$$

which is simply the proportion of data points in region R_ℓ which do not belong to the most common class. Other common splitting criteria are the *Gini index*

$$Q_\ell = \sum_{m=1}^{M} \widehat{\pi}_{\ell m}(1 - \widehat{\pi}_{\ell m}) \tag{2.7b}$$

and the *entropy* criterion,

$$Q_\ell = - \sum_{m=1}^{M} \widehat{\pi}_{\ell m} \ln \widehat{\pi}_{\ell m}. \tag{2.7c}$$

In Example 2.6 we illustrate how to construct a classification tree using recursive binary splitting and with the entropy as the splitting criterion.

Example 2.6 Learning a classification tree (continuation of Example 2.5)

We consider the same setup as in Example 2.5, but now with the following dataset:
We want to learn a classification tree by using the entropy criterion in (2.7c) and growing the tree until there are no regions with more than five data points left.

First split: There are infinitely many possible splits we can make, but all splits which give the same partition of the data points are equivalent. Hence, in practice we only have nine different splits to consider in this dataset. The data (dots) and these possible splits (dashed lines) are visualised in Figure 2.8.

We consider all nine splits in turn. We start with the split at $x_1 = 2.5$, which splits the input space into two regions, $R_1 = x_1 < 2.5$ and $R_2 = x_1 \geq 2.5$. In region R_1 we

x_1	x_2	y
9.0	2.0	Blue
1.0	4.0	Blue
4.0	6.0	Blue
4.0	1.0	Blue
1.0	2.0	Blue
1.0	8.0	Red
6.0	4.0	Red
7.0	9.0	Red
9.0	8.0	Red
9.0	6.0	Red

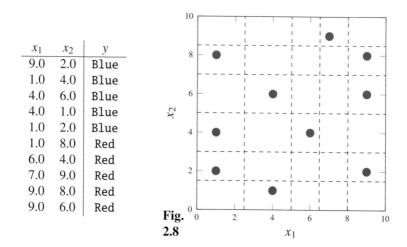

Fig. 2.8

have two blue data points and one red, in total $n_1 = 3$ data points. The proportion of the two classes in region R_1 will therefore be $\widehat{\pi}_{1B} = 2/3$ and $\widehat{\pi}_{1R} = 1/3$. The entropy is calculated as

$$Q_1 = -\widehat{\pi}_{1B} \ln(\widehat{\pi}_{1B}) - \widehat{\pi}_{1R} \ln(\widehat{\pi}_{1R}) = -\frac{2}{3} \ln\left(\frac{2}{3}\right) - \frac{1}{3} \ln\left(\frac{1}{3}\right) = 0.64.$$

In region R_2 we have $n_2 = 7$ data points with the proportions $\widehat{\pi}_{2B} = 3/7$ and $\widehat{\pi}_{2R} = 4/7$. The entropy for this region will be

$$Q_2 = -\widehat{\pi}_{2B} \ln(\widehat{\pi}_{2B}) - \widehat{\pi}_{2R} \ln(\widehat{\pi}_{2R}) = -\frac{3}{7} \ln\left(\frac{3}{7}\right) - \frac{4}{7} \ln\left(\frac{4}{7}\right) = 0.68,$$

and inserted in (2.6), the total weighted entropy for this split becomes

$$n_1 Q_1 + n_2 Q_2 = 3 \cdot 0.64 + 7 \cdot 0.68 = 6.69.$$

We compute the costs for all other splits in the same manner and summarise them in the table below:

Split (R_1)	n_1	$\widehat{\pi}_{1B}$	$\widehat{\pi}_{1R}$	Q_1	n_2	$\widehat{\pi}_{2B}$	$\widehat{\pi}_{2R}$	Q_2	$n_1 Q_1 + n_2 Q_2$
$x_1 < 2.5$	3	2/3	1/3	0.64	7	3/7	4/7	0.68	6.69
$x_1 < 5.0$	5	4/5	1/5	0.50	5	1/5	4/5	0.50	5.00
$x_1 < 6.5$	6	4/6	2/6	0.64	4	1/4	3/4	0.56	6.07
$x_1 < 8.0$	7	4/7	3/7	0.68	3	1/3	2/3	0.64	6.69
$x_2 < 1.5$	1	1/1	0/1	0.00	9	4/9	5/9	0.69	6.18
$x_2 < 3.0$	3	3/3	0/3	0.00	7	2/7	5/7	0.60	**4.18**
$x_2 < 5.0$	5	4/5	1/5	0.50	5	1/5	4/5	0.06	5.00
$x_2 < 7.0$	7	5/7	2/7	0.60	3	0/3	3/3	0.00	**4.18**
$x_2 < 8.5$	9	5/9	4/9	0.69	1	0/1	1/1	0.00	6.18

From the table, we can read that the two splits at $x_2 < 3.0$ and $x_2 < 7.0$ are both equally good. We choose to continue with $x_2 < 3.0$.

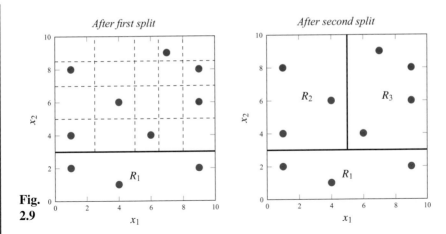

Fig. 2.9

Second split: We note that only the upper region has more than five data points. Also, there is no point splitting region R_1 further since it only contains data points from the same class. In the next step, we therefore split the upper region into two new regions, R_2 and R_3. All possible splits are displayed in Figure 2.9 to the left (dashed lines), and we compute their costs in the same manner as before:

Splits (R_1)	n_2	$\widehat{\pi}_{2B}$	$\widehat{\pi}_{2R}$	Q_2	n_3	$\widehat{\pi}_{3B}$	$\widehat{\pi}_{3R}$	Q_3	$n_2Q_2 + n_3Q_3$
$x_1 < 2.5$	2	1/2	1/2	0.69	5	1/5	4/5	0.50	3.89
$x_1 < 5.0$	3	2/3	1/3	0.63	4	0/4	4/4	0.00	**1.91**
$x_1 < 6.5$	4	2/4	2/4	0.69	3	0/3	3/3	0.00	2.77
$x_1 < 8.0$	5	2/5	3/5	0.67	2	0/2	2/2	0.00	3.37
$x_2 < 5.0$	2	1/2	1/2	0.69	5	1/5	4/5	0.50	3.88
$x_2 < 7.0$	4	2/4	2/4	0.69	3	0/3	3/3	0.00	2.77
$x_2 < 8.5$	6	2/6	4/6	0.64	1	0/1	1/1	0.00	3.82

The best split is the one at $x_1 < 5.0$, visualised above to the right. None of the three regions has more than five data points. Therefore, we terminate the training. The final tree and its partitions were displayed in Example 2.5. If we want to use the tree for prediction, we predict blue if $\mathbf{x}_\star \in R_1$ or $\mathbf{x}_\star \in R_2$ since the blue training data points are in the majority in each of these two regions. Similarly, we predict red if $\mathbf{x}_\star \in R_3$.

When choosing between the different splitting criteria mentioned above, the misclassification rate sounds like a reasonable choice since that is typically the criterion we want the final model to do well on.[6] However, one drawback is that it does not favour pure nodes. By pure nodes we mean nodes where most of the data points belong to a certain class. It is usually an advantage to favour pure nodes in the greedy procedure that we use to grow the tree, since this can lead to fewer splits

---

[6]This is not always true, for example for imbalanced and asymmetric classification problems; see Section 4.5.

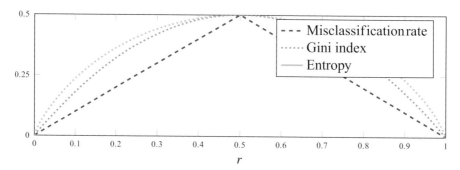

Figure 2.10 Three splitting criteria for classification trees as a function of the proportion of the first class $r = \pi_{\ell 1}$ in a certain region R_ℓ as given in (2.8). The entropy criterion has been scaled such that it passes through (0.5,0.5).

in total. Both the entropy criterion and the Gini index favour node purity more than the misclassification rate does.

This advantage can also be illustrated in Example 2.6. Consider the first split in this example. If we were to use the misclassification rate as the splitting criterion, both the split $x_2 < 5.0$ and the split $x_2 < 3.0$ would provide a total misclassification rate of 0.2. However, the split at $x_2 < 3.0$, which the entropy criterion favoured, provides a pure node R_1. If we now went with the split $x_2 < 5.0$, the misclassification after the second split would still be 0.2. If we continued to grow the tree until no data points were misclassified, we would need three splits if we used the entropy criterion, whereas we would need five splits if we used the misclassification criterion and started with the split at $x_2 < 5.0$.

To generalise this discussion, consider a problem with two classes, where we denote the proportion of the first class as $\pi_{\ell 1} = r$ and hence the proportion of the second class as $\pi_{\ell 2} = 1 - r$. The three criteria (2.7) can then be expressed in terms of r as

$$\text{Misclassification rate:} \quad Q_\ell = 1 - \max(r, 1 - r),$$

$$\text{Gini index:} \quad Q_\ell = 2r(1 - r), \tag{2.8}$$

$$\text{Entropy:} \quad Q_\ell = -r \ln r - (1 - r) \ln(1 - r).$$

These functions are shown in Figure 2.10. All three citeria are similar in the sense that they provide zero loss if all data points belong to either of the two classes and maximum loss if the data points are equally divided between the two classes. However, the Gini index and entropy have a higher loss for all other proportions. In other words, the gain of having a pure node (r close to 0 or 1) is higher for the Gini index and the entropy than for the misclassification rate. As a consequence, the Gini index and the entropy both tend to favour making one of the two nodes pure (or close to pure) since that provides a smaller total loss, which can make a good combination with the greedy nature of the recursive binary splitting.

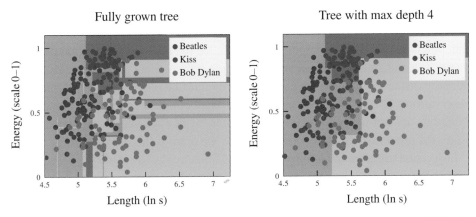

(a) Decision boundaries for the music classification problem for a fully grown classification tree with the Gini index. This model overfits the data.

(b) The same problem and data as in 2.11a for which a tree restricted to depth 4 has been learned, again using the Gini index. This models will hopefully make better predictions for new data.

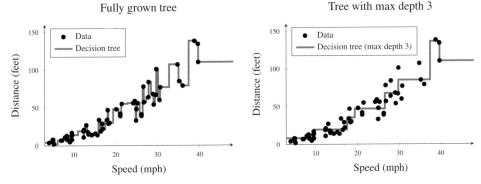

(c) The prediction for a fully grown regression tree. As for the classification problem above, this model overfits to the training data.

(d) The same problem and data as in 2.11c for which a tree restricted to depth 3 has been learned.

Figure 2.11 Decision trees applied to the music classification Example 2.1 (a and b) and the car stopping distance Example 2.2 (c and d).

How Deep Should a Decision Tree be?

The depth of a decision tree (the maximum distance between the root node and any leaf node) has a big impact on the final predictions. The tree depth impacts the predictions in a somewhat similar way to the hyperparameter k in k-NN. We again use the music classification and car stopping distance problems from Examples 2.1 and 2.2 to study how the decision boundaries change depending on the depth of the trees. In Figure 2.11, the decision boundaries are illustrated for two different trees. In Figure 2.11a and c, we have not restricted the depth of the tree and have grown it until each region contains only data points with the same output value – a so-called fully grown tree. In Figure 2.11b and d, the maximum depth is restricted to 4 and 3, respectively.

35

Similarly to choosing $k = 1$ in k-NN, for a fully grown tree, all training data points will, by construction, be correctly predicted since each region only contains data points with the same output. As a result, for the music classification problem, we get thin and small regions adapted to single training data points, and for the car stopping distance problem, we get a very irregular line passing exactly through the observations. Even though these trees give excellent performance on the training data, they are not likely to be the best models for new, as yet unseen data. As we discussed previously in the context of k-NN, we refer to this as overfitting.

In decision trees, we can mitigate overfitting by using shallower trees. Consequently, we get fewer and larger regions with an increased averaging effect, resulting in decision boundaries that are less adapted to the noise in the training data. This is illustrated in Figure 2.11b and d for the two example problems. As for k in k-NN, the optimal size of the tree depends on many properties of the problem, and it is a trade-off between flexibility and rigidity. Similar trade-offs have to be made for almost all methods presented in this book, and they will be discussed systematically in Chapter 4.

How can the user control the growth of the tree? Here we have different strategies. The most straightforward strategy is to adjust the stopping criterion, that is, the condition that should be fulfilled for not proceeding with further splits in a certain node. As mentioned earlier, this criterion could be that we do not attempt further splits if there are less than a certain number of training data points in the corresponding region, or, as in Figure 2.11, we can stop splitting when we reach a certain depth. Another strategy to control the depth is to use *pruning*. In pruning, we start with a fully grown tree, and then in a second post-processing step, prune it back to a smaller one. We will, however, not discuss pruning further here.

2.4 Further Reading

The reason why we started this book by k-NN is that it is perhaps the most intuitive and straightforward way to solve a classification problem. The idea is at least a thousand years old and was described already by Ḥassan Ibn al-Haytham (latinised as Alhazen) around the year 1030 in *Kitāb al-Manāẓir* (*Book of Optics*) (Pelillo 2014), as an explanation of how the human brain perceives objects. As with many good ideas, the nearest neighbour idea has been re-invented many times, and a more modern description of k-NN can be found in Cover and Hart (1967).

Also, the basic idea of decision trees is relatively simple, but there are many possible ways to improve and extend them as well as different options for how to implement them in detail. A somewhat longer introduction to decision trees is found in Hastie et al. (2009), and a historically oriented overview can be found in Loh (2014). Of particular significance is perhaps CART (Classification and Regression Trees, Breiman et al. (1984)), as well as ID3 and C4.5 (Quinlan 1986), Quinlan (1993).

3 Basic Parametric Models and a Statistical Perspective on Learning

In the previous chapter, we introduced the supervised machine learning problem, as well as two methods for solving it. In this chapter, we will consider a generic approach to learning referred to as *parametric* modelling. In particular, we will introduce *linear regression* and *logistic regression*, which are two such parametric models. The key point of a parametric model is that it contains some parameters θ, which are learned from training data. However, once the parameters are learned, the training data may be discarded, since the prediction only depends on θ.

3.1 Linear Regression

Regression is one of the two fundamental tasks of supervised learning (the other one is classification). We will now introduce the *linear regression* model, which might (at least historically) be the most popular method for solving regression problems. Despite its relative simplicity, it is a surprisingly useful and is an important stepping stone for more advanced methods, such as deep learning (see Chapter 6).

As discussed in the previous chapter, regression amounts to learning the relationships between some input variables $\mathbf{x} = [x_1 \ x_2 \ \ldots \ x_p]^\mathsf{T}$ and a numerical output variable y. The inputs can be either categorical or numerical, but we will start by assuming that all p inputs are numerical as well, and discuss categorical inputs later. In a more mathematical framework, regression is about learning a *model f*,

$$y = f(\mathbf{x}) + \varepsilon, \tag{3.1}$$

mapping the input to the output, where ε is an error term that describes everything about the input–output relationship that cannot be captured by the model. With a statistical perspective, we consider ε as a random variable, referred to as *noise*, that is independent of $\mathbf{x}$ and has mean value of zero. As a running example of regression, we will use the car stopping distance regression problem introduced in the previous chapter as Example 2.2.

The Linear Regression Model

The linear regression model assumes that the output variable y (a scalar) can be described as an affine[1] combination of the p input variables $x_1, x_2, \ldots, x_p$ plus a noise term ε,

$$y = \theta_0 + \theta_1 x_1 + \theta_2 x_2 + \cdots + \theta_p x_p + \varepsilon. \tag{3.2}$$

We refer to the coefficients $\theta_0, \theta_1, \ldots \theta_p$ as the *parameters* of the model, and we sometimes refer to θ_0 specifically as the intercept (or offset) term. The noise term ε accounts for random errors in the data not captured by the model. The noise is assumed to have mean zero and to be independent of $\mathbf{x}$. The zero-mean assumption is nonrestrictive, since any (constant) non-zero mean can be incorporated in the offset term θ_0.

To have a more compact notation, we introduce the parameter vector $\boldsymbol{\theta} = [\theta_0 \ \theta_1 \ \cdots \ \theta_p]^\mathsf{T}$ and extend the vector $\mathbf{x}$ with a constant one in its first position, such that we can write the linear regression model (3.2) compactly as

$$y = \theta_0 + \theta_1 x_1 + \theta_2 x_2 + \cdots + \theta_p x_p + \varepsilon = \begin{bmatrix} \theta_0 & \theta_1 & \cdots & \theta_p \end{bmatrix} \begin{bmatrix} 1 \\ x_1 \\ \vdots \\ x_p \end{bmatrix} + \varepsilon = \boldsymbol{\theta}^\mathsf{T} \mathbf{x} + \varepsilon. \tag{3.3}$$

This notation means that the symbol $\mathbf{x}$ is used both for the $p+1$ and the p-dimensional versions of the input vector, with or without the constant one in the leading position, respectively. This is only a matter of book-keeping for handling the intercept term θ_0. Which definition is used will be clear from the context and carries no deeper meaning.

The linear regression model is a *parametric* function of the form (3.3). The parameters $\boldsymbol{\theta}$ can take arbitrary values, and the actual values that we assign to them will control the input–output relationship described by the model. *Learning* of the model therefore amounts to finding suitable values for $\boldsymbol{\theta}$ based on observed training data. Before discussing how to do this, however, let us first look at how to use the model for predictions once it has been learned.

The goal in supervised machine learning is making predictions $\widehat{y}(\mathbf{x}_\star)$ for new, previously unseen, test inputs $\mathbf{x}_\star = [1 \ x_{\star 1} \ x_{\star 2} \ \cdots \ x_{\star p}]^\mathsf{T}$. Let us assume that we have already learned some parameter values $\widehat{\boldsymbol{\theta}}$ for the linear regression model (how this is done will be described next). We use the symbol $\widehat{}$ to indicate that $\widehat{\boldsymbol{\theta}}$ contains learned values of the unknown parameter vector $\boldsymbol{\theta}$. Since we assume that the noise

---

[1] An affine function is a linear function plus a constant offset.

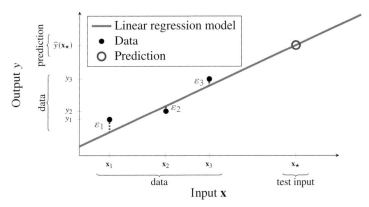

Figure 3.1 Linear regression with $p = 1$: The black dots represent $n = 3$ data points, from which a linear regression model (blue line) is learned. The model does not fit the data perfectly, so there is a remaining error corresponding to the noise ε (red). The model can be used to *predict* (blue circle) the output $\widehat{y}(\mathbf{x}_\star)$ for a test input $\mathbf{x}_\star$.

term ε is random with zero mean and independent of all observed variables, it makes sense to replace ε with 0 in the prediction. That is, a prediction from the linear regression model takes the form

$$\widehat{y}(\mathbf{x}_\star) = \widehat{\theta}_0 + \widehat{\theta}_1 x_{\star 1} + \widehat{\theta}_2 x_{\star 2} + \cdots + \widehat{\theta}_p x_{\star p} = \widehat{\boldsymbol{\theta}}^\mathsf{T} \mathbf{x}_\star. \tag{3.4}$$

The noise term ε is often referred to as an *irreducible error* or an *aleatoric*[2] uncertainty in the prediction. We illustrate the predictions made by a linear regression model in Figure 3.1.

Training a Linear Regression Model from Training Data

Let us now discuss how to train a linear regression model, that is to learn $\boldsymbol{\theta}$, from training data $\mathcal{T} = \{\mathbf{x}_i, y_i\}_{i=1}^n$. We collect the training data, which consists of n data point with inputs $\mathbf{x}_i$ and outputs y_i, in the $n \times (p + 1)$ matrix $\mathbf{X}$ and n-dimensional vector $\mathbf{y}$,

$$\mathbf{X} = \begin{bmatrix} \mathbf{x}_1^\mathsf{T} \\ \mathbf{x}_2^\mathsf{T} \\ \vdots \\ \mathbf{x}_n^\mathsf{T} \end{bmatrix}, \quad \mathbf{y} = \begin{bmatrix} y_1 \\ y_2 \\ \vdots \\ y_n \end{bmatrix}, \quad \text{where each } \mathbf{x}_i = \begin{bmatrix} 1 \\ x_{i1} \\ x_{i2} \\ \vdots \\ x_{ip} \end{bmatrix}. \tag{3.5}$$

---

[2] From the Latin word *aleator*, meaning dice-player.

Example 3.1 Car stopping distances

We continue Example 2.2 and train a linear regression model for the car stopping distance data. We start by forming the matrices $\mathbf{X}$ and $\mathbf{y}$. Since we only have one input and one output, both x_i and y_i are scalar. We get

$$\mathbf{X} = \begin{bmatrix} 1 & 4.0 \\ 1 & 4.9 \\ 1 & 5.0 \\ 1 & 5.1 \\ 1 & 5.2 \\ \vdots & \vdots \\ 1 & 39.6 \\ 1 & 39.7 \end{bmatrix}, \quad \boldsymbol{\theta} = \begin{bmatrix} \theta_0 \\ \theta_1 \end{bmatrix}, \quad \text{and} \quad \mathbf{y} = \begin{bmatrix} 4.0 \\ 8.0 \\ 8.0 \\ 4.0 \\ 2.0 \\ \vdots \\ 134.0 \\ 110.0 \end{bmatrix}. \tag{3.6}$$

Altogether we can use this vector and matrix notation to describe the linear regression model for all training data points $\mathbf{x}_i$, $i = 1, \ldots, n$ in one equation as a matrix multiplication,

$$\mathbf{y} = \mathbf{X}\boldsymbol{\theta} + \boldsymbol{\epsilon}, \tag{3.7}$$

where $\boldsymbol{\epsilon}$ is a vector of errors/noise terms. Moreover, we can also define a vector of predicted outputs for the training data $\widehat{\mathbf{y}} = \begin{bmatrix} \widehat{y}(\mathbf{x}_1) & \widehat{y}(\mathbf{x}_2) & \cdots & \widehat{y}(\mathbf{x}_n) \end{bmatrix}^{\mathsf{T}}$, which also allows a compact matrix formulation,

$$\widehat{\mathbf{y}} = \mathbf{X}\boldsymbol{\theta}. \tag{3.8}$$

Note that whereas $\mathbf{y}$ is a vector of recorded training data values, $\widehat{\mathbf{y}}$ is a vector whose entries are functions of $\boldsymbol{\theta}$. Learning the unknown parameters $\boldsymbol{\theta}$ amounts to finding values such that $\widehat{\mathbf{y}}$ is similar to $\mathbf{y}$. That is, the predictions given by the model should fit the training data well. There are multiple ways to define what 'similar' or 'well' actually means, but it somehow amounts to finding $\boldsymbol{\theta}$ such that $\widehat{\mathbf{y}} - \mathbf{y} = \boldsymbol{\epsilon}$ is small. We will approach this by formulating a loss function, which gives a mathematical meaning to 'fitting the data well'. We will thereafter interpret the loss function from a statistical perspective, by understanding this as selecting the value of $\boldsymbol{\theta}$ which makes the observed training data $\mathbf{y}$ as likely as possible with respect to the model – the so-called *maximum likelihood* solution. Later, in Chapter 9, we will also introduce a conceptually different way of learning $\boldsymbol{\theta}$.

Loss Functions and Cost Functions

A principled way to define the learning problem is to introduce a *loss function* $L(\widehat{y}, y)$ which measures how close the model's prediction $\widehat{y}$ is to the observed data y. If the model fits the data well, so that $\widehat{y} \approx y$, then the loss function should take a small value, and vice versa. Based on the chosen loss function, we also define the *cost function* as the average loss over the training data. Training a model then amounts to finding the parameter values that minimise the cost

$$
\widehat{\theta} = \arg\min_{\theta} \underbrace{\frac{1}{n} \sum_{i=1}^{n} \overbrace{L(\widehat{y}(\mathbf{x}_i; \theta), y_i)}^{\text{loss function}}}_{\text{cost function } J(\theta)}. \tag{3.9}
$$

Note that each term in the expression above corresponds to evaluating the loss function for the prediction $\widehat{y}(\mathbf{x}_i; \theta)$, given by (3.4), for the training point with index i and the true output value y_i at that point. To emphasise that the prediction depends on the parameters θ, we have included θ as an argument to $\widehat{y}$ for clarity. The operator arg min$_\theta$ means 'the value of θ for which the cost function attains it minimum'. The relationship between loss and cost functions (3.9) is general for all cost functions in this book.

Least Squares and the Normal Equations

For regression, a commonly used loss function is the *squared error* loss

$$
L(\widehat{y}(\mathbf{x}; \theta), y) = (\widehat{y}(\mathbf{x}; \theta) - y)^2. \tag{3.10}
$$

This loss function is 0 if $\widehat{y}(\mathbf{x}; \theta) = y$ and grows fast (quadratically) as the difference between y and the prediction $\widehat{y}(\mathbf{x}; \theta) = \theta^\mathsf{T}\mathbf{x}$ increases. The corresponding cost function for the linear regression model (3.7) can be written with matrix notation as

$$
J(\theta) = \frac{1}{n} \sum_{i=1}^{n} (\widehat{y}(\mathbf{x}_i; \theta) - y_i)^2 = \frac{1}{n} \|\widehat{\mathbf{y}} - \mathbf{y}\|_2^2 = \frac{1}{n} \|\mathbf{X}\theta - \mathbf{y}\|_2^2 = \frac{1}{n} \|\boldsymbol{\epsilon}\|_2^2, \tag{3.11}
$$

where $\| \cdot \|_2$ denotes the usual Euclidean vector norm and $\| \cdot \|_2^2$ its square. Due to the square, this particular cost function is also commonly referred to as the *least squares* cost. It is illustrated in Figure 3.2. We will discuss other loss functions in Chapter 5.

When using the squared error loss for learning a linear regression model from $\mathcal{T}$, we thus need to solve the problem

$$
\widehat{\theta} = \arg\min_{\theta} \frac{1}{n} \sum_{i=1}^{n} (\theta^\mathsf{T}\mathbf{x}_i - y_i)^2 = \arg\min_{\theta} \frac{1}{n} \|\mathbf{X}\theta - \mathbf{y}\|_2^2. \tag{3.12}
$$

From a linear algebra point of view, this can be seen as the problem of finding the closest vector to $\mathbf{y}$ (in an Euclidean sense) in the subspace of $\mathbb{R}^n$ spanned by the columns of $\mathbf{X}$. The solution to this problem is the orthogonal projection of $\mathbf{y}$ onto this subspace, and the corresponding $\widehat{\theta}$ can be shown (see Section 3.A) to fulfill

$$
\mathbf{X}^\mathsf{T}\mathbf{X}\widehat{\theta} = \mathbf{X}^\mathsf{T}\mathbf{y}. \tag{3.13}
$$

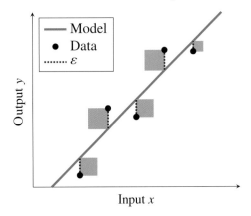

Figure 3.2 A graphical explanation of the squared error loss function: the goal is to choose the model (blue line) such that the sum of the squares (light red) of each error ε is minimised. That is, the blue line is to be chosen so that the amount of red colour is minimised. This motivates the name *least squares*. The black dots, the training data, are fixed.

Equation (3.13) is often referred to as the *normal equations* and gives the solution to the least squares problem (3.12). If $\mathbf{X}^{\mathsf{T}}\mathbf{X}$ is invertible, which is often the case, then $\widehat{\boldsymbol{\theta}}$ has the closed form expression

$$\widehat{\boldsymbol{\theta}} = (\mathbf{X}^{\mathsf{T}}\mathbf{X})^{-1}\mathbf{X}^{\mathsf{T}}\mathbf{y}. \tag{3.14}$$

The fact that this closed-form solution exists is important and is probably the reason for why the linear regression with squared error loss is so extremely common in practice. Other loss functions lead to optimisation problems that often lack closed-form solutions.

We now have everything in place for using linear regression, and we summarise it as Method 3.1 and illustrate it by Example 3.2.

Learn linear regression with squared error loss

Data: Training data $\mathcal{T} = \{\mathbf{x}_i, y_i\}_{i=1}^{n}$
Result: Learned parameter vector $\widehat{\boldsymbol{\theta}}$

1 Construct the matrix $\mathbf{X}$ and vector $\mathbf{y}$ according to (3.5).
2 Compute $\widehat{\boldsymbol{\theta}}$ by solving (3.13).

Predict with linear regression

Data: Learned parameter vector $\widehat{\boldsymbol{\theta}}$ and test input $\mathbf{x}_{\star}$
Result: Prediction $\widehat{y}(\mathbf{x}_{\star})$

1 Compute $\widehat{y}(\mathbf{x}_{\star}) = \widehat{\boldsymbol{\theta}}^{\mathsf{T}}\mathbf{x}_{\star}$.

Method 3.1 Linear regression

> **Time to reflect 3.1** *What does it mean in practice if $\mathbf{X}^\mathsf{T}\mathbf{X}$ is not invertible?*

> **Time to reflect 3.2** *If the columns of $\mathbf{X}$ are linearly independent, and $p = n - 1$, $\mathbf{X}$ spans the entire $\mathbb{R}^n$. If that is the case, $\mathbf{X}$ is invertible, and (3.14) reduces to $\theta = \mathbf{X}^{-1}\mathbf{y}$. Hence, a unique solution exists such that $\mathbf{y} = \mathbf{X}\theta$ exactly, that is, the model fits the training data perfectly. Why would that not be a desired property in practice?*

Example 3.2 Car stopping distances

By inserting the matrices (3.6) from Example 3.1 into the normal equations (3.14), we obtain $\widehat{\theta}_0 = -20.1$ and $\widehat{\theta}_1 = 3.14$. Plotting the resulting model gives us Figure 3.3.

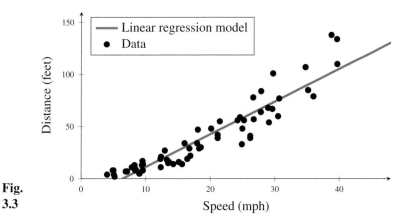

Fig. 3.3

This can be compared to how k-NN and decision trees solves the same problem (Figures 2.5 and 2.11). Clearly, the linear regression model behaves differently than these models; linear regression does not share the 'local' nature of k-NN and decision trees (only training data points close to $\mathbf{x}_\star$ affect $\widehat{y}(\mathbf{x}_\star)$), which is related to the fact that linear regression is a parametric model.

The Maximum Likelihood Perspective

To get another perspective on the squared error loss, we will now reinterpret the least squares method above as a *maximum likelihood* solution. The word 'likelihood' refers to the statistical concept of the likelihood function, and maximising the likelihood function amounts to finding the value of θ that makes observing $\mathbf{y}$ as likely as possible. That is, instead of (somewhat arbitrarily) selecting a loss function, we start with the problem

$$\widehat{\theta} = \arg\max_\theta p(\mathbf{y} \mid \mathbf{X}; \theta). \tag{3.15}$$

Here $p(\mathbf{y} \mid \mathbf{X}; \boldsymbol{\theta})$ is the probability density of all observed outputs $\mathbf{y}$ in the training data, given all inputs $\mathbf{X}$ and parameters $\boldsymbol{\theta}$. This determines mathematically what 'likely' means, but we need to specify it in more detail. We do that by considering the noise term ε as a stochastic variable with a certain distribution. A common assumption is that the noise terms are independent, each with a Gaussian distribution (also known as a normal distribution) with mean zero and variance σ_ε^2,

$$\varepsilon \sim \mathcal{N}\left(0, \sigma_\varepsilon^2\right). \tag{3.16}$$

This implies that the n observed training data points are independent, and $p(\mathbf{y} \mid \mathbf{X}; \boldsymbol{\theta})$ factorises as

$$p(\mathbf{y} \mid \mathbf{X}; \boldsymbol{\theta}) = \prod_{i=1}^{n} p(y_i \mid \mathbf{x}_i, \boldsymbol{\theta}). \tag{3.17}$$

Considering the linear regression model from (3.3), $y = \boldsymbol{\theta}^\mathsf{T}\mathbf{x} + \varepsilon$, together with the Gaussian noise assumption (3.16), we have

$$p(y_i \mid \mathbf{x}_i, \boldsymbol{\theta}) = \mathcal{N}\left(y_i; \boldsymbol{\theta}^\mathsf{T}\mathbf{x}_i, \sigma_\varepsilon^2\right) = \frac{1}{\sqrt{2\pi\sigma_\varepsilon^2}} \exp\left(-\frac{1}{2\sigma_\varepsilon^2}\left(\boldsymbol{\theta}^\mathsf{T}\mathbf{x}_i - y_i\right)^2\right). \tag{3.18}$$

Recall that we want to maximise the likelihood with respect to $\boldsymbol{\theta}$. For numerical reasons, it is usually better to work with the logarithm of $p(\mathbf{y} \mid \mathbf{X}; \boldsymbol{\theta})$,

$$\ln p(\mathbf{y} \mid \mathbf{X}; \boldsymbol{\theta}) = \sum_{i=1}^{n} \ln p(y_i \mid \mathbf{x}_i, \boldsymbol{\theta}). \tag{3.19}$$

Since the logarithm is a monotonically increasing function, maximising the log-likelihood (3.19) is equivalent to maximising the likelihood itself. Putting (3.18) and (3.19) together, we get

$$\ln p(\mathbf{y} \mid \mathbf{X}; \boldsymbol{\theta}) = -\frac{n}{2}\ln(2\pi\sigma_\varepsilon^2) - \frac{1}{2\sigma_\varepsilon^2}\sum_{i=1}^{n}\left(\boldsymbol{\theta}^\mathsf{T}\mathbf{x}_i - y_i\right)^2. \tag{3.20}$$

Removing terms and factors independent of $\boldsymbol{\theta}$ does not change the maximising argument, and we see that we can rewrite (3.15) as

$$\widehat{\boldsymbol{\theta}} = \arg\max_{\boldsymbol{\theta}} p(\mathbf{y} \mid \mathbf{X}; \boldsymbol{\theta}) = \arg\max_{\boldsymbol{\theta}} - \sum_{i=1}^{n}\left(\boldsymbol{\theta}^\mathsf{T}\mathbf{x}_i - y_i\right)^2 = \arg\min_{\boldsymbol{\theta}} \frac{1}{n}\sum_{i=1}^{n}\left(\boldsymbol{\theta}^\mathsf{T}\mathbf{x}_i - y_i\right)^2. \tag{3.21}$$

This is indeed linear regression with the least squares cost (the cost function implied by the squared error loss function (3.10)). Hence, using the squared error loss is equivalent to assuming a Gaussian noise distribution in the maximum likelihood formulation. Other assumptions on ε lead to other loss functions, as we will discuss further in Chapter 5.

Categorical Input Variables

The regression problem is characterised by a numerical output y and inputs $\mathbf{x}$ of arbitrary type. We have, however, only discussed the case of numerical inputs so far. To see how we can handle categorical inputs in the linear regression model, assume that we have an input variable that only takes two different values. We refer to those two values as A and B. We can then create a *dummy variable* x as

$$x = \begin{cases} 0 & \text{if A,} \\ 1 & \text{if B,} \end{cases} \tag{3.22}$$

and use this variable in any supervised machine learning method as if it was numerical. For linear regression, this effectively gives us a model which looks like

$$y = \theta_0 + \theta_1 x + \varepsilon = \begin{cases} \theta_0 + \varepsilon & \text{if A,} \\ \theta_0 + \theta_1 + \varepsilon & \text{if B.} \end{cases} \tag{3.23}$$

The model is thus able to learn and predict two different values depending on whether the input is A or B.

If the categorical variable takes more than two values, let us say A, B, C, and D, we can make a so-called *one-hot encoding* by constructing a four-dimensional vector

$$\mathbf{x} = \begin{bmatrix} x_A & x_B & x_C & x_D \end{bmatrix}^\mathsf{T} \tag{3.24}$$

where $x_A = 1$ if A, $x_B = 1$ if B, and so on. That is, only one element of $\mathbf{x}$ will be 1, the rest are 0. Again, this construction can be used for any supervised machine learning method and is not restricted to linear regression.

3.2 Classification and Logistic Regression

After presenting a parametric method for solving the regression problem, we now turn our attention to classification. As we will see, with a modification of the linear regression model, we can apply it to the classification problem as well; however, this is the cost of not being able to use the convenient normal equations. Instead, we have to resort to numerical optimisation for learning the parameters of the model.

A Statistical View of the Classification Problem

Supervised machine learning amounts to predicting the output from the input. From a statistical perspective, classification amounts to predicting the conditional class probabilities

$$p(y = m \mid \mathbf{x}), \tag{3.25}$$

where y is the output $(1, 2, \ldots,$ or $M)$ and $\mathbf{x}$ is the input.[3] In words, $p(y = m \mid \mathbf{x})$ describes *the probability for class m given that we know the input* $\mathbf{x}$. Talking

---

[3] We use the notation $p(y \mid \mathbf{x})$ to denote probability masses (y discrete) as well as probability densities (y continuous).

about $p(y\,|\,\mathbf{x})$ implies that we think about the class label y as a random variable. Why? Because we choose to model the real world, from where the data originates, as involving a certain amount of randomness (much like the random error ε in regression). Let us illustrate this with an example.

Example 3.3 Describing voting behavior using probabilities

We want to construct a model that can predict voting preferences ($= y$, the categorical output) for different population groups ($= \mathbf{x}$, the input). However, we then have to face the fact that not everyone in a certain population group will vote for the same political party. We can therefore think of y as a random variable which follows a certain probability distribution. If we know that the vote count in the group of 45 year old women ($= \mathbf{x}$) is 13% for the cerise party, 39% for the turquoise party, and 48% for the purple party (here we have $M = 3$), we could describe it as

$$p(y = \text{cerise party}\,|\,\mathbf{x} = \text{45 year old women}) = 0.13,$$
$$p(y = \text{turqoise party}\,|\,\mathbf{x} = \text{45 year old women}) = 0.39,$$
$$p(y = \text{purple party}\,|\,\mathbf{x} = \text{45 year old women}) = 0.48.$$

In this way, the probabilities $p(y\,|\,\mathbf{x})$ describe the non-trivial fact that

(a) all 45 year old women do not vote for the same party, but

(b) the choice of party does not appear to be completely random among 45 year old women either; the purple party is the most popular, and the cerise party is the least popular.

Thus, it can be useful to have a classifier which predicts not only a class $\widehat{y}$ (one party) but a distribution over classes $p(y\,|\,\mathbf{x})$.

We now aim to construct a classifier which can not only predict classes but also learn the class probabilities $p(y\,|\,\mathbf{x})$. More specifically, for binary classification problems ($M = 2$, and y is either 1 or -1), we train a model $g(\mathbf{x})$ for which

$$\boxed{p(y = 1\,|\,\mathbf{x}) \text{ is modelled by } g(\mathbf{x}).} \tag{3.26a}$$

By the laws of probabilities, it holds that $p(y = 1\,|\,\mathbf{x}) + p(y = -1\,|\,\mathbf{x}) = 1$, which means that

$$\boxed{p(y = -1\,|\,\mathbf{x}) \text{ is modelled by } 1 - g(\mathbf{x}).} \tag{3.26b}$$

Since $g(\mathbf{x})$ is a model for a probability, it is natural to require that $0 \leq g(\mathbf{x}) \leq 1$ for any $\mathbf{x}$. We will see how this constraint can be enforced below.

For the multiclass problem, we instead let the classifier return a vector-valued function $\mathbf{g}(\mathbf{x})$, where

$$\boxed{\begin{bmatrix} p(y = 1\,|\,\mathbf{x}) \\ p(y = 2\,|\,\mathbf{x}) \\ \vdots \\ p(y = M\,|\,\mathbf{x}) \end{bmatrix} \text{ is modelled by } \begin{bmatrix} g_1(\mathbf{x}) \\ g_2(\mathbf{x}) \\ \vdots \\ g_M(\mathbf{x}) \end{bmatrix} = \mathbf{g}(\mathbf{x}).} \tag{3.27}$$

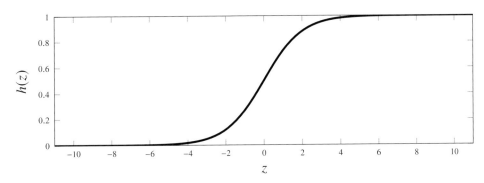

Figure 3.4 The logistic function $h(z) = \frac{e^z}{1+e^z}$.

In words, each element $g_m(\mathbf{x})$ of $\mathbf{g}(\mathbf{x})$ corresponds to the conditional class probability $p(y = m \mid \mathbf{x})$. Since $\mathbf{g}(\mathbf{x})$ models a probability vector, we require that each element $g_m(\mathbf{x}) \geq 0$ and that $\|\mathbf{g}(\mathbf{x})\|_1 = \sum_{m=1}^{M} |g_m(\mathbf{x})| = 1$ for any $\mathbf{x}$.

The Logistic Regression Model for Binary Classification

We will now introduce the logistic regression model, which is one possible way of modelling conditional class probabilities. Logistic regression can be viewed as a modification of the linear regression model so that it fits the classification (instead of the regression) problem.

Let us start with binary classification. We wish to learn a function $g(\mathbf{x})$ that approximates the conditional probability of the positive class, see (3.26). To this end, we start with the linear regression model which, without the noise term, is given by

$$z = \theta_0 + \theta_1 x_1 + \theta_2 x_2 + \cdots + \theta_p x_p = \boldsymbol{\theta}^\mathsf{T} \mathbf{x}. \tag{3.28}$$

This is a mapping which takes $\mathbf{x}$ and returns z, which in this context is called the *logit*. Note that z takes values on the entire real line, whereas we need a function which instead returns a value in the interval $[0, 1]$. The key idea of logistic regression is to 'squeeze' z from (3.28) to the interval $[0, 1]$ by using the *logistic function* $h(z) = \frac{e^z}{1+e^z}$, see Figure 3.4. This results in

$$g(\mathbf{x}) = \frac{e^{\boldsymbol{\theta}^\mathsf{T} \mathbf{x}}}{1 + e^{\boldsymbol{\theta}^\mathsf{T} \mathbf{x}}}, \tag{3.29a}$$

which is restricted to $[0, 1]$ and hence can be interpreted as a probability. The function (3.29a) is the logistic regression model for $p(y = 1 \mid \mathbf{x})$. Note that this implicitly also gives a model for $p(y = -1 \mid \mathbf{x})$,

$$1 - g(\mathbf{x}) = 1 - \frac{e^{\boldsymbol{\theta}^\mathsf{T} \mathbf{x}}}{1 + e^{\boldsymbol{\theta}^\mathsf{T} \mathbf{x}}} = \frac{1}{1 + e^{\boldsymbol{\theta}^\mathsf{T} \mathbf{x}}} = \frac{e^{-\boldsymbol{\theta}^\mathsf{T} \mathbf{x}}}{1 + e^{-\boldsymbol{\theta}^\mathsf{T} \mathbf{x}}}. \tag{3.29b}$$

In a nutshell, the logistic regression model is linear regression appended with the logistic function. This is the reason for the (somewhat confusing) name, but despite

47

the name, logistic regression is a method for classification, not regression! The reason why there is no noise term ε in (3.28), as we had in the linear regression model (3.3), is that the randomness in classification is statistically modelled by the class probability construction $p(y = m \mid \mathbf{x})$ instead of an additive noise ε.

As for linear regression, we have a model (3.29) which contains unknown parameters $\boldsymbol{\theta}$. Logistic regression is thereby also a parametric model, and we need to learn the parameters from training data. How this can be done is the topic for the next section.

Training the Logistic Regression Model by Maximum Likelihood

By using the logistic function, we have transformed linear regression (a model for regression problems) into logistic regression (a model for classification problems). The price to pay is that we will not be able to use the convenient normal equations for learning $\boldsymbol{\theta}$ (as we could for linear regression if we used the squared error loss), due to the nonlinearity of the logistic function.

In order to derive a principled way of learning $\boldsymbol{\theta}$ in (3.29) from training data $\mathcal{T} = \{\mathbf{x}_i, y_i\}_{i=1}^{n}$, we start with the maximum likelihood approach. From a maximum likelihood perspective, learning a classifier amounts to solving

$$\widehat{\boldsymbol{\theta}} = \arg \max_{\boldsymbol{\theta}} p(\mathbf{y} \mid \mathbf{X}; \boldsymbol{\theta}) = \arg \max_{\boldsymbol{\theta}} \sum_{i=1}^{n} \ln p(y_i \mid \mathbf{x}_i; \boldsymbol{\theta}), \tag{3.30}$$

where similarly to linear regression (3.19), we assume that the training data points are independent, and we consider the logarithm of the likelihood function for numerical reasons. We have also added $\boldsymbol{\theta}$ explicitly to the notation to emphasise the dependence on the model parameters. Remember that our model of $p(y = 1 \mid \mathbf{x}; \boldsymbol{\theta})$ is $g(\mathbf{x}; \boldsymbol{\theta})$, which gives

$$\ln p(y_i \mid \mathbf{x}_i; \boldsymbol{\theta}) = \begin{cases} \ln g(\mathbf{x}_i; \boldsymbol{\theta}) & \text{if } y_i = 1, \\ \ln (1 - g(\mathbf{x}_i; \boldsymbol{\theta})) & \text{if } y_i = -1. \end{cases} \tag{3.31}$$

It is common to turn the maximisation problem (3.30) into an equivalent minimisation problem by using the negative log-likelihood as cost function, $J(\boldsymbol{\theta}) = -\frac{1}{n} \sum \ln p(y_i \mid \mathbf{x}_i; \boldsymbol{\theta})$, that is,

$$J(\boldsymbol{\theta}) = \frac{1}{n} \sum_{i=1}^{n} \underbrace{\begin{cases} -\ln g(\mathbf{x}_i; \boldsymbol{\theta}) & \text{if } y_i = 1, \\ -\ln (1 - g(\mathbf{x}_i; \boldsymbol{\theta})) & \text{if } y_i = -1. \end{cases}}_{\text{Binary cross-entropy loss } L(g(\mathbf{x}_i; \boldsymbol{\theta}), y_i)} \tag{3.32}$$

The loss function in the expression above is called the *cross-entropy loss*. It is not specific to logistic regression but can be used for any binary classifier that predicts class probabilities $g(\mathbf{x}; \boldsymbol{\theta})$.

However, we will now consider specifically the logistic regression model, for which we can write out the cost function (3.32) in more detail. In doing so, the particular choice of labelling $\{-1, 1\}$ turns out to be convenient. For $y_i = 1$, we can write

$$g(\mathbf{x}_i; \boldsymbol{\theta}) = \frac{e^{\boldsymbol{\theta}^\mathsf{T}\mathbf{x}_i}}{1 + e^{\boldsymbol{\theta}^\mathsf{T}\mathbf{x}_i}} = \frac{e^{y_i\boldsymbol{\theta}^\mathsf{T}\mathbf{x}_i}}{1 + e^{y_i\boldsymbol{\theta}^\mathsf{T}\mathbf{x}_i}}, \tag{3.33a}$$

and for $y_i = -1$,

$$1 - g(\mathbf{x}_i; \boldsymbol{\theta}) = \frac{e^{-\boldsymbol{\theta}^\mathsf{T}\mathbf{x}_i}}{1 + e^{-\boldsymbol{\theta}^\mathsf{T}\mathbf{x}_i}} = \frac{e^{y_i\boldsymbol{\theta}^\mathsf{T}\mathbf{x}_i}}{1 + e^{y_i\boldsymbol{\theta}^\mathsf{T}\mathbf{x}_i}}. \tag{3.33b}$$

Hence, we get the same expression in both cases and can write (3.32) compactly as

$$J(\boldsymbol{\theta}) = \frac{1}{n} \sum_{i=1}^{n} -\ln \frac{e^{y_i\boldsymbol{\theta}^\mathsf{T}\mathbf{x}_i}}{1 + e^{y_i\boldsymbol{\theta}^\mathsf{T}\mathbf{x}_i}} = \frac{1}{n} \sum_{i=1}^{n} -\ln \frac{1}{1 + e^{-y_i\boldsymbol{\theta}^\mathsf{T}\mathbf{x}_i}}$$

$$= \frac{1}{n} \sum_{i=1}^{n} \underbrace{\ln\left(1 + e^{-y_i\boldsymbol{\theta}^\mathsf{T}\mathbf{x}_i}\right)}_{\text{Logistic loss } L(\mathbf{x}_i, y_i, \boldsymbol{\theta})}. \tag{3.34}$$

The loss function $L(\mathbf{x}, y_i, \boldsymbol{\theta})$ above, which is a special case of the cross-entropy loss, is called the *logistic loss* (or sometimes binomial deviance). Learning a logistic regression model thus amounts to solving

$$\widehat{\boldsymbol{\theta}} = \arg\min_{\boldsymbol{\theta}} \frac{1}{n} \sum_{i=1}^{n} \ln\left(1 + e^{-y_i\boldsymbol{\theta}^\mathsf{T}\mathbf{x}_i}\right). \tag{3.35}$$

Contrary to linear regression with squared error loss, the problem (3.35) has no closed-form solution, so we have to use numerical optimisation instead. Solving nonlinear optimisation problems numerically is central to the training of many machine learning models, not just logistic regression, and we will come back to this topic in Chapter 5. For now, however, it is enough to note that there exist efficient algorithms for solving (3.35) numerically to find $\widehat{\boldsymbol{\theta}}$.

Predictions and Decision Boundaries

So far, we have discussed logistic regression as a method for predicting class probabilities for a test input $\mathbf{x}_\star$ by first learning $\boldsymbol{\theta}$ from training data and thereafter computing $g(\mathbf{x}_\star)$, our model for $p(y = 1 \mid \mathbf{x}_\star)$. However, sometimes we want to make a 'hard' prediction for the test input $\mathbf{x}_\star$, that is, predicting $\widehat{y}(\mathbf{x}_\star) = -1$ or $\widehat{y}(\mathbf{x}_\star) = 1$ in binary classification, just like with k-NN or decision trees. We then have to add a final step to the logistic regression model, in which the predicted probabilities are turned into a class prediction. The most common approach is to *let $\widehat{y}(\mathbf{x}_\star)$ be the most probable class*. For binary classification, we can express this as[4]

$$\widehat{y}(\mathbf{x}_\star) = \begin{cases} 1 & \text{if } g(\mathbf{x}) > r \\ -1 & \text{if } g(\mathbf{x}) \leq r \end{cases}, \tag{3.36}$$

---

[4]It is arbitrary what happens if $g(\mathbf{x}) = 0.5$.

Learn binary logistic regression

Data: Training data $\mathcal{T} = \{\mathbf{x}_i, y_i\}_{i=1}^{n}$ (with output classes $y = \{-1, 1\}$)
Result: Learned parameter vector $\widehat{\theta}$

1 Compute $\widehat{\theta}$ by solving (3.35) numerically.

Predict with binary logistic regression

Data: Learned parameter vector $\widehat{\theta}$ and test input $\mathbf{x}_{\star}$
Result: Prediction $\widehat{y}(\mathbf{x}_{\star})$

1 Compute $g(\mathbf{x}_{\star})$ (3.29a).
2 If $g(\mathbf{x}_{\star}) > 0.5$, return $\widehat{y}(\mathbf{x}_{\star}) = 1$, otherwise return $\widehat{y}(\mathbf{x}_{\star}) = -1$.

Method 3.2 Logistic regression

with decision threshold $r = 0.5$, which is illustrated in Figure 3.5. We now have everything in place for summarising binary logistic regression in Method 3.2.

In some applications, however, it can be beneficial to explore different thresholds than $r = 0.5$. It can be shown that *if* $g(\mathbf{x}) = p(y = 1 \mid \mathbf{x})$, that is, the model provides a correct description of the real-world class probabilities, then the choice $r = 0.5$ will give the smallest possible number of misclassifications on average. In other words, $r = 0.5$ minimises the so-called *misclassification rate*. The misclassification rate is, however, not always the most important aspect of a classifier. Many classification problems are asymmetric (it is more important to correctly predict some classes than others) or imbalanced (the classes occur with very different frequencies). In a medical diagnosis application, for example, it can be more important not to falsely predict the negative class (that is, by mistake predict a sick patient being healthy) than to falsely predict the positive class (by mistake predict a healthy patient as sick). For such a problem, minimising the misclassification rate might not lead to the desired performance. Furthermore, the medical diagnosis problem could be imbalanced if the disorder is very rare, meaning that the vast majority of the data points (patients) belong to the negative class. By only considering the misclassification rate in such a situation, we implicitly value accurate predictions of the negative class higher than accurate predictions of the positive class, simply because the negative class is more common in the data. We will discuss how we can evaluate such situations more systematically in Section 4.5. In the end, however, the decision threshold r is a choice that the user has to make.

The decision boundary for binary classification can be computed by solving the equation

$$g(\mathbf{x}) = 1 - g(\mathbf{x}). \tag{3.37}$$

The solutions to this equation are points in the input space for which the two classes are predicted to be equally probable. Therefore, these points lie on the decision boundary. For binary logistic regression, this means

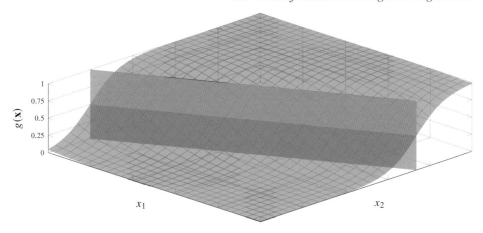

Figure 3.5 In binary classification ($y = -1$ or 1), logistic regression predicts $g(\mathbf{x}_\star)$ ($\mathbf{x}$ is two-dimensional here), which is an attempt to determine $p(y = 1 \mid \mathbf{x}_\star)$. This implicitly also gives a prediction for $p(y = -1 \mid \mathbf{x}_\star)$ as $1 - g(\mathbf{x}_\star)$. To turn these probabilities into actual class predictions ($\widehat{y}(\mathbf{x}_\star)$ is either -1 or 1), the class which is modelled to have the highest probability can be taken as the prediction, as in Equation (3.36). The point(s) where the prediction changes from from one class to another is the decision boundary (grey plane).

$$\frac{e^{\boldsymbol{\theta}^\mathsf{T}\mathbf{x}}}{1 + e^{\boldsymbol{\theta}^\mathsf{T}\mathbf{x}}} = \frac{1}{1 + e^{\boldsymbol{\theta}^\mathsf{T}\mathbf{x}}} \Leftrightarrow e^{\boldsymbol{\theta}^\mathsf{T}\mathbf{x}} = 1 \Leftrightarrow \boldsymbol{\theta}^\mathsf{T}\mathbf{x} = 0. \tag{3.38}$$

The equation $\boldsymbol{\theta}^\mathsf{T}\mathbf{x} = 0$ parameterises a (linear) hyperplane. Hence, the decision boundaries in logistic regression always have the shape of a (linear) hyperplane.

From the derivation above, it can be noted that the sign of the expression $\boldsymbol{\theta}^\mathsf{T}\mathbf{x}$ determines if we are predicting the positive or the negative class. Hence, we can compactly write (3.36), with the threshold $r = 0.5$, as

$$\widehat{y}(\mathbf{x}_\star) = \mathrm{sign}(\boldsymbol{\theta}^\mathsf{T}\mathbf{x}_\star). \tag{3.39}$$

In general we distinguish between different types of classifiers by the shape of their decision boundaries.

> A classifier whose decision boundaries are linear hyperplanes is a *linear classifier.*

All other classifiers are *non-linear classifiers*. Logistic regression is an example of a linear classifier, whereas k-NN and decision trees are non-linear classifiers. Note that the term 'linear' is used in a different sense for linear regression: linear regression is a model which is linear in its parameters, whereas a linear classifier is a model whose decision boundaries are linear.

The same arguments and constructions as above can be generalised to the multiclass setting. Predicting according to the most probable class then amounts to computing the prediction as

$$\widehat{y}(\mathbf{x}_\star) = \arg\max_m g_m(\mathbf{x}_\star). \tag{3.40}$$

51

As in the binary case, it is possible to modify this when working with an asymmetric or imbalanced problem. The decision boundaries will be given by a combination of $M - 1$ (linear) hyperplanes for a multiclass logistic regression model.

Logistic Regression for More Than Two Classes

Logistic regression can be used also for the multiclass problem when there are more than two classes, $M > 2$. There are several ways of generalising logistic regression to this setting. We will follow one path using the so-called softmax function, which will also be useful later when introducing deep learning models in Chapter 6.

For the binary problem, we used the logistic function to design a model for $g(\mathbf{x})$, a scalar-valued function representing $p(y = 1 \mid \mathbf{x})$. For the multiclass problem, we instead have to design a vector-valued function $\mathbf{g}(\mathbf{x})$, whose elements should be non-negative and sum to one. For this purpose, we first use M instances of (3.28), each denoted z_m and each with a different set of parameters $\boldsymbol{\theta}_m$, $z_m = \boldsymbol{\theta}_m^\mathsf{T}\mathbf{x}$. We stack all z_m into a vector of logits $\mathbf{z} = [z_1 \ z_2 \ \dots \ z_M]^\mathsf{T}$ and use the *softmax function* as a vector-valued generalisation of the logistic function,

$$\text{softmax}(\mathbf{z}) \triangleq \frac{1}{\sum_{m=1}^{M} e^{z_m}} \begin{bmatrix} e^{z_1} \\ e^{z_2} \\ \vdots \\ e^{z_M} \end{bmatrix}. \tag{3.41}$$

Note that the argument $\mathbf{z}$ to the softmax function is an M-dimensional vector and that it also returns a vector of the same dimension. By construction, the output vector from the softmax function always sums to 1, and each element is always ≥ 0. Similarly to how we combined linear regression and the logistic function for the binary classification problem (3.29), we have now combined linear regression and the softmax function to model the class probabilities:

$$\mathbf{g}(\mathbf{x}) = \text{softmax}(\mathbf{z}), \qquad \text{where } \mathbf{z} = \begin{bmatrix} \boldsymbol{\theta}_1^\mathsf{T}\mathbf{x} \\ \boldsymbol{\theta}_2^\mathsf{T}\mathbf{x} \\ \vdots \\ \boldsymbol{\theta}_M^\mathsf{T}\mathbf{x} \end{bmatrix}. \tag{3.42}$$

Equivalently, we can write out the individual class probabilities, that is, the elements of the vector $\mathbf{g}(\mathbf{x})$, as

$$g_m(\mathbf{x}) = \frac{e^{\boldsymbol{\theta}_m^\mathsf{T}\mathbf{x}}}{\sum_{j=1}^{M} e^{\boldsymbol{\theta}_j^\mathsf{T}\mathbf{x}}}, \qquad m = 1, \dots, M. \tag{3.43}$$

This is the multiclass logistic regression model. Note that this construction uses M parameter vectors $\boldsymbol{\theta}_1, \dots, \boldsymbol{\theta}_M$ (one for each class), meaning that the number of parameters to learn grows with M. As for binary logistic regression, we can learn these parameters using the maximum likelihood method. We use $\boldsymbol{\theta}$ to denote *all*

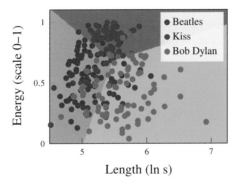

Figure 3.6 Logistic regression applied to the music classification problem from Example 2.1. The decision boundaries are linear, but unlike trees (Figure 2.11a), they are not perpendicular to the axes.

model parameters, $\boldsymbol{\theta} = \{\boldsymbol{\theta}_1, \ldots, \boldsymbol{\theta}_M\}$. Since $g_m(\mathbf{x}_i; \boldsymbol{\theta})$ is our model for $p(y_i = m \mid \mathbf{x}_i)$, the cost function for the cross-entropy (equivalently, negative log-likelihood) loss for the multiclass problem is

$$J(\boldsymbol{\theta}) = \frac{1}{n} \sum_{i=1}^{n} \underbrace{-\ln g_{y_i}(\mathbf{x}_i; \boldsymbol{\theta})}_{\substack{\text{Multiclass cross-entropy} \\ \text{loss } L(\mathbf{g}(\mathbf{x}_i; \boldsymbol{\theta}), y_i)}}. \tag{3.44}$$

Note that we use the training data labels y_i as index variables to select the correct conditional probability for the loss function. That is, the ith term of the sum is the negative logarithm of the y_ith element of the vector $\mathbf{g}(\mathbf{x}_i; \boldsymbol{\theta})$. We illustrate the meaning of this in Example 3.4.

Inserting the model (3.43) into the loss function (3.44) gives the cost function to optimise when learning multiclass logistic regression:

$$J(\boldsymbol{\theta}) = \frac{1}{n} \sum_{i=1}^{n} \left(-\boldsymbol{\theta}_{y_i}^{\mathsf{T}} \mathbf{x}_i + \ln \sum_{j=1}^{M} e^{\boldsymbol{\theta}_j^{\mathsf{T}} \mathbf{x}_i} \right). \tag{3.45}$$

We apply this to the music classification problem in Figure 3.6.

Example 3.4 The cross-entropy loss for multiclass problems

Consider the following (very small) data set with $n = 6$ data points, $p = 2$ input dimensions, and $M = 3$ classes, which we want to use to train a multiclass classifier:

$$\mathbf{X} = \begin{bmatrix} 0.20 & 0.86 \\ 0.41 & 0.18 \\ 0.96 & -1.84 \\ -0.25 & 1.57 \\ -0.82 & -1.53 \\ -0.31 & 0.58 \end{bmatrix}, \quad \mathbf{y} = \begin{bmatrix} 2 \\ 3 \\ 1 \\ 2 \\ 1 \\ 3 \end{bmatrix}.$$

Multiclass logistic regression with softmax (or any other multiclass classifier which predicts a vector of conditional class probabilities) return a three-dimensional probability vector $\mathbf{g}(\mathbf{x}; \boldsymbol{\theta})$ for any $\mathbf{x}$ and $\boldsymbol{\theta}$. If we stack the logarithms of the transpose of all vectors $\mathbf{g}(\mathbf{x}_i; \boldsymbol{\theta})$ for $i = 1, \ldots, 6$, we obtain the matrix

$$\mathbf{G} = \begin{bmatrix} \ln g_1(\mathbf{x}_1; \boldsymbol{\theta}) & \ln g_2(\mathbf{x}_1; \boldsymbol{\theta}) & \ln g_3(\mathbf{x}_1; \boldsymbol{\theta}) \\ \ln g_1(\mathbf{x}_2; \boldsymbol{\theta}) & \ln g_2(\mathbf{x}_2; \boldsymbol{\theta}) & \ln g_3(\mathbf{x}_2; \boldsymbol{\theta}) \\ \ln g_1(\mathbf{x}_3; \boldsymbol{\theta}) & \ln g_2(\mathbf{x}_3; \boldsymbol{\theta}) & \ln g_3(\mathbf{x}_3; \boldsymbol{\theta}) \\ \ln g_1(\mathbf{x}_4; \boldsymbol{\theta}) & \ln g_2(\mathbf{x}_4; \boldsymbol{\theta}) & \ln g_3(\mathbf{x}_4; \boldsymbol{\theta}) \\ \ln g_1(\mathbf{x}_5; \boldsymbol{\theta}) & \ln g_2(\mathbf{x}_5; \boldsymbol{\theta}) & \ln g_3(\mathbf{x}_5; \boldsymbol{\theta}) \\ \ln g_1(\mathbf{x}_6; \boldsymbol{\theta}) & \ln g_2(\mathbf{x}_6; \boldsymbol{\theta}) & \ln g_3(\mathbf{x}_6; \boldsymbol{\theta}) \end{bmatrix}.$$

Computing the multi-class cross-entropy cost (3.44) now simply amounts to taking the average of all circled elements and multiplying that by -1. The element that we have circled in row i is given by the training label y_i. Training the model amounts to finding $\boldsymbol{\theta}$ such that this negated average is minimised.

Time to reflect 3.3 Can you derive (3.32) as a special case of (3.44)? Hint: think of the binary classifier as a special case of the multiclass classifier with $\mathbf{g}(\mathbf{x}) = \begin{bmatrix} g(\mathbf{x}) \\ 1 - g(\mathbf{x}) \end{bmatrix}$.

Time to reflect 3.4 The softmax-based logistic regression is actually over-parameterised, in the sense that we can construct an equivalent model with fewer parameters. That is often not a problem in practice, but compare the multiclass model (3.42) for the case $M = 2$ with binary logistic regression (3.29), and see if you can spot the over-parametrisation!

3.3 Polynomial Regression and Regularisation

In comparison to k-NN and decision trees studied in Chapter 2, linear and logistic regression might appear to be rigid and non-flexible models with their straight lines (such as Figures 3.1 and 3.5). However, both models are able to adapt to the training data well if the input dimension p is large relative to the number of data points n.

A common way of increasing the input dimension in linear and logistic regression, which we will discuss more thoroughly in Chapter 8, is to make a non-linear transformation of the input. A simple non-linear transformation is to replace a one-dimensional input x with itself raised to different powers, which makes the linear regression model a polynomial:

$$y = \theta_0 + \theta_1 x + \theta_2 x^2 + \theta_3 x^3 + \cdots + \varepsilon. \tag{3.46}$$

This is called *polynomial regression*. The same polynomial expansion can also be applied to the expression for the logit in logistic regression. Note that if we let $x_1 = x$, $x_2 = x^2$ and $x_3 = x^3$, this is still a linear model (3.2) with input $\mathbf{x} = [1 \ x \ x^2 \ x^3]$, but we have 'lifted' the input from being one-dimensional ($p = 1$) to three-dimensional ($p = 3$). Using non-linear input transformations can be very useful in practice, but it effectively increases p, and we can easily end up with *overfitting* the model to the noise – rather than the interesting patterns – in the training data, as in the example below.

Example 3.5 Car stopping distances with polynomial regression

We return to Example 2.2, but this time we also add the squared speed as an input and thereby use a second-order polynomial in linear regression. This gives the new matrices (compared to Example 3.1)

$$\mathbf{X} = \begin{bmatrix} 1 & 4.0 & 16.0 \\ 1 & 4.9 & 24.0 \\ 1 & 5.0 & 25.0 \\ \vdots & \vdots & \vdots \\ 1 & 39.6 & 1568.2 \\ 1 & 39.7 & 1576.1 \end{bmatrix}, \qquad \boldsymbol{\theta} = \begin{bmatrix} \theta_0 \\ \theta_1 \\ \theta_2 \end{bmatrix}, \qquad \mathbf{y} = \begin{bmatrix} 4.0 \\ 8.0 \\ 8.0 \\ \vdots \\ 134.0 \\ 110.0 \end{bmatrix}, \tag{3.47}$$

and when we insert these into the normal equations (3.13), the new parameter estimates are $\widehat{\theta}_0 = 1.58$, $\widehat{\theta}_1 = 0.42$, and $\widehat{\theta}_2 = 0.07$. (Note that also $\widehat{\theta}_0$ and $\widehat{\theta}_1$ change, compared to Example 3.2.)

In a completely analogous way, we also learn a 10th order polynomial, and we illustrate them all in Figure 3.7.

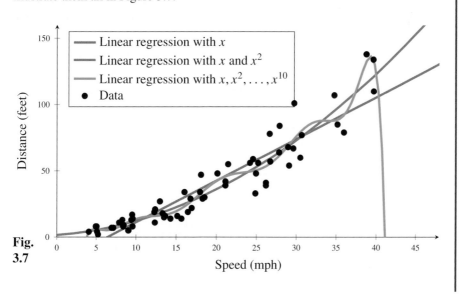

Fig. 3.7

The second-order polynomial (red line) appears sensible, and using a second-order polynomial seems to give some advantage compared to plain linear regression (blue line, from Example 3.2). However, using a tenth-order polynomial (green line) seems to make the model less useful than even plain linear regression due to overfitting. In conclusion, there is merit to the idea of polynomial regression, but it has to be applied carefully.

One way to avoid issues with overfitting when augmenting the input with non-linear transformation is to carefully select which inputs (transformations) to include. There are various strategies for doing this, for instance by adding inputs one at a time (forward selection) or by starting with a large number of inputs and then gradually removing the ones that are considered redundant (backward elimination). Different candidate models can be evaluated and compared using cross-validation, as we discuss in Chapter 4. See also Chapter 11, where we discuss input selection further.

An alternative approach to explicit input selection which can also be used to mitigate overfitting is *regularisation*. The idea of regularisation can be described as 'keeping the parameters $\widehat{\boldsymbol{\theta}}$ small unless the data really convinces us otherwise', or alternatively 'if a model with small parameter values $\widehat{\boldsymbol{\theta}}$ fits the data almost as well as a model with larger parameter values, the one with small parameter values should be preferred'. There are several ways to implement this idea mathematically, which lead to different regularisation methods. We will give a more complete treatment of this in Section 5.3 and only discuss the so-called L^2 regularisation for now. When paired with regularisation, the idea of using non-linear input transformations can be very powerful and enables a whole family of supervised machine learning methods that we will properly introduce and discuss in Chapter 8.

To keep $\widehat{\boldsymbol{\theta}}$ small, an extra penalty term $\lambda\|\boldsymbol{\theta}\|_2^2$ is added to the cost function when using L^2 regularisation. Here, $\lambda \geq 0$, referred to as the regularisation parameter, is a hyperparameter chosen by the user which controls the strength of the regularisation effect. The purpose of the penalty term is to prevent overfitting. Whereas the original cost function only rewards the fit to the training data (which encourages overfitting), the regularisation term prevents overly large parameter values at the cost of a slightly worse fit. It is therefore important to choose the regularisation parameter λ wisely, to obtain the right amount of regularisation. With $\lambda = 0$, the regularisation has no effect, whereas $\lambda \rightarrow \infty$ will force all parameters $\widehat{\boldsymbol{\theta}}$ to 0. A common approach is to use cross-validation (see Chapter 4) to select λ.

If we add L^2 regularisation to the previously studied linear regression model with squared error loss (3.12), the resulting optimisation problem becomes[5]

$$\widehat{\boldsymbol{\theta}} = \arg\min_{\boldsymbol{\theta}} \frac{1}{n}\|\mathbf{X}\boldsymbol{\theta} - \mathbf{y}\|_2^2 + \lambda\|\boldsymbol{\theta}\|_2^2. \tag{3.48}$$

---

[5]In practice, it can be wise to exclude θ_0, the intercept, from the regularisation.

It turns out that, just like the non-regularised problem, (3.48) has a closed-form solution given by a modified version of the normal equations,

$$(\mathbf{X}^\mathsf{T}\mathbf{X} + n\lambda\mathbf{I}_{p+1})\widehat{\boldsymbol{\theta}} = \mathbf{X}^\mathsf{T}\mathbf{y}, \tag{3.49}$$

where $\mathbf{I}_{p+1}$ is the identity matrix of size $(p+1)\times(p+1)$. This particular application of L^2 regularisation is referred to as *ridge regression*.

Regularisation is not restricted to linear regression, however. The same L^2 penalty can be applied to any method that involves optimising a cost function. For instance, for logistic regression, we get the optimisation problem

$$\widehat{\boldsymbol{\theta}} = \arg\min_{\boldsymbol{\theta}} \frac{1}{n}\sum_{i=1}^{n}\ln\left(1 + \exp\left(-y_i\boldsymbol{\theta}^\mathsf{T}\mathbf{x}_i\right)\right) + \lambda\|\boldsymbol{\theta}\|_2^2. \tag{3.50}$$

It is common in practice to train logistic regression models using (3.50) instead of (3.29). One reason is to decrease possible issues with overfitting, as discussed above. Another reason is that for the non-regularised cost function, (3.29), the optimal $\widehat{\boldsymbol{\theta}}$ is not finite if the training data is linearly separable (meaning there exists a linear decision boundary which separates the classes perfectly). In practice, it this means that logistic regression training diverges with some datasets unless (3.50) (with $\lambda > 0$) is used instead of (3.29). Finally, the regularisation term implies that there is a unique solution to the optimisation problem, despite the fact that the softmax model is overparameterised as discussed above.

3.4 Generalised Linear Models

In this chapter we have introduced two basic parametric models for regression and classification: linear regression and logistic regression, respectively. The latter model was presented as a way of adapting linear regression to the categorical nature of the output y encountered in a classification problem. This was done by passing the linear regression through a non-linear (in this case, logistic) function, allowing us to interpret the output as a class probability.

The same principle can be generalised to adapt the linear regression model to other properties of the output as well, resulting in what are referred to as *generalised linear models*. In the discussion above, we have focused on two specific problems corresponding to two different types of output data: real-valued regression ($y \in \mathbb{R}$) and classification ($y \in \{1,\ldots,M\}$). These are the most common instances of supervised learning problems, and, indeed, they will be central to most of the discussion and methods presented in this book.

However, in various applications, we might encounter data with other properties, not well described by either of the two standard problems. For instance, assume that the output y corresponds to the count of some quantity, such as the number of earthquakes in a certain area during a fixed time interval, the number of persons diagnosed with a specific illness in a certain region, or the number of patents granted to a tech company. In such cases, y is a natural number taking one of the values $0, 1, 2, \ldots$ (formally, $y \in \mathbb{N}$). Such *count data*, despite being numerical in nature, is not well described by a linear regression model of the form (3.2).[6] The reason is that linear regression models are not restricted to discrete values or to being non-negative, even though we know that this is the case for the actual output y that we are trying to model. Neither does this scenario correspond to a classification setting, since y is numerical (that is, the values can be ordered), and there is no fixed upper limit on how large y can be.

To address this issue, we will extend our notion of parametric models to encompass various probability distributions that can be used to model the conditional output distribution $p(y \mid \mathbf{x}; \boldsymbol{\theta})$. The first step is to choose a suitable *form* for the conditional distribution $p(y \mid \mathbf{x}; \boldsymbol{\theta})$. This is part of the model design, guided by the properties of the data. Specifically, we should select a distribution with support corresponding to that of the data (such as the natural numbers). Naturally, we still want to allow the distribution to depend on the input variable $\mathbf{x}$ – modelling the relationship between the input and the output variables is the fundamental task of supervised learning after all! However, this can be accomplished by first computing a linear regression term $z = \boldsymbol{\theta}^\mathsf{T}\mathbf{x}$ and then letting the conditional distribution $p(y \mid \mathbf{x}; \boldsymbol{\theta})$ depend on z in some appropriate way. We illustrate with an example.

Example 3.6 Poisson regression

A simple model for count data is to use a Poisson likelihood. The Poisson distribution is supported on the natural numbers (including 0) and has the probability mass function

$$\text{Pois}(y; \lambda) = \frac{\lambda^y e^{-\lambda}}{y!}, \qquad y = 0, 1, 2, \ldots$$

The so-called rate parameter λ controls the shape of the distribution and also corresponds to its mean value, $\mathbb{E}[y] = \lambda$. To use this likelihood in a regression model for count data, we can let λ depend on the input variable $\mathbf{x}$ and the model parameters $\boldsymbol{\theta}$ through a linear regression $z = \boldsymbol{\theta}^\mathsf{T}\mathbf{x}$. However, the rate parameter λ is restricted to being positive. To ensure that this constraint is satisfied, we model λ according to

$$\lambda = \exp(\boldsymbol{\theta}^\mathsf{T}\mathbf{x}).$$

The exponential function maps the output from the linear regression component to the positive real line, resulting in a valid rate parameter for any $\mathbf{x}$ and $\boldsymbol{\theta}$. Thus, we get the model

$$p(y \mid \mathbf{x}; \boldsymbol{\theta}) = \text{Pois}\left(y; \exp(\boldsymbol{\theta}^\mathsf{T}\mathbf{x})\right),$$

referred to a *Poisson regression* model.

---

[6]Simply assuming that the distribution of the additive noise ε is discrete is not enough, since the regression function itself $\boldsymbol{\theta}^\mathsf{T}\mathbf{x}$ can take arbitrary real values.

In the Poisson regression model, we can write the conditional mean of the output as

$$\mathbb{E}[y \mid \mathbf{x}; \theta] = \phi^{-1}(z),$$

where $z = \theta^{\mathsf{T}}\mathbf{x}$ and $\phi(\mu) \overset{\text{def}}{=} \log(\mu)$. The idea of providing an explicit link between the linear regression term and the conditional mean of the output in this way is what underlies the generic framework of generalised linear models. Specifically, a generalised linear model consists of:

(i) A choice of output distribution $p(y \mid \mathbf{x}; \theta)$ from the exponential family of distributions.[7]

(ii) A linear regression term $z = \theta^{\mathsf{T}}\mathbf{x}$.

(iii) A strictly increasing, so-called *link function* ϕ, such that $\mathbb{E}[y \mid \mathbf{x}; \theta] = \phi^{-1}(z)$.

By convention, we map the linear regression output through the *inverse* of the link function to obtain the mean of the output. Equivalently, if μ denotes the mean of $p(y \mid \mathbf{x}; \theta)$, we can express the model as $\phi(\mu) = \theta^{\mathsf{T}}\mathbf{x}$.

Different choices of conditional distributions and link functions result in different models with varying properties. In fact, as hinted at above, we have already seen another example of a generalised linear model, namely the logistic regression model. In binary logistic regression, the output distribution $p(y \mid \mathbf{x}; \theta)$ is a Bernoulli distribution,[8] the logit is computed as $z = \theta^{\mathsf{T}}\mathbf{x}$, and the link function ϕ is given by the inverse of the logistic function, $\phi(\mu) = \log(\mu/(1 - \mu))$. Other examples include negative binomial regression (a more flexible model for count data than Poisson regression) and exponential regression (for non-negative real-valued outputs). Hence, the generalised linear model framework can be used to model output variables y with many different properties, and it allows us to describe these models in a common language.

Since generalised linear models are defined in terms of the conditional distribution $p(y \mid \mathbf{x}; \theta)$, that is, the likelihood, it is natural to adopt the maximum likelihood formulation for training. That is, we train the model by finding the parameter values such that the negative log-likelihood of the training data is minimised:

$$\widehat{\theta} = \arg\min_{\theta} \left[-\frac{1}{n} \sum_{i=1}^{n} \ln p(y_i \mid \mathbf{x}_i; \theta) \right]. \tag{3.51}$$

A regularisation penalty can be added to the cost function, similarly to (3.50). Regularisation is discussed in more detail in Section 5.3.

---

[7]The exponential family is a class of probability distributions that can be written on a particular exponential form. It includes many of the commonly used probability distributions, such as Gaussian, Bernoulli, Poisson, exponential, gamma, etc.

[8]The generalised linear model interpretation of logistic regression is more straightforward if we encode the classes as $0/1$ instead of $-1/1$, in which case the output is modelled with a Bernoulli distribution with mean $\mathbb{E}[y \mid x; \theta] = p(y = 1 \mid \mathbf{x}; \theta) = g_\theta(\mathbf{x})$.

In general, just as for logistic regression, the training objective (3.51) is a nonlinear optimisation problem without a closed-form solution. However, an important aspect of generalised linear models is that efficient numerical optimisation algorithms exist for solving the maximum likelihood problem. Specifically, under certain assumptions on the link function, the problem becomes convex, and Newton's method can be used to compute $\widehat{\theta}$, efficiently. These are concepts that we will return to in Section 5.4 when we discuss numerical optimisation in more detail.

3.5 Further Reading

Compared to the thousand-year-old k-NN idea (Chapter 2), the linear regression model with least squares cost is much younger and can 'only' be traced back a little over two hundred years. It was introduced by Adrien-Marie Legendre in his 1805 book *Nouvelles méthodes pour la détermination des orbites des cométes (New methods for the determination of the orbits of comets)* as well as Carl Friedrich Gauss in his 1809 book *Theoria Motus Corporum Coelestium in Sectionibus Conicis Solem Ambientium (Theory of the motion of the heavenly bodies moving about the sun in conic sections*; in that book he claims to have been using it since 1795). Gauss also made the interpretation of it as the maximum likelihood solution when the noise was assumed to have a Gaussian distribution (hence the name of the distribution), although the general maximum likelihood approach was introduced much later by the work of Ronald Fisher (Fisher 1922). The history of logistic regression is almost as old as linear regression and is described further by Cramer (2003). An in-depth account of generalised linear models is given in the classical textbook by McCullagh and Nelder (2018).

3.A Derivation of the Normal Equations

The normal equations (3.13)

$$\mathbf{X}^\mathsf{T}\mathbf{X}\widehat{\theta} = \mathbf{X}^\mathsf{T}\mathbf{y}$$

can be derived from (3.12) (the scaling $\frac{1}{n}$ does not affect the minimising argument),

$$\widehat{\theta} = \arg\min_{\theta} \ \|\mathbf{X}\theta - \mathbf{y}\|_2^2,$$

in different ways. We will present one based on (matrix) calculus and one based on geometry and linear algebra.

No matter how (3.13) is derived, if $\mathbf{X}^\mathsf{T}\mathbf{X}$ is invertible, it (uniquely) gives

$$\widehat{\theta} = (\mathbf{X}^\mathsf{T}\mathbf{X})^{-1}\mathbf{X}^\mathsf{T}\mathbf{y}.$$

If $\mathbf{X}^\mathsf{T}\mathbf{X}$ is not invertible, then (3.13) has infinitely many solutions $\widehat{\theta}$, which are all equally good solutions to the problem (3.12).

A Calculus Approach

Let

$$V(\boldsymbol{\theta}) = \|\mathbf{X}\boldsymbol{\theta} - \mathbf{y}\|_2^2 = (\mathbf{X}\boldsymbol{\theta} - \mathbf{y})^\mathsf{T}(\mathbf{X}\boldsymbol{\theta} - \mathbf{y}) = \mathbf{y}^\mathsf{T}\mathbf{y} - 2\mathbf{y}^\mathsf{T}\mathbf{X}\boldsymbol{\theta} + \boldsymbol{\theta}^\mathsf{T}\mathbf{X}^\mathsf{T}\mathbf{X}\boldsymbol{\theta}, \qquad (3.52)$$

and differentiate $V(\boldsymbol{\theta})$ with respect to the vector $\boldsymbol{\theta}$:

$$\frac{\partial}{\partial\boldsymbol{\theta}}V(\boldsymbol{\theta}) = -2\mathbf{X}^\mathsf{T}\mathbf{y} + 2\mathbf{X}^\mathsf{T}\mathbf{X}\boldsymbol{\theta}. \qquad (3.53)$$

Since $V(\boldsymbol{\theta})$ is a positive quadratic form, its minimum must be attained at $\frac{\partial}{\partial\boldsymbol{\theta}}V(\boldsymbol{\theta}) = 0$, which characterises the solution $\widehat{\boldsymbol{\theta}}$ as

$$\frac{\partial}{\partial\boldsymbol{\theta}}V(\widehat{\boldsymbol{\theta}}) = 0 \Leftrightarrow -2\mathbf{X}^\mathsf{T}\mathbf{y} + 2\mathbf{X}^\mathsf{T}\mathbf{X}\boldsymbol{\theta} = 0 \Leftrightarrow \mathbf{X}^\mathsf{T}\mathbf{X}\widehat{\boldsymbol{\theta}} = \mathbf{X}^\mathsf{T}\mathbf{y}, \qquad (3.54)$$

which are the normal equations.

A Linear Algebra Approach

Denote the $p + 1$ columns of $\mathbf{X}$ as $c_j, j = 1, \ldots, p + 1$. We first show that $\|\mathbf{X}\boldsymbol{\theta} - \mathbf{y}\|_2^2$ is minimised if $\boldsymbol{\theta}$ is chosen such that $\mathbf{X}\boldsymbol{\theta}$ is the orthogonal projection of $\mathbf{y}$ onto the (sub)space spanned by the columns c_j of $\mathbf{X}$, and then show that the orthogonal projection is found by the normal equations.

Let us decompose $\mathbf{y}$ as $\mathbf{y}_\perp + \mathbf{y}_\|$, where $\mathbf{y}_\perp$ is orthogonal to the (sub)space spanned by all columns c_i, and $\mathbf{y}_\|$ is in the (sub)space spanned by all columns c_j. Since $\mathbf{y}_\perp$ is orthogonal to both $\mathbf{y}_\|$ and $\mathbf{X}\boldsymbol{\theta}$, it follows that

$$\|\mathbf{X}\boldsymbol{\theta} - \mathbf{y}\|_2^2 = \|\mathbf{X}\boldsymbol{\theta} - (\mathbf{y}_\perp + \mathbf{y}_\|)\|_2^2 = \|(\mathbf{X}\boldsymbol{\theta} - \mathbf{y}_\|) - \mathbf{y}_\perp\|_2^2 \geq \|\mathbf{y}_\perp\|_2^2, \qquad (3.55)$$

and the triangle inequality also gives us

$$\|\mathbf{X}\boldsymbol{\theta} - \mathbf{y}\|_2^2 = \|\mathbf{X}\boldsymbol{\theta} - \mathbf{y}_\perp - \mathbf{y}_\|\|_2^2 \leq \|\mathbf{y}_\perp\|_2^2 + \|\mathbf{X}\boldsymbol{\theta} - \mathbf{y}_\|\|_2^2. \qquad (3.56)$$

This implies that if we choose $\boldsymbol{\theta}$ such that $\mathbf{X}\boldsymbol{\theta} = \mathbf{y}_\|$, the criterion $\|\mathbf{X}\boldsymbol{\theta} - \mathbf{y}\|_2^2$ must have reached its minimum. Thus, our solution $\widehat{\boldsymbol{\theta}}$ must be such that $\mathbf{X}\widehat{\boldsymbol{\theta}} - \mathbf{y}$ is orthogonal to the (sub)space spanned by all columns c_i, meaning that

$$(\mathbf{y} - \mathbf{X}\widehat{\boldsymbol{\theta}})^\mathsf{T}c_j = 0, j = 1, \ldots, p + 1 \qquad (3.57)$$

(remember that two vectors $\mathbf{u}, \mathbf{v}$ are, by definition, orthogonal if their scalar product, $\mathbf{u}^\mathsf{T}\mathbf{v}$, is 0). Since the columns c_j together form the matrix $\mathbf{X}$, we can write this compactly as

$$(\mathbf{y} - \mathbf{X}\widehat{\boldsymbol{\theta}})^\mathsf{T}\mathbf{X} = 0, \qquad (3.58)$$

where the right hand side is the $p + 1$-dimensional zero vector. This can equivalently be written as

$$\mathbf{X}^\mathsf{T}\mathbf{X}\widehat{\boldsymbol{\theta}} = \mathbf{X}^\mathsf{T}\mathbf{y},$$

which are the normal equations.

4 Understanding, Evaluating, and Improving Performance

So far, we have encountered four different methods for supervised machine learning, and more are to come in later chapters. We always train the models by adapting them to training data and hoping that the models will thereby also give us good predictions when faced with new, previously unseen data. But can we really expect that to work? This is a very important question for the practical usefulness of machine learning. In this chapter, we will discuss this question in a rather general sense, before diving into more advanced methods in later chapters. By doing so, we will unveil some interesting concepts and also discover some practical tools for evaluating, improving, and choosing between different supervised machine learning methods.

4.1 Expected New Data Error E_{new}: Performance in Production

We start by introducing some concepts and notation. First, we define an error function $E(\widehat{y}, y)$ which encodes the purpose of classification or regression. The error function compares a prediction $\widehat{y}(\mathbf{x})$ to a measured data point, y, and returns a small value (possibly zero) if $\widehat{y}(\mathbf{x})$ is a good prediction of y and a larger value otherwise. Similarly to how we can use different loss functions when training a model, we can consider many different error functions, depending on what properties of the prediction are most important for the application at hand. However, unless otherwise stated, our default choices are misclassification and squared error, respectively:

$$\text{Misclassification:} \quad E(\widehat{y}, y) \triangleq \mathbb{I}\{\widehat{y} \neq y\} = \begin{cases} 0 & \text{if } \widehat{y} = y \\ 1 & \text{if } \widehat{y} \neq y \end{cases} \quad \text{(classification)} \quad (4.1a)$$

$$\text{Squared error:} \quad E(\widehat{y}, y) \triangleq (\widehat{y} - y)^2 \quad \text{(regression).} \quad (4.1b)$$

When we compute the average misclassification (4.1a), we usually refer to it as the *misclassification rate* (or 1 minus the misclassification rate as the *accuracy*). The misclassification rate is often a natural quantity to consider in classification, but for imbalanced or asymmetric problems, other aspects might be more important, as we discuss in Section 4.5.

The error function $E(\widehat{y}, y)$ has similarities to a loss function $L(\widehat{y}, y)$. However, they are used differently: A loss function is used when *learning* (or, equivalently, training) a model, whereas we use the error function to *analyse performance* of an already learned model. There are reasons for choosing $E(\widehat{y}, y)$ and $L(\widehat{y}, y)$ differently, which we will come back to soon.

In the end, supervised machine learning amounts to designing a method which performs well when faced with an endless stream of new, unseen data. Imagine, for example, all real-time recordings of street views that have to be processed by a vision system in a self-driving car once it is sold to a customer, or all incoming patients that have to be classified by a medical diagnosis system once it is implemented in clinical practice. The performance on fresh unseen data can, in mathematical terms, be understood as the average of the error function – how often the classifier is right, or how well the regression method predicts. To be able to mathematically describe the endless stream of new data, we introduce a *distribution over data* $p(\mathbf{x}, y)$. In most other chapters, we only consider the output y as a random variable, whereas the input $\mathbf{x}$ is considered fixed. In this chapter, however, we have to also think of the input $\mathbf{x}$ as a random variable with a certain probability distribution. In any real-world machine learning scenario, $p(\mathbf{x}, y)$ can be extremely complicated and practically impossible to write down. We will nevertheless use $p(\mathbf{x}, y)$ to *reason* about supervised machine learning methods, and the bare notion of $p(\mathbf{x}, y)$ (even though it is unknown in practice) will be helpful for that.

No matter which specific classification or regression method we consider, once it has been learned from training data $\mathcal{T} = \{\mathbf{x}_i, y_i\}_{i=1}^n$, it will return predictions $\widehat{y}(\mathbf{x}_\star)$ for any new input $\mathbf{x}_\star$ we feed into it. In this chapter, we will write $\widehat{y}(\mathbf{x}; \mathcal{T})$ to emphasise the fact that the model depends on the training data $\mathcal{T}$. Indeed, if we were to use a different training data set to learn the same (type of) model, this would typically result in a different model with different predictions.

In the other chapters, we mostly discuss how a model predicts the output for one, or a few, test inputs $\mathbf{x}_\star$. Let us take that to the next level by integrating (averaging) the error function (4.1) over *all* possible test data points with respect to the distribution $p(\mathbf{x}, y)$. We refer to this as the *expected new data error*,

$$\boxed{E_{\text{new}} \triangleq \mathbb{E}_\star \left[E(\widehat{y}(\mathbf{x}_\star; \mathcal{T}), y_\star) \right],} \tag{4.2}$$

where the expectation $\mathbb{E}_\star$ is the expectation over all possible test data points with respect to the distribution $(\mathbf{x}_\star, y_\star) \sim p(\mathbf{x}, y)$, that is,

$$\mathbb{E}_\star \left[E(\widehat{y}(\mathbf{x}_\star; \mathcal{T}), y_\star) \right] = \int E(\widehat{y}(\mathbf{x}_\star; \mathcal{T}), y_\star) p(\mathbf{x}_\star, y_\star) \, d\mathbf{x}_\star dy_\star. \tag{4.3}$$

Remember that the model (regardless of whether it is a linear regression, a classification tree, an ensemble of trees, a neural network, or something else) is trained on a given training dataset $\mathcal{T}$ and represented by $\widehat{y}(\cdot; \mathcal{T})$. What is happening in equation (4.2) is an averaging over possible test data points $(\mathbf{x}_\star, y_\star)$. Thus, E_{new} describes how well the model *generalises* from the training data $\mathcal{T}$ to new situations.

We also introduce the *training error*,

$$E_{train} \triangleq \frac{1}{n} \sum_{i=1}^{n} E(\widehat{y}(\mathbf{x}_i; \mathcal{T}), y_i), \qquad (4.4)$$

where $\{\mathbf{x}_i, y_i\}_{i=1}^{n}$ is the training data $\mathcal{T}$. E_{train} simply describes how well a method performs on the specific data on which it was trained, but in general this gives no information on how well the method will perform for new unseen data points.[1]

> ***Time to reflect 4.1*** What is E_{train} for k-NN with $k = 1$?

Whereas the training error E_{train} describes how well the method is able to 'reproduce' the data from which it was learned, the expected new data error E_{new} tells us how well a method performs when we put it 'into production'. For instance, what are the rates of false and missed pedestrian detections that we can expect a vision system in a self-driving car to make? Or, how large a proportion of all future patients will a medical diagnosis system get wrong?

> The overall goal in supervised machine learning is to achieve as small an E_{new} as possible.

This sheds some additional light on the comment we made previously, that the loss function $L(\widehat{y}, y)$ and the error function $E(\widehat{y}, y)$ do not have to be the same. As we will discuss thoroughly in this chapter, a model which fits the training data well and consequently has a small E_{train} might still have a large E_{new} when faced with new, unseen data. The best strategy to achieve a small E_{new} is therefore not necessarily to minimise E_{train}. Besides the fact that the misclassification (4.1a) is unsuitable for use as an optimisation objective (it is discontinuous and has derivative zero almost everywhere), it can also, depending on the method, be argued that E_{new} can be made smaller by a smarter choice of loss function. Examples of when this is the case include gradient boosting (Chapter 7) and support vector machines (Chapter 8). Finally, it is worth noting that not all methods are trained by explicitly minimising a loss function (k-NN is one such example), but the idea of evaluating the performance of the model using an error function still applies, no matter how it is trained.

Unfortunately, in practical cases, we can never compute E_{new} to assess how well we are doing. The reason is that $p(\mathbf{x}, y)$ – which we do not know in practice – is part of the definition of E_{new}. However, E_{new} is too important a quantity to be abandoned just because we cannot compute it exactly. Instead, we will spend quite some time

---

[1] The term 'risk function' is used in some literature for the expected loss, which is the same as the new data error E_{new} if the loss function and the error function are chosen to be the same. The training error E_{train} is then referred to as 'empirical risk' and the idea of minimising the cost function as 'empirical risk minimisation'.

and effort on *estimating* E_{new} from data, as well as on analysing how E_{new} behaves to better understand how we can decrease it.

We emphasise that E_{new} is a property of a trained model together with a specific machine learning problem. That is, we cannot talk about 'E_{new} for logistic regression' in general, but instead we have to make more specific statements, like 'E_{new} for the handwritten digit recognition problem with a logistic regression classifier trained on the MNIST data'.[2]

4.2 Estimating E_{new}

There are multiple reasons for a machine learning engineer to be interested in E_{new}, such as:

- judging if the performance is satisfying (whether E_{new} is small enough), or if more work should be put into the solution and/or more training data should be collected;

- choosing between different methods;

- choosing hyperparameters (such as k in k-NN, the regularisation parameter in ridge regression; or the number of hidden layers in deep learning) in order to minimise E_{new};

- reporting the expected performance to the customer.

As discussed above, we can unfortunately not compute E_{new} in any practical situation. We will, therefore, explore various ways of *estimating* E_{new}, which will lead us to a very useful concept known as cross-validation.

$E_{train} \not\approx E_{new}$: We Cannot Estimate E_{new} from Training Data

We have introduced both the expected new data error, E_{new}, and the training error E_{train}. In contrast to, E_{new}, we can always compute E_{train}.

We assume for now that $\mathcal{T}$ consists of samples (data points) from $p(\mathbf{x}, y)$. This means that the training data is assumed to have been collected under similar circumstances to the ones under which the trained model will be used, which is a common assumption.

When an expected value, such as in the definition of E_{new} in (4.2), cannot be computed in closed form, one option is to approximate the expected value by a sample average. Effectively this means that we approximate the integral (expected value) by a finite sum. Now, the question is if the integral in E_{new} can be well approximated by the sum in E_{train}, like this:

$$E_{new} = \int E(\widehat{y}(\mathbf{x}; \mathcal{T}), y))p(\mathbf{x}, y)d\mathbf{x}dy \overset{??}{\approx} \frac{1}{n} \sum_{i=1}^{n} E(\widehat{y}(\mathbf{x}_i; \mathcal{T}), y_i) = E_{train}. \quad (4.5)$$

---

[2]http://yann.lecun.com/exdb/mnist/

Put differently: Can we expect a method to perform equally well when faced with new, previously unseen data as it did on the training data?

The answer is, unfortunately, **no**.

> ***Time to reflect 4.2*** *Why can we not expect the performance on training data* (E_{train}) *to be a good approximation for how a method will perform on new, previously unseen data* (E_{new})*, even though the training data is drawn from the distribution* $p(\mathbf{x}, y)$*?*

Equation (4.5) does *not* hold, and the reason is that the samples used to approximate the integral are given by the training data points. However, these data points are also used to train the model and, indeed, there is an explicit dependence on the complete training data set $\mathcal{T}$ in the first factor of the integrand. We can, therefore, not use these data points to also approximate the integral. Put differently, the expected value in (4.5) should be computed *conditionally* on a fixed training data set $\mathcal{T}$.

In fact, as we will discuss more thoroughly later, the typical behavior is that $E_{train} < E_{new}$ (although this is not always the case). Hence, a method often performs worse on new, unseen data than on training data. *The performance on training data E_{train} is therefore not a reliable estimate of E_{new}.*

$E_{\text{hold-out}} \approx E_{\text{new}}$: We Can Estimate E_{new} from Hold-Out Validation Data

We could not use the training data directly to approximate the integral in (4.2) (that is, estimating E_{new} by E_{train}) since this would imply that we effectively use the training data twice: first, to train the model ($\widehat{y}$ in (4.4)) and second, to evaluate the error function (the sum in (4.4)). A remedy is to set aside some *hold-out validation data* $\{\mathbf{x}'_j, y'_j\}_{j=1}^{n_v}$, which is not in $\mathcal{T}$ used for training, and then use this only for estimating the model performance as the *hold-out validation error*,

$$E_{\text{hold-out}} \triangleq \frac{1}{n_v} \sum_{j=1}^{n_v} E(\widehat{y}(\mathbf{x}'_j; \mathcal{T}), y'_j). \tag{4.6}$$

In this way, not all data will be used for training, but some data points will be saved and used only for computing $E_{\text{hold-out}}$. This simple procedure for estimating E_{new} is illustrated in Figure 4.1.

Be aware! *When splitting your data, always do it randomly, for instance by shuffling the data points before the training–validation split! Someone might – intentionally or unintentionally – have sorted the dataset for you. If you do not split randomly, your binary classification problem might end up with one class in your training data and the other class in your hold-out validation data ...*

Assuming that all (training and validation) data points are drawn from $p(\mathbf{x}, y)$, it follows that $E_{\text{hold-out}}$ is an unbiased estimate of E_{new} (meaning that if the entire

All available data

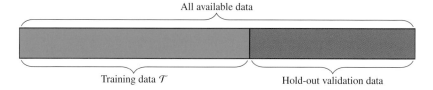

Training data $\mathcal{T}$ | Hold-out validation data

Figure 4.1 The hold-out validation dataset approach: If we split the available data into two sets and train the model on the training set, we can compute $E_{\text{hold-out}}$ using the hold-out validation set. $E_{\text{hold-out}}$ is an unbiased estimate of E_{new}, and the more data there is in the hold-out validation dataset, the less variance there will be in $E_{\text{hold-out}}$, (better estimate) but the less data is left for training the model (larger E_{new}).

procedure is repeated multiple times, each time with new data, the average value of $E_{\text{hold-out}}$ will be E_{new}). That is reassuring, at least on a theoretical level, but it does not tell us how close $E_{\text{hold-out}}$ will be to E_{new} in a single experiment. However, the variance of $E_{\text{hold-out}}$ decreases when the size of the hold-out validation dataset n_v increases; a small variance of $E_{\text{hold-out}}$ means that we can expect it to be close to E_{new}. Thus, if we make the hold-out validation dataset large enough, $E_{\text{hold-out}}$ will be close to E_{new}. However, setting aside a large validation dataset means that the dataset left for training becomes small. It is reasonable to assume that the more training data, the smaller E_{new} (which we will discuss later in Section 4.3). This is bad news since achieving a small E_{new} is our ultimate goal.

Sometimes there is *a lot* of available data. When we really have a lot of data, we can often afford to set aside a few percent to create a reasonably large hold-out validation dataset without sacrificing the size of the training dataset too much. *In such data-rich situations, the hold-out validation data approach is sufficient.*

If the amount of available data is more limited, this becomes more of a problem. We are, in practice, faced with the following dilemma: *the better we want to know* E_{new} (more hold-out validation data gives less variance in $E_{\text{hold-out}}$), *the worse we have to make it* (less training data increases E_{new}). That is not very satisfying, and we need to look for an alternative to the hold-out validation data approach.

k-Fold Cross-Validation: $E_{k\text{-fold}} \approx E_{\text{new}}$ Without Setting Aside Validation Data

To avoid setting aside validation data but still obtaining an estimate of E_{new}, one could suggest a two-step procedure of

(i) splitting the available data into one training and one hold-out validation set, training the model on the training data, and computing $E_{\text{hold-out}}$ using the hold-out validation data (as in Figure 4.1); and then

(ii) training the model again, this time using the entire dataset.

By such a procedure, we get an estimate of E_{new} at the same time as a model trained on the entire dataset. That is not bad, but not perfect either. Why? To achieve a small

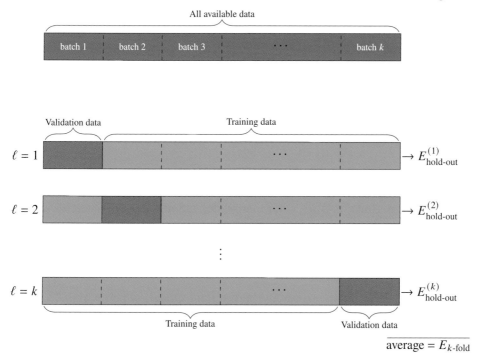

Figure 4.2 Illustration of k-fold cross-validation. The data is split into k batches of similar sizes. When looping over $\ell = 1, 2, \ldots, k$, batch ℓ is held out as validation data, and the model is trained on the remaining $k - 1$ data batches. Each time, the trained model is used to compute the average error $E_{k\text{-fold}}^{(\ell)}$ for the validation data. The final model is trained using all available data, and the estimate of E_{new} for that model is $E_{k\text{-fold}}$, the average of all $E_{k\text{-fold}}^{(\ell)}$.

variance in the estimate, we have to put a lot of data in the hold-out validation dataset in step (i). Unfortunately, this means that the model trained in (i) will possibly be quite different from the one obtained in step (ii), and the estimate of E_{new} concerns the model from step (i), not the possibly very different model from step (ii). Hence, this will not give us a good estimate of E_{new}. However, we can build on this idea to obtain the useful *k-fold cross-validation* method.

We would like to use all available data to train a model and at the same time have a good estimate of E_{new} for that model. By *k-fold* cross-validation, we can approximately achieve this goal. The idea of k-fold cross-validation is simply to repeat the hold-out validation dataset approach multiple times with a *different* hold-out dataset each time, in the following way:

(i) split the dataset into k batches of similar size (see Figure 4.2), and let $\ell = 1$;

(ii) take batch ℓ as the hold-out validation data and the remaining batches as training data;

(iii) train the model on the training data, and compute $E_{hold\text{-out}}^{(\ell)}$ as the average error on the hold-out validation data, as in (4.6);

(iv) if $\ell < k$, set $\ell \leftarrow \ell + 1$ and return to (ii). If $\ell = k$, compute the *k-fold cross-validation error*

$$E_{k\text{-fold}} \triangleq \frac{1}{k} \sum_{\ell=1}^{k} E_{\text{hold-out}}^{(\ell)} \tag{4.7}$$

(v) train the model again, this time using the entire dataset.

This procedure is illustrated in Figure 4.2.

With k-fold cross-validation, we get a model which is trained on all data as well as an approximation of E_{new} for that model, namely $E_{k\text{-fold}}$. Whereas $E_{\text{hold-out}}$ (Section 4.2) was an unbiased estimate of E_{new} (at the cost of setting aside hold-out validation data), this is not the case for $E_{k\text{-fold}}$. However, with k large enough, it turns out to often be a sufficiently good approximation. Let us try to understand why k-fold cross-validation works.

First, we have to distinguish between the final model, which is trained on all data in step (v), and the intermediate models which are trained on all except a $1/k$ fraction of the data in step (iii). The key in k-fold cross-validation is that if k is large enough, the intermediate models are quite similar to the final model (since they are trained on almost the same dataset: only a fraction $1/k$ of the data is missing). Furthermore, each intermediate $E_{\text{hold-out}}^{(\ell)}$ is an unbiased but high-variance estimate of E_{new} *for the corresponding ℓth intermediate model*. Since all intermediate models and the final model are similar, $E_{k\text{-fold}}$ (4.7) is approximately the average of k high-variance estimates of E_{new} for the final model. When averaging estimates, the variance decreases, and $E_{k\text{-fold}}$ will thus become a better estimate of E_{new} than the intermediate $E_{\text{hold-out}}^{(\ell)}$.

Be aware! *For the same reason as with the hold-out validation data approach, it is important to always split the data randomly for cross-validation to work! A simple solution is to first randomly permute the entire dataset, and thereafter split it into batches.*

We usually talk about training (or learning) as a procedure that is executed once. However, in k-fold cross-validation, the training is repeated k (or even $k + 1$) times. A special case is $k = n$, which is also called *leave-one-out cross-validation*. For methods such as linear regression, the actual training (solving the normal equations) is usually done within milliseconds on modern computers, and doing it an extra n times might not be a problem in practice. If the training is computationally demanding (as for deep neural networks, for instance), it becomes a rather cumbersome procedure, and a choice like $k = 10$ might be more practically feasible. If there is much data available, it is also an option to use the computationally less demanding hold-out validation approach.

Using a Test Dataset

A very important use of $E_{k\text{-fold}}$ (or $E_{\text{hold-out}}$) in practice is to choose between methods and select different types of hyperparameters such that $E_{k\text{-fold}}$ (or $E_{\text{hold-out}}$) becomes as small as possible. Typical hyperparameters to choose in this way are k in k-NN, tree depths, or regularisation parameters. However, much as we cannot use the training data error E_{train} to estimate the new data error E_{new}, selecting models and hyperparameters based on $E_{k\text{-fold}}$ (or $E_{\text{hold-out}}$) will invalidate its use as an estimator of E_{new}. Indeed, if hyperparameters are selected to minimise $E_{k\text{-fold}}$, there is a risk of overfitting to the validation data, resulting in $E_{k\text{-fold}}$ being an overly optimistic estimate of the actual new data error. If it is important to have a good estimate of the final E_{new}, it is wise to first set aside another hold-out dataset, which we refer to as a *test set*. This test set should be used only once (after selecting models and hyperparameters), to estimate E_{new} for the final model.

In problems where the training data is expensive, it is common to increase the training dataset using more or less artificial techniques. Such techniques can be to duplicate the data and add noise to the duplicated versions, to use simulated data, or to use data from a different but related problem, as we discuss in more depth in Chapter 11. With such techniques (which indeed can be very successful), the training data $\mathcal{T}$ is no longer drawn from $p(\mathbf{x}, y)$. In the worst case (if the artificial training data is very poor), $\mathcal{T}$ might not provide any information about $p(\mathbf{x}, y)$, and we cannot really expect the model to learn anything useful. It can therefore be very useful to have a good estimate of E_{new} if such techniques were used during training, but a reliable estimate of E_{new} can only be achieved from data that we *know* is drawn from $p(\mathbf{x}, y)$ (that is, collected under 'production-like' circumstances). If the training data is extended artificially, it is therefore extra important to set aside a test dataset *before* that extension is done.

The error function evaluated on the test data set could indeed be called 'test error'. To avoid confusion, however, we do not use the term 'test error' since it is commonly used (ambiguously) both as a name for the error on the test dataset as well as another name for E_{new}.

4.3 The Training Error–Generalisation Gap Decomposition of E_{new}

Designing a method with small E_{new} is a central goal in supervised machine learning, and cross-validation helps in estimating E_{new}. However, we can gain valuable insights and better understand the behavior of supervised machine learning methods by further analysing E_{new} mathematically. To be able to reason about E_{new}, we have to introduce another abstraction level, namely the *training-data averaged* versions of E_{new} and E_{train}. To make the notation more explicit, we here write $E_{\text{new}}(\mathcal{T})$ and

$E_{\text{train}}(\mathcal{T})$ to emphasise the fact that they both are conditional on a specific training dataset $\mathcal{T}$. Let us now introduce

$$\bar{E}_{\text{new}} \triangleq \mathbb{E}_{\mathcal{T}}[E_{\text{new}}(\mathcal{T})], \quad \text{and} \tag{4.8a}$$

$$\bar{E}_{\text{train}} \triangleq \mathbb{E}_{\mathcal{T}}[E_{\text{train}}(\mathcal{T})]. \tag{4.8b}$$

Here, $\mathbb{E}_{\mathcal{T}}$ denotes the expected value with respect to the training dataset $\mathcal{T} = break\{\mathbf{x}_i, y_i\}_{i=1}^n$ (of a fixed size n), assuming that this consists of independent draws from $p(\mathbf{x}, y)$. Thus $\bar{E}_{\text{new}}$ *is the average E_{new} if we were to train the model multiple times on different training datasets*, all of size n, and similarly for $\bar{E}_{\text{train}}$. The point of introducing these quantities is that it is easier to reason about the *average* behaviour $\bar{E}_{\text{new}}$ and $\bar{E}_{\text{train}}$ than about the errors E_{new} and E_{train} obtained when the model is trained on one specific training dataset $\mathcal{T}$. Even though we most often care about E_{new} in the end (the training data is usually fixed), insights from studying $\bar{E}_{\text{new}}$ are still useful.

> ***Time to reflect 4.3*** $E_{new}(\mathcal{T})$ *is the new data error when the model is trained on a specific training dataset $\mathcal{T}$, whereas $\bar{E}_{new}$ is averaged over all possible training datasets. Considering the fact that in the procedure of k-fold cross-validation, the model is trained each time on an (at least slightly) different training dataset, does $E_{k\text{-}fold}$ actually estimate E_{new}, or is it rather $\bar{E}_{new}$? And is that different for different values of k? How could $\bar{E}_{train}$ be estimated?*

We have already discussed the fact that E_{train} cannot be used in estimating E_{new}. In fact, it usually holds that

$$\bar{E}_{\text{train}} < \bar{E}_{\text{new}}. \tag{4.9}$$

Put into words, this means that on average, a method usually performs worse on new, unseen data than on training data. A method's ability to perform well on unseen data after being trained is often referred to as its ability to *generalise* from training data. We consequently call the difference between $\bar{E}_{\text{new}}$ and $\bar{E}_{\text{train}}$ the *generalisation gap*:[3]

$$\text{generalisation gap} \triangleq \bar{E}_{\text{new}} - \bar{E}_{\text{train}}. \tag{4.10}$$

The generalisation gap is the difference between the expected performance on training data and the expected performance 'in production' on new, previously unseen data.

---

[3] With stricter terminology, we should perhaps refer to $\bar{E}_{\text{new}} - \bar{E}_{\text{train}}$ as the *expected* generalisation gap, whereas $E_{\text{new}} - E_{\text{train}}$ would be the *conditional* generalisation gap. We will, however, use the same term for both.

With the decomposition of $\bar{E}_{new}$ into

$$\bar{E}_{new} = \bar{E}_{train} + \text{generalisation gap}, \qquad (4.11)$$

we also have an opening for digging deeper and trying to understand what affects $\bar{E}_{new}$ in practice. We will refer to (4.11) as the *training error–generalisation gap decomposition of $\bar{E}_{new}$*.

What Affects the Generalisation Gap?

The generalisation gap depends on the method and the problem. Concerning the method, one can typically say that *the more a method adapts to training data, the larger the generalisation gap*. A theoretical framework for how much a method adapts to training data is given by the so-called Vapnik–Chervonenkis (VC) dimension. From the VC dimension framework, probabilistic bounds on the generalisation gap can be derived, but those bounds are unfortunately rather conservative, and we will not pursue that approach any further. Instead, we only use the vague terms *model complexity* or *model flexibility* (we use them interchangeably), by which we mean the ability of a method to adapt to patterns in the training data. A model with high complexity (such as a fully connected deep neural network, deep trees, or k-NN with small k) can describe complicated input–output relationships, whereas a model with low complexity (such as logistic regression) is less flexible in what functions it can describe. For parametric models, the model complexity is somewhat related to the number of learnable parameters, but is also affected by regularisation techniques. As we will come back to later, the idea of model complexity is an oversimplification and does not capture the full nature of various supervised machine learning methods, but it nevertheless carries some useful intuition.

Typically, *higher model complexity implies a larger generalisation gap*. Furthermore, $\bar{E}_{train}$ decreases as the model complexity increases, whereas $\bar{E}_{new}$ typically attains a minimum for some intermediate model complexity value: too low *and* too high model complexity both raise $\bar{E}_{new}$. This is illustrated in Figure 4.3. A too high model complexity, meaning that $\bar{E}_{new}$ is higher than it had been with a less complex model, is called *overfitting*. The other situation, when the model complexity is too low, is sometimes called *underfitting*. In a consistent terminology, the point where $\bar{E}_{new}$ attains it minimum could be referred to as a balanced fit. Since the goal is to minimise $\bar{E}_{new}$, we are interested in finding this sweet spot. We also illustrate this by Example 4.1.

Note that we are discussing the usual behavior of $\bar{E}_{new}$, $\bar{E}_{train}$, and the generalisation gap. We use the term 'usual' because there are so many supervised machine learning methods and problems that it is almost impossible to make any claim that is *always* true for all possible situations, and pathological counter-examples also exist. One should also keep in mind that claims about $\bar{E}_{train}$ and $\bar{E}_{new}$ are about the *average* behavior when the model is retrained and evaluated on (hypothetical) new training data sets, see Example 4.1.

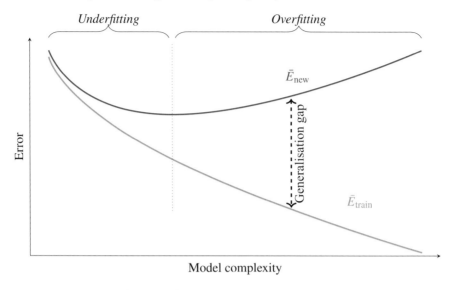

Figure 4.3 Behavior of $\bar{E}_{\text{train}}$ and $\bar{E}_{\text{new}}$ for many supervised machine learning methods, as a function of model complexity. We have not made a formal definition of complexity, but a rough proxy is the number of parameters that are learned from the data. The difference between the two curves is the generalisation gap. The training error $\bar{E}_{\text{train}}$ decreases as the model complexity increases, whereas the new data error $\bar{E}_{\text{new}}$ typically has a U-shape. If the model is so complex that $\bar{E}_{\text{new}}$ is larger than it had been with a less complex model, the term *overfit* is commonly used. Somewhat less common is the term *underfitting*, used for the opposite situation. The level of model complexity which gives the minimum $\bar{E}_{\text{new}}$ (at the dotted line) could be called a balanced fit. When, for example, we use cross-validation to select hyperparameters (that is, tuning the model complexity), we are searching for a balanced fit.

Example 4.1 The training error–generalisation gap decomposition for k-NN

We consider a simulated binary classification example with a two-dimensional input **x**. Contrary to all real world machine learning problems, in a simulated example like this, we know $p(\mathbf{x}, y)$. In this example, $p(\mathbf{x})$ is a uniform distribution on the square $[-1, 1]^2$, and $p(y \mid \mathbf{x})$ is defined as follows: all points above the dotted curve in Figure 4.4 are blue with probability 0.8, and points below the curve are red with probability 0.8. (The optimal classifier, in terms of minimal E_{new}, would have the dotted line as its decision boundary and achieve $E_{\text{new}} = 0.2$.)

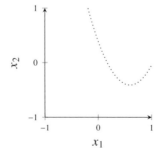

Fig. 4.4

We have $n = 200$ in the training data and learn three classifiers: k-NN with $k = 70$, $k = 20$, and $k = 2$, respectively. In model complexity sense, $k = 70$ gives the least flexible model and $k = 2$ the most flexible model. We plot their decision boundaries, together with the training data, in Figure 4.5.

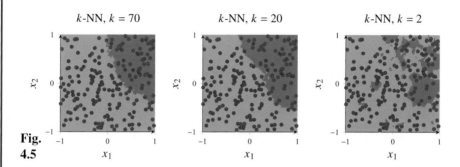

Fig. 4.5

We see in Figure 4.5 that $k = 2$ (right) adapts too much to the data. With $k = 70$ (left), on the other hand, the model is rigid enough not to adapt to the noise, but appears to possibly be too inflexible to adapt well to the true dotted line in Figure 4.4.

We can compute E_{train} by counting the fraction of misclassified training data points in Figure 4.5. From left to right, we get $E_{train} = 0.27, 0.24, 0.22$. Since this is a simulated example, we can also access E_{new} (or rather estimate it numerically by simulating a lot of test data), and from left to right, we get $E_{new} = 0.26, 0.23, 0.33$. This pattern resembles Figure 4.3, except for the fact that E_{new} is actually smaller than E_{train} for some values of k. However, this does not contradict the theory. What we have discussed in the main text is the *average* $\bar{E}_{new}$ and $\bar{E}_{train}$, *not* the E_{new} and E_{train} for one particular set of training data. To study $\bar{E}_{new}$ and $\bar{E}_{train}$, we therefore repeat this entire experiment 100 times and compute the average over those 100 experiments:

	k-NN with $k = 70$	k-NN with $k = 20$	k-NN with $k = 2$
$\bar{E}_{train}$	0.24	0.22	0.17
$\bar{E}_{new}$	0.25	0.23	0.30

This table follows Figure 4.3 well: The generalisation gap (difference between $\bar{E}_{new}$ and $\bar{E}_{train}$) is positive and increases with model complexity (decreasing k in k-NN), whereas $\bar{E}_{train}$ decreases with model complexity. Among these values for k, $\bar{E}_{new}$ has its minimum for $k = 20$. This suggests that k-NN with $k = 2$ suffers from overfitting for this problem, whereas $k = 70$ is a case of underfitting.

We have so far been concerned about the relationship between the generalisation gap and the model complexity. Another very important aspect is the size of the training dataset, n. We can in general expect that *the more training data, the smaller the generalisation gap*. On the other hand, $\bar{E}_{train}$ typically increases as n increases, since most models are unable to fit all training data points well if there are too many of them. A typical behavior of $\bar{E}_{train}$ and $\bar{E}_{new}$ is sketched in Figure 4.6.

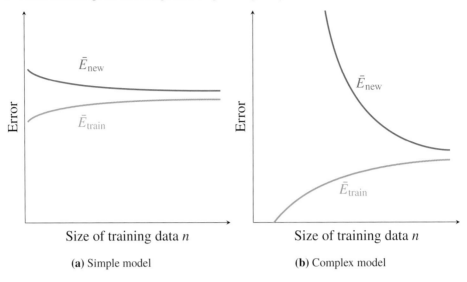

(a) Simple model   (b) Complex model

Figure 4.6 Typical relationship between $\bar{E}_{new}$, $\bar{E}_{train}$, and the number of data points n in the training dataset for a simple model (low model flexibility, left) and a complex model (high model flexibility, right). The generalisation gap (difference between $\bar{E}_{new}$ and $\bar{E}_{train}$) decreases, at the same time as $\bar{E}_{train}$ increases. Typically, a more complex model (right panel) will for large enough n attain a smaller $\bar{E}_{new}$ than a simpler model (left panel) would on the same problem (the figures should be thought of as having the same scales on the axes). However, the generalisation gap is typically larger for a more complex model, in particular when the training dataset is small.

Reducing E_{new} in Practice

Our overall goal is to achieve a small error 'in production', that is, a small E_{new}. To achieve that, according to the decomposition $E_{new} = E_{train} + $ generalisation gap, we need to have both E_{train} and the generalisation gap be small. Let us draw two conclusions from what we have seen so far:

- The new data error E_{new} will, on average, not be smaller than the training error E_{train}. Thus, if E_{train} is much bigger than the E_{new} you need for your model to be successful for the application at hand, you do not even need to waste time on implementing cross-validation for estimating E_{new}. Instead, you should re-think the problem and which method you are using.

- The generalisation gap and E_{new} typically decrease as n increases. Thus, if possible, increasing the size of the training data may help a lot with reducing E_{new}.

Making the model more flexible decreases E_{train} but often increases the generalisation gap. Making the model less flexible, on the other hand, typically decreases the generalisation gap but increases E_{train}. The optimal trade-off, in terms of small E_{new}, is often obtained when neither the generalisation gap nor the training error E_{train} is zero. Thus, by monitoring E_{train} and estimating E_{new} with cross-validation, we also get the following advice:

- If $E_{hold-out} \approx E_{train}$ (small generalisation gap; possibly underfitting), it might be beneficial to increase the model flexibility by loosening the regularisation, increasing the model order (more parameters to learn), etc.

- If E_{train} is close to zero and $E_{hold-out}$ is not (possibly overfitting), it might be beneficial to decrease the model flexibility by tightening the regularisation, decreasing the order (fewer parameters to learn), etc.

Shortcomings of the Model Complexity Scale

When there is one hyperparameter to choose, the situation sketched in Figure 4.3 is often a relevant picture. However, when there are multiple hyperparameters (or even competing methods) to choose, it is important to realise that the one-dimensional model complexity scale in Figure 4.3 does not do justice to the space of all possible choices. For a given problem, one method can have a smaller generalisation gap than another method *without* having a larger training error. Some methods are simply better for certain problems. The one-dimensional complexity scale can be particularly misleading for intricate deep learning models, but as we illustrate in Example 4.2, it is not even sufficient for the relatively simple problem of jointly choosing the degree of polynomial regression (higher degree means more flexibility) and the regularisation parameter (more regularisation means less flexibility).

Example 4.2 Training error and generalisation gap for a regression problem

To illustrate how the training error and generalisation gap can behave, we consider a simulated problem so that we can compute E_{new}. We let $n = 10$ data points be generated as $x \sim \mathcal{U}[-5, 10]$, $y = \min(0.1x^2, 3) + \varepsilon$, and $\varepsilon \sim \mathcal{N}(0, 1)$, and consider the following regression methods:

- Linear regression with L^2 regularisation
- Linear regression with a quadratic polynomial and L^2 regularisation
- Linear regression with a third order polynomial and L^2 regularisation
- Regression tree
- A random forest (Chapter 7) with 10 regression trees

For each of these methods, we try a few different values of the hyperparameters (regularisation parameter and tree depth, respectively) and compute $\bar{E}_{train}$ and the generalisation gap.

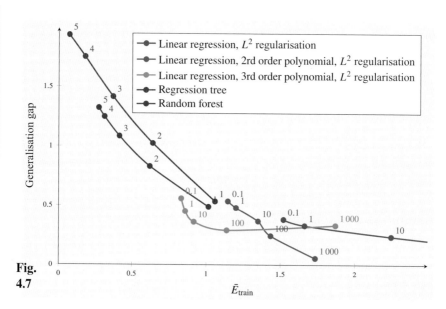

Fig. 4.7

For each method, the hyperparameter that minimises $\bar{E}_{new}$ is the value which is closest (in the 1-norm sense) to the origin in Figure 4.7, since $\bar{E}_{new} = \bar{E}_{train}$ + generalisation gap. Having decided on a certain model and only having one hyperparameter left to choose, corresponds well to the situation in Figure 4.3.

However, when we compare the *different* methods, a more complicated situation is revealed than is described by the one-dimensional model complexity scale. Compare, for example, the second (red) to the third order polynomial (green) linear regression in Figure 4.7: for some values of the regularisation parameter, the training error decreases *without* increasing the generalisation gap. Similarly, the generalisation gap is smaller, while the training error remains the same, for the random forest (purple) than for the tree (black) for a maximum tree depth of 2. The main takeaway from this is that these relationships are quite intricate, problem-dependent, and impossible to describe using the simplified picture in Figure 4.3. However, as we shall see, the picture becomes somewhat clearer when we next introduce another decomposition of $\bar{E}_{new}$, namely the bias–variance decomposition, in particular in Example 4.4.

In any real problem, we cannot make a plot such as in Example 4.2. This is only possible for simulated examples where we have full control over the data generating process. In practice, we instead have to make a decision based on the much more limited information available. It is good to choose models that are known to work well for a specific type of data and use experience from similar problems. We can also use cross-validation for selecting between different models and choosing hyperparameters. Despite the simplified picture, the intuition about under- and overfitting from Figure 4.3 can still be very helpful when deciding on what method or hyperparameter value to explore next with cross-validation.

4.4 The Bias–Variance Decomposition of E_{new}

We will now introduce another decomposition of $\bar{E}_{new}$ into a (squared) *bias* and a *variance* term, as well as an unavoidable component of irreducible noise. This decomposition is somewhat more abstract than the training–generalisation gap but provides some additional insights into E_{new} and how different models behave.

Let us first give a short reminder of the general concepts of bias and variance. Consider an experiment with an unknown constant z_0, which we would like to estimate. To assist us in estimating z_0, we have a random variable z. Think, for example, of z_0 as being the (true) position of an object and z of being noisy GPS measurements of that position. Since z is a random variable, it has some mean $\mathbb{E}[z]$, which we denote by $\bar{z}$. We now define

$$\text{Bias: } \bar{z} - z_0 \qquad (4.12a)$$

$$\text{Variance: } \mathbb{E}\left[(z - \bar{z})^2\right] = \mathbb{E}\left[z^2\right] - \bar{z}^2. \qquad (4.12b)$$

The *variance* describes how much the experiment varies each time we perform it (the amount of noise in the GPS measurements), whereas the *bias* describes the systematic error in z that remains no matter how many times we repeat the experiment (a possible shift or offset in the GPS measurements). If we consider the expected squared error between z and z_0 as a metric of how good the estimator z is, we can re-write it in terms of the variance and the squared bias:

$$\mathbb{E}\left[(z - z_0)^2\right] = \mathbb{E}\left[\left((z - \bar{z}) + (\bar{z} - z_0)\right)^2\right] =$$

$$= \underbrace{\mathbb{E}\left[(z - \bar{z})^2\right]}_{\text{Variance}} + \underbrace{2\left(\mathbb{E}[z] - \bar{z}\right)(\bar{z} - z_0)}_{0} + \underbrace{(\bar{z} - z_0)^2}_{\text{bias}^2}. \qquad (4.13)$$

In words, the average squared error between z and z_0 is the sum of the squared bias and the variance. The main point here is that to obtain a small expected squared error, we have to consider both the bias *and* the variance. Only a small bias *or* little variance in the estimator is not enough, but both aspects are important.

We will now apply the bias and variance concept to our supervised machine learning setting. For mathematical simplicity, we will consider the regression problem with the squared error function. The intuition, however, also carries over to the classification problem. In this setting, z_0 corresponds to the true relationship between inputs and output, and the random variable z corresponds to the model learned from training data. Note that, since the training data collection includes randomness, the model learned from it will also be random.

We first make the assumption that the true relationship between input $\mathbf{x}$ and output y can be described as some (possibly very complicated) function $f_0(\mathbf{x})$ plus independent noise ε:

$$y = f_0(\mathbf{x}) + \varepsilon, \quad \text{with } \mathbb{E}[\varepsilon] = 0 \text{ and } \text{var}(\varepsilon) = \sigma^2. \qquad (4.14)$$

In our notation, $\widehat{y}(\mathbf{x}; \mathcal{T})$ represents the model when it is trained on training data $\mathcal{T}$. This is our random variable, corresponding to z above. We now also introduce the *average trained model*, corresponding to $\bar{z}$:

$$\bar{f}(\mathbf{x}) \triangleq \mathbb{E}_{\mathcal{T}}[\widehat{y}(\mathbf{x}; \mathcal{T})]. \tag{4.15}$$

As before, $\mathbb{E}_{\mathcal{T}}$ denotes the expected value over n training data points drawn from $p(\mathbf{x}, y)$. Thus, $\bar{f}(\mathbf{x})$ is the (hypothetical) average model we would achieve, if we could re-train the model an infinite number of times on different training datasets, each one of size n, and compute the average.

Remember that the definition of $\bar{E}_{\text{new}}$ (for regression with squared error) is

$$\bar{E}_{\text{new}} = \mathbb{E}_{\mathcal{T}}\left[\mathbb{E}_\star\left[(\widehat{y}(\mathbf{x}_\star; \mathcal{T}) - y_\star)^2\right]\right]. \tag{4.16}$$

We can change the order of integration and write (4.16) as

$$\bar{E}_{\text{new}} = \mathbb{E}_\star\left[\mathbb{E}_{\mathcal{T}}\left[(\widehat{y}(\mathbf{x}_\star; \mathcal{T}) - f_0(\mathbf{x}_\star) - \varepsilon)^2\right]\right]. \tag{4.17}$$

With a slight extension of (4.13) to also include the zero-mean noise term ε (which is independent of $\widehat{y}(\mathbf{x}_\star; \mathcal{T})$), we can rewrite the expression inside the expected value $\mathbb{E}_\star$ in (4.17) as

$$\mathbb{E}_{\mathcal{T}}\left[\left(\underbrace{\widehat{y}(\mathbf{x}_\star; \mathcal{T})}_{\text{``}z\text{''}} - \underbrace{f_0(\mathbf{x}_\star) - \varepsilon}_{\text{``}z_0\text{''}}\right)^2\right]$$

$$= (\bar{f}(\mathbf{x}_\star) - f_0(\mathbf{x}_\star))^2 + \mathbb{E}_{\mathcal{T}}\left[(\widehat{y}(\mathbf{x}_\star; \mathcal{T}) - \bar{f}(\mathbf{x}_\star))^2\right] + \varepsilon^2. \tag{4.18}$$

This is (4.13) applied to supervised machine learning. In $\bar{E}_{\text{new}}$, which we are interested in decomposing, we also have the expectation over new data points $\mathbb{E}_\star$. By also incorporating that expected value in the expression, we can decompose $\bar{E}_{\text{new}}$ as

$$\bar{E}_{\text{new}} = \underbrace{\mathbb{E}_\star\left[(\bar{f}(\mathbf{x}_\star) - f_0(\mathbf{x}_\star))^2\right]}_{\text{Bias}^2} + \underbrace{\mathbb{E}_\star\left[\mathbb{E}_{\mathcal{T}}\left[(\widehat{y}(\mathbf{x}_\star; \mathcal{T}) - \bar{f}(\mathbf{x}_\star))^2\right]\right]}_{\text{Variance}} + \underbrace{\sigma^2}_{\substack{\text{Irreducible} \\ \text{error}}}. \tag{4.19}$$

The squared bias term $\mathbb{E}_\star\left[(\bar{f}(\mathbf{x}_\star) - f_0(\mathbf{x}_\star))^2\right]$ now describes how much the average trained model $\bar{f}(\mathbf{x}_\star)$ differs from the true $f_0(\mathbf{x}_\star)$, averaged over all possible test data points $\mathbf{x}_\star$. In a similar fashion, the variance term $\mathbb{E}_\star\left[\mathbb{E}_{\mathcal{T}}[(\widehat{y}(\mathbf{x}_\star; \mathcal{T}) - \bar{f}(\mathbf{x}_\star))^2]\right]$ describes how much $\widehat{y}(\mathbf{x}; \mathcal{T})$ varies each time the model is trained on a different training dataset. For the bias term to be small, the model has to be flexible enough such that $\bar{f}(\mathbf{x})$ can be close to $f_0(\mathbf{x})$, at least in regions where $p(\mathbf{x})$ is large. If the variance term is small, the model is not very sensitive to exactly which data points that happened to be in the training data, and vice versa. The irreducible error σ^2 is simply an effect of the assumption (4.14) – it is not possible to predict ε since it is a random error independent of all other variables. There is not much more to say about the irreducible error, so we will focus on the bias and variance terms.

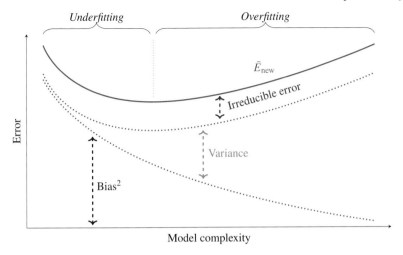

Figure 4.8 The bias–variance decomposition of $\bar{E}_{new}$, instead of the training error–generalisation gap decomposition in Figure 4.3. Low model complexity means high bias. The more complicated the model is, the more it adapts to (noise in) the training data, and the higher the variance. The irreducible error is independent of the particular choice of model and is therefore constant. The problem of achieving a small E_{new} by selecting a suitable model complexity level is often called the bias–variance tradeoff.

What Affects the Bias and Variance?

We have not properly defined model complexity, but we can actually use the bias and variance concept to give it a more concrete meaning: A high model complexity means low bias and high variance, and a low model complexity means high bias and low variance, as illustrated by Figure 4.8.

This resonates well with intuition. The more flexible a model is, the more it will adapt to the training data $\mathcal{T}$ – not only to the interesting patterns but also to the actual data points and noise that happened to be in $\mathcal{T}$. That is exactly what is described by the variance term. On the other hand, a model with low flexibility can be too rigid to capture the true relationship $f_0(\mathbf{x})$ between inputs and outputs well. This effect is described by the squared bias term.

Figure 4.8 can be compared to Figure 4.3, which builds on the training error–generalisation gap decomposition of $\bar{E}_{new}$ instead. From Figure 4.8, we can also talk about the challenge of finding the right model complexity level as the *bias–variance tradeoff*. We give an example of this in Example 4.3.

The squared bias term is more a property of the model than of the training dataset, and we may think of the bias term as independent of the number of data points n in the training data. The variance term, on the other hand, varies highly with n.[4] As we know, $\bar{E}_{new}$ typically decreases as n increases, and the reduction in $\bar{E}_{new}$ is largely because of the reduction of the variance. Intuitively, the more data, the more

---

[4]This is not exactly true. The average model $\bar{f}$ might indeed be different if all training datasets (which we average over) contain $n = 2$ or $n = 100\,000$ data points, but we neglect that effect here.

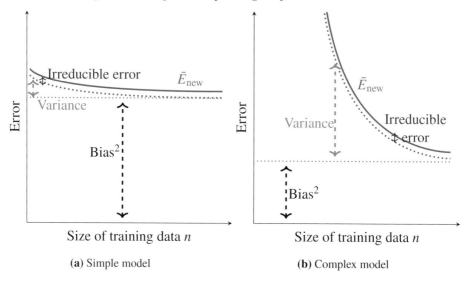

Figure 4.9 The typical relationship between bias, variance, and the size n of the training dataset. The bias is (approximately) constant, whereas the variance decreases as the size of the training dataset increases. This figure can be compared with Figure 4.6.

information we have about the parameters, resulting in a smaller variance. This is summarised by Figure 4.9, which can be compared to Figure 4.6.

Example 4.3 The bias–variance tradeoff for L^2 regularised linear regression

Let us consider a simulated regression example. We let $p(x, y)$ follow from $x \sim \mathcal{U}[0, 1]$ and

$$y = 5 - 2x + x^3 + \varepsilon, \quad \varepsilon \sim \mathcal{N}(0, 1). \tag{4.20}$$

We let the training data consist of only $n = 10$ data points. We now try to model the data using linear regression with a 4th order polynomial,

$$y = \beta_0 + \beta_1 x + \beta_2 x^2 + \beta_3 x^3 + \beta_4 x^4 + \varepsilon. \tag{4.21}$$

Since (4.20) is a special case of (4.21), and the squared error loss corresponds to Gaussian noise, we actually have zero bias for this model if we train it using squared error loss. However, learning 5 parameters from only 10 data points leads to very high variance, so we decide to train the model with squared error loss and L^2 regularisation, which will decrease the variance (but increase the bias). The more regularisation (bigger λ), the more bias and less variance.

Since this is a simulated example, we can repeat the experiment multiple times and estimate the bias and variance terms (since we can simulate as much training and test data as needed). We plot them in Figure 4.10 using the same style as Figures 4.3 and 4.8 (note the reversed x-axis: a smaller regularisation parameter corresponds to a higher model complexity). For this problem, the optimal value of λ would have

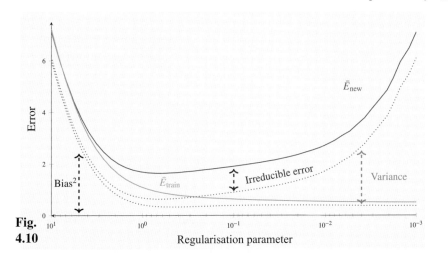

Fig. 4.10

been about 0.7 since $\bar{E}_{\text{new}}$ attains its minimum there. Finding this optimal λ is a typical example of the bias–variance tradeoff.

Connections Between Bias, Variance, and the Generalisation Gap

The bias and variance are theoretically well-defined properties but are often intangible in practice since they are defined in terms of $p(\mathbf{x}, y)$. In practice, we mostly have an estimate of the generalisation gap (for example as $E_{\text{hold-out}} - E_{\text{train}}$), whereas the bias and variance require additional tools for their estimation.[5] It is, therefore, interesting to explore what E_{train} and the generalisation gap say about the bias and variance.

Consider the regression problem. Assume that the squared error is used both as error function and loss function and that the global minimum is found during training. We can then write

$$\sigma^2 + \text{bias}^2 = \mathbb{E}_\star\left[(\bar{f}(\mathbf{x}_\star) - y_\star)^2\right] \approx \frac{1}{n}\sum_{i=1}^{n}(\bar{f}(\mathbf{x}_i) - y_i)^2$$

$$\geq \frac{1}{n}\sum_{i=1}^{n}(\widehat{y}(\mathbf{x}_i;\mathcal{T}) - y_i)^2 = E_{\text{train}}. \tag{4.22}$$

In the approximate equality, we approximate the expected value by a sample average using the training data points.[6] If, furthermore, we assume that $\widehat{y}$ can possibly be $\bar{f}$,

---

[5] The bias and variance can, to some extent, be estimated using the bootstrap, as we will introduce in Chapter 7.

[6] Since neither $\bar{f}(x_\star)$ nor $y_\star$ depends on the training data $\{x_i, y_i\}_{i=1}^{n}$, we can use $\{x_i, y_i\}_{i=1}^{n}$ to approximate the integral.

together with the above assumption of having the squared error as loss function and the learning of $\widehat{y}$ always finding the global minimum, we have the inequality in the next step. Remembering that $\bar{E}_{\text{new}} = \sigma^2 + \text{bias}^2 + \text{variance}$, and allowing ourselves to write $\bar{E}_{\text{new}} - E_{\text{train}} = \text{generalisation gap}$, we have

$$\text{generalisation gap} \gtrsim \text{variance}, \tag{4.23a}$$

$$E_{\text{train}} \lesssim \text{bias}^2 + \sigma^2. \tag{4.23b}$$

The assumptions in this derivation are not always met in practice, but it at least gives us some rough idea.

As we discussed previously, the choice of method is crucial for what E_{new} is obtained. Again, the one-dimensional scale in Figure 4.8 and the notion of a bias–variance tradeoff is a simplified picture; decreased bias does not *always* lead to increased variance, and vice versa. However, in contrast to the decomposition of E_{new} into training error and generalisation gap, the bias and variance decomposition can shed some more light on why E_{new} decreases for different methods: sometimes, the superiority of one method over another can be attributed to either a lower bias or a lower variance.

A simple (and useless) way to increase the variance without decreasing the bias in linear regression is to first learn the parameters using the normal equations and thereafter add zero-mean random noise to them. The extra noise does not affect the bias, since the noise has zero mean and hence leaves the average model $\bar{f}$ unchanged, but the variance increases. (This also affects the training error and the generalisation gap, but in a less clear way.) This way of training linear regression would be pointless in practice since it increases E_{new}, but it illustrates the fact that increased variance does *not* automatically lead to decreased bias.

A much more useful way of dealing with bias and variance is the meta-method called bagging, discussed in Chapter 7. It makes use of several copies (an *ensemble*) of a base model, each trained on a slightly different version of the training dataset. Since bagging averages over many base models, it reduces the variance, but the bias remains essentially unchanged. Hence, by using bagging instead of the base model, the variance is decreased without significantly increasing the bias, often resulting in an overall decrease in E_{new}.

To conclude, the world is more complex than just the one-dimensional model complexity scale used in Figure 4.3 and 4.8, which we illustrate by Example 4.4.

Time to reflect 4.4 *Can you modify linear regression such that the bias increases without decreasing the variance?*

Example 4.4 Bias and variance for a regression problem

We consider the exact same setting as in Example 4.2 but decompose $\bar{E}_{\text{new}}$ into bias and variance instead. This gives us Figure 4.11.

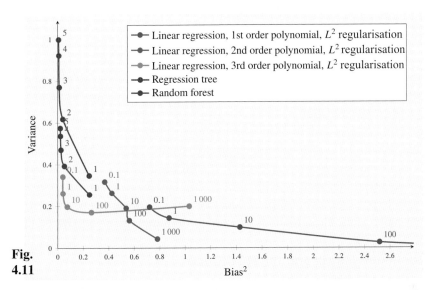

Fig. 4.11

There are clear resemblances to Example 4.2, as expected from (4.23). The effect of bagging (used in the random forest; see Chapter 7) is, however, clearer, namely that it reduces the variance compared to the regression tree with no noteworthy increase in bias.

For another illustration of what bias and variance means, we illustrate some of these cases in more detail in Figure 4.12. First we plot some of the linear regression models. The dashed red line is the true $f_0(\mathbf{x})$ the dotted blue lines are different models $\widehat{y}(\mathbf{x}_\star; \mathcal{T})$ learned from different training datasets $\mathcal{T}$ and the solid blue line their mean $\bar{f}(\mathbf{x})$. In these figures, bias is the difference between the dashed red and solid blue lines, whereas variance is the spread of the dotted blue lines around the solid blue. The variance appears to be roughly the same for all three models, perhaps somewhat smaller for the first order polynomial, whereas the bias is clearly smaller for the higher order polynomials. This can be compared to Figure 4.11.

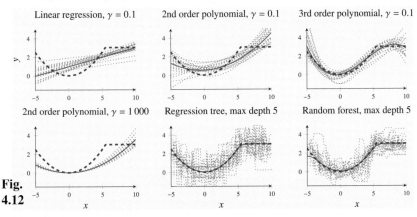

Fig. 4.12

Comparing the second order polynomial with little ($\gamma = 0.1$) and heavy ($\gamma = 1\,000$) regularisation, it is clear that regularisation reduces variance but also increases bias. Furthermore, the random forest has a smaller variance than the regression tree but without any noticeable change in the solid line $\bar{f}(\mathbf{x})$ and hence no change in bias.

4.5 Additional Tools for Evaluating Binary Classifiers

For classification, and in particular binary classification, there are a wide range of additional tools for inspecting the performance beyond the misclassification rate. For simplicity we consider the binary problem and use a hold-out validation dataset approach, but some of the ideas can be extended to the multiclass problem as well as to k-fold cross-validation.

Some of these tools are in particular useful for *imbalanced* and/or *asymmetric* problems, which we will discuss later in this section. Remember that in binary classification, we have either $y = \{-1, 1\}$. If a binary classifier is used to detect the presence of something, such as a disease, an object on the radar, etc., the convention is that $y = 1$ (positive) denotes presence, and $y = -1$ (negative) denotes absence. This convention is the background for a lot of the terminology we will introduce now.

The Confusion Matrix and the ROC Curve

If we learn a binary classifier and evaluate it on a hold-out validation dataset, a simple yet useful way to inspect the performance beyond just computing $E_{\text{hold-out}}$ is a *confusion matrix*. By separating the validation data in four groups depending on y (the actual output) and $\hat{y}(\mathbf{x})$ (the output predicted by the classifier), we can make the confusion matrix:

	$y = -1$	$y = 1$	*total*
$\hat{y}(\mathbf{x}) = -1$	True neg (TN)	False neg (FN)	N*
$\hat{y}(\mathbf{x}) = 1$	False pos (FP)	True pos (TP)	P*
total	N	P	n

Of course, TN, FN, FP, and TP (and also N*, P*, N, P and n) should be replaced by the actual numbers, as in Example 4.5. Note that P (N) denotes the total number of positive (negative) examples in the data set, whereas P* (N*) denotes the total number of positive (negative) predictions made by the model. The confusion matrix provides a quick and informative overview of the characteristics of a classifier. For asymmetric problems, which we will soon introduce, it is important to distinguish between false positive (FP, also called *type I error*) and false negative (FN, also called *type II error*). Ideally they should both be 0, but in practice, there is usually a tradeoff between these two errors, and the confusion matrix is a helpful tool in visualising them both. That tradeoff between false negatives and false positives can often be done by tuning a decision threshold r, which is present in many binary classifiers (3.36).

There is also a wide body of terminology related to the confusion matrix, which is summarised in Table 4.1. Some particularly common terms are the

$$recall = \frac{TP}{P} = \frac{TP}{TP + FN} \quad \text{and the} \quad precision = \frac{TP}{P^*} = \frac{TP}{TP + FP}.$$

Recall describes how large a proportion of the positive data points are correctly predicted as positive. A high recall (close to 1) is good, and a low recall (close to 0)

Table 4.1 Some common terms related to the quantities (TN, FN, FP, TP) in the confusion matrix. The terms written in italics are discussed in the text.

Ratio	Name
FP/N	False positive rate, Fall-out, Probability of false alarm
TN/N	True negative rate, Specificity, Selectivity
TP/P	True positive rate, Sensitivity, Power, *Recall*, Probability of detection
FN/P	False negative rate, Miss rate
TP/P*	Positive predictive value, *Precision*
FP/P*	False discovery rate
TN/N*	Negative predictive value
FN/N*	False omission rate
P/n	Prevalence
(FN + FP)/n	*Misclassification rate*
(TN + TP)/n	Accuracy, 1 − misclassification rate
$2\text{TP}/(\text{P}^* + \text{P})$	F_1 *score*
$(1 + \beta^2)\text{TP}/((1 + \beta^2)\text{TP} + \beta^2\text{FN} + \text{FP})$	F_β *score*

indicates a problem with many false negatives. Precision describes what the ratio of true positive points are among the ones predicted as positive. A high precision (close to 1) is good, and a low precision (close to 0) indicates a problem with many false positives.

Many classifiers contains a threshold r (3.36). If we want to compare different classifiers for a certain problem without specifying a certain decision threshold r, the *ROC curve* can be useful. The abbreviation ROC means 'receiver operating characteristics' and is due to its history from communications theory.

To plot an ROC curve, the recall/true positive rate (TP/P; a large value is good) is drawn against the false positive rate (FP/N; a small value is good) for all values of $r \in [0, 1]$. The curve typically looks as shown in Figure 4.13a. An ROC curve for a perfect classifier (always predicting the correct value for all $r \in (0, 1)$) touches the upper left corner, whereas a classifier which only assigns random guesses[7] gives a straight diagonal line.

A compact summary of the ROC curve is the *area under the ROC curve, ROC-AUC*. From Figure 4.13a, we conclude that a perfect classifier has ROC-AUC = 1, whereas a classifier which only assigns random guesses has ROC-AUC = 0.5. The ROC-AUC thus summarises the performance of a classifier for *all* possible values of the decision threshold r in a single number.

The F_1 Score and the Precision–Recall Curve

Many binary classification problems have particular characteristics, in that they are imbalanced, or asymmetric, or both. We say that a problem is

---

[7]That is, predicts $\widehat{y} = -1$ with probability r.

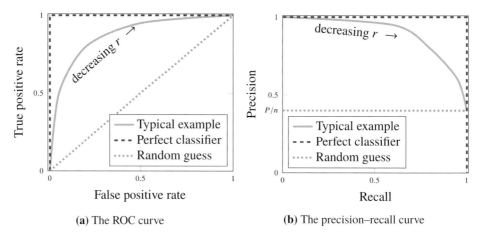

(a) The ROC curve   **(b)** The precision–recall curve

Figure 4.13 The ROC (left) and the precision–recall (right) curves. Both plots summarise the performance of a classifier for *all* decision thresholds r (see (3.36)), but the ROC curve is most relevant for balanced problems, whereas the precision–recall curve is more informative for imbalanced problems.

(i) *imbalanced* if the vast majority of the data points belong to one class, typically the negative class $y = -1$. This imbalance implies that a (useless) classifier which always predicts $\widehat{y}(\mathbf{x}) = -1$ will score very well in terms of misclassification rate (4.1a).

(ii) *asymmetric* if a false negative is considered more severe than a false positive, or vice versa. That asymmetry is not taken into account in the misclassifcation rate (4.1a);

A typical imbalanced problem is the prediction of a rare disease (most patients do not have it – that is, most data points are negative). That problem could also be an asymmetric problem if it is, say, considered more problematic to predict an infected patient as healthy than vice versa.

To start with, the confusion matrix offers a good opportunity to inspect the false negatives and positives in a more explicit fashion. It can, however, sometimes be useful to also summarise the performance into a single number. For that purpose, the misclassification rate is not very helpful; in a severely imbalanced problem, it can, for instance, favour a useless predictor that always predicts -1 over any realistically useful predictor.

For imbalanced problems, where the negative class $y = -1$ is the most common class, the F_1 score is therefore preferable to the misclassification rate (or accuracy). The F_1 score summarises the precision and recall by their harmonic means,

$$F_1 = \frac{2 \cdot precision \cdot recall}{precision + recall}, \tag{4.24}$$

which is a number between zero and one (higher is better).

For asymmetric problems, however, the F_1 score is not sufficient since it does not factor in the preference of having one type of error considered more serious than the other. For that purpose, a generalisation of the F_1 score, namely the F_β score, can be used. The F_β score weighs together precision and recall by considering recall to be β times as important as precision:

$$F_\beta = \frac{(1 + \beta^2)precision \cdot recall}{\beta^2 \cdot precision + recall}. \tag{4.25}$$

Much as the the misclassification rate might be misleading for imbalanced problems, the ROC curve might also be misleading for such problems. Instead, the precision–recall curve can (for imbalanced problems where $y = -1$ is the most common class) be more useful. As the name suggests, the precision–recall curve plots the precision (TP/P*; a large value is good) against the recall (TP/P; a large value is good) for all values of $r \in [0, 1]$, much like the ROC curve. The precision–recall curve for the perfect classifier touches the upper right corner, and a classifier which only assigns random guesses gives a horizontal line at the level P/n, as shown in Figure 4.13b.

Also for the precision–recall curve, we can define the *area under the precision–recall curve, PR-AUC*. The best possible PR-AUC is 1, and the classifier which only makes random guesses has PR-AUC equal to P/n.

We summarise this section with an example of an imbalanced and asymmetric problem in medicine. The evaluation of real-world classification problems, which most often are both imbalanced and asymmetric, is however, a challenging topic with certain dilemmas that are discussed further in Chapter 12.

Example 4.5 The confusion matrix in thyroid disease detection

The thyroid is an endocrine gland in the human body. The hormones it produces influences the metabolic rate and protein synthesis, and thyroid disorders may have serious implications. We consider the problem of detecting thyroid diseases, using the dataset provided by the UCI Machine Learning Repository (Dheeru and Karra Taniskidou 2017). The dataset contains 7 200 data points, each with 21 medical indicators as inputs (both qualitative and quantitative). It also contains the qualitative diagnosis {normal, hyperthyroid, hypothyroid}. For simplicity, we convert this into the binary problem with the output classes {normal, abnormal}. The dataset is split into training and hold-out validation sets, with 3 772 and 3 428 data points, respectively. The problem is imbalanced since only 7% of the data points are abnormal. Hence, the naive (and useless) classifier which always predicts normal will obtain a misclassification rate of around 7%. The problem is possibly also asymmetric, if false negatives (not indicating the disease) are considered more problematic than false positives (falsely indicating the disease). We train a logistic regression classifier and evaluate it on the validation dataset (using the default decision threshold $r = 0.5$, see (3.36)). We obtain the confusion matrix

	$y =$ normal	$y =$ abnormal
$\widehat{y}(\mathbf{x}) =$ normal	3 177	237
$\widehat{y}(\mathbf{x}) =$ abnormal	1	13

Most validation data points are correctly predicted as normal, but a large part of the abnormal data is also falsely predicted as normal. This might indeed be undesired in the application. The accuracy (1-misclassification) rate is 0.931, and the F_1 score is 0.106. (The useless predictor of always predicting normal has a very similar accuracy of 0.927, but worse F_1 score of 0.)

To change the picture, we lower the decision threshold to $r = 0.15$ in (3.36). That is, we predict the positive (abnormal) class whenever the predicted class probability exceeds this value, $g(\mathbf{x}) > 0.15$. This results in new predictions with the following confusion matrix:

	$y = $ normal	$y = $ abnormal
$\widehat{y} = $ normal	3 067	165
$\widehat{y} = $ abnormal	111	85

This change gives more true positives (85 instead of 13 patients are correctly predicted as abnormal), but this happens at the expense of more false positives (111 instead of 1 patients are now falsely predicted as abnormal). As expected, the accuracy is now lower at 0.919, but the F_1 score is higher at 0.381. Remember, however, that the F_1 score does not take the asymmetry into account but only the imbalance. We have to decide ourselves whether this classifier is a good tradeoff between the false negative and false positive rates, by considering which type of error has the more severe consequences.

4.6 Further Reading

This chapter was to a large extent inspired by the introductory machine learning textbook by Abu-Mostafa et al. (2012). There are also several other textbooks on machine learning, including Vapnik (2000) and Mohri et al. (2018), in which the central theme is understanding the generalisation gap using formal definitions of model flexibility such as the VC dimension or Rademacher complexity. The understanding of model flexibility for deep neural networks (Chapter 6) is, however, still subject to research; see for example, C. Zhang et al. (2017), Neyshabur et al. (2017), Belkin et al. (2019), and B. Neal et al. (2019) for some directions. Furthermore, the bias–variance decomposition is most often (including in this chapter) presented only for regression, but a possible generalisation to the classification problem is suggested by Domingos (2000). An alternative to the precision–recall curve, the so-called precision–recall–gain curve, is presented by Flach and Kull (2015).

5 Learning Parametric Models

In this chapter, we elaborate on the concept of parametric modelling. We start by generalising the notion of a parametric model and outline basic principles for learning these models from data. The chapter then resolves around three central concepts, namely loss functions, regularisation, and optimisation. We have touched upon all of them already, mostly in connection with parametric models in Chapter 3, linear and logistic regression. These topics are, however, central to many supervised machine learning methods, in fact even beyond parametric models, and deserve a more elaborate discussion.

5.1 Principles of Parametric Modelling

In Chapter 3, we introduced two basic parametric models for regression and classification, linear regression and logistic regression, respectively. We also briefly discussed how generalised linear models could be used to handle different types of data. The concept of parametric modelling is, however, not restricted to these cases. We therefore start this chapter by introducing a general framework for parametric modelling and discuss basic principles for learning these models from data.

Non-linear Parametric Functions

Consider the regression model (3.1), repeated here for convenience:

$$y = f_\theta(\mathbf{x}) + \varepsilon. \tag{5.1}$$

Here we have introduced an explicit dependence on the parameters θ in the notation to emphasise that the equation above should be viewed as our *model* of the true input–output relationship. To turn this model into a linear regression model, which could be trained using least squares with a closed form solution, we made two assumptions in Chapter 3. First, the function f_θ was assumed to be linear in the model parameters, $f_\theta(\mathbf{x}) = \theta^\mathsf{T}\mathbf{x}$. Second, the noise term ε was assumed to be Gaussian, $\varepsilon \sim \mathcal{N}(0, \sigma_\varepsilon^2)$. The latter assumption is sometimes implicit, but as we saw in Chapter 3, it makes the maximum likelihood formulation equivalent to least squares.

Both of these assumptions can be relaxed. Based on the expression above, the perhaps most obvious generalisation is to allow the function f_θ to be some arbitrary non-linear function. Since we still want the function to be learnt from training data, we require that it is adaptable. Similarly to the linear case, this can be accomplished by letting the function depend on some model parameters $\boldsymbol{\theta}$ that control the shape of the function. Different values of the model parameters will then result in different functions $f_{\boldsymbol{\theta}}(\cdot)$. Training the model amounts to finding a suitable value for the parameter vector $\boldsymbol{\theta}$, such that the function $f_{\boldsymbol{\theta}}$ accurately describes the true input–output relationship. In mathematical terms, we say that we have a *parametric family* of functions

$$\{f_{\boldsymbol{\theta}}(\cdot) : \boldsymbol{\theta} \in \Theta\},$$

where Θ is the space containing all possible parameter vectors. We illustrate with an example:

Example 5.1 Michaelis–Menten kinetics

A simple example of a non-linear parametric function is the Michaelis–Menten equation for modelling enzyme kinetics. The model is given by

$$y = \underbrace{\frac{\theta_1 x}{\theta_2 + x}}_{=f_{\boldsymbol{\theta}}(x)} + \varepsilon,$$

where y corresponds to a reaction rate and x a substrate concentration. The model is parameterised by the maximum reaction rate $\theta_1 > 0$ and the so-called Michaelis constant of the enzyme $\theta_2 > 0$. Note that $f_{\boldsymbol{\theta}}(x)$ depends non-linearly on the parameter θ_2 appearing in the denominator.

Typically the model is written as a deterministic relationship without the noise term ε, but here we include the noise as an error term for consistency with our statistical regression framework.

In the example above, the parameters θ_1 and θ_2 have physical interpretations and are restricted to be positive. Thus, Θ corresponds to the positive quadrant in $\mathbb{R}^2$. However, in machine learning we typically lack such physical interpretations of the parameters. The model is more of a 'black box' which is adapted to fit the training data as well as possible. For simplicity, we will therefore assume that $\Theta = \mathbb{R}^d$, meaning that $\boldsymbol{\theta}$ is a d-dimensional vector of real-valued parameters. The archetypes of such non-linear black-box models are neural networks, which we will discuss in more detail in Chapter 6. If we need to restrict a parameter value in some way, for example to be positive, then this can be accomplished by a suitable transformation of that parameter. For instance, in the Michaelis–Menten equation, we can replace θ_1 and θ_2 with $\exp(\theta_1)$ and $\exp(\theta_2)$, respectively, where the parameters are now allowed to take arbitrary real values.

Note that the likelihood corresponding to the model (5.1) is governed by the noise term ε. As long as we stick with the assumption that the noise is additive and Gaussian with zero mean and variance σ_ε^2, we obtain a Gaussian likelihood function

$$p(y \mid \mathbf{x}; \boldsymbol{\theta}) = \mathcal{N}\left(f_{\boldsymbol{\theta}}(\mathbf{x}), \sigma_\varepsilon^2 \right). \tag{5.2}$$

The only difference between this expression and the likelihood used in the linear regression model (3.18) is that the mean of the Gaussian distribution is now given by the arbitrary non-linear function $f_\theta(\mathbf{x})$.

Non-linear classification models can be constructed in a very similar way, as a generalisation of the logistic regression model (3.29). In binary logistic regression, we first compute the logit $z = \theta^\mathsf{T}\mathbf{x}$. The probability of the positive class, that is $p(y = 1 \mid \mathbf{x})$, is then obtained by mapping the logit value through the logistic function, $h(z) = \frac{e^z}{1+e^z}$. To turn this into a non-linear classification model, we can simply replace the expression for the logit with $z = f_\theta(\mathbf{x})$ for some arbitrary real-valued non-linear function f_θ. Hence, the non-linear logistic regression model becomes

$$g(\mathbf{x}) = \frac{e^{f_\theta(\mathbf{x})}}{1 + e^{f_\theta(\mathbf{x})}}. \tag{5.3}$$

Analogously, we can construct a multiclass non-linear classifier by generalising the multiclass logistic regression model (3.42). That is, we compute a vector of logits $\mathbf{z} = [z_1 \; z_2 \; \cdots \; z_M]^\mathsf{T}$ according to $\mathbf{z} = \mathbf{f}_\theta(\mathbf{x})$, where $\mathbf{f}_\theta$ is some arbitrary function that maps $\mathbf{x}$ to an M-dimensional real-valued vector $\mathbf{z}$. Propagating this logit vector through the softmax function results in a non-linear model for the conditional class probabilities, $\mathbf{g}_\theta(\mathbf{x}) = \text{softmax}(\mathbf{f}_\theta(\mathbf{x}))$. We will return to non-linear classification models of this form in Chapter 6, where we use neural networks to construct the function $\mathbf{f}_\theta$.

Loss Minimisation as a Proxy for Generalisation

Having specified a certain model class – that is, a parametric family of functions defining the model – learning amounts to finding suitable values for the parameters so that the model as accurately as possible describes the actual input–output relationship. For parametric models, this learning objective is typically formulated as an optimisation problem, such as

$$\widehat{\theta} = \arg\min_\theta \frac{1}{n} \sum_{i=1}^n \overbrace{L(y_i, f_\theta(\mathbf{x}_i))}^{\text{loss function}}. \tag{5.4}$$

$$\underbrace{\phantom{\widehat{\theta} = \arg\min_\theta \frac{1}{n} \sum_{i=1}^n L(y_i, f_\theta(\mathbf{x}_i))}}_{\text{cost function } J(\theta)}$$

That is, we seek to minimise a cost function defined as the average of some (user-chosen) loss function L evaluated on the training data. In some special cases (such as linear regression with squared loss), we can compute the the solution to this optimisation problem exactly. However, in most cases, and in particular when working with non-linear parametric models, this is not possible, and we need to resort to *numerical optimisation*. We will discuss such algorithms in more detail in Section 5.4, but it is useful to note already now that these optimisation algorithms are often iterative. That is, the algorithm is run over many iterations, and at each iteration, the current approximate solution to the optimisation problem (5.4) is updated to a new (hopefully better) approximate solution. This leads to a computational trade-off. The longer we run the algorithm, the better solution we expect to find, but at the cost of a longer training time.

Finding the value of θ which is such that the model fits the training data as well as possible is a natural idea. However, as we discussed in the previous chapter, the ultimate goal of machine learning is *not* to fit the training data as well as possible but rather to find a model that can *generalise to new data*, not used for training the model. Put differently, the problem that we are actually interested in solving is not (5.4) but rather

$$\widehat{\theta} = \arg \min_{\theta} E_{\text{new}}(\theta), \qquad (5.5)$$

where $E_{\text{new}}(\theta) = \mathbb{E}_{\star}\left[E(\widehat{y}(\mathbf{x}_{\star}; \theta), y_{\star})\right]$ is the expected new data error (for some error function E of interest; see Chapter 4). The issue is, of course, that the expected new data error is unknown to us. The 'true' data generating distribution is not available, and we thus cannot compute the expected error with respect to new data, nor can we optimise the objective (5.5) explicitly. However, this insight is still of practical importance, because it means that

> the training objective (5.4) is only a proxy for the actual objective of interest, (5.5).

This view of the training objective as a proxy has implications for how we approach the optimisation problem (5.4) in practice. We make the following observations.

Optimisation accuracy vs. statistical accuracy: The cost function $J(\theta)$ is computed based on the training data and is thus subject to noise in the data. It can be viewed as a random approximation of the 'true' expected loss (obtained as $n \to \infty$). Hence, it is not meaningful to *optimise $J(\theta)$ with greater accuracy than the statistical error in the estimate*. This is particularly relevant in situations when we need to spend a lot of computational effort to obtain a very accurate solution to the optimisation problem. This is unnecessary as long as we are within the statistical accuracy of the estimate. In practice, however, it can be difficult to determine what the statistical accuracy is (and we will not elaborate on methods that can be used for estimating it in this book), but this trade-off between optimisation accuracy and statistical accuracy is still useful to have in the back of the mind.

Loss function $\neq$ error function As discussed in Chapter 4, we can use an error function E for evaluating the performance of a model, which is different from the loss function L used during training. In words, when training the model, we minimise an objective which is different from the one that we are actually interested in. This might seem counter-intuitive, but based on the proxy view on the training objective, it makes perfect sense and, in fact, provides the machine learning engineer with additional flexibility in designing a useful training objective. There are many reasons why we might want to use a loss function that is different from the error function. First, it can result in a model which is expected to generalise better. The typical example is when evaluating a classification model based on accuracy (equivalently, misclassification error). If we were to train the model by minimising the misclassification loss, we would only care about placing the decision boundaries to get as many training data points as possible on the right side, but without taking the distances to the decision boundaries into account. However, due to the noise in the data, having some *margin* to the decision boundary can result in better generalisation, and there are loss functions that explicitly encourage this. Second, we can choose the loss function with the aim of making the optimisation problem (5.4) easier to solve, for instance by using a convex loss function (see Section 5.4). Third, certain loss functions can encourage other favorable properties of the final model, such as making the model less computationally demanding to use 'in production'.

Early stopping When optimising the objective (5.4) using an *iterative numerical optimisation method*, this can be thought of as generating a sequence of candidate models. At each iteration of the optimsation algorithm, we have access to the current estimate of the parameter vector, and we thus obtain a 'path' of parameter values. Interestingly, it is not necessarily the end point of this path that is closest to the solution of (5.5). Indeed, the path of parameter values can pass a useful solution (with good generalisation properties) before drifting off to a worse solution (for example due to overfitting). Based on this observation, there is another reason for stopping the optimisation algorithm prematurely, apart from the purely computational reason mentioned above. By *early stopping* of the algorithm, we can obtain a final model with superior performance to the one we would obtain if we ran the algorithm until convergence. We refer to this as *implicit regularisation* and discuss the details of how it can be implemented in practice in Section 5.3.

Explicit regularisation Another strategy is to explicitly modify the cost function (5.4) by adding a term independent of the training data. We refer to this technique as explicit regularisation. The aim is to make the final model generalise better – that is, we hope to make the solution to the modified problem closer to the solution of (5.5). We saw an example of this already in Section 3.3 where we introduced L^2 regularisation. The underlying idea is the law of parsimony: that the simplest explanation of an observed phenomenon is usually the right one. In the context of machine learning, this means that if both a 'simple' and a 'complicated' model fit the data (more or less) equally well, then the 'simple' one will typically have superior generalisation properties and should therefore be preferred. In explicit regularisation the vague notions of 'simple' and 'complicated' are reduced to simply mean small and large parameter values, respectively. In order to favour a simple model, an extra term is added to the cost function that penalises large parameter values. We will discuss regularisation further in Section 5.3.

5.2 Loss Functions and Likelihood-Based Models

Which loss function L to use in the training objective (5.4) is a design choice, and different loss functions will give rise to different solutions $\widehat{\theta}$. This will in turn result in models with different characteristics. There is in general no 'right' or 'wrong' loss function, but for a given problem, one particular choice can be superior to another in terms of small E_{new} (note that there is a similar design choice involved in E_{new}, namely how to choose the error function which defines how we measure the performance of the model). Certain combinations of models and loss functions have proven particularly useful and have historically been branded as specific methods. For example, the term 'linear regression' most often refers to the combination of a linear-in-the-parameter model and the squared error loss, whereas the term 'support vector classification' (see Chapter 8) refers to a linear-in-the-parameter model trained using the hinge loss. In this section, however, we provide a general discussion about different loss functions and their properties, without connections to a specific method.

One important aspect of a loss function is its *robustness*. Robustness is tightly connected to outliers, meaning spurious data points that do not describe the relationship we are interested in modelling. If outliers in the training data only have a minor impact on the learned model, we say that the loss function is robust. Conversely, a loss function is not robust if the outliers have a major impact on the learned model. Robustness is therefore a very important property in applications where the training data is contaminated with outliers. It is not a binary property, however, and loss functions can be robust to a greater or lesser extent. Some of the commonly used loss functions, including the squared error loss, are unfortunately not particularly robust, and it is therefore important for the user to make an active and informed decision before resorting to these 'default' options.

From a statistical perspective, we can link the loss function to statistical properties of the learnt model. First, the maximum likelihood approach provides a formal connection between the loss function and the probabilistic assumptions on the (noise in the) data. Second, even for loss functions that are not derived from a likelihood perspective, we can relate the so-called *asymptotic minimiser* of the loss function to the statistical properties of the model. The asymptotic minimiser refers to the model that minimises the expected loss when averaged over the true data-generating distribution. Equivalently, we can think about the asymptotic minimiser as the solution to the optimisation problem (5.4) as the number of training data points

$n \to \infty$ (hence the name 'asymptotic'). If there is a unique asymptotic minimiser from which we can recover the true conditional distribution $p(y \mid \mathbf{x})$, then the loss function is said to be *strictly proper*. We will return to this concept below, specifically in the context of binary classification.

Loss Functions for Regression

In Chapter 3 we introduced the *squared error loss*[1]

$$L(y, \widehat{y}) = (\widehat{y} - y)^2, \tag{5.6}$$

which is the default choice for linear regression since it simplifies the training to only solving the normal equations. The squared error loss is often also used for other regression models, such as neural networks. Another common choice is the *absolute error loss*,

$$L(y, \widehat{y}) = |\widehat{y} - y|. \tag{5.7}$$

The absolute error loss is more robust to outliers than the squared error loss since it grows more slowly for large errors; see Figure 5.1. In Chapter 3 we introduced the maximum likelihood motivation of the squared error loss by assuming that the output y is measured with additive noise ε from a Gaussian distribution, $\varepsilon \sim \mathcal{N}(0, \sigma_\varepsilon^2)$. We can similarly motivate the absolute error loss by instead assuming ε to have a Laplace distribution, $\varepsilon \sim \mathcal{L}(0, b_\varepsilon)$. We elaborate and expand on the idea of deriving the loss function from the maximum likelihood objective and certain statistical modelling assumptions below. However, there are also some commonly used loss functions for regression which are not very natural to derive from a maximum likelihood perspective.

It is sometimes argued that the squared error loss is a good choice because of its quadratic shape, which penalises small errors ($\varepsilon < 1$) less than linearly. After all, the Gaussian distribution appears (at least approximately) quite often in nature. However, the quadratic shape for large errors ($\varepsilon > 1$) is the reason for its non-robustness, and the *Huber loss* has therefore been suggested as a hybrid between the absolute loss and squared error loss:

$$L(y, \widehat{y}) = \begin{cases} \frac{1}{2}(\widehat{y} - y)^2 & \text{if } |\widehat{y} - y| < 1, \\ |\widehat{y} - y| - \frac{1}{2} & \text{otherwise.} \end{cases} \tag{5.8}$$

Another extension to the absolute error loss is the *ϵ-insensitive loss*,

$$L(y, \widehat{y}) = \begin{cases} 0 & \text{if } |\widehat{y} - y| < \epsilon, \\ |\widehat{y} - y| - \epsilon & \text{otherwise,} \end{cases} \tag{5.9}$$

---

[1] As you might already have noticed, the arguments to the loss function (here y and $\widehat{y}$) vary with context. The reason for this is that different loss functions are most naturally expressed in terms of different quantities, for example the prediction $\widehat{y}$, the predicted conditional class probability $g(\mathbf{x})$, the classifier margin, etc.

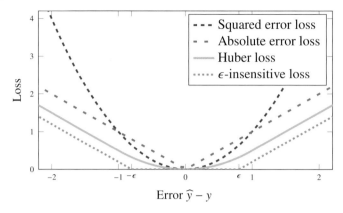

Figure 5.1 The loss functions for regression presented in the text, each as a function of the error $\widehat{y} - y$.

where ϵ is a user-chosen design parameter. This loss places a tolerance of width 2ϵ around the observed y and behaves like the absolute error loss outside this region. The robustness properties of the ϵ-insensitive loss are very similar to those of the absolute error loss. The ϵ-insensitive loss turns out to be useful for support vector regression in Chapter 8. We illustrate all these loss functions for regression in Figure 5.1.

Loss Functions for Binary Classification

An intuitive loss function for binary classification is provided by the *misclassification loss*,

$$L(y, \widehat{y}) = \mathbb{I}\{\widehat{y} \neq y\} = \begin{cases} 0 & \text{if } \widehat{y} = y, \\ 1 & \text{if } \widehat{y} \neq y. \end{cases} \tag{5.10}$$

However, even though a small misclassification loss might be the ultimate goal in practice, this loss function is rarely used when training models. As mentioned in Section 5.1, there are at least two reasons for this. First, using a different loss function can result in a model that generalises better from the training data. This can be understood by noting that the final prediction $\widehat{y}$ does not reveal all aspects of the classifier. Intuitively, we may prefer to not have the decision boundary close to the training data points, even if they are correctly classified, but instead push the boundary further away to have some margin. To achieve this, we can formulate the loss function not just in terms of the hard class prediction $\widehat{y}$ but based on the predicted class probability $g(\mathbf{x})$ or some other continuous quantity used to compute the class prediction. The second reason for not using misclassification loss as the training objective, which is also important, is that it would result in a cost function that is piecewise constant. From a numerical optimisation perspective, this is a difficult objective since the gradient is zero everywhere, except where it is undefined.

For a binary classifier that predicts conditional class probabilities $p(y = 1 \mid \mathbf{x})$ in terms of a function $g(\mathbf{x})$, the *cross-entropy loss*, as introduced in Chapter 3, is a natural choice:

$$L(y, g(\mathbf{x})) = \begin{cases} \ln g(\mathbf{x}) & \text{if } y = 1, \\ \ln(1 - g(\mathbf{x})) & \text{if } y = -1. \end{cases} \tag{5.11}$$

This loss was derived from a maximum likelihood perspective, but unlike regression (where we had to specify a distribution for ε), there are no user choices left in the cross-entropy loss, other than what model to use for $g(\mathbf{x})$. Indeed, for a binary classification problem, the model $g(\mathbf{x})$ provides a complete statistical description of the conditional distribution of the output given the input.

While cross entropy is commonly used in practice, there are also other loss functions for binary classification that are useful. To define an entire family of loss functions, let us first introduce the concept of *margins* in binary classification. Many binary classifiers $\widehat{y}(\mathbf{x})$ can be constructed by thresholding some real-valued function[2] $f(\mathbf{x})$ at 0. That is, we can write the class prediction

$$\widehat{y}(\mathbf{x}) = \text{sign}\{f(\mathbf{x})\}. \tag{5.12}$$

Logistic regression, for example, can be brought into this form by simply using $f(\mathbf{x}) = \boldsymbol{\theta}^{\mathsf{T}}\mathbf{x}$, as shown in (3.39). More generally, for a non-linear generalisation of the logistic regression model where the probability of the positive class is modelled as in (5.3), the prediction (5.12) corresponds to the most likely class. Not all classifiers have a probabilistic interpretation, however, but often they can still be expressed as in (5.12) for some underlying function $f(\mathbf{x})$.

The decision boundary for any classifier of the form (5.12) is given by the values of $\mathbf{x}$ for which $f(\mathbf{x}) = 0$. To simplify our discussion, we will assume that none of the data points fall exactly on the decision boundary (which always gives rise to an ambiguity). This will imply that we can assume that $\widehat{y}(\mathbf{x})$ as defined above is always either -1 or $+1$. Based on the function $f(\mathbf{x})$, we say that

> the margin of a classifier for a data point $(\mathbf{x}, y)$ is $y \cdot f(\mathbf{x})$.

It follows that if y and $f(\mathbf{x})$ have the same sign, meaning that the classification is correct, then the margin is positive. Analogously, for an incorrect classification, y and $f(\mathbf{x})$ will have different signs, and the margin will be negative. The margin can be viewed as a measure of certainty in a prediction, where data points with small margins are in some sense (not necessarily Euclidean) close to the decision boundary. The margin plays a similar role for binary classification as the prediction error $\widehat{y} - y$ does for regression.

We can now define loss functions for binary classification in terms of the margin, by assigning a small loss to positive margins (correct classifications) and a large

---

[2]In general, the function $f(\mathbf{x})$ depends on the model parameters $\boldsymbol{\theta}$, but in the presentation below we will drop this dependence from the notation for brevity.

loss to negative margins (misclassifications). We can, for instance, re-formulate the logistic loss (3.34) in terms of the margin as

$$L(y \cdot f(\mathbf{x})) = \ln\left(1 + \exp\left(-y \cdot f(\mathbf{x})\right)\right), \tag{5.13}$$

where, in line with the discussion above, the linear logistic regression model corresponds to $f(\mathbf{x}) = \theta^\mathsf{T}\mathbf{x}$. Analogously to the derivation of the logistic loss in Chapter 3, this is just another way of writing the cross entropy (or negative log-likelihood) loss (5.11), assuming that the probability of the positive class is modelled according to (5.3). However, from an alternative point of view, we can consider (5.13) as a generic margin-based loss, without linking it to the probabilistic model (5.3). That is, we simply postulate a classifier according to (5.12) and learn the parameters of $f(\mathbf{x})$ by minimising (5.13). This is, of course, equivalent to logistic regression, except for the fact that we have seemingly lost the notion of a conditional class probability estimate $g(\mathbf{x})$ and only have a 'hard' prediction $\widehat{y}(\mathbf{x})$. We will, however, recover the class probability estimate later when we discuss the asymptotic minimiser of the logistic loss.

We can also re-formulate the misclassification loss in terms of the margin,

$$L(y \cdot f(\mathbf{x})) = \begin{cases} 1 & \text{if } y \cdot f(\mathbf{x}) < 0, \\ 0 & \text{otherwise.} \end{cases} \tag{5.14}$$

More important, however, is that the margin view allows us to easily come up with other loss functions with possibly favourable properties. In principle, any decreasing function is a candidate loss function. However, most loss functions used in practice are also convex, which is useful when optimising the training loss numerically.

One example is the *exponential loss*, defined as

$$L(y \cdot f(\mathbf{x})) = \exp(-y \cdot f(\mathbf{x})), \tag{5.15}$$

which turns out to be a useful loss function when we derive the AdaBoost algorithm in Chapter 7. The downside of the exponential loss is that it is not particularly robust against outliers, due to its exponential growth for negative margins, compared to, for example, the linear asymptotic growth of the logistic loss.[3] We also have the *hinge loss*, which we will use for support vector classification in Chapter 8:

$$L(y \cdot f(\mathbf{x})) = \begin{cases} 1 - y \cdot f(\mathbf{x}) & \text{for } y \cdot f(\mathbf{x}) \leq 1, \\ 0 & \text{otherwise.} \end{cases} \tag{5.16}$$

As we will see in Chapter 8, the hinge loss has an attractive so-called support vector property. However, a downside of the hinge loss is that it is not a *strictly proper* loss function, which means that it is not possible to interpret the learnt classification

---

[3] For $yf(\mathbf{x}) \ll 0$, it holds that $\ln\left(1 + \exp\left(-yf(\mathbf{x})\right)\right) \approx -yf(\mathbf{x})$.

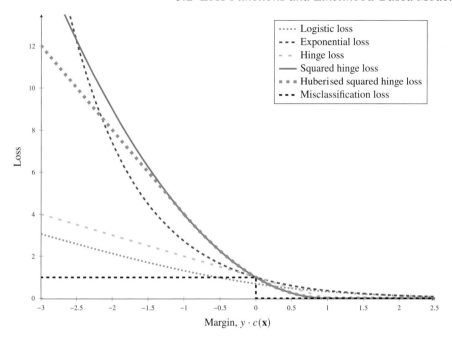

Figure 5.2 Comparison of some common loss functions for classification, plotted as a function of the margin.

model probabilistically when using this loss (we elaborate on this below). As a remedy, one may instead consider the *squared hinge loss*

$$L(y \cdot f(\mathbf{x})) = \begin{cases} (1 - y \cdot f(\mathbf{x}))^2 & \text{for } y \cdot f(\mathbf{x}) \leq 1, \\ 0 & \text{otherwise,} \end{cases} \qquad (5.17)$$

which on the other hand is less robust than the hinge loss (quadratic instead of linear growth). A more elaborate alternative is therefore the *Huberised squared hinge* loss

$$L(y \cdot f(\mathbf{x})) = \begin{cases} -4y \cdot f(\mathbf{x}) & \text{for } y \cdot f(\mathbf{x}) \leq -1, \\ (1 - y \cdot f(\mathbf{x}))^2 & \text{for } -1 \leq y \cdot f(\mathbf{x}) \leq 1, \quad \text{(squared hinge loss)} \\ 0 & \text{otherwise,} \end{cases}$$

$$(5.18)$$

whose name refers to its similarities to the Huber loss for regression, namely that the quadratic function is replaced with a linear function for margins <-1. The three loss functions presented above are all particularly interesting for support vector classification, due to the fact that they are all exactly 0 for margins >1.

We summarise this cascade of loss functions for binary classification in Figure 5.2, which illustrates all these losses as a function of the margin.

When learning models for imbalanced or asymmetric problems, it is possible to modify the loss function to account for imbalance or asymmetry. For example, to

101

reflect that not predicting $y = 1$ correctly is a 'C times more severe mistake' than not predicting $y = -1$ correctly, the misclassification loss can be modified into

$$L(y, \widehat{y}) = \begin{cases} 0 & \text{if } \widehat{y} = y, \\ 1 & \text{if } \widehat{y} \neq y \text{ and } y = -1, \\ C & \text{if } \widehat{y} \neq y \text{ and } y = 1. \end{cases} \quad (5.19)$$

The other loss functions can be modified in a similar fashion. A similar effect can also be achieved by, for this example, simply duplicating all positive training data points C times in the training data, instead of modifying the loss function.

We have already made some claims about robustness. Let us motivate them using Figure 5.2. One characterisation of an outlier is as a data point on the wrong side of and far away from the decision boundary. From a margin perspective, that is equivalent to a large negative margin. The robustness of a loss function is therefore tightly connected to the shape of the loss function for large negative margins. The steeper the slope and heavier the penalisation of large negative margins, the more sensitive it is to outliers. We can therefore tell from Figure 5.2 that the exponential loss is expected to by sensitive to outliers, due to its exponential growth, whereas the squared hinge loss is somewhat more robust with a quadratic growth instead. However, even more robust are the Huberised squared hinge loss, the hinge loss, and the logistic loss which all have an asymptotic behavior which is linear. Most robust is the misclassification loss, but as already discussed, that loss has other disadvantages.

Multiclass Classification

So far, we have only discussed the binary classification problem, with $M = 2$. The cross-entropy (equivalently, negative log-likelihood) loss is straightforward to generalise to the multiclass problem, that is, $M > 2$, as we did in Chapter 3 for logistic regression. This is a useful property of the likelihood-based loss since it allows us to systematically treat both binary and multiclass classification in the same coherent framework.

Generalising the other loss functions discussed above requires a generalisation of the margin to the multiclass problem. That is possible, but we do not elaborate on it in this book. Instead we mention a pragmatic approach, which is to reformulate the problem as several binary problems. This reformulation can be done using either a one-versus-rest or one-versus-one scheme.

The one-versus-rest (or one-versus-all or binary relevance) idea is to train M binary classifiers. Each classifier in this scheme is trained for predicting one class against all the other classes. To make a prediction for a test data point, all M classifiers are used, and the class which, for example, is predicted with the largest margin is taken as the predicted class. This approach is a pragmatic solution, which may turn out to work well for some problems.

The one-versus-one idea is instead to train one classifier for each pair of classes. If there are M classes in total, there are $\frac{1}{2}M(M-1)$ such pairs. To make a prediction, each classifier predicts either of its two classes, and the class which overall obtains most 'votes' is chosen as the final prediction. The predicted margins can be used to break a tie if that happens. Compared to one-versus-rest, the one-versus-one approach has the disadvantage of involving $\frac{1}{2}M(M-1)$ classifiers, instead of only M. On the other hand, each of these classifiers is trained on much smaller datasets (only the data points that belong to either of the two classes), compared to one-versus-rest, which uses the entire original training dataset for all M classifiers.

Likelihood-Based Models and the Maximum Likelihood Approach

The maximum likelihood approach is a generic way of constructing a loss function based on a statistical model of the observed data. In general, maximising the data likelihood is equivalent to minimising a cost function based on the *negative log-likelihood loss*,

$$J(\boldsymbol{\theta}) = -\frac{1}{n} \sum_{i=1}^{n} \ln p(y_i \mid \mathbf{x}_i; \boldsymbol{\theta}).$$

Hence, in all cases where we have a probabilistic model of the conditional distribution $p(y \mid \mathbf{x})$, the negative log-likelihood is a plausible loss function. For classification problems, this takes a particularly simple form since $p(y \mid \mathbf{x})$ then corresponds to a probability vector over the M classes, and the negative log-likelihood is then equivalent to the cross-entropy loss (3.44) (or (3.32) in the case of binary classification).

Also, in the regression case there is a duality between certain common loss functions and the maximum likelihood approach, as we have previously observed. For instance, in a regression model with additive noise as in (5.1), the squared error loss is equivalent to the negative log-likelihood if we assume a Gaussian noise distribution, $\varepsilon \sim \mathcal{N}(0, \sigma_\varepsilon^2)$. Similarly, we noted above that the absolute error loss corresponds to an implicit assumption of Laplace distributed noise, $\varepsilon \sim \mathcal{L}(0, b_\varepsilon)$.[4] This statistical perspective is one way to understand the fact that the absolute error loss is more robust (less sensitive to outliers) than the squared error loss, since the Laplace distribution has thicker tails compared to the Gaussian distribution. The Laplace distribution therefore encodes sporadic large noise values (that is, outliers) as more probable, compared to the Gaussian distribution.

Using the maximum likelihood approach, other assumptions about the noise or insights into its distribution can be incorporated in a similar way in the regression model (5.1). For instance, if we believe that the error is non-symmetric, in the sense that the probability of observing a large positive error is larger than the probability of observing a large negative error, then this can be modelled by a skewed noise

---

[4]This can be verified from the definition of the Laplace probability density function, which is an exponential of the negative absolute deviation from the mean.

distribution. Using the negative log-likelihood loss is then a systematic way of incorporating this skewness into the training objective.

Relaxing the Gaussian assumption in (5.1) gives additional flexibility to the model. However, the noise is still assumed to be additive and independent of the input **x**. The real power of the likelihood perspective for designing a loss function comes when these basic assumptions are dropped. For instance, in Section 3.4, we introduced generalised linear models as a way to handle output variables with specific properties, such as count data (that is, y takes values in the set of natural numbers $0, 1, 2, \ldots$). In such situations, to build a model we often start from a specific form of the likelihood $p(y \mid \mathbf{x})$, which is chosen to capture the key properties of the data (for instance, having support only on the natural numbers). Hence, the likelihood becomes an integral part of the model, and this approach therefore lends itself naturally to training by maximum likelihood.

In generalised linear models (see Section 3.4), the likelihood is parameterised in a very particular way, but when working with non-linear parametric models, this is not strictly necessary. A more direct approach to (non-linear) likelihood-based parametric modelling is therefore to

> model the conditional distribution $p(y \mid \mathbf{x}; \boldsymbol{\theta})$ directly as a function parameterised by $\boldsymbol{\theta}$.

More specifically, once we have assumed a certain form for the likelihood (such as a Gaussian, a Poisson, or some other distribution), its shape will be controlled by some parameters (such as the mean and the variance of the Gaussian, or the rate of a Poisson distribution, not to be confused with $\boldsymbol{\theta}$). The idea is then to construct a parametric model $\mathbf{f}_{\boldsymbol{\theta}}(\mathbf{x})$, such that the output of this model is a *vector of parameters* controlling the shape of the distribution $p(y \mid \mathbf{x}; \boldsymbol{\theta})$.

As an example, assume that we are working with unbounded real-valued outputs and want to use a Gaussian likelihood, similarly to the regression model (5.2). However, the nature of the data is such that the noise variance, that is the magnitude of the errors that we expect to see, varies with the input **x**. By directly working with the likelihood formulation, we can then hypothesise a model according to

$$p(y \mid \mathbf{x}; \boldsymbol{\theta}) = \mathcal{N}(f_{\boldsymbol{\theta}}(\mathbf{x}), \exp(h_{\boldsymbol{\theta}}(\mathbf{x}))),$$

where $f_{\boldsymbol{\theta}}$ and $h_{\boldsymbol{\theta}}$ are two arbitrary (linear or non-linear) real-valued regression functions parameterised by $\boldsymbol{\theta}$ (hence, following the notation above, $\mathbf{f}_{\boldsymbol{\theta}}(\mathbf{x}) = (f_{\boldsymbol{\theta}}(\mathbf{x}) \quad h_{\boldsymbol{\theta}}(\mathbf{x}))^{\mathsf{T}}$). The exponential function is used to ensure that the variance is always positive without explicitly constraining the function $h_{\boldsymbol{\theta}}(\mathbf{x})$. The two functions can be learned simultaneously by minimising the negative log-likelihood over the training data. Note that in this case the problem does not simplify to a squared error loss, despite the fact that the likelihood is Gaussian, since we need to take the dependence on the variance into account. More precisely, the negative log-likelihood loss becomes

$$L(y, \boldsymbol{\theta}) = -\ln \mathcal{N}(f_{\boldsymbol{\theta}}(\mathbf{x}), \exp(h_{\boldsymbol{\theta}}(\mathbf{x})))$$

$$\propto h_{\boldsymbol{\theta}}(\mathbf{x}) + \frac{(y - f_{\boldsymbol{\theta}}(\mathbf{x}))^2}{\exp(h_{\boldsymbol{\theta}}(\mathbf{x}))} + \text{const.}$$

Once the parameters have been learned, the resulting model is capable of predicting a different mean *and a different variance* for the output y, depending on the value of the input variable $\mathbf{x}$.[5]

Other situations that can be modelled using a direct likelihood model in a similar way include multimodality, quantisation, and truncated data. As long as the modeller can come up with a reasonable likelihood – that is, a distribution that *could have* generated the data under study – the negative log-likelihood loss can be used to train the model in a systematic way.

Strictly Proper Loss Functions and Asymptotic Minimisers

As mentioned earlier, the *asymptotic minimiser* of a loss function is an important theoretical concept for understanding its properties. The asymptotic minimiser is the model which minimises the cost function when the number of training data points $n \to \infty$ (hence the name asymptotic). To formalise this, assume that the model is expressed in terms of a function $f(\mathbf{x})$. As we have seen above, this captures not only regression but also classification, through the margin concept. The asymptotic minimiser $f^*(\mathbf{x})$ of a loss function $L(y, f(\mathbf{x}))$ is then defined as the function which minimises the expected loss:

$$f^*(\cdot) = \arg \min_f \mathbb{E}[L(y, f(\mathbf{x}))]. \tag{5.20}$$

There are a couple of things to note about this expression. First, we stated above that the asymptotic minimiser is obtained as the solution to the training objective (5.4) as $n \to \infty$, but this has now been replaced by an expected value. This is motivated by the law of large numbers stipulating that the cost function (5.4) will converge to the expected loss as $n \to \infty$, and the latter is more convenient to analyse mathematically. Note that the expected value is taken with respect to a ground truth data generating probability distribution $p(y, \mathbf{x})$, analogously to how we reasoned about a the new data error in Chapter 4. Second, when we talk about asymptotic minimisers, it is typically assumed that the model class is flexible enough to contain *any function* $f(\mathbf{x})$. Consequently, the minimisation in (5.20) is not with respect to a finite dimensional model parameter $\boldsymbol{\theta}$ but rather with respect to the function $f(\mathbf{x})$ itself. The reason for this, rather abstract, definition is that we want to derive the asymptotic minimiser as a property of the *loss function* itself, not of a particular combination of loss function and model class.

The expected value above is with respect to both inputs $\mathbf{x}$ and outputs y. However, by the law of total expectation, we can write $\mathbb{E}[L(y, f(\mathbf{x}))] = \mathbb{E}[\mathbb{E}[L(y, f(\mathbf{x})) \mid \mathbf{x}]]$,

---

[5]This property is referred to as *heteroskedasticity* (in contrast to the standard regression model (5.2) which is *homoskedastic* – that is, it has the same output variance for all possible inputs).

where the inner expectation is over y (conditionally on $\mathbf{x}$), and the outer expectation is over $\mathbf{x}$. Now, since $f(\cdot)$ is free to be any function, minimising the total expectation is equivalent to minimising the inner expectation point-wise for each value of $\mathbf{x}$. Therefore, we can replace (5.20) with

$$f^*(\mathbf{x}) = \underset{f(\mathbf{x})}{\arg\min} \, \mathbb{E}[L(y, f(\mathbf{x})) \mid \mathbf{x}], \qquad (5.21)$$

where the minimisation is now done independently for any fixed value of $\mathbf{x}$.

By computing the asymptotic minimiser of a loss function, we obtain information about the expected behaviour or properties of a model that is trained using this loss function. Although the asymptotic minimiser is an idealised theoretical concept (assuming infinite data and infinite flexibility), it reveals, in some sense, what the training algorithm is striving to achieve when minimising a particular loss.

The concept is useful for understanding both regression and classification losses. A few notable examples in the regression setting are the asymptotic minimisers of the squared error loss and the absolute error loss, respectively. For the former, the asymptotic minimiser can be shown to be equal to the conditional mean, $f^*(\mathbf{x}) = \mathbb{E}[y \mid \mathbf{x}]$. That is, a regression model trained using squared error loss will strive to predict y according to its true conditional mean under the data generating distribution $p(y, \mathbf{x})$ (although in practice this will be hampered by the limited flexibility of the model class and the limited amount of training data). For the absolute error loss, the asymptotic minimiser is given by the conditional median, $f^*(\mathbf{x}) = \text{Median}[y \mid \mathbf{x}]$. This is less sensitive to the tail probability of $p(y \mid \mathbf{x})$ than the conditional mean, providing yet another interpretation of the improved robustness of the absolute error loss.

Related to the concept of asymptotic minimisers is the notion of a *strictly proper* loss function. A loss function is said to be strictly proper[6] if its asymptotic minimiser is *(i)* unique and *(ii)* in one-to-one correspondence with the true conditional distribution $p(y \mid \mathbf{x})$. Put differently, for a strictly proper loss function, we can express $p(y \mid \mathbf{x})$ in terms of the asymptotic minimiser $f^*(\mathbf{x})$. Such a loss function will thus *strive to* recover a complete probabilistic characterisation of the true input–output relationship.

This requires a probabilistic interpretation of the model, in the sense that we can express $p(y \mid \mathbf{x})$ in terms of the model $f(\mathbf{x})$, which is not always obvious. One case which stands out in this respect is the maximum likelihood approach. Indeed, training by maximum likelihood requires a likelihood-based model since the corresponding loss is expressed directly in terms of the likelihood. As we have discussed above, the negative log-likelihood loss is a very generic loss function (it is applicable to regression, classification, and many other types of problems). We can now complement this by the theoretical statement that

> the negative-log likelihood loss is strictly proper.

---

[6]A loss function that is *proper* but not *strictly proper* is minimised by the true conditional distribution $p(y \mid \mathbf{x})$, but the minimising argument is not unique.

Note that this applies to any type of problem where the negative log-likelihood loss can be used. As noted above, the concept of a loss function being strictly proper is related to its asymptotic minimiser, which in turn is derived under the assumption of infinite flexibility and infinite data. Hence, what our claim above says is that *if the likelihood-based model is flexible enough to describe the true conditional distribution* $p(y \mid \mathbf{x})$, *then the optimal solution to the maximum likelihood problem as* $n \to \infty$ *is to learn this true distribution.*

Time to reflect 5.1 *To express the expected negative log-likelihood loss mathematically, we need to distinguish between the likelihood according to the model, which we can denote by* $q(y \mid \mathbf{x})$ *for the time being, and the likelihood with respect to the true data generating distribution* $p(y \mid \mathbf{x})$. *The expected loss becomes*

$$\mathbb{E}_{p(y \mid \mathbf{x})}\left[-\ln q(y \mid \mathbf{x}) \mid \mathbf{x} \right],$$

which is referred to as the (conditional) cross-entropy *of the distribution* $q(y \mid \mathbf{x})$ *with respect to the distribution* $p(y \mid \mathbf{x})$ *(which explains the alternative name* cross-entropy *loss commonly used in classification).*

What does our claim, that the negative log-likelihood loss is strictly proper, imply regarding the cross entropy?

That negative log-likelihood is strictly proper should not come as a surprise since it is tightly linked to the statistical properties of the data. What is perhaps less obvious is that there are other loss functions that are also strictly proper, as we will see next. To make the presentation below more concrete, we will focus on the case of binary classification for the remainder of this section. In binary classification, the conditional distribution $p(y \mid \mathbf{x})$ takes a particularly simple form, since it is completely characterised by a single number, namely the probability of the positive class, $p(y = 1 \mid \mathbf{x})$.

Returning to the margin-based loss functions discussed above, recall that any loss function that encourages positive margins can be used to train a classifier, which can then be used for making class predictions according to (5.12). However,

---

it is only when we use a strictly proper loss function that we can interpret the resulting classification model $g(\mathbf{x})$ as an estimate of the conditional class probability $p(y = 1 \mid \mathbf{x})$.

When choosing a loss function for classification, it is therefore instructive to consider its asymptotic minimiser, since this will determine whether or not the loss function is strictly proper. In turn, this will reveal whether or not it is sensible to use the resulting model to reason about conditional class probabilities.

We proceed by stating the asymptotic minimisers for some of the loss functions presented above. Deriving the asymptotic minimiser is most often a straightforward calculation, but for brevity we do not include the derivations here. Starting with the binary cross-entropy loss (5.11), its asymptotic minimiser can be shown to be $g^*(\mathbf{x}) = p(y = 1 \mid \mathbf{x})$. In other words, when $n \to \infty$, the loss function (5.11) is uniquely minimised when $g(\mathbf{x})$ is equal to the true conditional class probability. This is in agreement with the discussion above, since the binary cross-entropy loss is just another name for the negative log-likelihood.

Similarly, the asymptotic minimiser of the logistic loss (5.13) is $f^*(\mathbf{x}) = \ln \frac{p(y=1 \mid \mathbf{x})}{1 - p(y=1 \mid \mathbf{x})}$. This is an invertible function of $p(y = 1 \mid \mathbf{x})$ and hence the logistic loss is strictly proper. By inverting $f^*(\mathbf{x})$, we obtain $p(y = 1 \mid \mathbf{x}) = \frac{\exp f^*(\mathbf{x})}{1 + \exp f^*(\mathbf{x})}$, which shows how conditional class probability predictions can be obtained from $f^*(\mathbf{x})$. With the 'margin formulation' of logistic regression, we seemingly lost the class probability predictions $g(\mathbf{x})$. We have now recovered them. Again, this is not surprising since the logistic loss is a special case of negative log-likelihood when using a logistic regression model.

For the exponential loss (5.15), the asymptotic minimiser is $f^*(\mathbf{x}) = \frac{1}{2} \ln \frac{p(y=1 \mid \mathbf{x})}{1 - p(y=1 \mid \mathbf{x})}$, which is in fact the same expression as we got for the logistic loss apart from a constant factor $\frac{1}{2}$. The exponential loss is therefore also strictly proper, and $f^*(\mathbf{x})$ can be inverted and used for predicting conditional class probabilities.

Turning to the hinge loss (5.16), the asymptotic minimiser is

$$f^*(\mathbf{x}) = \begin{cases} 1 & \text{if } p(y = 1 \mid \mathbf{x}) > 0.5, \\ -1 & \text{if } p(y = 1 \mid \mathbf{x}) < 0.5. \end{cases}$$

This is a non-invertible transformation of $p(y = 1 \mid \mathbf{x})$, which means that it is not possible to recover $p(y = 1 \mid \mathbf{x})$ from the asymptotic minimiser $f^*(\mathbf{x})$. This implies that a classifier learned using hinge loss (such as support vector classification, Section 8.5) is *not able* to predict conditional class probabilities.

The squared hinge loss (5.17), on the other hand, is a strictly proper loss function, since its asymptotic minimiser is $f^*(\mathbf{x}) = 2p(y = 1 \mid \mathbf{x}) - 1$. This also holds for the Huberised square hinge loss (5.18). Recalling our robustness discussion, we see that by squaring the hinge loss, we make it strictly proper, but at the same time we impact its robustness. However, the 'Huberisation' (replacing the quadratic curve with a linear one for margins < -1) improves the robustness while keeping the property of being strictly proper.

We have now seen that some (but not all) loss functions are strictly proper, meaning they could potentially predict conditional class probabilities correctly. However, this is only under the assumption that the model is sufficiently flexible that $g(\mathbf{x})$ or $f(\mathbf{x})$ can actually take the shape of the asymptotic minimiser. This is possibly problematic; for instance, recall that $f(\mathbf{x})$ is a linear function in logistic regression, whereas $p(y = 1 \mid \mathbf{x})$ can be almost arbitrarily complicated in real world applications. It is therefore not sufficient to use a strictly proper loss function in order to accurately predict conditional class probabilities: our model also has to be flexible enough. This discussion is also only valid in the limit as $n \to \infty$. However, in practice n is always finite, and we may ask how large n has to be for a flexible enough model to at least approximately learn the asymptotic minimiser? Unfortunately, we cannot give any general numbers, but following the same principles as the overfitting discussion in Chapter 4, the more flexible the model, the larger n is required. If n is not large enough, the predicted conditional class probabilities tend to 'overfit' to the training data. In summary, using a strictly proper loss function will *encourage* the training procedure to learn a model that is faithful to the true statistical properties of the data, but in itself it is not enough to guarantee that these properties are well described by the model.

In many practical applications, having access to reliable uncertainty estimates regarding a model's predictions is necessary for robust and well-informed decision making. In such cases, it is thus important to validate the model, not only in terms of accuracy or expected errors but also in terms of its statistical properties. One approach is to evaluate the so-called *calibration* of the model, which is, however, beyond the scope of this book.

5.3 Regularisation

We will now take a closer look at regularisation, which was briefly introduced in Section 3.3 as a useful tool for avoiding overfitting if the model was too flexible, such as a polynomial of high degree. We have also discussed thoroughly in Chapter 4 the need for tuning the model flexibility, which effectively is the purpose of regularisation. Finding the right level of flexibility, and thereby avoiding overfit, is very important in practice.

The idea of regularisation in a parametric model is to 'keep the parameters $\widehat{\theta}$ small unless the data really convinces us otherwise', or alternatively 'if a model with small values of the parameters $\widehat{\theta}$ fits the data almost as well as a model with larger parameter values, the one with small parameter values should be preferred'. There are, however, many different ways to implement this idea, and we distinguish between *explicit regularisation* and *implicit regularisation*. We will first discuss explicit regularisation, which amounts to modifying the cost function, and in particular so-called L^2 and L^1 regularisation.

L^2 Regularisation

L^2 regularisation (also known as *Tikhonov regularisation, ridge regression*, and *weight decay*) amounts to adding an extra penalty term $\|\theta\|_2^2$ to the cost function. Linear regression with squared error loss and L^2 regularisation, as an example, amounts to solving

$$\widehat{\theta} = \arg \min_{\theta} \frac{1}{n} \|\mathbf{X}\theta - \mathbf{y}\|_2^2 + \lambda \|\theta\|_2^2. \tag{5.22}$$

By choosing the regularisation parameter $\lambda \geq 0$, a trade-off between the original cost function (fitting the training data as well as possible) and the regularisation term (keeping the parameters $\widehat{\theta}$ close to zero) is made. In setting $\lambda = 0$ we recover the original least squares problem (3.12), whereas $\lambda \to \infty$ will force all parameters $\widehat{\theta}$ to 0. A good choiceǎof lambda in practice is usually neither of those extremes but somewhere in between, and can be determined using cross-validation.

It is actually possible to derive a version of the normal equations for (5.22), namely

$$(\mathbf{X}^{\mathsf{T}}\mathbf{X} + n\lambda\mathbf{I}_{p+1})\widehat{\theta} = \mathbf{X}^{\mathsf{T}}\mathbf{y}, \tag{5.23}$$

where $\mathbf{I}_{p+1}$ is the identity matrix of size $(p + 1) \times (p + 1)$. For $\lambda > 0$, the matrix $\mathbf{X}^{\mathsf{T}}\mathbf{X} + n\lambda\mathbf{I}_{p+1}$ is always invertible, and we have the closed form solution

$$\widehat{\theta} = (\mathbf{X}^{\mathsf{T}}\mathbf{X} + n\lambda\mathbf{I}_{p+1})^{-1}\mathbf{X}^{\mathsf{T}}\mathbf{y}. \tag{5.24}$$

This also reveals another reason for using regularisation in linear regression, namely when $\mathbf{X}^{\mathsf{T}}\mathbf{X}$ is not invertible. When $\mathbf{X}^{\mathsf{T}}\mathbf{X}$ is not invertible, the ordinary normal equations (3.13) have no unique solution $\widehat{\theta}$, whereas the L^2-regularised version always has the unique solution (5.24) if $\lambda > 0$.

L^1 Regularisation

With L^1 regularisation (also called *LASSO*, an abbreviation for Least Absolute Shrinkage and Selection Operator), the penalty term $\|\theta\|_1$ is added to the cost function. Here $\|\theta\|_1$ is the 1-norm or 'taxicab norm' $\|\theta\|_1 = |\theta_0| + |\theta_1| + \cdots + |\theta_p|$. The L^1 regularised cost function for linear regression (with squared error loss) then becomes

$$\widehat{\theta} = \arg\min_{\theta} \frac{1}{n}\|\mathbf{X}\theta - \mathbf{y}\|_2^2 + \lambda\|\theta\|_1. \tag{5.25}$$

Contrary to linear regression with L^2 regularisation (3.48), there is no closed-form solution available for (5.25). However, as we will see in Section 5.4, it is possible to design an efficient numerical optimisation algorithm for solving (5.25).

As for L^2 regularisation, the regularisation parameter λ has to be chosen by the user and has a similar meaning: $\lambda = 0$ gives the ordinary least squares solution and $\lambda \to \infty$ gives $\widehat{\theta} = 0$. Between these extremes, however, L^1 and L^2 tend to give different solutions. Whereas L^2 regularisation pushes all parameters towards small values (but not necessarily exactly zero), L^1 tends to favour so-called *sparse* solutions, where only a few of the parameters are non-zero, and the rest are exactly zero. Thus, L^1 regularisation can effectively 'switch off' some inputs (by setting the corresponding parameter θ_k to zero), and it can therefore be used as an input (or feature) selection method.

Example 5.2 Regularisation for car stopping distance

Consider again Example 2.2 with the car stopping distance regression problem. We use the 10th order polynomial that was considered meaningless in Example 3.5 and apply L^2 and L^1 regularisation to it in turn. With manually chosen λ, we obtain the models shown in Figure 5.3.

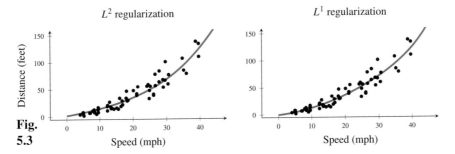

Fig. 5.3

Both models suffer less from overfitting than the non-regularised 10th order polynomial in Example 3.5. The two models here are, however, not identical. Whereas all parameters are relatively small but non-zero in the L^2-regularised model (left panel), only 4 (out of 11) parameters are non-zero in the L^1-regularised model (right panel). It is typical for L^1 regularisation to give sparse models, where some parameters are set exactly to zero.

General Explicit Regularisation

L^1 and L^2 regularisation are two common examples of what we refer to as explicit regularisation since they are both formulated as modifications of the cost function. They suggest a general pattern on which explicit regularisation can be formulated:

$$\widehat{\boldsymbol{\theta}} = \arg\min_{\boldsymbol{\theta}} \underbrace{J(\boldsymbol{\theta}; \mathbf{X}, \mathbf{y})}_{\text{(i)}} + \underbrace{\lambda}_{\text{(iii)}} \underbrace{R(\boldsymbol{\theta})}_{\text{(ii)}} . \tag{5.26}$$

This expression contains three important elements:

(i) the cost function, which encourages a good fit to the training data;

(ii) the regularisation term, which encourages small parameter values; and

(iii) the regularisation parameter λ, which determines the trade-off between (i) and (ii).

In this view, it is clear that explicit regularisation modifies the problem of fitting to the training data (minimising E_{train}) into something else, which hopefully minimises E_{new} instead. The actual design of the regularisation term $R(\boldsymbol{\theta})$ can be done in many ways. As a combination of the L^1 and L^2 terms, one option is $R(\boldsymbol{\theta}) = \|\boldsymbol{\theta}\|_1 + \|\boldsymbol{\theta}\|_2^2$, which often is referred to as elastic net regularisation. Regardless of the exact expression of the regularisation term, its purpose is to encourage small parameter values and thereby decrease the flexibility of the model, which might improve the performance and lower E_{new}.

Implicit Regularisation

Any supervised machine learning method that is trained by minimising a cost function can be regularised using (5.26). There are, however, alternative ways to achieve a similar effect without explicitly modifying the cost function. One such example of implicit regularisation is early stopping. Early stopping is applicable to any method that is trained using *iterative* numerical optimisation, which is the topic of the next section. It amounts to aborting the optimisation before it has reached the minimum of the cost function. Although it may appear counter-intuitive to prematurely abort an optimisation procedure, it has proven useful in practice, and early stopping has been shown to be of practical importance to avoid overfitting for some models, most notably deep learning (Chapter 6). Early stopping can be implemented by setting aside some hold-out validation data and computing $E_{hold-out}$ as in (4.6) for $\theta^{(t)}$ after each iteration t of the numerical optimisation.[7] It is typically observed that $E_{hold-out}$ decreases initially but eventually reaches a minimum and thereafter starts to increase, even though the cost function (by design of the optimisation algorithm) decreases monotonically. The optimisation is then aborted at the point when $E_{hold-out}$ reached its minimum, as we will illustrate in Example 5.7.

Early stopping is a commonly used implicit regularisation technique, but not the only one. Another technique with a regularising effect is dropout for neural networks, which we discuss in Chapter 6, and data augmentation, which we discuss in Chapter 11. For decision trees, the splitting criterion can be seen as a type of implicit regularisation. It has also been argued that the randomness of the stochastic gradient optimisation algorithm in itself also has the effect of implicit regularisation.

5.4 Parameter Optimisation

Many supervised machine learning methods, linear and logistic regression included, involve one (or more) optimisation problems, such as (3.12), (3.35), or (5.25). A machine learning engineer therefore needs to be familiar with the main strategies for how to solve optimisation problems fast. Starting with the optimisation problems from linear and logistic regression, we will introduce the ideas behind some of the optimisation methods commonly used in supervised machine learning. This section only gives a brief introduction to optimisation theory and, for example, we will only discuss unconstrained optimisation problems.

Optimisation is about finding the minimum or maximum of an *objective function*. Since the maximisation problem can be formulated as minimisation

---

[7]More practically, to reduce the computational overhead of early stopping, we can compute the validation error at regular intervals, for instance after each epoch.

of the negative objective function, we can limit ourselves to minimisation without any loss of generality.

There are primarily two ways in which optimisation is used in machine learning:

1. For training a model by minimising the cost function with respect to the model parameters $\boldsymbol{\theta}$. In this case, the objective function corresponds to the cost function $J(\boldsymbol{\theta})$, and the optimisation variables correspond to the model parameters.

2. For tuning hyperparameters, such as the regularisation parameter λ. For instance, by using a held-out validation dataset (see Chapter 4), we can select λ to minimise the hold-out validation error $E_{\text{hold-out}}$. In this case, the objective function is the validation error, and the optimisation variables correspond to the hyperparameters.

In the presentation below, we will use $\boldsymbol{\theta}$ to denote a general optimisation variable, but keep in mind that optimisation can also be used for selecting hyperparameters.

An important class of objective functions are *convex* functions. Optimisation is often easier to carry out for convex objective functions, and it is good practice to take some time to consider whether a non-convex optimisation problem can be re-formulated into a convex problem (which sometimes, but not always, is possible). The most important property of a convex function, for this discussion, is that a convex function has a unique minimum,[8] and no other local minima. Examples of convex functions are the cost functions for logistic regression, linear regression, and L^1-regularised linear regression. An example of a non-convex function is the cost function for a deep neural network. We illustrate this by Example 5.3.

Example 5.3 Examples of objective functions

Figure 5.4 contains examples of what an objective function can look like.

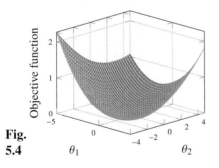 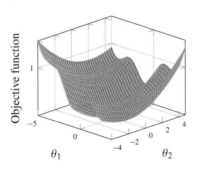

Fig. 5.4

Both examples are functions of a two-dimensional parameter vector $\boldsymbol{\theta} = [\theta_1 \ \theta_2]^{\mathsf{T}}$. The left is convex and has a finite unique global minimum, whereas the right is non-convex and has three local minima (of which only one is the global minimum).

---

[8]The minimum does, however, not have to be finite. The exponential function, for example, is convex but attains its minimum at $-\infty$. Convexity is a relatively strong property, and also non-convex functions may have only one minimum.

We will in the following examples illustrate these objective functions using contour plots instead, as shown in Figure 5.5.

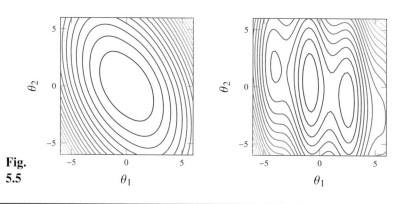

Fig. 5.5

Time to reflect 5.2 *After reading the rest of this book, return here and try to fill out this table, summarising how optimisation is used by the different methods.*

Method	What is optimisation used for?			What type of optimisation?			
	Training	Hyper-parameters	Nothing	Closed-form*	Grid search	Gradient-based	Stochastic gradient descent
k-NN							
Trees							
Linear regression							
Linear regression with L^2-regularisation							
Linear regression with L^1-regularisation							
Logistic regression							
Deep learning							
Random forests							
AdaBoost							
Gradient boosting							
Gaussian processes							

*including coordinate descent

Optimisation Using Closed-Form Expressions

For linear regression with squared error loss, training the model amounts to solving the optimisation problem (3.12)

$$\widehat{\boldsymbol{\theta}} = \arg\min_{\boldsymbol{\theta}} \frac{1}{n}\|\mathbf{X}\boldsymbol{\theta} - \mathbf{y}\|_2^2.$$

As we have discussed, and also proved in Appendix 3.A, the solution (3.14) to this problem can (under the assumption that $\mathbf{X}^\mathsf{T}\mathbf{X}$ is invertible) be derived analytically. If we just take the time to efficiently implement (3.14) once, for example using Cholesky or QR factorisation, we can use this every time we want to train a linear regression model with squared error loss. Each time we use it, we know that we have found the optimal solution in a computationally efficient way.

If we instead want to learn the L^1-regularised version, we have to solve (5.25)

$$\widehat{\boldsymbol{\theta}} = \arg\min_{\boldsymbol{\theta}} \frac{1}{n} \|\mathbf{X}\boldsymbol{\theta} - \mathbf{y}\|_2^2 + \lambda\|\boldsymbol{\theta}\|_1.$$

Unfortunately, this problem cannot be solved analytically. Instead we have to use computer power to solve it, by constructing an iterative procedure to find the solution. With a certain choice of such an optimisation algorithm, we can make use of some analytical expressions along the way, which turns out to offer an efficient way of solving it. Remember that $\boldsymbol{\theta}$ is a vector containing $p + 1$ parameters that we want to learn from the training data. As it turns out, if we seek the minimum for only one of these parameters, say θ_j, while keeping the other parameters fixed, we can find the optimum as

$$\arg\min_{\theta_j} \frac{1}{n} \|\mathbf{X}\boldsymbol{\theta} - \mathbf{y}\|_2^2 + \lambda\|\boldsymbol{\theta}\|_1 = \text{sign}(t)(|t| - \lambda),$$

$$\text{where } t = \sum_{i=1}^{n} x_{ij} \left(y_i - \sum_{k \neq j} x_{ik} \theta_k \right). \tag{5.27}$$

It turns out that making repeated 'sweeps' through the vector $\boldsymbol{\theta}$ and updating one parameter at a time according to (5.27) is a good way to solve (5.25). This type of algorithm, where we update one parameter at a time, is referred to as *coordinate descent*, and we illustrate it in Example 5.4.

It can be shown that the cost function in (5.25) is convex. Convexity alone is not sufficient to guarantee that coordinate descent will find its (global) minimum, but for the L^1-regularised cost function (5.25), it can be shown that coordinate descent actually finds the (global) minimum. In practice we know that we have found the global minimum when no parameters have changed during a full 'sweep' of the parameter vector.

It turns out that coordinate descent is a very efficient method for L^1-regularised linear regression (5.25). The keys are that (i) (5.27) exists and is cheap to compute, and (ii) many updates will simply set $\theta_j = 0$ due to the sparsity of the optimal $\widehat{\boldsymbol{\theta}}$. This makes the algorithm fast. For most machine learning optimisation problems, however, it *cannot* be said that coordinate descent is the preferred method. We will now have a look at some more general families of optimisation methods that are widely used in machine learning.

Example 5.4 Coordinate descent

We apply coordinate descent to the objective functions from Example 5.3 and show the result in Figure 5.6. For coordinate descent to be an efficient alternative in practice, closed-form solutions for updating one parameter at a time, similar to (5.27), have to be available.

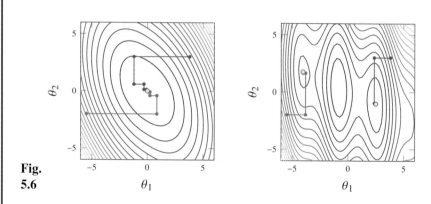

Fig. 5.6

Figure 5.6 shows how the parameters are updated in the coordinate descent algorithm, for two different initial parameter vectors (blue and green trajectory, respectively). It is clear from the figure that only one parameter is updated each time, which gives the trajectory a characteristic shape. The obtained minimum is marked with a yellow dot. Note how the different initialisations lead to different (local) minima in the non-convex case (right panel).

Gradient Descent

In many situations, we cannot do closed-form manipulations, but we do have access to the value of the objective function as well as its derivative (or gradient). Sometimes we even have access to the second derivative (the Hessian). In those situations, it is often a good idea to use a *gradient descent* method, which we will introduce now, or even *Newton's method*, which we will discuss later.

Gradient descent can be used for learning parameter vectors $\boldsymbol{\theta}$ of high dimension when the objective function $J(\boldsymbol{\theta})$ is simple enough such that its gradient is possible to compute. Let us therefore consider the parameter learning problem

$$\widehat{\boldsymbol{\theta}} = \arg\min_{\boldsymbol{\theta}} J(\boldsymbol{\theta}) \tag{5.28}$$

(even though gradient descent can potentially be used for hyperparameters as well). We will assume that the gradient of the cost function $\nabla_{\boldsymbol{\theta}} J(\boldsymbol{\theta})$ exists for all $\boldsymbol{\theta}$. As an example, the gradient of the cost function for logistic regression (3.34) is[9]

$$\nabla_{\boldsymbol{\theta}} J(\boldsymbol{\theta}) = -\frac{1}{n} \sum_{i=1}^{n} \left(\frac{1}{1 + e^{y_i \boldsymbol{\theta}^{\mathsf{T}} \mathbf{x}_i}} \right) y_i \mathbf{x}_i. \tag{5.29}$$

Note that $\nabla_{\boldsymbol{\theta}} J(\boldsymbol{\theta})$ is a vector of the same dimension as $\boldsymbol{\theta}$, which describes the direction in which $J(\boldsymbol{\theta})$ increases. Consequently, and more useful for us, $-\nabla_{\boldsymbol{\theta}} J(\boldsymbol{\theta})$

---

[9]This assumption is primarily made for the theoretical discussion. In practice, there are successful examples of gradient descent being applied to objective functions not differentiable everywhere, such as neural networks with ReLu activation functions (Chapter 6).

describes the direction in which $J(\boldsymbol{\theta})$ decreases. That is, if we take a small step in the direction of the negative gradient, this will reduce the value of the cost function,

$$J\big(\boldsymbol{\theta} - \gamma \nabla_{\boldsymbol{\theta}} J(\boldsymbol{\theta})\big) \leq J\big(\boldsymbol{\theta}\big) \tag{5.30}$$

for some (possibly very small) $\gamma > 0$. If $J(\boldsymbol{\theta})$ is convex, the inequality in (5.30) is strict except at the minimum (where $\nabla_{\boldsymbol{\theta}} J(\boldsymbol{\theta})$ is zero). This suggests that if we have $\boldsymbol{\theta}^{(t)}$ and want to select $\boldsymbol{\theta}^{(t+1)}$ such that $J(\boldsymbol{\theta}^{(t+1)}) \leq J(\boldsymbol{\theta}^{(t)})$, we should

$$\boxed{\text{update } \boldsymbol{\theta}^{(t+1)} = \boldsymbol{\theta}^{(t)} - \gamma \nabla_{\boldsymbol{\theta}} J(\boldsymbol{\theta}^{(t)})} \tag{5.31}$$

with some positive $\gamma > 0$. Repeating (5.31) gives the gradient descent algorithm, Algorithm 5.1.

Algorithm 5.1: Gradient descent

Input: Objective function $J(\boldsymbol{\theta})$, initial $\boldsymbol{\theta}^{(0)}$, learning rate γ
Result: $\widehat{\boldsymbol{\theta}}$
1 Set $t \leftarrow 0$
2 **while** $\|\boldsymbol{\theta}^{(t)} - \boldsymbol{\theta}^{(t-1)}\|$ *not small enough* **do**
3 $\quad$ Update $\boldsymbol{\theta}^{(t+1)} \leftarrow \boldsymbol{\theta}^{(t)} - \gamma \nabla_{\boldsymbol{\theta}} J(\boldsymbol{\theta}^{(t)})$
4 $\quad$ Update $t \leftarrow t + 1$
5 **end**
6 **return** $\widehat{\boldsymbol{\theta}} \leftarrow \boldsymbol{\theta}^{(t-1)}$

In practice we do not know γ, which determines how big the $\boldsymbol{\theta}$-step is at each iteration. It is possible to formulate the selection of γ as an internal optimisation problem that is solved at each iteration, a so-called *line-search problem*. This will result in a possibly different value for γ at each iteration of the algorithm. Here we will consider the simpler solution where we leave the choice of γ to the user, or more specifically view it as a hyperparameter.[10] In such cases, γ is often referred to as the *learning rate* or step-size. Note that the gradient $\nabla_{\boldsymbol{\theta}} J(\boldsymbol{\theta})$ will typically decrease and eventually attain 0 at a stationary point (possibly, but not necessarily, a minimum), so Algorithm 5.1 may converge if γ is kept constant. This is in contrast to what we will discuss when we introduce the *stochastic* gradient algorithm.

The choice of learning rate γ is important. Some typical situations with too small, too large and a good choice of learning rate are shown in Figure 5.7. With the intuition from these figures, we advise monitoring $J(\boldsymbol{\theta}^{(t)})$ during the optimisation, and to

---

[10]When viewed as a hyperparmeter, we can also optimise γ, for instance by using cross-validation, as discussed above. However, this is an 'external' optimisation problem, contrary to line-search which is an 'internal' optimisation problem.

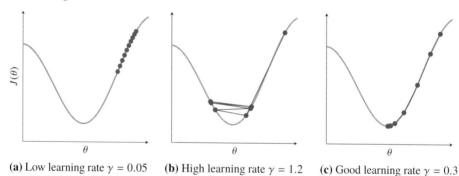

(a) Low learning rate $\gamma = 0.05$ **(b)** High learning rate $\gamma = 1.2$ **(c)** Good learning rate $\gamma = 0.3$

Figure 5.7 Optimisation using gradient descent of a cost function $J(\theta)$ where θ is a scalar parameter. In the different subfigures we use a too low learning rate (5.7a), a too high learning rate (5.7b), and a good learning rate (5.7c). Remember that a good value of γ is very much related to the shape of the cost function; $\gamma = 0.3$ might be too small (or large) for a different $J(\theta)$.

- decrease the learning rate γ if the cost function values $J(\theta^{(t)})$ are getting worse or oscillate widely (as in Figure 5.7b);

- increase the learning rate γ if the cost function values $J(\theta^{(t)})$ are fairly constant and only slowly decreasing (as in Figure 5.7a).

No general convergence guarantees can be given for gradient descent, basically because a bad learning rate γ may break the method. However, with the 'right' choice of γ, the value of $J(\boldsymbol{\theta})$ will decrease for each iteration (as suggested by (5.30)) until a point with zero gradient is found – that is, a stationary point. A stationary point is, however, not necessarily a minimum but can also be a maximum or a saddle-point of the objective function. In practice one typically monitors the value of $J(\boldsymbol{\theta})$ and terminates the algorithm when it seems not to be decreasing anymore, and hope it has arrived at a minimum.

In non-convex problems with multiple local minima, we cannot expect gradient descent to always find the global minimum. The initialisation is usually critical for determining which minimum (or stationary point) is found, as illustrated by Example 5.5. It can, therefore, be a good practice (if time and computational resources permit) to run the optimisation multiple times with different initialisations. For computationally heavy non-convex problems, such as training a deep neural network (Chapter 6), when we cannot afford to re-run the training, we usually employ method-specific heuristics and tricks to find a good initialisation point.

For convex problems, there is only one stationary point, which also is the global minimum. Hence, the initialisation for a convex problem can be done arbitrarily. However, by *warm-starting* the optimisation with a good initial guess, we may still save valuable computational time. Sometimes, such as when doing k-fold cross validation (Chapter 4), we have to train k models on similar (but not identical) datasets. In situations like this, we can typically make use of the situation by initialising Algorithm 5.1 with the parameters learned for the previous model.

For training a logistic regression model (3.35), gradient descent can be used. Since its cost function is convex, we know that once the gradient descent has converged to a minimum, it has reached the global minimum and we are done. For logistic regression there are, however, more advanced alternatives that usually perform better. We discuss these next.

Example 5.5 Gradient descent

We first consider the convex objective function from Example 5.3 and apply gradient descent to it with a seemingly reasonable learning rate. We show the result in Figure 5.8. Note that each step is perpendicular to the level curves at the point where it starts, which is a property of the gradient. As expected, we find the (global) minimum with both of the two different initialisations.

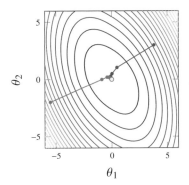

Fig. 5.8

For the non-convex objective function from Example 5.3, we apply gradient descent with two different learning rates and show the result in Figure 5.9. In the left plot, the learning rate seems well chosen and the optimisation converges nicely, albeit to different minima depending on the initialisation. Note that it *could* have converged also to one of the saddle points between the different minima. In the right plot, the learning rate is too big, and the procedure does not seem to converge.

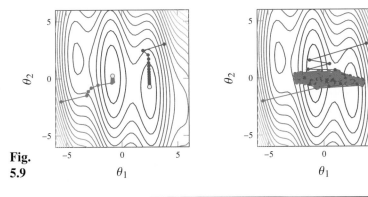

Fig. 5.9

Second Order Gradient Methods

We can think of gradient descent as approximating $J(\theta)$ with a first order Taylor expansion around $\theta^{(t)}$, that is, a (hyper-)plane. The next parameter $\theta^{(t+1)}$ is selected by taking a step in the steepest direction of the (hyper-)plane. Let us now see what happen if we instead use a second order Taylor expansion,

$$J(\theta + \mathbf{v}) \approx \underbrace{J(\theta) + \mathbf{v}^{\mathsf{T}}[\nabla_\theta J(\theta)] + \frac{1}{2}\mathbf{v}^{\mathsf{T}}[\nabla_\theta^2 J(\theta)]\mathbf{v}}_{\triangleq s(\theta, \mathbf{v})}, \tag{5.32}$$

where $\mathbf{v}$ is a vector of the same dimension as θ. This expression contains not only the gradient of the cost function $\nabla_\theta J(\theta)$ but also the Hessian matrix of the cost function $\nabla_\theta^2 J(\theta)$. Remember that we are searching for the minimum of $J(\theta)$. We will compute this by iteratively minimising the second order approximation $s(\theta, \mathbf{v})$. If the Hessian $\nabla_\theta^2 J(\theta)$ is positive definite, then the minimum of $s(\theta, \mathbf{v})$ with respect to $\mathbf{v}$ is obtained where the derivative of $s(\theta, \mathbf{v})$ is zero:

$$\frac{\partial}{\partial \mathbf{v}} s(\theta, \mathbf{v}) = \nabla_\theta J(\theta) + [\nabla_\theta^2 J(\theta)]\mathbf{v} = 0 \Leftrightarrow \mathbf{v} = -[\nabla_\theta^2 J(\theta)]^{-1}[\nabla_\theta J(\theta)]. \tag{5.33}$$

This suggests to update

$$\theta^{(t+1)} = \theta^{(t)} - [\nabla_\theta^2 J(\theta^{(t)})]^{-1}[\nabla_\theta J(\theta^{(t)})], \tag{5.34}$$

which is *Netwton's method* for minimisation. Unfortunately, no general convergence guarantees can be given for Newton's method either. For certain cases, Newton's method can be much faster than gradient descent. In fact, *if* the cost function $J(\theta)$ is a quadratic function in θ, then (5.32) is exact, and Newton's method (5.34) will find the optimum in only one iteration! Quadratic objective functions are, however, rare in machine learning.[11] It is not even guaranteed that the Hessian $\nabla_\theta^2 J(\theta)$ is always positive definite in practice, which may result in rather strange parameter updates in (5.34). To still make use of the potentially valuable second order information but at the same time also have a robust and practically useful algorithm, we have to introduce some modification of Newton's method. There are multiple options, and we will look at so-called *trust regions*.

We derived Newton's method using the second order Taylor expansion (5.32) as a model for how $J(\theta)$ behaves around $\theta^{(t)}$. We should perhaps not trust the Taylor expansion to be a good model for *all* values of θ but only for those in the vicinity of $\theta^{(t)}$. One natural restriction is, therefore, to trust the second order Taylor

---

[11] For regression, we often use the squared error loss $L(y, \widehat{y}) = (\widehat{y} - y)^2$, which is a quadratic function in $\widehat{y}$. That does *not* imply that $J(\theta)$ (the objective function) is necessarily a quadratic function in θ, since $\widehat{y}$ can depend non-linearly on θ. For linear regression with squared loss, however, the dependence is linear, and the cost function is indeed quadratic. This is why we can compute an explicit solution using the normal equations, which is of course the same solution that we would obtain after one iteration of Newton's method applied to this problem.

expansion (5.32) only within a ball of radius D around $\boldsymbol{\theta}^{(t)}$, which we refer to as our trust region. This suggests that we could make a Newton update (5.34) of the parameters, unless the step is longer than D, in which case we downscale the step to never leave our trust region. In the next iteration, the trust region is moved to be centered around the updated $\boldsymbol{\theta}^{(t+1)}$, and another step is taken from there. We can express this as

$$\text{update } \boldsymbol{\theta}^{(t+1)} = \boldsymbol{\theta}^{(t)} - \eta [\nabla_{\boldsymbol{\theta}}^2 J(\boldsymbol{\theta}^{(t)})]^{-1} [\nabla_{\boldsymbol{\theta}} J(\boldsymbol{\theta}^{(t)})], \qquad (5.35)$$

where $\eta \leq 1$ is chosen as large as possible such that $\|\boldsymbol{\theta}^{(t+1)} - \boldsymbol{\theta}^{(t)}\| \leq D$. The radius of the trust region D can be updated and adapted as the optimisation proceeds, but for simplicity we will consider D to be a user choice (much like the learning rate for gradient descent). We summarise this as Algorithm 5.2 and look at it in Example 5.6. The trust region Newton method, with a certain set of rules on how to update D, is actually one of the methods commonly used for training logistic regression in practice.

Algorithm 5.2: Trust region Newton's method

Input: Objective function $J(\boldsymbol{\theta})$, initial $\boldsymbol{\theta}^{(0)}$, trust region radius D
Result: $\widehat{\boldsymbol{\theta}}$

1   Set $t \leftarrow 0$
2   **while** $\|\boldsymbol{\theta}^{(t)} - \boldsymbol{\theta}^{(t-1)}\|$ *not small enough* **do**
3   Compute $\mathbf{v} \leftarrow [\nabla_{\boldsymbol{\theta}}^2 J(\boldsymbol{\theta}^{(t)})]^{-1} [\nabla_{\boldsymbol{\theta}} J(\boldsymbol{\theta}^{(t)})]$
4   Compute $\eta \leftarrow \frac{D}{\max(\|\mathbf{v}\|, D)}$
5   Update $\boldsymbol{\theta}^{(t+1)} \leftarrow \boldsymbol{\theta}^{(t)} - \eta \mathbf{v}$
6   Update $t \leftarrow t + 1$
7   **end**
8   **return** $\widehat{\boldsymbol{\theta}} \leftarrow \boldsymbol{\theta}^{(t-1)}$

It can be computationally expensive or even impossible to compute the inverse of the Hessian matrix $[\nabla_{\boldsymbol{\theta}}^2 J(\boldsymbol{\theta}^{(t)})]^{-1}$. To this end, there is an entire class of methods called *quasi-Newton methods* that all use different ways to *approximate* the inverse of the Hessian matrix $[\nabla_{\boldsymbol{\theta}}^2 J(\boldsymbol{\theta})]^{-1}$ in (5.34). This class includes, among others, the Broyden method and the BFGS method (an abbreviation of Broyden, Fletcher, Goldfarb, and Shanno). A further approximation of the latter, called limited-memory BFGS or L-BFGS, has proven to be another good choice for the logistic regression problem.

Example 5.6 Newton's method

We first apply Newton's method to the cost functions from Example 5.3 and show the result in Figure 5.10. Since the convex cost function (left) also happens to be close to a quadratic function, Newton's method works well and finds, for both initialisations, the minimum in only two iterations. For the non-convex problem (right), Newton's method diverges for both initialisations, since the second order

---

Taylor expansion (5.32) is a poor approximation of this function and leads the method astray.

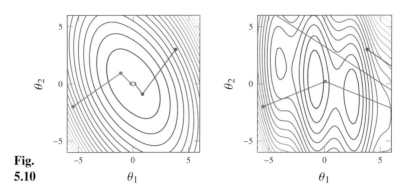

Fig. 5.10

We also apply the trust region Newton's method to both problems and show the result in Figure 5.11. Note that the first step direction is identical to the non-truncated version above, but the steps are now limited to stay within the trust region (here a circle of radius 2). This prevents the severe divergence problems for the non-convex case, and all cases converge nicely. Indeed, the convex case (left) requires more iterations than for the non-truncated version above, but that is a price we have to pay in order to have a robust method which also works for the non-convex case shown to the right.

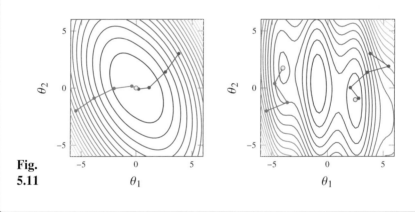

Fig. 5.11

Before we end this section, we will have a look at an example of early stopping for logistic regression when using a Newton-type of method. (It can in fact be shown that using early stopping when solving linear regression (with squared error loss) with gradient descent is equivalent to L^2 regularisation.[12]) Besides completing the discussion on early stopping from Section 5.3, this example also serves as a good reminder that it is actually not always the global optimum which is the goal when we use optimisation in machine learning.

---

[12]See, for example, Goodfellow, Bengio, et al. (2016, Section 7.8).

Example 5.7 Early stopping with logistic regression for the music classification example

We consider again the music classification problem from Example 2.1. We apply multi-class logistic regression and, to exaggerate the point of this example, we apply a 20 degree polynomial input transformation. The polynomial transformation means that instead of having $\theta_0 + \theta_1 x_1 + \theta_2 x_2$ within the logistic regression model, we now have $\theta_0 + \theta_1 x_1 + \theta_2 x_2 + \theta_3 x_1^2 + \theta_4 x_1 x_2 + \theta_5 x_2^2 + \cdots + \theta_{229} x_1 x_2^{19} + \theta_{230} x_2^{20}$. Such a setup with 231 parameters and a rather limited amount of data will most likely lead to overfitting if no regularisation is used.

Logistic regression is learned using a Newton-type numerical optimisation algorithm (Section 5.4). We can therefore apply early stopping to it. For this purpose we set aside some hold-out validation data and monitor how $E_{\text{hold-out}}$ (with misclassification error) evolves as the numerical optimisation proceeds.

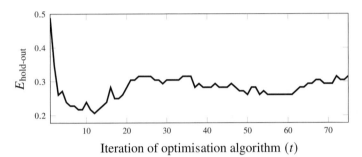

Fig. 5.12

Iteration of optimisation algorithm (t)

As seen in Figure 5.12, $E_{\text{hold-out}}$ reaches a minimum for $t = 12$ and seems to increase thereafter. We do, however, know that the cost function, and thereby probably also E_{train}, decreases monotonically as t increases. The picture, therefore, is that the model suffers from overfitting as t becomes large. The best model (in terms of $E_{\text{hold-out}}$ and, hopefully, in the end also E_{new}) is for this case found after a only a few initial runs of the optimisation, long before it has reached the minimum of the cost function. To illustrate what is happening, we plot in Figure 5.13 the decision boundaries after $t = 1, 12, 75$, and $10\,000$ iterations, respectively.

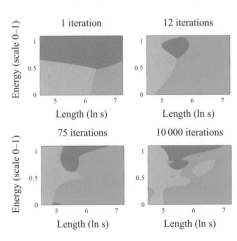

Fig. 5.13

123

It is clear that the shape of the decision boundaries becomes more complicated as t increases, and the number of iterations t can therefore, to some extent, be understood as a way to control the model flexibility. This example is indeed somewhat exaggerated, but the same effect can be seen in particular when training deep neural networks (Chapter 6).

5.5 Optimisation with Large Datasets

In machine learning, the training data may have n = millions (or more) of data points. Computing, for example, the gradient of the cost function

$$\nabla_\theta J(\theta) = \frac{1}{n} \sum_{i=1}^{n} \nabla_\theta L(\mathbf{x}_i, y_i, \theta) \tag{5.36}$$

thus can involve summing a million terms. Besides taking lot of time to sum, it can also be an issue to keep all data points in the computer memory at the same time. However, with that many data points, many of them are probably relatively similar, and in practice we might not need to consider all of them every time: looking at only a subset of them might give sufficient information. This is a general idea called *subsampling*, and we will have a closer look at how subsampling can be combined with gradient descent into a very useful optimisation method called *stochastic gradient descent*. It is, however, also possible to combine the subsampling idea with other methods.

Stochastic Gradient Descent

With very large n, we can expect the gradient computed only for the first half of the dataset $\nabla_\theta J(\theta) \approx \sum_{i=1}^{n/2} \nabla_\theta L(\mathbf{x}_i, y_i, \theta)$ to be almost identical to the gradient based on the second half of the dataset $\nabla_\theta J(\theta) \approx \sum_{i=n/2+1}^{n} \nabla_\theta L(\mathbf{x}_i, y_i, \theta)$. Consequently, it might be a waste of time to compute the gradient based on the whole training dataset at each iteration of gradient descent. Instead, we could compute the gradient based on the first half of the training dataset, update the parameters according to the gradient descent method Algorithm 5.1, and then compute the gradient for the new parameters based on the second half of the training data:

$$\theta^{(t+1)} = \theta^{(t)} - \gamma \frac{1}{n/2} \sum_{i=1}^{\frac{n}{2}} \nabla_\theta L(\mathbf{x}_i, y_i, \theta^{(t)}), \tag{5.37a}$$

$$\theta^{(t+2)} = \theta^{(t+1)} - \gamma \frac{1}{n/2} \sum_{i=\frac{n}{2}+1}^{n} \nabla_\theta L(\mathbf{x}_i, y_i, \theta^{(t+1)}). \tag{5.37b}$$

In other words, we use only a *subsample* of the training data when we compute the gradient. In this way we still make use of all the training data, but it is split into two consecutive parameter updates. Hence, (5.37) requires roughly half the computational time compared to two parameter updates of normal gradient descent. This computational saving illustrates the benefit of the subsampling idea.

We can extend on this idea and consider subsampling with even fewer data points used in each gradient computation. The extreme version of subsampling would be to use only one single data point each time we compute the gradient. In practice it is most common to do something in between. We call a small subsample of data a *mini-batch*, which typically can contain $n_b = 10$, $n_b = 100$, or $n_b = 1\,000$ data points. One complete pass through the training data is called an *epoch*, and consequently consists of n/n_b iterations.

When using mini-batches it is important to ensure that the different mini-batches are balanced and representative for the whole dataset. For example, if we have a big training dataset with a few different output classes, and the dataset is sorted with respect to the output, the mini-batch with the first n_b data points would only include one class and hence not give a good approximation of the gradient for the full dataset. For this reason, the mini-batches should be formed randomly. One implementation of this is to first randomly shuffle the training data, and thereafter divide it into mini-batches in an ordered manner. When we have completed one epoch, we do another random reshuffling of the training data and do another pass through the dataset. We summarise gradient descent with mini-batches, often called *stochastic gradient descent*, as Algorithm 5.3.

Stochastic gradient descent is widely used in machine learning, and there are many extensions tailored to different methods. For training deep neural networks

---

Algorithm 5.3: Stochastic gradient descent

Input: Objective function $J(\theta) = \frac{1}{n}\sum_{i=1}^{n} L(\mathbf{x}_i, y_i, \theta)$, initial $\theta^{(0)}$, learning rate $\gamma^{(t)}$

Result: $\widehat{\theta}$

1 Set $t \leftarrow 0$

2 **while** *Convergence criteria not met* **do**

3   **for** $i = 1, 2, \ldots, E$ **do**

4   Randomly shuffle the training data $\{\mathbf{x}_i, y_i\}_{i=1}^{n}$

5   **for** $j = 1, 2, \ldots, \frac{n}{n_b}$ **do**

6   Approximate the gradient using the mini-batch
$\{(\mathbf{x}_i, y_i)\}_{i=(j-1)n_b+1}^{jn_b}$, $\widehat{\mathbf{d}}^{(t)} = \frac{1}{n_b}\sum_{i=(j-1)n_b+1}^{jn_b} \nabla_\theta L(\mathbf{x}_i, y_i, \theta^{(t)})$.

7   Update $\theta^{(t+1)} \leftarrow \theta^{(t)} - \gamma^{(t)}\widehat{\mathbf{d}}^{(t)}$

8   Update $t \leftarrow t + 1$

9   **end**

10   **end**

11 **end**

12 **return** $\widehat{\theta} \leftarrow \theta^{(t-1)}$

(Chapter 6), some commonly used methods include automatic adaption of the learning rate and an idea called momentum to counteract the randomness caused by subsampling. The AdaGrad (short for adaptive gradient), RMSProp (short for root mean square propagation), and Adam (short for adaptive moments) methods are such examples. For logistic regression in the 'big data' setting, the stochastic average gradient (SAG) method, which averages over all previous gradient estimates, has proven useful, to mention but a few.

Learning Rate and Convergence for Stochastic Gradient Descent

Standard gradient descent converges if the learning rate is wisely chosen and constant, since the gradient itself is zero at the minimum (or any other stationary point). For stochastic gradient descent, on the other hand, we *cannot* obtain convergence with a constant learning rate. The reason is that we only use an *estimate* of the true gradient, and this estimate will not necessarily be zero at the minimum of the objective function, but there might still be a considerable amount of 'noise' in the gradient estimate due to the subsampling. As a consequence, the stochastic gradient descent algorithm with a constant learning rate will not converge towards a point but will continue to 'wander around', somewhat randomly. For the algorithm to work properly, we also need the gradient estimate to be *unbiased*. The intuitive reason is that the unbiased gradient ensures that the algorithm will on average step in the right direction in its search for the optimum.

By not using a constant learning rate but instead decreasing it gradually towards zero, the parameter updates will be smaller and smaller, and eventually converge. We hence start at $t = 0$ with a fairly high learning rate $\gamma^{(t)}$ (meaning that we take big steps), and then decay $\gamma^{(t)}$ as t increases. Under certain regularity conditions of the cost function and with a learning rate fulfilling the Robbins–Monro conditions $\sum_{t=0}^{\infty} \gamma^{(t)} = \infty$ and $\sum_{t=0}^{\infty} (\gamma^{(t)})^2 < \infty$, the stochastic gradient descent algorithm can be shown to almost surely converge to a local minimum. The Robbins–Monro conditions are, for example, fulfilled if using $\gamma^{(t)} = \frac{1}{t^{\alpha}}, \alpha \in (0.5, 1]$. For many machine learning problems, however, it has been found that better performance is often obtained in practice by not letting $\gamma^{(t)} \to 0$ but to cap it at some small value $\gamma_{min} > 0$. This will cause stochastic gradient descent not to exactly converge, and the Robbins–Monro conditions will not be fulfilled, but the algorithm will in fact walk around indefinitely (or until the algorithm is aborted by the user). For practical purposes, this seemingly undesirable property does not usually cause any major issue if γ_{min} is small enough, and one heuristic for setting the learning rate in practice is

$$\gamma^{(t)} = \gamma_{min} + (\gamma_{max} - \gamma_{min})e^{-\frac{t}{\tau}}. \tag{5.38}$$

Now the learning rate $\gamma^{(t)}$ starts at γ_{max} and goes to γ_{min} as $t \to \infty$. How to pick the parameters $\gamma_{min}, \gamma_{max}$, and τ is more art than science. As a rule of thumb, γ_{min} can be chosen approximately as 1% of γ_{max}. The parameter τ depends on the size of the dataset and the complexity of the problem, but it should be chosen such that multiple epochs have passed before we reach $\gamma_{\min}$. The strategy for picking $\gamma_{\max}$ can be chosen by monitoring the cost function as for standard gradient descent in Figure 5.7.

Example 5.8 Stochastic gradient descent

We apply the stochastic gradient descent method to the objective functions from Example 5.3. For the convex function in Figure 5.14, the choice of learning rate is not very crucial. Note, however, that the algorithm does not converge as nicely as, for example, gradient descent, due to the 'noise' in the gradient estimate caused by the subsampling. This is the price we have to pay for the substantial computational savings offered by the subsampling.

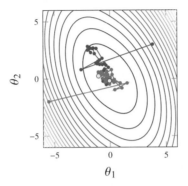

Fig. 5.14

For the objective function with multiple local minima, we apply stochastic gradient descent with two decaying learning rates but with different initial $\gamma^{(0)}$ in Figure 5.15. With a smaller learning rate, left, stochastic gradient descent converges to the closest minima, whereas a larger learning rate causes it to initially take larger steps, and it does not therefore necessarily converge to the closest minimum (right).

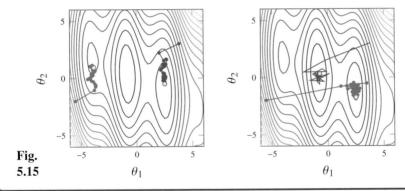

Fig. 5.15

Stochastic Second Order Gradient Methods

The idea of improving the stochastic gradient method by exploiting second order information is natural in settings involving ill-conditioning and significant non-linearity. At the same time, this will add complexity and computational time to the algorithm, which needs to be traded off in the design of these algorithms.

A popular and rather natural strand of algorithms is those falling under the name *stochastic quasi-Newton methods*. As mentioned above, the idea underlying the deterministic quasi-Newton methods is to compute an approximation of the Hessian using information in the gradients. For large-scale problems, we make use of a receding history of gradients. These ideas can also be employed in the stochastic setting, albeit with new algorithms as the result.

Adaptive Methods

The idea of using gradients from earlier steps is also exploited within the adaptive methods. By considering different ways of combining the gradients from earlier steps into suitable learning rates

$$\gamma_t = \gamma(\nabla J_t, \nabla J_{t-1}, \ldots \nabla J_0) \tag{5.39}$$

and search directions

$$d_t = d(\nabla J_t, \nabla J_{t-1}, \ldots \nabla J_0), \tag{5.40}$$

we obtain different members of this family of methods. In the basic stochastic gradient algorithms, d_t only depends on the current gradient ∇J_t. The resulting update rule for the adaptive stochastic gradient methods is

$$\theta_{(t+1)} = \theta_{(t)} - \gamma_t d_t. \tag{5.41}$$

The most popular member of this class of methods makes use of an *exponential moving average*, where recent gradients have higher weights than older gradients. Let $\beta_1 < 1$ and $\beta_2 < 1$ denote the exponential weights for the search direction and the learning rate, respectively. The ADAM optimiser then updates the search direction and the learning rate according to

$$d_t = (1 - \beta_1) \sum_{i=1}^{t} \beta_1^{t-i} \nabla J_i, \tag{5.42a}$$

$$\gamma_t = \frac{\eta}{\sqrt{t}} \left((1 - \beta_2) \mathrm{diag} \left(\sum_{i=1}^{t} \beta_2^{t-i} \|\nabla J_i\|^2 \right) \right)^{1/2}. \tag{5.42b}$$

Both of the tuning parameters β_1 and β_2 are typically set to be close to 1, and common values are $\beta_1 = 0.9, \beta_2 = 0.999$. The reason is simply that too small values will effectively result in an exponential forgetting of the past information and remove the – often very valuable – memory effect inherent in this method.

The first member of this adaptive family is called ADAGRAD, which makes use of the current gradient as its search direction $d_t = \nabla J_t$ and has a learning rate with a memory, but where all components are equally important:

$$\gamma_t = \frac{\eta}{\sqrt{t}} \left(\frac{1}{\sqrt{k}} \text{diag} \left(\sum_{i=1}^{t} \|\nabla J_i\|^2 \right) \right)^{1/2}.$$ (5.43)

5.6 Hyperparameter Optimisation

Besides the learning parameters of a model, there are quite often also a set of hyperparameters that have to be optimised. As a concrete example, we will use the regularisation parameter λ, but the discussion below applies to all hyperparameters, as long as they are not of too high dimensions. We can usually estimate E_{new} as, say, $E_{\text{hold-out}}$, and aim for minimising this.

Writing down an explicit form of $E_{\text{hold-out}}$ as a function of the hyperparameter λ can be quite tedious, not to mention taking its derivate. In fact, $E_{\text{hold-out}}$ includes an optimisation problem itself – learning $\widehat{\theta}$ for a given value of λ. However, we can nevertheless evaluate the objective function for any given λ, simply by running the entire learning procedure and computing the prediction errors on the validation dataset.

Perhaps the simplest way to solve such an optimisation problem is to 'try a few different parameter values and pick the one which works best'. That is the idea of *grid search* and its likes. The term 'grid' here refers to some (more or less arbitrarily chosen) set of different parameter values to try out, and we illustrate it in Example 5.9.

Although simple to implement, grid search can be computationally inefficient, in particular if the parameter vector has a high dimension. As an example, having a grid with a resolution of 10 grid points per dimension (which is a very coarse-grained grid) for a five-dimensional parameter vector requires $10^5 = 100\,000$ evaluations of the objective function. If possible one should avoid using grid search for this reason. However, with low-dimensional hyperparameters (in L^1 and L^2 regularisation, λ is one-dimensional, for example), grid search can be feasible. We summarise grid search in Algorithm 5.4, where we use it to determine a regularisation parameter λ.

Example 5.9 Grid search

We apply grid search to the objective functions from Example 5.3, with an arbitrarily chosen grid indicated by blue the marks in Figure 5.16. The discovered minimum, which is the grid point with the smallest value of the objective functions, is marked with a yellow dot.

Due to the unfortunate selection of the grid, the global minimum is not found in the non-convex problem (right of Figure 5.16). This problem could be handled by increasing the resolution of the grid, which however requires more computations (more evaluations of the objective function).

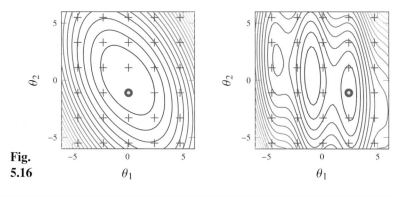

Fig. 5.16

Algorithm 5.4: Grid search for regularisation parameter λ

Input: Training data $\{\mathbf{x}_i, y_i\}_{i=1}^n$, validation data $\{\mathbf{x}_j, y_j\}_{j=1}^{n_v}$

Result: $\widehat{\lambda}$

1 **for** $\lambda = 10^{-3}, 10^{-2}, \ldots, 10^3$ *(as an example)* **do**
2   Learn $\widehat{\boldsymbol{\theta}}$ with regularisation parameter λ from training data
3   Compute error on validation data $E_{\text{val}}(\lambda) \leftarrow \frac{1}{n_v} \sum_{j=1}^{n_v} (\widehat{y}(\mathbf{x}_j; \widehat{\boldsymbol{\theta}}) - y_j)^2$
4 **end**
5 **return** $\widehat{\lambda}$ as $\arg\min_\lambda E_{\text{val}}(\lambda)$

Some hyperparameters (for example k in k-NN, Chapter 2) are integers, and sometimes it is feasible to simply try all reasonable integer values in grid search. However, most of the time the major challenge in grid search is to select a good grid. The grid used in Algorithm 5.4 is logarithmic between 0.001 and 1 000, but that is of course only an example. One could indeed do some manual work by first selecting a coarse grid to get an initial guess, and thereafter refine the grid only around the promising candidates, etc. In practice, if the problem has more than one dimension, it can also be beneficial to select the grid points randomly instead of using an equally spaced linear or logarithmic grid.

The manual procedure of choosing a grid might, however, become quite tedious, and one could wish for an automated method. That is, in fact, possible by treating the grid point selection problem as a machine learning problem itself. If we consider the points for which the objective function has already been evaluated as a training dataset, we can use a regression method to learn a model for the objective function. That model can, in turn, be used to answer questions on where to evaluate the objective function next, and thereby automatically select the next grid point. A concrete method built from this idea is the Gaussian process optimisation method, which uses Gaussian processes (Chapter 9) to train a model of the objective function.

5.7 Further Reading

A mathematically more thorough discussion on loss functions is provided by Gneiting and Raftery (2007). Some of the asymptotic minimisers, also referred to as population minimisers, are derived by Hastie et al. (2009, Section 10.5-10.6).

A standard reference for optimisation, covering much more than this chapter, is the book by Nocedal and Wright (2006). Stochastic gradient descent has its roots in the work on stochastic optimisation by Robbins and Monro (1951), and two overviews of its modern use in machine learning are given by Bottou et al. (2018) and Ruder (2017). For Gaussian process optimisation, see Frazier (2018) and Snoek et al. (2012).

L^2 regularisation was introduced independently in statistics by Hoerl and Kennard (1970) and earlier in numerical analysis by Andrey Nikolayevich Tikhonov. L^1 regularisation was first introduced by Tibshirani (1996). Early stopping has been used as a regulariser for long time in neural network practice and has been analysed by Bishop (1995) and Sjöberg and Ljung (1995). For the regularising effect of stochastic gradient descent, see Hardt et al. (2016) and Mandt et al. (2017). A lot has been written about adaptive methods, and many different algorithms are available. The ADAGRAD algorithm was introduced by Duchi et al. (2011), and ADAM was derived by D. P. Kingma and Ba (2015). Interesting insights about these algorithms are offered by Reddi et al. (2018).

6 Neural Networks and Deep Learning

In Chapter 3, we introduced linear regression and logistic regression as the two basic parametric models for solving the regression and classification problems. A neural network extends this by stacking multiple copies of these models to construct a hierarchical model that can describe more complicated relationships between inputs and outputs than linear or logistic regression models are able to. Deep learning is a subfield of machine learning that deals with such hierarchical machine learning models.

We will start in Section 6.1 by generalising linear regression to a two-layer neural network (that is, a neural network with one hidden layer), and then generalise it further to a deep neural network. In Section 6.3, we present a special neural network tailored for images, and in Section 6.2, we look into some details on how to train neural networks. Finally, in Section 6.4, we provide one technique for how to regularise neural networks.

6.1 The Neural Network Model

In Section 5.1, we introduced concept of non-linear parametric functions for modelling the relationship between the input variables $x_1, \ldots, x_p$ and the output y. We denote this non-linear relationship in its prediction form as

$$\widehat{y} = f_{\boldsymbol{\theta}}(x_1, \ldots, x_p), \tag{6.1}$$

where the function f is parametrised by $\boldsymbol{\theta}$. Such a non-linear function can be parametrised in many ways. In a neural network, the strategy is to use several *layers* of linear regression models and non-linear *activation functions*. We will explain carefully what that means step by step below.

Generalised Linear Regression

We start the description of the neural network model with the linear regression model

$$\widehat{y} = W_1 x_1 + W_2 x_2 + \cdots + W_p x_p + b. \tag{6.2}$$

Here we denote the parameters by the weights $W_1, \ldots, W_p$ and the offset term b. We choose to use this notation instead of the one used in (3.2) since we will later handle the weights slightly differently from the offset term. As before, $x_1, \ldots, x_p$ are the input variables. In Figure 6.1a, a graphical illustration of (6.2) is shown. Each input

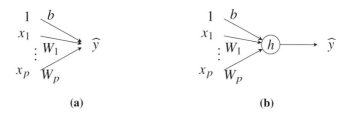

(a)   **(b)**

Figure 6.1 Graphical illustration of a linear regression model (Figure 6.1a) and a generalised linear regression model (Figure 6.1b). In Figure 6.1a, the output $\widehat{y}$ is described as the sum of all terms, b and $\{W_j x_j\}_{j=1}^{p}$, as in (6.2). In Figure 6.1b, the circle denotes addition and also transformation through the activation function h, as in (6.3).

variable x_j is represented by a node, and each parameter W_j by a link. Furthermore, the output $\widehat{y}$ is described as the sum of all the terms, $W_j x_j$. Note that we use the constant value 1 as the input variable corresponding to the offset term b.

To describe *non-linear* relationships between $\mathbf{x} = [1 \; x_1 \; x_2 \; \ldots \; x_p]^{\mathsf{T}}$ and $\widehat{y}$, we introduce a non-linear scalar function called the *activation function* $h : \mathbb{R} \rightarrow \mathbb{R}$. The linear regression model (6.2) is now modified into a generalised linear regression model (see Section 3.4) where the linear combination of the inputs is transformed by the activation function

$$\widehat{y} = h\big(W_1 x_1 + W_2 x_2 + \cdots + W_p x_p + b\big). \tag{6.3}$$

This extension to the generalised linear regression model is visualised in Figure 6.1b.

Common choices of activation function are the *logistic function* and the *rectified linear unit* (ReLU).

$$\text{Logistic: } h(z) = \frac{1}{1 + e^{-z}}, \qquad\qquad \text{ReLU: } h(z) = \max(0, z).$$

These are illustrated in Figure 6.2a and b, respectively. The logistic (or sigmoid) function has already been used in the context of logistic regression (Section 3.2). The logistic function is linear close to $z = 0$ and saturates at 0 and 1 as z decreases or increases. The ReLU is even simpler. The function is just equal to z for positive inputs and equal to zero for negative inputs. The logistic function used to be the standard choice of activation function in neural networks for many years, whereas the ReLU is now the standard choice in most neural network models, despite (and partly due to) its simplicity.

The generalised linear regression model (6.3) is very simple and is itself not capable of describing very complicated relationships between the input $\mathbf{x}$ and the output $\widehat{y}$. Therefore, we make two further extensions to increase the generality of the model: We first make use of *several* parallel generalised linear regression models to build a layer (which will lead us to the *two-layer* neural network) and then stack these layers in a *sequential* construction (which will result in a *deep* neural network).

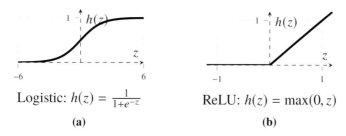

Logistic: $h(z) = \frac{1}{1+e^{-z}}$ ReLU: $h(z) = \max(0, z)$

(a)   (b)

Figure 6.2 Two common activation functions used in neural networks. The logistic (or sigmoid) function (Figure 6.2a) and the rectified linear unit (Figure 6.2b).

Two-Layer Neural Network

In (6.3), the output $\widehat{y}$ is constructed by one scalar regression model. To increase its flexibility and turn it into a two-layer neural network, we instead let its output be a sum of U such generalised linear regression models, each of which has its own set of parameters. The parameters for the kth regression model are $b_k, W_{k1}, \ldots, W_{kp}$, and we denote its output by q_k,

$$q_k = h\left(W_{k1}x_1 + W_{k2}x_2 + \cdots + W_{kp}x_p + b_k\right), \qquad k = 1, \ldots, U. \qquad (6.4)$$

These intermediate outputs q_k are so-called *hidden units*, since they are not the output of the whole model. The U different hidden units $\{q_k\}_{k=1}^{U}$ instead act as input variables to an additional linear regression model

$$\widehat{y} = W_1 q_1 + W_2 q_2 + \cdots + W_U q_U + b. \qquad (6.5)$$

To distinguish the parameters in (6.4) and (6.5), we add the superscripts (1) and (2), respectively. The equations describing this two-layer neural network (or equivalently, a neural network with one layer of hidden units) are thus

$$q_1 = h\left(W_{11}^{(1)}x_1 + W_{12}^{(1)}x_2 + \cdots + W_{1p}^{(1)}x_p + b_1^{(1)}\right),$$

$$q_2 = h\left(W_{21}^{(1)}x_1 + W_{22}^{(1)}x_2 + \cdots + W_{2p}^{(1)}x_p + b_2^{(1)}\right), \qquad (6.6a)$$

$$\vdots$$

$$q_U = h\left(W_{U1}^{(1)}x_1 + W_{U2}^{(1)}x_2 + \cdots + W_{Up}^{(1)}x_p + b_U^{(1)}\right),$$

$$\widehat{y} = W_1^{(2)}q_1 + W_2^{(2)}q_2 + \cdots + W_U^{(2)}q_U + b^{(2)}. \qquad (6.6b)$$

Extending the graphical illustration from Figure 6.1, this model can be depicted as a graph with two layers of links (illustrated using arrows); see Figure 6.3. As before, each link has a parameter associated with it. Note that we include an offset term not only in the input layer but also in the hidden layer.

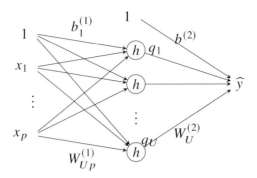

Figure 6.3 A two-layer neural network, or equivalently, a neural network with one intermediate layer of hidden units.

Vectorisation over Units

The two-layer neural network model in (6.6) can also be written more compactly using matrix notation, where the parameters in each layer are stacked in a *weight matrix* $\mathbf{W}$ and an *offset vector*[1] $\mathbf{b}$ as

$$\mathbf{W}^{(1)} = \begin{bmatrix} W_{11}^{(1)} & \cdots & W_{1p}^{(1)} \\ \vdots & & \vdots \\ W_{U1}^{(1)} & \cdots & W_{Up}^{(1)} \end{bmatrix}, \quad \mathbf{b}^{(1)} = \begin{bmatrix} b_1^{(1)} \\ \vdots \\ b_U^{(1)} \end{bmatrix},$$

$$\mathbf{W}^{(2)} = \begin{bmatrix} W_1^{(2)} & \cdots & W_U^{(2)} \end{bmatrix}, \quad \mathbf{b}^{(2)} = \begin{bmatrix} b^{(2)} \end{bmatrix}. \tag{6.7}$$

The full model can then be written as

$$\mathbf{q} = h\big(\mathbf{W}^{(1)}\mathbf{x} + \mathbf{b}^{(1)}\big), \tag{6.8a}$$

$$\widehat{y} = \mathbf{W}^{(2)}\mathbf{q} + \mathbf{b}^{(2)}, \tag{6.8b}$$

where we have also stacked the components in $\mathbf{x}$ and $\mathbf{q}$ as $\mathbf{x} = [x_1 \;\; \cdots \;\; x_p]^\mathsf{T}$ and $\mathbf{q} = [q_1 \;\; \cdots \;\; q_U]^\mathsf{T}$. Note that the activation function h in (6.8a) acts element-wise on the input vector and results in an output vector of the same dimension. The two weight matrices and the two offset vectors are the parameters of the model, which can be written as

$$\boldsymbol{\theta} = \big[\mathrm{vec}(\mathbf{W}^{(1)})^\mathsf{T} \quad \mathbf{b}^{(1)\mathsf{T}} \quad \mathrm{vec}(\mathbf{W}^{(2)})^\mathsf{T} \quad \mathbf{b}^{(2)\mathsf{T}}\big]^\mathsf{T}, \tag{6.9}$$

---

[1] The word 'bias' is often used for the offset vector in the neural network literature, but this is really just a model parameter and not a bias in the statistical sense. To avoid confusion, we refer to it as an offset instead.

where the operator vec takes all elements in the matrix and puts them into a vector. Overall, (6.8) describes a non-linear regression model of the form $\widehat{y} = f_{\theta}(\mathbf{x})$.

Deep Neural Network

The two-layer neural network is a useful model on its own, and a lot of research and analysis has been done on it. However, the real descriptive power of a neural network is realised when we stack multiple such layers of generalised linear regression models and thereby achieve a *deep* neural network. Deep neural networks can model complicated relationships (such as the one between an image and its class), and are one of the state-of-the-art methods in machine learning as of today.

We enumerate the layers with index $l \in \{1, \ldots, L\}$, where L is the number of layers. Each *layer* is parametrised with a weight matrix $\mathbf{W}^{(l)}$ and an offset vector $\mathbf{b}^{(l)}$, as for the two-layer case. For example, $\mathbf{W}^{(1)}$ and $\mathbf{b}^{(1)}$ belong to layer $l = 1$, $\mathbf{W}^{(2)}$ and $\mathbf{b}^{(2)}$ belong to layer $l = 2$, and so forth. We also have multiple *layers of hidden units* denoted by $\mathbf{q}^{(l)}$. Each such layer consists of U_l hidden units $\mathbf{q}^{(l)} = [q_1^{(l)} \; \cdots \; q_{U_l}^{(l)}]^\mathsf{T}$, where the dimensions $U_1, \ldots, U_{L-1}$ can be different across the various layers.

Each layer maps a hidden layer $\mathbf{q}^{(l-1)}$ to the next hidden layer $\mathbf{q}^{(l)}$ according to

$$\mathbf{q}^{(l)} = h\big(\mathbf{W}^{(l)}\mathbf{q}^{(l-1)} + \mathbf{b}^{(l)}\big). \tag{6.10}$$

This means that the layers are stacked such that the output of the first layer of hidden units $\mathbf{q}^{(1)}$ is the input to the second layer, the output of the second layer $\mathbf{q}^{(2)}$ (the second layer of hidden units) is the input to the third layer, etc. By stacking multiple layers we have constructed a *deep* neural network. A deep neural network of L layers can be described mathematically as

$$\begin{aligned}
\mathbf{q}^{(1)} &= h\big(\mathbf{W}^{(1)}\mathbf{x} + \mathbf{b}^{(1)}\big), \\
\mathbf{q}^{(2)} &= h\big(\mathbf{W}^{(2)}\mathbf{q}^{(1)} + \mathbf{b}^{(2)}\big), \\
&\;\;\vdots \\
\mathbf{q}^{(L-1)} &= h\big(\mathbf{W}^{(L-1)}\mathbf{q}^{(L-2)} + \mathbf{b}^{(L-1)}\big), \\
\widehat{y} &= \mathbf{W}^{(L)}\mathbf{q}^{(L-1)} + \mathbf{b}^{(L)}.
\end{aligned} \tag{6.11}$$

A graphical representation of this model is provided in Figure 6.4. The expression (6.11) for a deep neural network can be compared with the expression (6.8) for a two-layer neural network.

The weight matrix $\mathbf{W}^{(1)}$ for the first layer $l = 1$ has dimension $U_1 \times p$, and the corresponding offset vector $\mathbf{b}^{(1)}$ has dimension U_1. Since the output is scalar, in the last layer, the weight matrix $\mathbf{W}^{(L)}$ has dimension $1 \times U_{L-1}$, and the offset vector $\mathbf{b}^{(L)}$ has dimension 1. For all intermediate layers $l = 2, \ldots, L - 1$, $\mathbf{W}^{(l)}$ has dimension $U_l \times U_{l-1}$, and the corresponding offset vector has dimension U_l. The number of inputs p is given by the problem, but the number of layers L and the dimensions $U_1, U_2, \ldots$ are user design choices that determine the flexibility of the model.

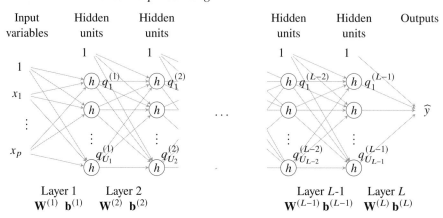

Figure 6.4 A deep neural network with L layers. Each layer l is parameterised by $\mathbf{W}^{(l)}$ and $\mathbf{b}^{(l)}$.

Vectorisation over Data Points

During training, the neural network model is used to compute the predicted output, not only for one input $\mathbf{x}$ but for several inputs $\{\mathbf{x}_i\}_{i=1}^n$. For example, for the two-layer neural network presented in Section 6.1, we have

$$\mathbf{q}_i^\mathsf{T} = h\left(\mathbf{x}_i^\mathsf{T}\mathbf{W}^{(1)\mathsf{T}} + \mathbf{b}^{(1)\mathsf{T}}\right), \tag{6.12a}$$

$$\widehat{y}_i = \mathbf{q}_i^\mathsf{T}\mathbf{W}^{(2)\mathsf{T}} + \mathbf{b}^{(2)\mathsf{T}}, \qquad i = 1,\ldots,n. \tag{6.12b}$$

Similar to the vectorisation over units explained earlier, we also want to vectorise these equations over the data points to allow for efficient computation of the model. Note that the equations (6.12) are transposed in comparison to the model in (6.8). With this notation, we can, similar to the linear regression model (3.5), stack all data points in matrices, where each data point represents one row:

$$\mathbf{y} = \begin{bmatrix} y_1 \\ \vdots \\ y_n \end{bmatrix}, \qquad \mathbf{X} = \begin{bmatrix} \mathbf{x}_1^\mathsf{T} \\ \vdots \\ \mathbf{x}_n^\mathsf{T} \end{bmatrix}, \quad \widehat{\mathbf{y}} = \begin{bmatrix} \widehat{y}_1 \\ \vdots \\ \widehat{y}_n \end{bmatrix}, \quad \text{and} \quad \mathbf{Q} = \begin{bmatrix} \mathbf{q}_1^\mathsf{T} \\ \vdots \\ \mathbf{q}_n^\mathsf{T} \end{bmatrix}. \tag{6.13}$$

We can then conveniently write (6.12) as

$$\mathbf{Q} = h\left(\mathbf{X}\mathbf{W}^{(1)\mathsf{T}} + \mathbf{b}^{(1)\mathsf{T}}\right), \tag{6.14a}$$

$$\widehat{\mathbf{y}} = \mathbf{Q}\mathbf{W}^{(2)\mathsf{T}} + \mathbf{b}^{(2)\mathsf{T}}, \tag{6.14b}$$

where we have also stacked the predicted output and the hidden units in matrices. Note that the transposed offset vectors $\mathbf{b}^{(1)\mathsf{T}}$ and $\mathbf{b}^{(2)\mathsf{T}}$ are added to each row in this notation.

The vectorised equations in (6.14) are also how the model would typically be implemented in languages that support array programming. For implementation, you may want to consider using the transposed versions of $\mathbf{W}$ and $\mathbf{b}$ as your weight matrix and offset vector to avoid transposing them in each layer.

Neural Networks for Classification

Neural networks can also be used for classification, where we have categorical outputs $y \in \{1, \ldots, M\}$ instead of numerical. In Section 3.2, we extended linear regression to logistic regression by simply adding the logistic function to the output. In the same manner, we can extend the neural network for regression presented in the previous section to a neural network for classification. In doing so, we use the multiclass version of logistic regression presented in Section 3.2 and more specifically the softmax parametrisation (3.41), repeated here for convenience:

$$\text{softmax}(\mathbf{z}) \triangleq \frac{1}{\sum_{j=1}^{M} e^{z_j}} \begin{bmatrix} e^{z_1} \\ e^{z_2} \\ \vdots \\ e^{z_M} \end{bmatrix}. \tag{6.15}$$

The model is constructed as in (6.11), but where the output is of dimension M. The softmax function now becomes an additional activation function acting on the final layer of the neural network:

$$\mathbf{q}^{(1)} = h\left(\mathbf{W}^{(1)}\mathbf{x} + \mathbf{b}^{(1)}\right), \tag{6.16a}$$

$$\vdots$$

$$\mathbf{q}^{(L-1)} = h\left(\mathbf{W}^{(L-1)}\mathbf{q}^{(L-2)} + \mathbf{b}^{(L-1)}\right), \tag{6.16b}$$

$$\mathbf{z} = \mathbf{W}^{(L)}\mathbf{q}^{(L-1)} + \mathbf{b}^{(L)}, \tag{6.16c}$$

$$\mathbf{g} = \text{softmax}(\mathbf{z}). \tag{6.16d}$$

The softmax function maps the output of the last layer $\mathbf{z} = [z_1, \ldots, z_M]^\mathsf{T}$ to $\mathbf{g} = [g_1, \ldots, g_M]^\mathsf{T}$, where g_m is a model of the class probability $p(y_i = m \mid \mathbf{x}_i)$. The input variables $z_1, \ldots, z_M$ to the softmax function are referred to as *logits*. Note that the softmax function does not come as a layer with additional parameters; it merely acts as a transformation of the output into the modelled class probabilities. By construction, the outputs of the softmax function will always be in the interval $g_m \in [0, 1]$ and sum to $\sum_{m=1}^{M} g_m = 1$, otherwise they could not be interpreted as probabilities. Since the output now has dimension M, the last layer of the weight matrix $\mathbf{W}^{(L)}$ has dimension $M \times U_{L-1}$, and the offset vector $\mathbf{b}^{(L)}$ has dimension M.

Example 6.1 Classification of hand-written digits – problem formulation

We consider the so-called MNIST dataset,[a] which is one of the most well studied datasets within machine learning and image processing. The dataset has 60 000 training data points and 10 000 validation data points. Each data point consists of a 28×28 pixel greyscale image of a handwritten digit. The digit has been size-normalised and centred within a fixed-sized image. Each image is also labelled with the digit 0, 1, . . . , 8, or 9 that it is depicting. Figure 6.5 shows a batch of 20 data points from this dataset.

Fig. 6.5

In this classification task, we consider the image as our input $\mathbf{x} = [x_1, \ldots x_p]^{\mathsf{T}}$. Each input variable x_j corresponds to a pixel in the image. In total we have $p = 28 \times 28 = 784$ input variables which we flatten out into one long vector.[b] The value of each x_j represents the intensity of that pixel. The intensity-value is within the interval $[0, 1]$, where $x_j = 0$ corresponds to a black pixel and $x_j = 1$ to a white pixel. Anything between 0 and 1 is a grey pixel with corresponding intensity. The output is the class $y_i \in \{0, \ldots, 9\}$. This means that we have in total 10 classes representing the 10 digits. Based on a set of training data $\{\mathbf{x}_i, y_i\}_{i=1}^n$ with images and labels, the problem is to find a good model for the class probabilities

$$p(y = m \mid \mathbf{x}), \qquad m = 0, \ldots, 9,$$

in other words, the probabilities that an unseen image $\mathbf{x}$ belongs to each of the $M = 10$ classes. Assume that we would like to use logistic regression to solve this problem with a softmax output. This is identical to a neural network with just one layer – that is, (6.16) where $L = 1$. The parameters of that model would be

$$\mathbf{W}^{(1)} \in \mathbb{R}^{784 \times 10} \qquad \mathbf{b}^{(1)} \in \mathbb{R}^{10},$$

which gives in total $784 \cdot 10 + 10 = 7\,850$ parameters. Assume that we would like to extend this model with a two-layer neural network with $U = 200$ hidden units. That would require two sets of weight matrices and offset vectors:

$$\mathbf{W}^{(1)} \in \mathbb{R}^{784 \times 200} \qquad \mathbf{b}^{(1)} \in \mathbb{R}^{200}, \qquad \mathbf{W}^{(2)} \in \mathbb{R}^{200 \times 10} \qquad \mathbf{b}^{(2)} \in \mathbb{R}^{10},$$

which is a model with $784 \cdot 200 + 200 + 200 \cdot 10 + 10 = 159\,010$ parameters. In the next section, we will learn how to fit all of these parameters to the training data.

---

[a] http://yann.lecun.com/exdb/mnist/
[b] By flattening, we actually remove quite some information from the data. In Section 6.3, we will look at another neural network model where this spatial information is preserved.

6.2 Training a Neural Network

A neural network is a parametric model, and we find its parameters by using the techniques explained in Chapter 5. The parameters in the model are all weight matrices and all offset vectors:

$$\theta = \left[\text{vec}(\mathbf{W}^{(1)})^{\mathsf{T}} \quad \mathbf{b}^{(1)\mathsf{T}} \quad \cdots \quad \text{vec}(\mathbf{W}^{(L)})^{\mathsf{T}} \quad \mathbf{b}^{(L)\mathsf{T}} \right]^{\mathsf{T}}. \tag{6.17}$$

To find suitable values for the parameters θ, we solve an optimisation problem of the form

$$\widehat{\theta} = \arg\min_{\theta} J(\theta), \qquad \text{where } J(\theta) = \frac{1}{n} \sum_{i=1}^{n} L(\mathbf{x}_i, y_i, \theta). \tag{6.18}$$

We denote the cost function as $J(\theta)$ and the loss function as $L(\mathbf{x}_i, \mathbf{y}_i, \theta)$. The functional form of the loss function depends on the problem at hand, mainly if it is a regression problem or a classification problem.

For the regression problems, we typically use the squared error loss (5.6) as we did in linear regression,

$$L(\mathbf{x}, y, \theta) = \left(y - f(\mathbf{x}; \theta)\right)^2, \tag{6.19}$$

where $f(\mathbf{x}; \theta)$ is the output of the neural network.

For the multiclass classification problem, we analogously use the cross-entropy loss function (3.44) as we did for multiclass logistic regression,

$$L(\mathbf{x}, y, \theta) = -\ln g_y\left(\mathbf{f}(\mathbf{x}; \theta)\right) = -z_y + \ln \sum_{j=1}^{M} e^{z_j}, \tag{6.20}$$

where $z_j = f_j(\mathbf{x}; \theta)$ is the jth logit – that is, the jth output of the last layer before the softmax function $\mathbf{g}(\mathbf{z})$. Also, similar to the notation in (3.44), we use the training data label y as an index variable to select the correct logit for the loss function. Also note that both linear regression and logistic regression can be seen as a special case of the neural network model where we only have one single layer in the network. Also note that we are not restricted to these two loss functions. Following the discussion in Section 5.2, we could use another loss function that suits our needs.

These optimisation problems cannot be solved in closed form, so numerical optimisation has to be used. In all numerical optimisation algorithms, the parameters are updated in an iterative manner. In deep learning, we typically use various versions of gradient based search:

1. Pick an initialisation θ_0.
2. Update the parameters as $\theta_{t+1} \leftarrow \theta_t - \gamma \nabla_\theta J(\theta_t)$ for $t = 0, 1, 2, \dots$. (6.21)
3. Terminate when some criterion is fulfilled, and take the last θ_t as $\widehat{\theta}$.

Solving the optimisation problem (6.18) has two main computational challenges.

- **Computational challenge 1 – n is large.** The first computational challenge is the big data problem. For many deep learning applications, the number of data points n is very large, making the computation of the cost function and its gradient very costly since it requires sums over all data points. As a consequence, we cannot afford to compute the exact gradient $\nabla_\theta J(\theta_t)$ at each iteration. Instead, we compute an approximation of this gradient by only considering a random subset of the training data at each iteration, which we refer to as a mini-batch. This optimisation procedure is called stochastic gradient descent and was further explained in Section 5.5.

- **Computational challenge 2 – dim($\boldsymbol{\theta}$) is large.** The second computational challenge is that the number of parameters dim($\boldsymbol{\theta}$) is also very large for deep learning problems. To efficiently compute the gradient $\nabla_{\boldsymbol{\theta}} J(\boldsymbol{\theta}_t)$, we apply the chain rule of calculus and reuse the partial derivatives needed to compute this gradient. This is called the backpropagation algorithm, which is further explained in the next section.

Backpropagation

The backpropagation algorithm is an important ingredient in almost all training procedures of neural networks. As outlined above, it is not a complete training algorithm in the sense that it takes training data and trains a model. Backpropagation is an algorithm that efficiently computes the cost function and its gradient with respect to all the parameters in a neural network. The cost function and its gradient are then used in the stochastic gradient descent algorithms explained in Section 5.5.

The parameters in this model are all weight matrices and all offset vectors. Hence, at each iteration in our gradient based search algorithm (6.21), we also need to find the gradient of the cost function with respect to all elements in these matrices and vectors. To summarise, we want to find

$$d\mathbf{W}^{(l)} \triangleq \nabla_{\partial \mathbf{W}^{(l)}} J(\boldsymbol{\theta}) = \begin{bmatrix} \dfrac{\partial J(\boldsymbol{\theta})}{\partial w_{11}^{(l)}} & \cdots & \dfrac{\partial J(\boldsymbol{\theta})}{\partial w_{1,U^{(l-1)}}^{(l)}} \\ \vdots & & \vdots \\ \dfrac{\partial J(\boldsymbol{\theta})}{\partial w_{U^{(l)},1}^{(l)}} & \cdots & \dfrac{\partial J(\boldsymbol{\theta})}{\partial w_{U^{(l)},U^{(l-1)}}^{(l)}} \end{bmatrix} \quad \text{and}$$

$$d\mathbf{b}^{(l)} \triangleq \nabla_{\partial \mathbf{b}^{(l)}} J(\boldsymbol{\theta}) = \begin{bmatrix} \dfrac{\partial J(\boldsymbol{\theta})}{\partial b_1^{(l)}} \\ \vdots \\ \dfrac{\partial J(\boldsymbol{\theta})}{\partial b_{U^{(l)}}^{(l)}} \end{bmatrix}. \tag{6.22}$$

for all $l = 1, \ldots, L$. Note that the cost function $J(\boldsymbol{\theta})$ here only includes the losses in the current mini-batch. When these gradients are computed, we can update the weight matrices and offset vectors accordingly:

$$\mathbf{W}_{t+1}^{(l)} \leftarrow \mathbf{W}_t^{(l)} - \gamma d\mathbf{W}_t^{(l)}, \tag{6.23a}$$

$$\mathbf{b}_{t+1}^{(l)} \leftarrow \mathbf{b}_t^{(l)} - \gamma d\mathbf{b}_t^{(l)}. \tag{6.23b}$$

To compute all these gradients efficiently, backpropagation exploits the structure of the model instead of naively computing the derivatives with respect to each single parameter separately. To do that, backpropagation uses the chain rule of calculus.

First, we describe how backpropagation works for one single data point $(\mathbf{x}, y)$. In Algorithm 6.1, we later generalise this to multiple data points. The backpropagation algorithm consists of two steps, the forward propagation and the backward propagation. In the forward propagation, we simply evaluate the cost function using the neural network model we presented in Section 6.1. We start with the input $\mathbf{x}$ and evaluate each layer sequentially from layer 1 to the last layer L: hence, we propagate forwards:

$$\mathbf{q}^{(0)} = \mathbf{x}, \tag{6.24a}$$

$$\begin{cases} \mathbf{z}^{(l)} = \mathbf{W}^{(l)}\mathbf{q}^{(l-1)} + \mathbf{b}^{(l)}, \\ \mathbf{q}^{(l)} = h(\mathbf{z}^{(l)}), \end{cases} \quad \text{for } l = 1, \ldots, L - 1 \tag{6.24b}$$

$$\mathbf{z}^{(L)} = \mathbf{W}^{(L)}\mathbf{q}^{(L-1)} + \mathbf{b}^{(L)}, \tag{6.24c}$$

$$J(\boldsymbol{\theta}) = \begin{cases} \left(y - z^{(L)}\right)^2, & \text{if regression problem,} \\ -z_y^{(L)} + \ln \sum_{j=1}^M e^{z_j^{(L)}}, & \text{if classification problem.} \end{cases} \tag{6.24d}$$

Note that, since we only consider one data point, the cost function $J(\boldsymbol{\theta})$ will only include one loss term.

When it comes to backward propagation, we need to introduce some additional notation, namely the gradient of the cost J with respect to the hidden units $\mathbf{z}^{(l)}$ and $\mathbf{q}^{(l)}$, given by

$$d\mathbf{z}^{(l)} \triangleq \nabla_{\mathbf{z}^{(l)}} J(\boldsymbol{\theta}) = \begin{bmatrix} \frac{\partial J(\boldsymbol{\theta})}{\partial z_1^{(l)}} \\ \vdots \\ \frac{\partial J(\boldsymbol{\theta})}{\partial z_{U^{(l)}}^{(l)}} \end{bmatrix} \quad \text{and} \quad d\mathbf{q}^{(l)} \triangleq \nabla_{\mathbf{q}^{(l)}} J(\boldsymbol{\theta}) = \begin{bmatrix} \frac{\partial J(\boldsymbol{\theta})}{\partial q_1^{(l)}} \\ \vdots \\ \frac{\partial J(\boldsymbol{\theta})}{\partial q_{U^{(l)}}^{(l)}} \end{bmatrix}. \tag{6.25}$$

In the backward propagation, we compute the gradients $d\mathbf{z}^{(l)}$ and $d\mathbf{q}^{(l)}$ for all layers. We do this recursively, in the opposite direction to what we did in the forward propagation – that is, starting from the last layer L, we propagate back to the first layer. To start these recursions, we first need to compute $d\mathbf{z}^{(L)}$, the gradient of the cost function with respect to the hidden units in the last hidden layer. This obviously depends on our choice of loss function (6.24d). If we have a regression problem and choose the squared error loss, we get

$$dz^{(L)} = \frac{\partial J(\boldsymbol{\theta})}{\partial z^{(L)}} = \frac{\partial}{\partial z^{(L)}} \left(y - z^{(L)}\right)^2 = -2\left(y - z^{(L)}\right). \tag{6.26a}$$

For a multiclass classification problem, we instead use the cross-entropy loss (6.20), and we get

$$dz_j^{(L)} = \frac{\partial J(\boldsymbol{\theta})}{\partial z_j^{(L)}} = \frac{\partial}{\partial z_j^{(l)}} \left(-z_y^{(L)} + \ln \sum_{k=1}^M e^{z_k^{(L)}}\right) = -\mathbb{I}\{y = j\} + \frac{e^{z_j^{(L)}}}{\sum_{k=1}^M e^{z_k^{(L)}}}. \tag{6.26b}$$

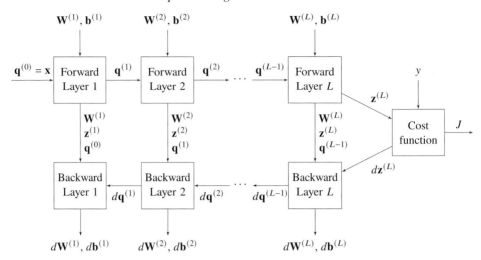

Figure 6.6 A computational graph of the backpropagation algorithm. We start with the input in the upper left corner and propagate forward and evaluate the cost function. Along the way, we also cache the values for the hidden units $\mathbf{q}^{(l)}$ and $\mathbf{z}^{(l)}$. We then propagate the gradients $d\mathbf{q}^{(l)}$ and $d\mathbf{z}^{(l)}$ backwards and compute the gradients for the parameters $\mathbf{W}^{(l)}$, $\mathbf{b}^{(l)}$. The equations behind this computational graph are given in (6.24), (6.26), and (6.27).

The backwards propagation now proceeds with the following recursions:

$$d\mathbf{z}^{(l)} = d\mathbf{q}^{(l)} \odot h'(\mathbf{z}^{(l)}), \tag{6.27a}$$

$$d\mathbf{q}^{(l-1)} = \mathbf{W}^{(l)\mathsf{T}} d\mathbf{z}^{(l)}, \tag{6.27b}$$

where $\odot$ denotes the element-wise product and where $h'(z)$ is the derivative of the activation function $h(z)$. Similar to the notation in (6.24b), $h'(\mathbf{z})$ acts element-wise on the vector $\mathbf{z}$. Note that the first line (6.27a) is not executed for layer L since that layer does not have an activation function; see (6.24c).

With $d\mathbf{z}^{(l)}$, we can now compute the gradients of the weight matrices and offset vectors as

$$d\mathbf{W}^{(l)} = d\mathbf{z}^{(l)} \mathbf{q}^{(l-1)\mathsf{T}}, \tag{6.27c}$$

$$d\mathbf{b}^{(l)} = d\mathbf{z}^{(l)}. \tag{6.27d}$$

All equations for the backward propagation (6.27) can be derived from the chain rule of calculus; for further details see Appendix 6.A. A computational graph of the backpropagation algorithm is summarised in Figure 6.6.

So far, we have only considered backpropagation for one data point $(\mathbf{x}, y)$. However, we do want to compute the cost function $J(\boldsymbol{\theta})$ and its gradients $d\mathbf{W}^{(l)}$ and $d\mathbf{b}^{(l)}$ for the whole mini-batch $\{\mathbf{x}_i, y_i\}_{i=(j-1)n_b+1}^{jn_b}$. Therefore, we run the equations (6.24), (6.26), and (6.27) for all data points in the current mini-batch and average their results for J, $d\mathbf{W}^{(l)}$, and $d\mathbf{b}^{(l)}$. To do this in a computationally efficient manner, we process all n_b data points in the mini-batch simultaneously by stacking them in matrices as we did in (6.14), where each row represent one data point:

Algorithm 6.1: Backpropagation

Input: Parameters $\boldsymbol{\theta} = \{\mathbf{W}^{(l)}, \mathbf{b}^{(l)}\}_{l=1}^{L}$, activation function h, and data $\mathbf{X}$, $\mathbf{y}$, with n_b rows, where each row corresponds to one data point in the current mini-batch.

Result: $J(\boldsymbol{\theta})$, $\nabla_{\boldsymbol{\theta}} J(\boldsymbol{\theta})$ of the current mini-batch.

1 *Forward propagation*
2 Set $\mathbf{Q}^0 \leftarrow \mathbf{X}$
3 **for** $l = 1, \ldots, L$ **do**
4 $\quad$ $\mathbf{Z}^{(l)} = \mathbf{Q}^{(l-1)} \mathbf{W}^{(l)\mathsf{T}} + \mathbf{b}^{(l)\mathsf{T}}$
5 $\quad$ $\mathbf{Q}^{(l)} = h(\mathbf{Z}^{(l)})$ $\qquad$ *Do not execute this line for last layer $l = L$*
6 **end**

7 *Evaluate cost function*
8 **if** *Regression problem* **then**
9 $\quad$ $J(\boldsymbol{\theta}) = \frac{1}{n_b} \sum_{i=1}^{n_b} \left(y_i - Z_i^{(L)} \right)^2$
10 $\quad$ $d\mathbf{Z}^{(L)} = -2 \left(\mathbf{y} - \mathbf{Z}^{(L)} \right)$
11 **else if** *Classification problem*[2] **then**
12 $\quad$ $J(\boldsymbol{\theta}) = \frac{1}{n_b} \sum_{i=1}^{n_b} \left(-Z_{i, y_i}^{(L)} + \ln \left(\sum_{j=1}^{M} \exp \left(Z_{ij}^{(L)} \right) \right) \right)$
13 $\quad$ $dZ_{ij}^{(L)} = -\mathbb{I}\{y_i = j\} + \dfrac{\exp \left(Z_{ij}^{(L)} \right)}{\sum_{j=1}^{M} \exp \left(Z_{ij}^{(L)} \right)}$ $\qquad$ $\forall i, j$

14 *Backward propagation*
15 **for** $l = L, \ldots, 1$ **do**
16 $\quad$ $d\mathbf{Z}^{(l)} = d\mathbf{Q}^{(l)} \odot h'(\mathbf{Z}^{(l)})$ $\qquad$ *Do not execute this line for last layer $l = L$*
17 $\quad$ $d\mathbf{Q}^{(l-1)} = d\mathbf{Z}^{(l)} \mathbf{W}^{(l)}$
18 $\quad$ $d\mathbf{W}^{(l)} = \frac{1}{n_b} d\mathbf{Z}^{(l)\mathsf{T}} \mathbf{Q}^{(l-1)}$
19 $\quad$ $db_j^{(l)} = \frac{1}{n_b} \sum_{i=1}^{n_b} dZ_{ij}^{(l)}$ $\qquad$ $\forall j$
20 **end**
21 $\nabla_{\boldsymbol{\theta}} J(\boldsymbol{\theta}) = \begin{bmatrix} \text{vec}(d\mathbf{W}^{(1)})^\mathsf{T} & db^{(1)\mathsf{T}} & \cdots & \text{vec}(d\mathbf{W}^{(L)})^\mathsf{T} & db^{(L)\mathsf{T}} \end{bmatrix}$
22 **return** $J(\boldsymbol{\theta})$, $\nabla_{\boldsymbol{\theta}} J(\boldsymbol{\theta})$

$$\mathbf{Q} = \begin{bmatrix} \mathbf{q}_1^\mathsf{T} \\ \vdots \\ \mathbf{q}_{n_b}^\mathsf{T} \end{bmatrix}, \qquad \mathbf{Z} = \begin{bmatrix} \mathbf{z}_1^\mathsf{T} \\ \vdots \\ \mathbf{z}_{n_b}^\mathsf{T} \end{bmatrix}, \qquad d\mathbf{Q} = \begin{bmatrix} d\mathbf{q}_1^\mathsf{T} \\ \vdots \\ d\mathbf{q}_{n_b}^\mathsf{T} \end{bmatrix} \quad \text{and} \quad d\mathbf{Z} = \begin{bmatrix} d\mathbf{z}_1^\mathsf{T} \\ \vdots \\ d\mathbf{z}_{n_b}^\mathsf{T} \end{bmatrix}. \quad (6.28)$$

The complete algorithm we then get is summarised as Algorithm 6.1.

---

[2] One might want to consider normalizing the logits $Z_{ij}^{(L)} \leftarrow Z_{ij}^{(L)} - \max_j Z_{ij}^{(L)}$ before computing the cost to avoid potential overflow while computing $\exp \left(Z_{ij}^{(L)} \right)$. Note that this normalisation does not change the value of the cost function.

Initialisation

Most of the previous optimisation problems (such as L^1 regularisation and logistic regression) that we have encountered have been convex. This means that we can guarantee global convergence regardless of what initialisation θ_0 we use. In contrast, the cost functions for training neural networks are usually non-convex. This means that the training is sensitive to the value of the initial parameters. Typically, we initialise all the parameters to small random numbers to enable the different hidden units to encode different aspects of the data. If ReLU activation functions are used, the offset elements b_0 are typically initialised to a small positive value such that they operate in the non-negative range of the ReLU.

Example 6.2 Classification of hand-written digits – first attempt

We consider the example of classifying hand-written digits, introduced in Example 6.1. Based on the presented data, we train the two models mentioned at the end of that example: a logistic regression model (or equivalently a one-layer neural network) and a two-layer neural network.

We use stochastic gradient descent, explained in Algorithm 5.3, with learning rate $\gamma = 0.5$ and a mini-batch size of $n_b = 100$ data points. Since we have $n = 60\,000$ training data points in total, one epoch is completed after $6\,000/100 = 600$ iterations. We run the algorithm for 15 epochs, i.e., $9\,000$ iterations.

As explained earlier, at each iteration of the algorithm, the cost function is evaluated for the current mini-batch of the training data. The value for this cost function is illustrated in blue in the left parts of Figures 6.7 and 6.8. In addition, we also compute the miscalssification rate for the 100 data points in the current mini-batch. This is illustrated in the right parts of Figures 6.7 and 6.8. Since the current mini-batch consists of 100 randomly selected training data points, the performance fluctuates depending on which mini-batch is considered.

However, the important measure is how we perform on data which has not been used during training. Therefore, at every 100th iteration, we also evaluate the cost function and the misclassification error on the whole validation dataset of $10\,000$ data points. This performance is illustrated in red in Figures 6.7 and 6.8.

Logistic regression model
Figure 6.7 illustrates the training of the logistic regression model.

Cost function   Misclassification rate

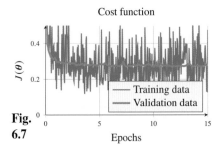
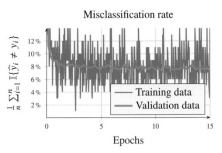

Fig. 6.7

We can see that the performance on validation data improves, and already after a few epochs we do not see any additional improvements, and we get a misclassification rate of approximately 8% on the validation data.

Two-layer neural network
In Figure 6.8, the training of the two-layer neural network with $U = 200$ hidden units is illustrated. We use the ReLU as activation function in this model.

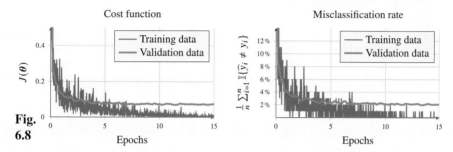

Fig. 6.8

Adding this layer of hidden units significantly reduces the misclassification rate down to 2% on the validation data. We can also see that during the later epochs, we often get all 100 data points in the current mini-batch correct. The discrepancy between training error and validation error indicates that we are overfitting our model. One way to circumvent this overfitting, and hence improve the performance on validation data even further, is to change the neural network layers to other types of layers which are tailored for image data. These types of neural network layers are explained in the following section.

6.3 Convolutional Neural Networks

Convolutional neural networks (CNN) are a special kind of neural network originally tailored for problems where the input data has a grid-like structure. In this text we will focus on images, where the pixels reside on a two-dimensional grid. Images are also the most common type of input data in applications where CNNs are applied. However, CNNs can be used for any input data on a grid, also in one dimension (e.g. audio waveform data) and three dimensions. (volumetric data, e.g. computer tomography (CT) scans or video data). We will focus on greyscale images, but the approach can easily be extended to colour images as well.

Data Representation of an Image

Digital greyscale images consist of pixels ordered in a matrix. Each pixel can be represented as a range from 0 (total absence, black) to 1 (total presence, white), and values between 0 and 1 represent different shades of grey. In Figure 6.9, this is

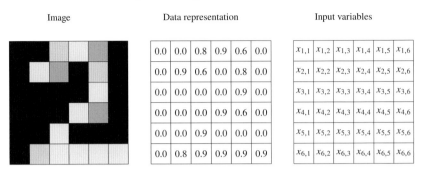

Figure 6.9 Data representation of a greyscale image with 6×6 pixels. Each pixel is represented by a number encoding the intensity of that pixel. These pixel values are stored in a matrix with the elements $x_{j,k}$.

illustrated for an image with 6×6 pixels. In an image classification problem, an image is the input $\mathbf{x}$, and the pixels in the image are the input variables $x_{1,1}$, $x_{1,2}$, $\ldots$, $x_{6,6}$. The two indices j and k determine the position of the pixel in the image, as illustrated in Figure 6.9.

If we put all input variables representing the image pixels in a long vector, as we did in Example 6.1 and Example 6.2, we can use the network architecture presented in Section 6.1. However, by doing that, a lot of the structure present in the image data will be lost. For example, we know that two pixels close to each other typically have more in common than two pixels further apart. This information would be destroyed by such a vectorisation. In contrast, CNNs preserve this information by representing both the input variables and the hidden layers as matrices. The core component in a CNN is the convolutional layer, which will be explained next.

The Convolutional Layer

Following the input layer, we use a hidden layer with as many hidden units as there are input variables. For the image with 6×6 pixels, we consequently have $6 \times 6 = 36$ hidden units. We choose to order the hidden units in a 6×6 matrix, in the same manner as we did for the input variables; see Figure 6.10a.

The network layers presented in earlier sections (like the one in Figure 6.3) have been *dense layers*. This means that each input variable is connected to all hidden units in the subsequent layer, and each such connection has a unique parameter W_{jk} associated to it. These layers have empirically been found to provide too much flexibility for images, and we might not be able to capture the patterns of real importance, and hence the models will not generalise and perform well on unseen data. Instead, a convolutional layer exploits the structure present in images to find a more efficiently parameterised model. In contrast to a dense layer, a convolutional layer leverages two important concepts – *sparse interactions* and *parameter sharing* – to achieve such a parametrisation.

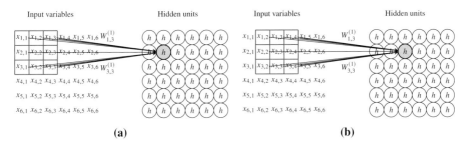

(a)   (b)

Figure 6.10 An illustration of the interactions in a convolutional layer: Each hidden unit (circle) is only dependent on the pixels in a small region of the image (red boxes), here of size 3×3 pixels. The location of the hidden unit corresponds to the location of the region in the image: if we move to a hidden unit one step to the right, the corresponding region in the image also moves one step to the right – compare Figure 6.10a and b. Furthermore, the nine parameters $W_{1,1}^{(1)}, W_{1,2}^{(1)}, \ldots, W_{3,3}^{(1)}$ are the *same* for all hidden units in the layer.

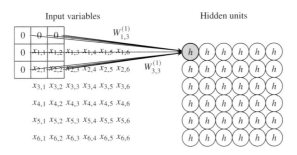

Figure 6.11 An illustration of zero-padding used when the region is partly outside the image. With zero-padding, the size of the image can be preserved in the following layer.

Sparse Interactions

By sparse interactions we mean that most of the parameters in a corresponding dense layer are forced to be equal to zero. More specifically, a hidden unit in a convolutional layer only depends on the pixels in a small region of the image and not on all pixels. In Figure 6.10, this region is of size 3×3. The position of the region is related to the position of the hidden unit in its matrix representation. If we move to a hidden unit one step to the right, the corresponding region in the image also moves one step to the right, as illustrated by comparing Figure 6.10a and b. For the hidden units on the border, the corresponding region is partly located outside the image. For these border cases, we typically use zero-padding, where the missing pixels are simply replaced with zeros. Zero-padding is illustrated in Figure 6.11.

Parameter Sharing

In a dense layer, each link between an input variable and a hidden unit has its own unique parameter. With parameter sharing, we instead let the same parameter

149

be present in multiple places in the network. In a convolutional layer, the set of parameters for the different hidden units are all *the same*. For example, in Figure 6.10a, we use the same set of parameters to map the 3×3 region of pixels to the hidden unit as we do in Figure 6.10b. Instead of learning separate sets of parameters for every position, we only learn one set of a few parameters, and use it for all links between the input layer and the hidden units. We call this set of parameters a *filter*. The mapping between the input variables and the hidden units can be interpreted as a convolution between the input variables and the filter, hence the name convolutional neural network. Mathematically, this convolution can be written as

$$q_{ij} = h \left(\sum_{k=1}^{F} \sum_{l=1}^{F} x_{i+k-1,j+l-1} W_{k,l} \right), \tag{6.29}$$

where $x_{i,j}$ denotes the zero-padded input to the layer, q_{ij} the output of the layer, and $W_{k,l}$ the filter with F rows and F columns. The sparse interactions and parameter sharing in a convolutional layer makes the CNN relatively invariant to translations of objects in the image. If the parameters in the filter are sensitive to a certain detail (such as a corner, an edge, etc.), a hidden unit will react to this detail (or not) *regardless of where in the image that detail is present*! Furthermore, a convolutional layer uses significantly fewer parameters compared to the corresponding dense layer. In Figure 6.10, only $3 \cdot 3 + 1 = 10$ parameters are required (including the offset parameter). If we instead had used a dense layer, $(36 + 1) \cdot 36 = 1\,332$ parameters would have been needed! Another way of interpreting this is: with the same amount of parameters, a convolutional layer can encode more properties of an image than a dense layer.

Convolutional Layer with Strides

In the convolutional layer presented above, we have as many hidden units as we have pixels in the image. However, when we add more layers, we want to reduce the number of hidden units and only store the most important information computed in the previous layers. One way of doing this is by not applying the filter to every pixel but to, say, every two pixels. If we apply the filter to every two pixels, both row-wise and column-wise, the hidden units will only have half as many rows and half as many columns. For a 6×6, image we get 3×3 hidden units. This concept is illustrated in Figure 6.12.

The *stride* controls how many pixels the filter shifts over the image at each step. In Figure 6.10, the stride is $s = 1$ since the filter moves by one pixel both row- and column-wise. In Figure 6.12, the stride is $s = 2$ since it moves by two pixels row- and column-wise. Note that the convolutional layer in Figure 6.12 still requires 10 parameters, just as the convolutional layer in Figure 6.10 does. Mathematically, the convolutional layer with stride can be expressed as

$$q_{ij} = h \left(\sum_{k=1}^{F} \sum_{l=1}^{F} x_{s(i-1)+k,s(j-1)+l} W_{k,l} \right). \tag{6.30}$$

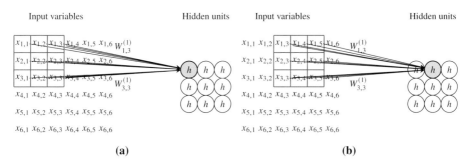

(a) (b)

Figure 6.12 A convolutional layer with stride 2 and filter size 3 × 3.

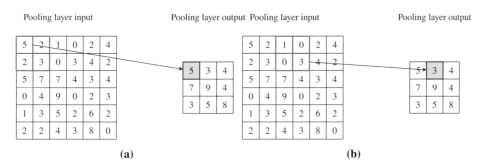

(a) (b)

Figure 6.13 A max pooling layer with stride 2 and pooling filter size 2 × 2.

Not in particular that this is equivalent to (6.29) if we were to use $s = 1$ in the equation above.

Pooling Layer

Another way of summarising the information in previous layers is achieved by using *pooling*. A pooling layer acts as an additional layer after the convolutional layer. Similar to the convolutional layer, it only depends on a region of pixels. However, in contrast to convolutional layers, the pooling layer does not come with any extra trainable parameters. In pooling layers, we also use strides to condense the information, meaning that region is shifted by $s > 1$ pixels. Two common versions of pooling are average pooling and max pooling. In average pooling, the average of the units in the corresponding region is computed. Mathematically, this means

$$\tilde{q}_{ij} = \frac{1}{F^2} \sum_{k=1}^{F} \sum_{l=1}^{F} q_{s(i-1)+k,s(j-1)+l}, \tag{6.31}$$

where $q_{i,j}$ is the input to the pooling layer, $\tilde{q}_{ij}$ is the output, F is the pooling size, and s is the stride used in the pooling layer. In max pooling, we instead take the maximum of the pixels. Max pooling is illustrated in Figure 6.13.

In comparison to convolution with strides, pooling layers can make the model more invariant to small translations of the input, meaning that if we translate the input by a small amount, many of the pooling outputs do not change. For example, in Figure 6.13, if we shift the input units one step to the right (and replace the first column with 0's), the output of the pooling layer would be the same except for the 7 and 3 in the first column, which would become a 5 and a 2. However, using a convolutional layer with stride $s = 2$ requires four times fewer computations than a computational layer (with stride $s = 1$) and after that a pooling layer with stride $s = 2$, since for the first option the convolution is shifted two steps row- and column-wise, whereas in the second option the convolution is still shifted by one step.

> **Time to reflect 6.1** *What would the pooling layer output be in Figure 6.13 if we applied average pooling instead of max pooling?*

Multiple Channels

The networks presented in Figures 6.10 and 6.12 only have 10 parameters each. Even though this parameterisation comes with several important advantages, one filter is probably not sufficient to encode all interesting properties of the images in our dataset. To extended the network, we add multiple filters, each with their own set of parameters. Each filter produces its own set of hidden units – a so-called *channel* – using the same convolution operation as explained in Section 6.3. Hence, each layer of hidden units in a CNN is organised into a so-called tensor with dimension (rows × columns × channels). In Figure 6.14, the first layer of hidden units has four channels, and that hidden layer consequently has dimension $6 \times 6 \times 4$.

When we continue to stack convolutional layers, each filter depends not only on one channel but on all the channels in the previous layer. This is displayed in the second convolutional layer in Figure 6.14. As a consequence, each filter is a tensor of dimension (filter rows × filter columns × input channels). For example, each filter in the second convolutional layer in Figure 6.14 is of size $3 \times 3 \times 4$. If we collect all filter parameters in one weight tensor $\mathbf{W}$, that tensor will be of dimension (filter rows × filter columns × input channels × output channels). In the second convolutional layer in Figure 6.14, the corresponding weight matrix $\mathbf{W}^{(2)}$ is a tensor of dimension $3 \times 3 \times 4 \times 6$. With multiple filters in each convolutional layer, each of them can be sensitive to different features in the image, such as certain edges, lines, or circles, enabling a rich representation of the images in our training data.

The convolutional layer with multiple input channels and output channels can be described mathematically as

$$q_{ijn}^{(l)} = h\left(\sum_{k=1}^{F_l}\sum_{l=1}^{F_l}\sum_{m=1}^{U_{l-1}} q_{s_l(i-1)+k-1,\,s_l(j-1)+l,\,m}^{(l-1)} W_{k,l,m,n}^{(l)}\right), \tag{6.32}$$

where $q_{ijm}^{(l-1)}$ is the input to layer l, $q_{ijn}^{(l)}$ is the output from layer l, U_{l-1} is the number of input channels, F_l is the filter rows/columns, s_l is the stride, and $W_{k,l,m,n}^{(l)}$ is the weight tensor.

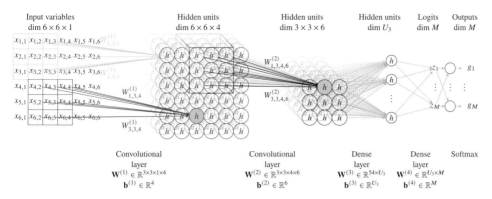

Figure 6.14 A full CNN architecture for classification of greyscale 6×6 images. In the first convolutional layer, four filters, each of size 3×3, produce a hidden layer with four channels. The first channel (in the back) is visualised in red, and the forth channel (in the front) is visualised in blue. We use stride 1, which maintains the number of rows and columns. In the second convolutional layer, six filters of size $3 \times 3 \times 4$ and stride 2 are used. They produce a hidden layer with 3 rows, 3 columns, and 6 channels. After the two convolutional layers follows a dense layer where all $3 \cdot 3 \cdot 6 = 54$ hidden units in the second hidden layer are densely connected to all U_3 hidden units in the third layer, where all links have their unique parameters. We add an additional dense layer mapping down to the M logits. The network ends with a softmax function to provide predicted class probabilities as output. Note that the arrows corresponding to the offset parameters are not included here in order to make the figure less cluttered.

Full CNN Architecture

A full CNN architecture consists of multiple convolutional layers. For predictive tasks, we decrease the number of rows and columns in the hidden layers as we proceed through the network but instead increase the number of channels to enable the network to encode more high level features. After a few convolutional layers, we usually end the network with one or more dense layers. If we consider an image classification task, we place a softmax layer at the very end to get outputs in the range [0,1]. The loss function when training a CNN will be the same as in the regression and classification networks explained earlier, depending on what type of problem we have at hand. Figure 6.14 shows a small example of a full CNN architecture.

Example 6.3 Classification of hand-written digits – convolutional neural network

In the previous models explained in Examples 6.1 and 6.2, we placed all the 28×28 pixels of each image into a long vector with 784 elements. With this action, we did not exploit the information that two neighbouring pixels are more likely to be correlated than two pixels further apart. Instead, we now keep the matrix structure of the data and use a CNN with three convolutional layers and two dense layers. The settings for the layers are given in the table below.

| | Convolutional layers | | | Dense layers | |
	Layer 1	**Layer 2**	**Layer 3**	**Layer 4**	**Layer 5**
Number of filters/output channels	4	8	12	–	–
Filter rows and columns	(5×5)	(5×5)	(4×4)	–	–
Stride	1	2	2	–	–
Number of hidden units	3 136	1 568	588	200	10
Number of parameters (including offset vector)	104	808	1 548	117 800	2 010

In a high-dimensional parameter space, saddle points in the cost function are frequent. Since the gradients are zero also at these saddle points, stochastic gradient descent might get stuck there. Therefore, we train this model using an extension of stochastic gradient descent called Adam (short for adaptive moment estimation). Adam uses running averages on the gradients and their second order moments and can pass these saddle points more easily. For the Adam optimiser, we use a learning rate of $\gamma = 0.002$. In Figure 6.15, the cost function and the misclassification rate on the current training mini-batch and the validation data are displayed. The shaded red line is the performance on the validation data for the two-layer network that was presented in Example 6.2.

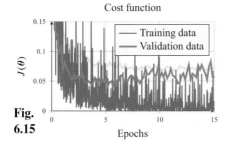

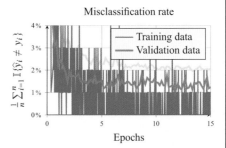

Fig. 6.15

In comparison to the result on the dense two-layer network, we can see an improvement going from 2% down to just over 1% misclassification on the validation data. From Figure 6.15 we can also see that the performance on validation data does not quite settle but is fluctuating in the span 1–1.5%. As explained in Section 5.5, this is due to the randomness introduced by stochastic gradient descent itself. To

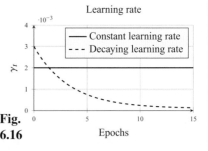

Fig. 6.16

circumvent this effect, we use decaying learning rate. We use the scheme suggested in (5.38), with $\gamma_{max} = 0.003$, $\gamma_{min} = 0.0001$, and $\tau = 2\,000$ (Figure 6.16).

After employing the adaptive learning rate in Figure 6.17, the misclassification rate on validation data settles around 1% rather than only sometimes bouncing down to 1% as it did before we applied a decaying learning rate. However, we can do more. In the last epochs, we get almost all data points correct in the current mini-batch. In addition, looking at the plot for the cost function evaluated for the validation data, it

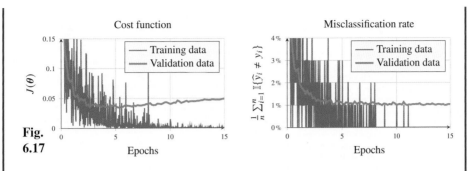

Fig. 6.17

starts increasing after five epochs. Hence, we see signs of overfitting as we did at the end of Example 6.2 . To circumvent this overfitting, we can add regularisation. One popular regularisation method for neural networks is dropout, which is explained in the following section.

> **Time to reflect 6.2** *In the table in Example 6.3, the number of parameters for all five layers, as well as the number of hidden units for the three convolutional layers, can all be computed from the remaining numbers in that table and previously stated information. Can you do this computation?*

6.4 Dropout

Like all models presented in this course, neural network models can suffer from overfitting if we have too flexible a model in relation to the complexity of the data. One way to reduce the variance, and by that also reduce the risk of overfitting, is by training not just one model but multiple models and averaging their predictions. This is the main idea behind *bagging*, which we present in more detail in Chapter 7. To set the terminology, we say that we train an *ensemble* of models, and each model we refer to as an *ensamble member*.

Bagging is also applicable to neural networks. However, it comes with some practical problems. A large neural network model usually takes quite some time to train, and it has many parameters to store. To train not just one but an entire ensemble of many large neural networks would thus be very costly, both in terms of runtime and memory. *Dropout* is a bagging-like technique that allows us to combine many neural networks without the need to train them separately. The trick is to let the different models share parameters with each other, which reduces the computational cost and memory requirement.

Ensemble of Sub-networks

Consider a dense neural network like the one in Figure 6.18a. In dropout, we construct the equivalent to an ensemble member by randomly removing some of

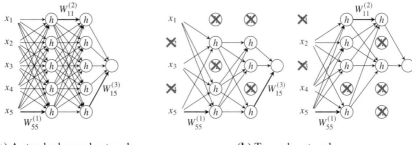

(a) A standard neural network **(b)** Two sub-networks

Figure 6.18 A neural network with two hidden layers (a) and two sub-networks with dropped units (b). The collection of units that have been dropped are independent between the two sub-networks.

the hidden units. We say that we drop the units, hence the name dropout. When a unit is removed, we also remove all of its incoming and outgoing connections. With this procedure, we obtain a sub-network that only contains a subset of the units and parameters present in the original network. Two such sub-networks are displayed in Figure 6.18b.

Mathematically, we can write this as sampling a *mask* $\mathbf{m}^{(l-1)} = [m_1^{(l-1)} \ \ldots \ m_{U_{l-1}}^{(l-1)}]$ for each layer, multiplying that mask element-wise with the hidden units $\mathbf{q}^{(l-1)}$, and then feeding the masked hidden units $\tilde{\mathbf{q}}^{(l-1)}$ to the next layer:

$$m_j^{(l-1)} = \begin{cases} 1 & \text{with probability} \quad r \\ 0 & \text{with probability} \quad 1-r, \end{cases} \quad \text{for all} \quad j = 1,\ldots,U_{l-1}, \quad (6.33a)$$

$$\tilde{\mathbf{q}}^{(l-1)} = \mathbf{m}^{(l-1)} \odot \mathbf{q}^{(l-1)}, \quad (6.33b)$$

$$\mathbf{q}^{(l)} = h(\mathbf{W}^{(l)}\tilde{\mathbf{q}}^{(l-1)} + \mathbf{b}^{(l)}). \quad (6.33c)$$

The probability r of keeping a unit is a hyperparameter set by the user. We can choose to apply dropout to all layers or only some of them and can also use different probabilities r for the different layers. We can also apply dropout to the input variables as we do in Figure 6.18b. However, we do not apply dropout on the output units. Since all sub-networks stem from the very same original network, the different sub-networks share some parameters with each other. For example, in Figure 6.18b, the parameter $W_{55}^{(1)}$ is present in both sub-networks. The fact that they share parameters with each other allows us to train the ensemble of sub-networks in an efficient manner.

Training with Dropout

To train with dropout, we use stochastic gradient descent as described in Algorithm 5.3. In each gradient step, a mini-batch of data is used to compute an approximation

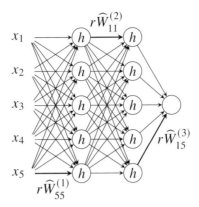

Figure 6.19 The network used for prediction after being trained with dropout. All units and links are present (no dropout), but the weights going out from a certain unit are multiplied by the probability of that unit being included during training. This is to compensate for the fact that some of them were dropped during training. Here all units have been kept with probability r during training (and consequently dropped with probability $1 - r$).

of the gradient, as normally done in stochastic gradient descent. However, instead of computing the gradient for the full network, we generate a random sub-network by randomly dropping units as described above. We compute the gradient for that sub-network and then do a gradient step. This gradient step only updates the parameters present in the sub-network. The parameters that are associated with the dropped units do not affect the output of that sub-network and are hence left untouched. In the next gradient step, we use another mini-batch of data, remove another randomly selected collection of units, and update the parameters present in that sub-network. We proceed in this manner until some terminal condition is fulfilled.

Prediction at Test Time

After we have trained the sub-networks, we want to make a prediction based on an unseen input data point $\mathbf{x}_\star$. If this was an ensemble method, we would evaluate all possible sub-networks and average their predictions. Since each unit can be either in our out, there are 2^U such sub-networks, where U is the total number of units in the network. Hence, due to this large number, evaluating all of them would be infeasible. However, there is a simple trick to approximately achieve the same result. Instead of evaluating all possible sub-networks, we simply evaluate the full network containing all the parameters. To compensate for the fact that the model was trained with dropout, we multiply each estimated parameter going out from a unit by the probability of that unit being kept during training. This ensures that the expected value of the input to the next unit is the same during training and testing. If during training, we kept a unit in layer $l-1$ with probability r, then during prediction we multiply the following weight matrix $\mathbf{W}^{(l)}$ with r, that is

$$\tilde{\mathbf{W}}^{(l)} = r\mathbf{W}^{(l)}, \tag{6.34a}$$

$$\mathbf{q}^{(l)} = h(\tilde{\mathbf{W}}^{(l)}\mathbf{q}^{(l-1)} + \mathbf{b}^{(l)}). \tag{6.34b}$$

This is also illustrated in Figure 6.19, where we have kept a unit with probability r in all layers during training. This adjustment of the weights can, of course, be done just once after we are done training and then these adjusted weights used as usual during all coming predictions.

This procedure of approximating the average over all ensemble members has been shown to work surprisingly well in practice even though there is not yet any solid theoretical argument for the accuracy of this approximation.

Dropout vs. Bagging

As already pointed out, dropout has similarities with the ensamble method called bagging. If you have already learned about bagging in Chapter 7, there are a few important differences to point out:

- In bagging, all models are independent in the sense that they have their own parameters. In dropout, the different models (the sub-networks) share parameters.

- In bagging, each model is trained until convergence. In dropout, most of the U^2 sub-networks are not trained at all (since they have not been sampled), and those that have been trained have most likely only been trained for one singe gradient step. However, since they share parameters, all models will also be updated when the other sub-networks are trained.

- Similar to bagging, in dropout, we train each model on a dataset that has been randomly selected from our training data. However, in bagging, we usually do it on a bootstrapped version of the whole dataset, whereas in dropout, each model is trained on a randomly selected mini-batch of data.

Even though dropout differs from bagging in some aspects, it has empirically been shown to enjoy similar properties as bagging in terms of avoiding overfitting and reducing the variance of the model.

Dropout as a Regularisation Method

As a way to reduce the variance and avoid overfitting, dropout can be seen as a regularisation method. There are plenty of other regularisation methods for neural networks, including explicit regularisation (like L^1 and L^2 regularisation; see Chapter 5), early stopping (the training is stopped before the parameters have converged; see Chapter 5), and various sparse representations (for example, CNNs can be seen as a regularisation method where most parameters are forced to be zero), just to mention a few. Since its invention, dropout has become one of the most popular regularisation techniques due to its simplicity, the fact that it is computationally cheap, and its good performance. In fact, a good practice of designing a neural network is often to extended the network until it overfits, then extend it a bit more, and finally add a regularisation like dropout to avoid that overfitting.

Example 6.4 Classification of hand-written digits – regularising with dropout

We return to the last model in Example 6.3, where we used a CNN trained with an adaptive learning rate. In the results, we could see clear indications of overfitting. To reduce this overfitting, we employ dropout during the training procedure. We use dropout in the final hidden layer and keep only $r = 75\%$ of the 200 hidden units in that layer at each iteration. The result for this regularised model is presented in Figure 6.20. In shaded red, we also present the performance on validation data for the non-regularised version which was already presented at the end of Example 6.3.

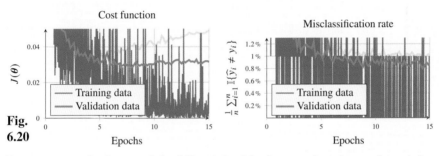

Fig. 6.20

In contrast to the last model of Example 6.3, the cost function evaluated for the validation data is (almost) no longer increasing, and we also reduce the misclassification rate by an additional 0.1% to 0.2%.

6.5 Further Reading

Although the first conceptual ideas of neural networks date back to the 1940s (McCulloch and Pitts 1943), they had their first main success stories in the late 1980s and early 1990s with the use of the so-called backpropagation algorithm. At that stage, neural networks could, for example, be used to classify handwritten digits from low-resolution images (LeCun, Boser, et al. 1989). However, in the late 1990s, neural networks were largely forsaken because it was widely believed that they could not be used to solve any challenging problems in computer vision and speech recognition. In these areas, neural networks could not compete with hand-crafted solutions based on domain-specific prior knowledge.

This situation has changed dramatically since the late 2000s under the name deep learning. Progress in software, hardware, and algorithm parallelisation made it possible to address more complicated problems, which were unthinkable only a couple of decades ago. For example, in image recognition, these deep models are now the dominant methods in use, and they reach human or even super-human performance on some specific tasks. An accessible introduction to and overview of deep learning is provided by LeCun, Bengio, et al. (2015), and via the textbook by Goodfellow, Bengio, et al. (2016).

6.A Derivation of the Backpropagation Equations

To derive the backpropagation equations (6.27), consider the non-vectorised version of layer l:

$$\begin{cases} z_j^{(l)} = \sum_k W_{jk}^{(l)} q_k^{(l-1)} + b_j^{(l)} \\ q_j^{(l)} = h(z_j^{(l)}) \end{cases}, \qquad \forall j = 1, \dots U^{(l)}. \tag{6.35}$$

Assume that we want to compute the derivatives of the cost function with respect to the parameters $W_{jk}^{(l)}$ and $b_j^{(l)}$. Note that the cost function $J(\boldsymbol{\theta})$ depends on both $W_{jk}^{(l)}$ and $b_j^{(l)}$ only via the hidden unit $z_j^{(l)}$ (and non of the other hidden units in that layer). We can use the chain rule of calculus to write

$$\frac{\partial J}{\partial b_j^{(l)}} = \frac{\partial J}{\partial z_j^{(l)}} \underbrace{\frac{\partial z_j^{(l)}}{\partial b_j^{(l)}}}_{=1} = \frac{\partial J}{\partial z_j^{(l)}},$$

$$\frac{\partial J}{\partial W_{jk}^{(l)}} = \frac{\partial J}{\partial z_j^{(l)}} \underbrace{\frac{\partial z_j^{(l)}}{\partial W_{jk}^{(l)}}}_{=q_k^{(l-1)}} = \frac{\partial J}{\partial z_j^{(l)}} q_k^{(l-1)}, \qquad \forall j = 1, \dots U^{(l)}, \tag{6.36}$$

where the partial derivatives of $z_j^{(l)}$ with respect to $W_{jk}^{(l)}$ and $b_j^{(l)}$ can be directly derived from (6.35).

Similarly, we can also use the chain rule to compute the partial derivative of $J(\boldsymbol{\theta})$ with respect to the post-activation hidden unit $q_k^{(l-1)}$ for layer $l - 1$. Note, $J(\boldsymbol{\theta})$ depends on $q_k^{(l-1)}$ via all of the pre-activation hidden units $\{z_j^{(l)}\}_{j=1}^{U^{(l)}}$ in layer l; hence we get

$$\frac{\partial J}{\partial q_k^{(l-1)}} = \sum_j \frac{\partial J}{\partial z_j^{(l)}} \underbrace{\frac{\partial z_j^{(l)}}{\partial q_k^{(l-1)}}}_{W_{jk}^{(l)}} = \sum_j \frac{\partial J}{\partial z_j^{(l)}} W_{jk}^{(l)}, \qquad \forall k = 1, \dots U^{(l-1)}. \tag{6.37}$$

Finally, we can also use the chain rule to express

$$\frac{\partial J}{\partial z_j^{(l)}} = \frac{\partial J}{\partial q_j^{(l)}}\frac{\partial q_j^{(l)}}{\partial z_j^{(l)}} = \frac{\partial J}{\partial q_j^{(l)}}h'(z_j^{(l)}), \qquad \forall j = 1,\dots U^{(l)}, \tag{6.38}$$

where h' is the derivative of the activation function. With the vectorised notation for $d\mathbf{W}$, $d\mathbf{b}$, $d\mathbf{z}$, and $d\mathbf{q}$ introduced in (6.2) and (6.25), we get that Equation (6.38) gives (6.27a), Equation (6.37) gives (6.27b), and Section 6.A gives (6.27c)–(6.27d).

7 Ensemble Methods
Bagging and Boosting

In the preceding chapters, we have seen several examples of different machine learning models, from k-NN to deep neural networks. In this chapter, we will introduce a new way of constructing models, by combining multiple instances of some basic model. We refer to this as an *ensemble of base models*, and the resulting methods are consequently referred to as *ensemble methods*. The key idea behind ensemble methods is the 'wisdom of crowds': by training each base model in a slightly different way, they can all contribute to learning the input–output relationship. Specifically, to obtain a prediction from an ensemble, we let each base model make its own prediction and then use a (possibly weighted) average or majority vote to obtain the final prediction. With a carefully constructed ensemble, the prediction obtained in this way is better than the predictions of the individual base models.

We start in Section 7.1 by introducing a general technique referred to as bootstrap aggregating, or *bagging* for short. The bagging idea is to first create multiple slightly different 'versions' of the training data by, essentially, randomly sampling overlapping subsets of the training data (the so-called bootstrap). Thereafter, one base model is trained from each such 'version' of the training data. In this way, an ensemble of similar, but not identical, base models is obtained. With this procedure it is possible to *reduce the variance* (without any notable increase in bias) compared to using only a single base model trained on the entire training dataset. In practice, this means that by using bagging, the risk of overfitting decreases compared to using the base model itself. In Section 7.2 we introduce an extension to bagging only applicable when the base model is a classification or regression tree, which results in a powerful off-the-shelf method called random forests. In random forests, each tree is randomly perturbed in order to obtain additional variance reduction, beyond what is already obtained by the bagging procedure itself.

In Sections 7.3–7.4 we introduce another ensemble method known as *boosting*. Boosting is different from bagging and random forests, since its base models are trained sequentially, one after the other, where each model tries to 'correct' for the 'mistakes' made by the previous ones. Contrary to bagging, the main effect of boosting is *bias reduction* compared to the base model. Thus, boosting is able to turn an ensemble of 'weak' base models (e.g., linear classifiers) into one 'strong' ensemble model (e.g., a heavily non-linear classifier).

7.1 Bagging

As already discussed in Chapter 4, a central concept in machine learning is the bias–variance trade-off. Roughly speaking, the more flexible a model is, the lower its bias will be. That is, a flexible model is capable of representing complicated input–output relationships. Examples of simple yet flexible models are k-NN with a small value of k and a classification tree that is grown deep. Such highly flexible models are sometimes needed for solving real-world machine learning problems, where relationships are far from linear. The downside, however, is the risk of overfitting, or equivalently, high model variance. Despite their high variance, those models are not useless. By using them as base models in bootstrap aggregating, or *bagging*, we can

> reduce the variance of the base model without increasing its bias.

We outline the main idea of bagging with the example below.

Example 7.1 Using bagging for a regression problem

Consider the data (black dots) that are drawn from a function (dashed line) plus noise in Figure 7.1a. As always in supervised machine learning, we want to train a model from the data which is able to predict new data points well. Being able to predict new data points well means, among other things, that the model should predict the dotted line at $x_\star$ (the empty blue circle) well.

To solve this problem, we could use any regression method. Here, we use a regression tree which is grown until each leaf node only contains one data point, whose prediction is shown to the lower left in Figure 7.1c (blue line and dot). This is a typical low-bias high-variance model, and the overfit to the training data is apparent from the figure. We could decrease its variance, and hence the overfitting, by using a shallower tree, but that would on the other hand increase the bias. Instead, we lower the variance (without increasing the bias much) by using bagging with the regression tree as base model.

The rationale behind bagging goes as follows: Because of the noise in the training data, we may think of the prediction $\hat{y}(x_\star)$ (the blue dot) as a random variable. In bagging, we learn an ensemble of base models (Figure 7.1b), where each base model is trained on a different 'version' of the training data, obtained using the bootstrap. We may therefore think of each base model as a different realisation of the random variable $\hat{y}(x_\star)$. The average of multiple realisations of a random variable has a lower variance than the random variable itself, which means that by taking the average (Figure 7.1d) of all the base models, we obtain a prediction with less variance than the base model itself. That is, the bagged regression tree (Figure 7.1d) has lower variance than a single prediction tree (Figure 7.1c). Since the base model itself also has low bias, the averaged prediction will have low bias *and* low variance. We can visually confirm that the prediction is better (blue dot and circle are closer to each other) for bagging than for the single regression tree.

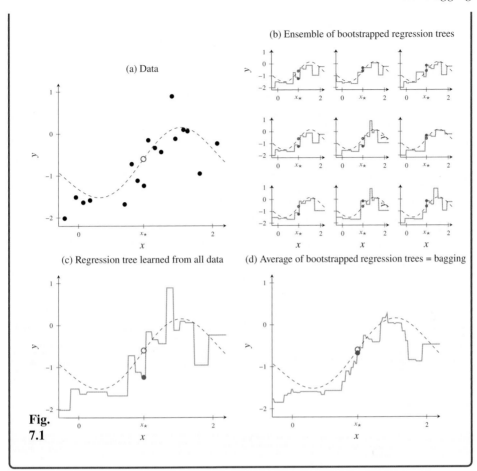

(a) Data

(b) Ensemble of bootstrapped regression trees

(c) Regression tree learned from all data

(d) Average of bootstrapped regression trees = bagging

Fig. 7.1

The Bootstrap

As outlined in Example 7.1, the idea of bagging is to average over multiple base models, each learned from a different training dataset. Therefore, we first have to construct different training datasets. In the best of worlds, we would just collect multiple datasets, but most often we cannot do that and instead we have to make the most of the limited data available. For this purpose, the bootstrap is useful.

The bootstrap is a method for artificially creating multiple datasets (of size n) out of one dataset (also of size n). The traditional usage of the bootstrap is to quantify uncertainties in statistical estimators (such as confidence intervals), but it turns out that it can also be used to construct machine learning models. We denote the original dataset $\mathcal{T} = \{\mathbf{x}_i, y_i\}_{i=1}^{n}$ and assume that $\mathcal{T}$ provides a good representation of the real-world data generating process, in the sense that *if* we were to collect more training data, these data points would likely be similar to the training data points already contained in $\mathcal{T}$. We can thus argue that randomly picking data points from $\mathcal{T}$ is a reasonable way to simulate a 'new' training dataset. In statistical terms, instead of sampling from the population (collecting more data), we sample from the available training data, which is assumed to provide a good representation of the population.

The bootstrap is stated in Algorithm 7.1 and illustrated in Example 7.2 below. Note that the sampling is done with replacement, meaning that the resulting bootstrapped dataset may contain multiple copies of some of the original training data points, whereas other data points may not be included at all.

Algorithm 7.1: The bootstrap.

Data: Training dataset $\mathcal{T} = \{\mathbf{x}_i, y_i\}_{i=1}^n$

Result: Bootstrapped data $\widetilde{\mathcal{T}} = \{\widetilde{\mathbf{x}}_i, \widetilde{y}_i\}_{i=1}^n$

1 **for** $i = 1, \ldots, n$ **do**

2 $\quad$ Sample ℓ uniformly on the set of integers $\{1, \ldots, n\}$

3 $\quad$ Set $\widetilde{\mathbf{x}}_i = \mathbf{x}_\ell$ and $\widetilde{y}_i = y_\ell$

4 **end**

> **Time to reflect 7.1** *What would happen if the sampling was done without replacement in the bootstrap?*

Example 7.2 The bootstrap

We have a small training dataset with $n = 10$ data points, with a two-dimensional input $\mathbf{x} = [x_1 \ x_2]$ and a binary output $y \in \{\text{Blue}, \text{Red}\}$ (see Figure 7.2).

Original training data, $\mathcal{T} = \{\mathbf{x}_i, y_i\}_{i=1}^{10}$

Index	x_1	x_2	y
1	9.0	2.0	Blue
2	1.0	4.0	Blue
3	4.0	6.0	Blue
4	4.0	1.0	Blue
5	1.0	2.0	Blue
6	1.0	8.0	Red
7	6.0	4.0	Red
8	7.0	9.0	Red
9	9.0	8.0	Red
10	9.0	6.0	Red

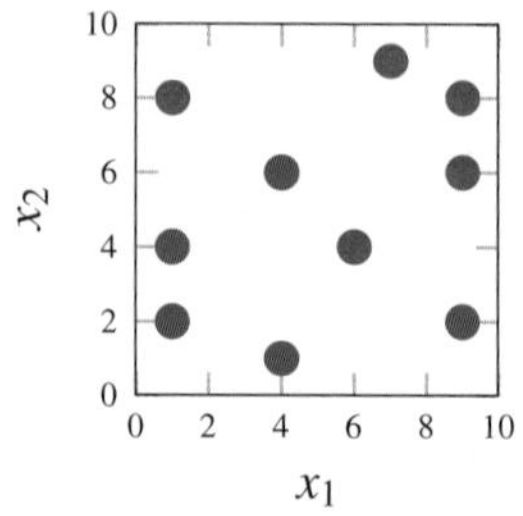

Fig. 7.2

To generate a bootstrapped dataset $\widetilde{\mathcal{T}} = \{\widetilde{\mathbf{x}}_i, \widetilde{y}_i\}_{i=1}^{10}$, we simulate 10 times with replacement from the index set $\{1, \ldots, 10\}$, resulting in the indices $\{2, 10, 10, 5, 9, 2, 5, 10, 8, 10\}$. Thus, $(\widetilde{\mathbf{x}}_1, \widetilde{y}_1) = (\mathbf{x}_2, y_2)$, $(\widetilde{\mathbf{x}}_2, \widetilde{y}_2) = (\mathbf{x}_{10}, y_{10})$, etc. We end up with the dataset in Figure 7.3, where the numbers in parentheses in the right panel indicate that there are multiple copies of some of the original data points in the bootstrapped data.

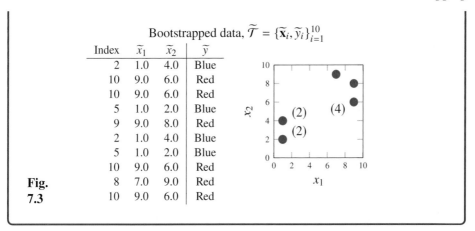

Fig. 7.3

Variance Reduction by Averaging

By running the bootstrap (Algorithm 7.1) repeatedly B times, we obtain B random but *identically distributed* bootstrapped datasets $\widetilde{\mathcal{T}}^{(1)}, \ldots, \widetilde{\mathcal{T}}^{(B)}$. We can then use those bootstrapped datasets to train an ensemble of B base models. We thereafter average their predictions

$$\widehat{y}_{\text{bag}}(\mathbf{x}_\star) = \frac{1}{B}\sum_{b=1}^{B}\widetilde{y}^{(b)}(\mathbf{x}_\star) \quad \text{or} \quad \mathbf{g}_{\text{bag}}(\mathbf{x}_\star) = \frac{1}{B}\sum_{b=1}^{B}\widetilde{\mathbf{g}}^{(b)}(\mathbf{x}_\star), \tag{7.1}$$

depending on whether we are concerned with regression (predicting an output value $\widehat{y}_{\text{bag}}(\mathbf{x}_\star)$) or classification (predicting class probabilities $\mathbf{g}_{\text{bag}}(\mathbf{x}_\star)$). The latter expression assumes that each base classifier outputs a vector of class probabilities. If this is not the case, we can instead obtain a 'hard' class prediction by taking a majority vote among the ensemble members. Note that it is natural to take a plain average across the ensemble (each member is weighted equally) in (7.1) due to the fact that all ensemble members are constructed in the same way, that is, they are identically distributed.

In (7.1), $\widetilde{y}^{(1)}(\mathbf{x}_\star), \ldots, \widetilde{y}^{(B)}(\mathbf{x}_\star)$ and $\widetilde{\mathbf{g}}^{(1)}(\mathbf{x}_\star), \ldots, \widetilde{\mathbf{g}}^{(B)}(\mathbf{x}_\star)$ denote the predictions from the individual ensemble members. The averaged prediction, denoted $\widehat{y}_{\text{bag}}(\mathbf{x}_\star)$ or $\mathbf{g}_{\text{bag}}(\mathbf{x}_\star)$, is the final prediction obtained from bagging. We summarise this by Method 7.1. (For classification, the prediction could alternatively be decided by majority vote among the ensemble members, but that typically degrades the performance slightly compared to averaging the predicted class probabilities.)

We will now give some more details on the variance reduction that happens in (7.1), which is the entire point of bagging. We focus on regression, but the intuition also works for classification.

First we make a basic observation regarding random variables, namely that averaging reduces variance. To formalise this, let $z_1, \ldots, z_B$ be a collection of identically distributed (but possibly dependent) random variables with mean value $\mathbb{E}[z_b] = \mu$ and variance $\text{Var}[z_b] = \sigma^2$ for $b = 1, \ldots, B$. Furthermore, assume that

167

Learn all base models

Data: Training dataset $\mathcal{T} = \{\mathbf{x}_i, y_i\}_{i=1}^n$
Result: B base models

1 **for** $b = 1, \ldots, B$ **do**
2   Run Algorithm 7.1 to obtain a bootstrapped training dataset $\widetilde{\mathcal{T}}^{(b)}$
3   Learn a base model from $\widetilde{\mathcal{T}}^{(b)}$
4 **end**
5 Obtain $\widehat{y}_{\text{bag}}(\mathbf{x}_\star)$ or $\mathbf{g}_{\text{bag}}(\mathbf{x}_\star)$ by averaging (7.1).

Predict with the base models

Data: B base models and test input $\mathbf{x}_\star$
Result: A prediction $\widehat{y}_{\text{bag}}(\mathbf{x}_\star)$ or $\mathbf{g}_{\text{bag}}(\mathbf{x}_\star)$

1 **for** $b = 1, \ldots, B$ **do**
2   Use base model b to predict $\widetilde{y}^{(b)}(\mathbf{x}_\star)$ or $\widetilde{\mathbf{g}}^{(b)}(\mathbf{x}_\star)$
3 **end**
4 Obtain $\widehat{y}_{\text{bag}}(\mathbf{x}_\star)$ or $\mathbf{g}_{\text{bag}}(\mathbf{x}_\star)$ by averaging (7.1).

Method 7.1 Bagging

the average correlation[1] between any pair of variables is ρ. Then, computing the mean and the variance of *the average* $\frac{1}{B}\sum_{b=1}^{B} z_b$ of these variables, we get

$$\mathbb{E}\left[\frac{1}{B}\sum_{b=1}^{B} z_b\right] = \mu, \tag{7.2a}$$

$$\text{Var}\left[\frac{1}{B}\sum_{b=1}^{B} z_b\right] = \frac{1-\rho}{B}\sigma^2 + \rho\sigma^2. \tag{7.2b}$$

The first equation (7.2a) tells us that the mean is unaltered by averaging a number of identically distributed random variables. Furthermore, the second equation (7.2b) tells us that the variance is reduced by averaging if the correlation $\rho < 1$. The first term in the variance expression (7.2b) can be made arbitrarily small by increasing B, whereas the second term is only determined by the correlation ρ and variance σ^2.

To make a connection between bagging and (7.2), consider the predictions $\widetilde{y}^{(b)}(\mathbf{x}_\star)$ from the base models as random variables. All base models, and hence their predictions, originate from the same data $\mathcal{T}$ (via the bootstrap), and $\widetilde{y}^{(b)}(\mathbf{x}_\star)$ are therefore identically distributed but correlated. By averaging the predictions, we decrease the variance, according to (7.2b). If we choose B large enough, the achieved variance reduction will be limited by the correlation ρ. Experience has shown that ρ

---

[1] That is, $\frac{1}{B(B-1)}\sum_{b\neq c}\mathbb{E}[(z_b - \mu)(z_c - \mu)] = \rho\sigma^2$.

is often small enough such that the computational complexity of bagging (compared to only using the base model itself) pays off well in terms of decreased variance. To summarise, by averaging the identically distributed predictions from several base models as in (7.1), each with a low bias, the *bias remains low*[2] (according to (7.2a)), and *the variance is reduced* (according to (7.2b)).

At first glance, one might think that a bagging model (7.1) becomes more 'complex' as the number of ensemble members B increases, and that we therefore run a risk of overfitting if we use many ensemble members B. However, there is nothing in (7.2) which indicates any such problem (bias remains low; variance decreases), and we confirm this by Example 7.3.

Example 7.3 Bagging for regression (continued)

We consider the problem from Example 7.1 again and explore how the number of base models B affects the result. We measure the squared error between the 'true' function value at $x_\star$ and the predicted $\widehat{y}^{\text{bag}}(x_\star)$ when using different values of B. (Because of the bootstrap, there is a certain amount of randomness in the bagging algorithm itself. To avoid that 'noise', we average the result over multiple runs of the bagging algorithm.)

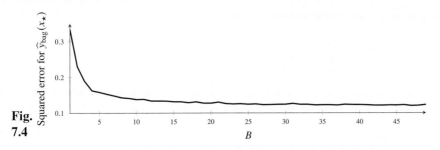

Fig. 7.4

What we see in Figure 7.4 is that the squared error eventually reaches a plateau as $B \to \infty$. Had there been an overfitting issue with $B \to \infty$, the squared error would have started to increase again for some large value of B.

Despite the fact that the number of parameters in the model increases as B increases, the lack of overfitting as $B \to \infty$ according to Example 7.3 is the expected (and intended) behaviour. It is important to understand that from the construction of bagging, *more ensemble members does not make the resulting model more flexible* but only reduces the variance. This can be understood by noting that the addition of an ensemble member to the bagging model is *not* done in order to obtain a better fit to the training data. On the contrary, if each ensemble member overfits to its own perturbed version of the training data, the averaging across the ensemble will result

---

[2] Strictly speaking, (7.2a) implies that the bias is identical for a single ensemble member and the ensemble average. The use of the bootstrap might, however, affect the bias, in that a base model trained on the original data might have a smaller bias than a base model trained on a bootstrapped version of the training data. Most often, this is not an issue in practice.

in a smoothing effect which typically results in a larger training error (compared to the individual ensemble members' training errors) but also better generalisation. We can also understand this by considering the limiting behavior as $B \to \infty$. By the law of large numbers and the fact that the ensemble members are identically distributed, the bagging model becomes

$$\widehat{y}_{\text{bag}}(x_\star) = \frac{1}{B} \sum_{b=1}^{B} \widetilde{y}^{(b)}(x_\star) \xrightarrow{B \to \infty} \mathbb{E}\left[\widetilde{y}^{(b)}(x_\star) \mid \mathcal{T}\right], \tag{7.3}$$

where the expectation is with respect to the randomness of the bootstrapping algorithm. As B increases, we expect the bagging model to converge to the hypothetical (limited flexibility) model on the right hand side. With this in mind, in practice the choice of B is mainly guided by computational constraints. The larger B is, the better, but increasing B when there is no further reduction in test error is computationally wasteful.

Be aware! *Bagging can still suffer from overfitting since each individual ensemble member can overfit. The only claim we have made is that the overfitting is not caused by (or made worse by) using too many ensemble members and, conceptually, there is no problem with taking $B \to \infty$.*

Out-of-Bag Error Estimation

When using bagging (or random forests, which we discuss below), it turns out that there is a way to estimate the expected new data error E_{new} *without* using cross-validation. The first observation we have to make is that not all data points from the original dataset $\mathcal{T}$ will have been used for training all ensemble members. It can be shown that with the bootstrap, on average only 63% of the original training data points in $\mathcal{T} = \{x_i, y_i\}_{i=1}^{n}$ will be present in a bootstrapped training dataset $\widetilde{\mathcal{T}} = \{\widetilde{x}_i, \widetilde{y}_i\}_{i=1}^{n}$. Roughly speaking, this means that for any given $\{x_i, y_i\}$ in $\mathcal{T}$, about one third of the ensemble members will not have seen that data point during training. We refer to these (roughly $B/3$) ensemble members as being out-of-bag for data point i, and we let them form their own ensemble: the ith out-of-bag-ensemble. Note that the out-of-bag-ensemble is different for each data point $\{x_i, y_i\}$.

The next key insight is that for the out-of-bag-ensemble i, the data point $\{x_i, y_i\}$ can act as a test data point since it has not yet been seen by any of its ensemble members. By computing the (e.g., squared or misclassification) error when the out-of-bag-ensemble i predicts $\{x_i, y_i\}$, we thus get an estimate of E_{new} for this out-of-bag-ensemble, which we denote $E_{\text{OOB}}^{(i)}$. Since $E_{\text{OOB}}^{(i)}$ is based on only one data point, it will be a fairly poor estimate of E_{new}. However, if we repeat this for all data points $\{x_i, y_i\}$ in the training data $\mathcal{T}$ and average $E_{\text{OOB}} = \frac{1}{n} \sum_{i=1}^{n} E_{\text{OOB}}^{(i)}$, we get a better estimate of E_{new}. Indeed, E_{OOB} will be an estimate of E_{new} for an ensemble with only $B/3$ (and not B) members, but as we have seen (Example 7.3), the performance of bagging plateaus after a certain number of ensemble members.

Hence, if B is large enough so that ensembles with B and $B/3$ members perform similarly, E_{OOB} provides an estimate of E_{new} which can be at least as good as the estimate $E_{k\text{-fold}}$ from k-fold cross-validation. Most importantly, however, E_{OOB} comes almost for free in bagging, whereas $E_{k\text{-fold}}$ requires much more computation when re-training k times.

7.2 Random Forests

In bagging, we reduce the variance by averaging over an ensemble of models. Unfortunately, the variance reduction is limited by the correlation between the individual ensemble members (compare this with the dependence on the average correlation ρ in (7.2b)). However, using a simple trick, it is possible to reduce the correlation beyond what is achieved by the bootstrap, resulting in a method referred to as *random forests*.

While bagging is a general technique that in principle can be used to reduce the variance of any base model, random forests assume that these base models are classification or regression trees. The idea is to inject additional randomness when constructing each tree, in order to further reduce the correlation among the base models. At first this might seem like a silly idea: randomly perturbing the training of a model should intuitively degrade its performance. There is a rationale for this perturbation, however, which we will discuss below, but first we present the details of the algorithm.

Let $\widetilde{\mathcal{T}}^{(b)}$ be one of the B bootstrapped datasets in bagging. To train a classification or regression tree on this data, we proceed as usual (see Section 2.3) but with one difference. Throughout the training, whenever we are about to split a node, we do not consider all possible input variables $x_1, \ldots, x_p$ as splitting variables. Instead, we pick a random subset consisting of $q \leq p$ inputs and only consider these q variables as possible splitting variables. At the next splitting point, we draw a new random subset of q inputs to use as possible splitting variables, and so on. Naturally, this random subset selection is done independently for each of the B ensemble members, so that we (with high probability) end up using different subsets for the different trees. This additional random constraint when training is what turns bagging into *random forests*. This will cause the B trees to be less correlated, and averaging their predictions can therefore result in a larger variance reduction compared to bagging. It should be noted, however, that this random perturbation of the training procedure will increase the variance[3] of each *individual tree*. In the notation of Equation (7.2b), the random forest decreases ρ (good) but increases σ^2 (bad) compared to bagging. Experience has, however, shown that the reduction in correlation is the dominant

---

[3] And possibly also the bias, in a similar manner as the bootstrap might increase the bias; see Footnote 2, page 169.

effect, so that the averaged prediction variance is often reduced. We illustrate this in Example 7.4 below.

To understand why it can be a good idea to only consider a subset of inputs as splitting variables, recall that tree-building is based on recursive binary splitting, which is a greedy algorithm. This means that the algorithm can make choices early on that appear to be good but which nevertheless turn out to be suboptimal further down the splitting procedure. For instance, consider the case when there is one dominant input variable. If we construct an ensemble of trees using plain bagging, it is then very likely that all of the ensemble members will pick this dominant variable as the first splitting variable, making all trees identical (that is, perfectly correlated) after the first split. If we instead apply a random forest, some of the ensemble members will not even have access to this dominant variable at the first split, since it most likely will not be present in the random subset of q inputs selected at the first split for some of the ensemble members. This will force those members to split according to some other variable. While there is no reason for why this would improve the performance of the individual tree, it *could* prove to be useful further down the splitting process, and since we average over many ensemble members, the overall performance could therefore be improved.

Example 7.4 Random forests and bagging for a binary classification problem

Consider the binary classification with $p = 2$ using the data in Figure 7.5. The different classes are blue and red. The $n = 200$ input values were randomly sampled from $[0, 2] \times [0, 2]$ and labelled red with probability 0.98 if above the dotted line, and vice versa. We use two different classifiers: bagging with classification trees (which is equivalent to a random forest with $q = p = 2$) and a random forest with $q = 1$, each with $B = 9$ ensemble members. In Figure 7.5, we plot the decision boundary for each ensemble member as well as the majority-voted final decision boundary.

The most apparent difference is the higher individual variation of the random forest ensemble members compared to bagging. Roughly half of the random forest ensemble members have been forced to make the first split along the horizontal axis, which has led to an increased variance and a decreased correlation compared to bagging, where all ensemble members make the first split along the vertical axis.

Since it is hard to visually compare the final decision boundaries for bagging and random forest (top right), we also compute E_{new} for different numbers of ensemble members B. Since the learning itself has a certain amount of randomness, we average over multiple learned models to avoid being confused by that random effect. Indeed, we see that the random forest performs better than bagging, except for very small B, and we conclude that the positive effect of the reduced correlation between the ensemble members outweighs the negative effect of additional variance. The poor performance of random forest with only one ensemble member is expected, since this single model has higher variance, and no averaging is taking place when $B = 1$.

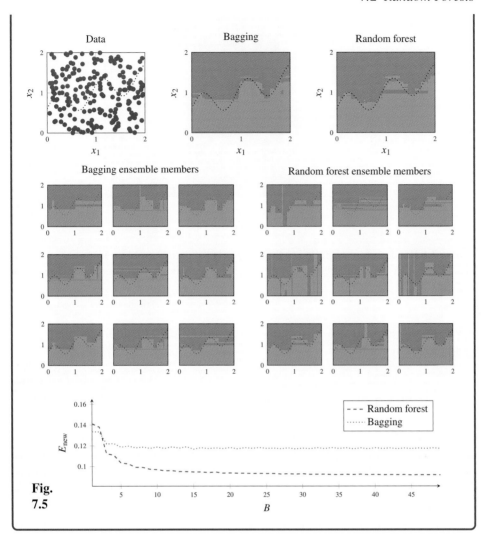

Fig. 7.5

Since the random forest is a bagging method, the tools and properties from Section 7.1 apply also to random forests, such as out-of-bag error estimation. As for bagging, taking $B \to \infty$ does not lead to overfitting in random forests. Hence, the only reason to choose B small is to reduce the computational cost. Compared to using a single tree, a random forest requires approximately B times as much computation. Since all trees are identically distributed, it is, however, possible to parallelise the implementation of random forest learning.

The choice of q is a tuning parameter, where for $q = p$, we recover the basic bagging method described previously. As a rule-of-thumb, we can set $q = \sqrt{p}$ for classification problems and $q = p/3$ for regression problems (values rounded down to closest integer). A more systematic way of selecting q is to use out-of-bag error estimation or cross-validation and select q such that E_{OOB} or $E_{k\text{-fold}}$ is minimised.

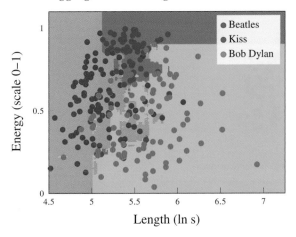

Figure 7.6 Random forest applied to the music classification problem from Example 2.1. This figure can be compared to Figure 2.11a, which is the decision boundary from a single tree.

We finally apply random forests to the music classification problem from Example 2.1 in Figure 7.6.

7.3 Boosting and AdaBoost

As we have seen above, bagging is an ensemble method for reducing the variance in high-variance base models. Boosting is another ensemble method, which is primarily used for reducing bias in high-bias base models. A typical example of a simple (or, in other words, weak) high-bias model is a classification tree of depth one (sometimes called a classification stump). Boosting is built on the idea that even a weak high-bias model can often capture *some* of the relationship between the inputs and the output. Thus, by training multiple weak models, each describing part of the input–output relationship, it might be possible to combine the predictions of these models into an overall better prediction. Hence, the intention is to *reduce the bias* by turning an ensemble of weak models into one strong model.

Boosting shares some similarities with bagging. They are both ensemble methods, in the sense that they are based on combining the predictions from multiple models (an ensemble). Both bagging and boosting can also be viewed as meta-algorithms, in the sense that they can be used to combine essentially any regression or classification algorithm – they are algorithms built on top of other algorithms. However, there are also important differences between boosting and bagging which we will discuss below.

The main difference is how the base models are trained. In bagging, we train B identically distributed models in parallel. Boosting, on the other hand, uses a *sequential* construction of the ensemble members. Informally, this is done in such a way that each model tries to correct the mistakes made by the previous one. This is accomplished by modifying the training dataset at each iteration in order to put more emphasis on the data points for which the model (so far) has performed poorly. The final prediction is obtained from a weighted average or a weighted majority vote among the models. We look at the simple Example 7.5 to illustrate this idea.

Example 7.5 Boosting illustration

We consider a binary classification problem with a two-dimensional input $\mathbf{x} = [x_1 \ x_2]$. The training data consists of $n = 10$ data points, 5 from each of the two classes. We use a decision stump, a classification tree of depth one, as a simple (weak) base classifier. A decision stump amounts to selecting one of the input variables, x_1 or x_2, and splitting the input space into two half spaces to minimise the training error. The first panel in Figure 7.7 shows the training data, illustrated by red and blue dots for the two classes. In the panel below that in Figure 7.7, the coloured regions show the decision boundary for a decision stump $\widehat{y}^{(1)}(\mathbf{x})$ trained on this data.

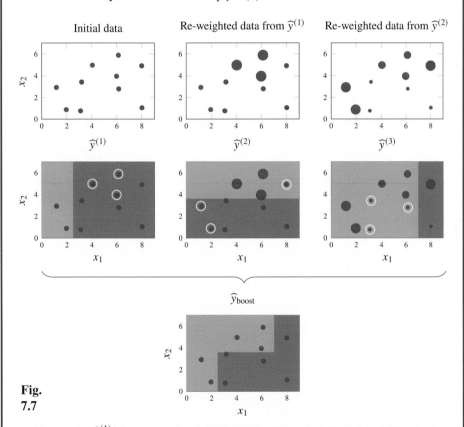

Fig. 7.7

The model $\widehat{y}^{(1)}(\mathbf{x})$ incorrectly classifies three data points (red dots falling in the blue region), which are circled in the figure. To improve the performance of the classifier, we want to find a model that can distinguish these three points from the blue class. To put emphasis on the three misclassified points when training the next decision stump, we assign *weights* $\{w_i^{(2)}\}_{i=1}^n$ to the data, which are shown in the upper middle panel in Figure 7.7 (larger radius = higher weight). The points correctly classified by $\widehat{y}^{(1)}(\mathbf{x})$ are down-weighted, whereas the three points misclassified by

$\widehat{y}^{(1)}(\mathbf{x})$ are up-weighted. We train another decision stump, $\widehat{y}^{(2)}(\mathbf{x})$, on the weighted data. The classifier $\widehat{y}^{(2)}(\mathbf{x})$ is found by minimising the *weighted* misclassification error, $\frac{1}{n}\sum_{i=1}^{n} w_i^{(2)}\mathbb{I}\{\widehat{y}^{(2)}(\mathbf{x}_i) \neq y_i\}$, resulting in the decision boundary shown in the lower middle panel. This procedure is repeated for a third and final iteration: we update the weights based on the hits and misses of $\widehat{y}^{(2)}(\mathbf{x})$ and train a third decision stump $\widehat{y}^{(3)}(\mathbf{x})$ shown in the lower right panel in Figure 7.7.

The final classifier $\widehat{y}_{\text{boost}}(\mathbf{x})$, in the bottom panel in Figure 7.7, is then obtained as a weighted majority vote of the three decision stumps. Note that its decision boundary is non-linear, whereas the decision boundary for each ensemble member is linear. This illustrates the concept of turning an ensemble of three weak (high-bias) base models into a stronger (low-bias) model.

The example illustrates the idea of boosting, but there are still important details left to be specified in order to have a complete algorithm. Specifically, how to compute the weights of the training data points at each iteration and how to combine the ensemble members to get the final model. Next, we will have a look at the AdaBoost algorithm, which is one approach for filling in these missing details. AdaBoost was the first successful implementation of the boosting idea, so it is interesting in its own right but also because it is simple enough to allow for closed form derivations. However, there are also more modern approaches to boosting, so after discussing AdaBoost, we will introduce the more general framework of gradient boosting.

Throughout this section, we will restrict our attention to binary classification, but boosting is also applicable to multiclass classification and regression problems.

AdaBoost

What we have discussed so far is a general idea, but there are still a few technical design choices left. Let us now derive an actual boosting method, the AdaBoost (Adaptive Boosting) algorithm for binary classification. AdaBoost was the first successful practical implementation of the boosting idea and led the way for its popularity.

As we outlined in Example 7.5, boosting attempts to construct a sequence of B (weak) binary classifiers $\widehat{y}^{(1)}(\mathbf{x})$, $\widehat{y}^{(2)}(\mathbf{x})$, ..., $\widehat{y}^{(B)}(\mathbf{x})$. In this procedure, we will only consider the final 'hard' prediction $\widehat{y}(\mathbf{x})$ from the base models and not their predicted class probabilities $g(\mathbf{x})$. Any classification model can, in principle, be used as base classifier – shallow classification trees are common in practice. The individual predictions of the B ensemble members are then combined into a final prediction. Unlike bagging, all ensemble members are not treated equally. Instead, we assign some positive coefficients $\{\alpha^{(b)}\}_{b=1}^{B}$ and construct the boosted classifier using a *weighted* majority vote:

$$\widehat{y}_{\text{boost}}^{(B)}(\mathbf{x}) = \text{sign}\left\{\sum_{b=1}^{B} \alpha^{(b)}\widehat{y}^{(b)}(\mathbf{x})\right\}. \tag{7.4}$$

Each ensemble member votes either -1 or $+1$, and the output from the boosted classifier is $+1$ if the weighted sum of the individual votes is positive and -1 if it is negative. The coefficient $\alpha^{(b)}$ can be thought of as a degree of confidence in the predictions made by the bth ensemble member.

The construction of the AdaBoost classifier in (7.4) follows the general form of a binary classifier from (5.12). That is, we obtain the class prediction by thresholding a real-valued function $f(\mathbf{x})$ at zero, where in this case the function is given by the weighted sum of predictions made by all the ensemble members. In AdaBoost, the ensemble members and their coefficients $\alpha^{(b)}$ are trained greedily by minimising the *exponential loss* of the boosted classifier at each iteration. Recall from (5.15) that the exponential loss is given by

$$L(y \cdot f(\mathbf{x})) = \exp(-y \cdot f(\mathbf{x})), \tag{7.5}$$

where $y \cdot f(\mathbf{x})$ is the *margin* of the classifier. The ensemble members are added one at a time, and when member b is added, this is done to minimise the exponential loss (7.5) of the entire ensemble constructed so far (that is, the boosted classifier consisting of the first b members). The main reason for choosing the exponential loss, and not one of the other loss functions discussed in Section 5.2, is that it results in convenient closed form expressions (much like the squared error loss in linear regression), as we will see when deriving the AdaBoost procedure below.

Let us write the boosted classifier after b iterations as $\widehat{y}_{\text{boost}}^{(b)}(\mathbf{x}) = \text{sign}\{f^{(b)}(\mathbf{x})\}$, where $f^{(b)}(\mathbf{x}) = \sum_{j=1}^{b} \alpha^{(j)}\widehat{y}^{(j)}(\mathbf{x})$. We can express $f^{(b)}(\mathbf{x})$ iteratively as

$$f^{(b)}(\mathbf{x}) = f^{(b-1)}(\mathbf{x}) + \alpha^{(b)}\widehat{y}^{(b)}(\mathbf{x}), \tag{7.6}$$

initialised with $f^0(\mathbf{x}) = 0$. The ensemble members (as well as the coefficients $\alpha^{(b)[j]}$) are constructed sequentially, meaning that at iteration b of the procedure, the function $f^{(b-1)}(\mathbf{x})$ is known and fixed. This is what makes this construction 'greedy'. Consequently, what remains to be learned at iteration b is the ensemble member $\widehat{y}^{(b)}(\mathbf{x})$ and its coefficient $\alpha^{(b)}$. We do this by minimising the exponential loss of the training data,

$$(\alpha^{(b)}, \widehat{y}^{(b)}) = \arg\min_{(\alpha,\widehat{y})} \sum_{i=1}^{n} L(y_i \cdot f^{(b)}(\mathbf{x}_i)) \tag{7.7a}$$

$$= \arg\min_{(\alpha,\widehat{y})} \sum_{i=1}^{n} \exp\left(-y_i\left(f^{(b-1)}(\mathbf{x}_i) + \alpha\widehat{y}(\mathbf{x}_i)\right)\right) \tag{7.7b}$$

$$= \arg\min_{(\alpha,\widehat{y})} \sum_{i=1}^{n} \underbrace{\exp\left(-y_i f^{(b-1)}(\mathbf{x}_i)\right)}_{=w_i^{(b)}} \exp\left(-y_i\alpha\widehat{y}(\mathbf{x}_i)\right), \tag{7.7c}$$

where for the first equality, we have used the definition of the exponential loss function (7.5) and the sequential structure of the boosted classifier (7.6). The last equality is where the convenience of the exponential loss appears, namely the fact that $\exp(a + b) = \exp(a)\exp(b)$. This allows us to define the quantities

$$w_i^{(b)} \stackrel{\text{def}}{=} \exp\left(-y_i f^{(b-1)}(\mathbf{x}_i)\right),$$ (7.8)

which can be interpreted as *weights* for the individual data points in the training dataset. Note that the weights $w_i^{(b)}$ are independent of α and $\widehat{y}$. That is, when learning $\widehat{y}^{(b)}(\mathbf{x})$ and its coefficient $\alpha^{(b)}$ by solving (7.7c), we can regard $\{w_i^{(b)}\}_{i=1}^n$ as constants.

To solve (7.7), we start by rewriting the objective function as

$$\sum_{i=1}^n w_i^{(b)} \exp\left(-y_i \alpha \widehat{y}(\mathbf{x}_i)\right) = e^{-\alpha} \underbrace{\sum_{i=1}^n w_i^{(b)} \mathbb{I}\{y_i = \widehat{y}(\mathbf{x}_i)\}}_{=W_c} + e^{\alpha} \underbrace{\sum_{i=1}^n w_i^{(b)} \mathbb{I}\{y_i \neq \widehat{y}(\mathbf{x}_i)\}}_{=W_e},$$
(7.9)

where we have used the indicator function to split the sum into two parts: the first ranging over all training data points correctly classified by $\widehat{y}$ and the second ranging over all points misclassified by $\widehat{y}$. (Remember that $\widehat{y}$ is the ensemble member we are to learn at this step.) Furthermore, for notational simplicity, we define W_c and W_e as the sums of weights of correctly classified and erroneously classified data points, respectively. Furthermore, let $W = W_c + W_e$ be the total weight sum, $W = \sum_{i=1}^n w_i^{(b)}$.

Minimising (7.9) is done in two stages: first with respect to $\widehat{y}$ and then with respect to α. This is possible since the minimising argument in $\widehat{y}$ turns out to be independent of the actual value of $\alpha > 0$, another convenient effect of using the exponential loss function. To see this, note that we can write the objective function (7.9) as

$$e^{-\alpha}W + (e^{\alpha} - e^{-\alpha})W_e.$$ (7.10)

Since the total weight sum W is independent of $\widehat{y}$, and since $e^{\alpha} - e^{-\alpha} > 0$ for any $\alpha > 0$, minimising this expression with respect to $\widehat{y}$ is equivalent to minimising W_e with respect to $\widehat{y}$. That is,

$$\widehat{y}^{(b)} = \arg\min_{\widehat{y}} \sum_{i=1}^n w_i^{(b)} \mathbb{I}\{y_i \neq \widehat{y}(\mathbf{x}_i)\}.$$ (7.11)

In words, the bth ensemble member should be trained by minimising the *weighted misclassification loss*, where each data point $(\mathbf{x}_i, y_i)$ is assigned a weight $w_i^{(b)}$. The intuition for these weights is that, at iteration b, we should focus our attention on the data points previously misclassified in order to 'correct the mistakes' made by the ensemble of the first $b - 1$ classifiers.

> ***Time to reflect 7.2*** *In AdaBoost, we use the exponential loss for training the boosting ensemble. How come we end up training the individual ensemble members using a weighted misclassification loss (and not the unweighted exponential loss)?*

How the problem (7.11) is solved in practice depends on the choice of base classifier that we use, that is, on the specific restrictions that we put on the function $\widehat{y}$ (for example a shallow classification tree). However, solving (7.11) is almost our standard classification problem, except for the weights $w_i^{(b)}$. Training the ensemble member b on a *weighted* classification problem is, for most base classifiers, straightforward. Since most classifiers are trained by minimising some cost function, this simply boils down to weighting the individual terms of the cost function and solving that slightly modified problem instead.

Once the bth ensemble member, $\widehat{y}^{(b)}(\mathbf{x})$, has been trained for solving the weighted classification problem (7.11), it remains to learn its coefficient $\alpha^{(b)}$. This is done by solving (7.7), which amounts to minimising (7.10) once $\widehat{y}$ has been trained. By differentiating (7.10) with respect to α and setting the derivative to zero, we get the equation

$$-\alpha e^{-\alpha}W + \alpha(e^\alpha + e^{-\alpha})W_e = 0 \Leftrightarrow W = \left(e^{2\alpha} + 1\right)W_e \Leftrightarrow \alpha = \frac{1}{2}\ln\left(\frac{W}{W_e} - 1\right).$$

Thus, by defining

$$E_{\text{train}}^{(b)} \stackrel{\text{def}}{=} \frac{W_e}{W} = \sum_{i=1}^n \frac{w_i^{(b)}}{\sum_{j=1}^n w_j^{(b)}}\mathbb{I}\{y_i \neq \widehat{y}^{(b)}(\mathbf{x}_i)\} \tag{7.12}$$

to be the weighted misclassification error for the bth classifier, we can express the optimal value for its coefficient as

$$\alpha^{(b)} = \frac{1}{2}\ln\left(\frac{1 - E_{\text{train}}^{(b)}}{E_{\text{train}}^{(b)}}\right). \tag{7.13}$$

The fact that $\alpha^{(b)}$ depends on the training error of the bth ensemble member is natural since, as mentioned above, we can interpret $\alpha^{(b)}$ as the confidence in this member's predictions. This completes the derivation of the AdaBoost algorithm, which is summarised in Method 7.2. In the algorithm we exploit the fact that the weights (7.8) can be computed recursively by using the expression (7.6) in line 6 in the learning section. Furthermore, we have added an explicit weight normalisation (line 7), which is convenient in practice and which does not affect the derivation of the method above.

The derivation of AdaBoost assumes that all coefficients $\{\alpha^{(b)}\}_{b=1}^{(B)}$ are positive. To see that this is indeed the case when the coefficients are computed according to

(7.13), note that the function $\ln((1 - x)/x)$ is positive for any $0 < x < 0.5$. Thus, $\alpha^{(b)}$ will be positive as long as the weighted training error for the bth classifier, $E_{\text{train}}^{(b)}$, is less than 0.5. That is, the classifier just has to be slightly better than a coin flip, which is always the case in practice (note that $E_{\text{train}}^{(b)}$ is the *training* error). (Indeed, if $E_{\text{train}}^{(b)} > 0.5$, then we could simply flip the sign of all predictions made by $\widehat{y}^{(b)}(\mathbf{x})$ to reduce the error below 0.5.)

Learn an AdaBoost classifier

Data: Training data $\mathcal{T} = \{\mathbf{x}_i, y_i\}_{i=1}^n$
Result: B weak classifiers

1 Assign weights $w_i^{(1)} = 1/n$ to all data points.
2 **for** $b = 1, \ldots, B$ **do**
3 $\quad$ Train a weak classifier $\widehat{y}^{(b)}(\mathbf{x})$ on the weighted training data $\{(\mathbf{x}_i, y_i, w_i^{(b)})\}_{i=1}^n$.
4 $\quad$ Compute $E_{\text{train}}^{(b)} = \sum_{i=1}^n w_i^{(b)} \mathbb{I}\{y_i \neq \widehat{y}^{(b)}(\mathbf{x}_i)\}$.
5 $\quad$ Compute $\alpha^{(b)} = 0.5 \ln((1 - E_{\text{train}}^{(b)})/E_{\text{train}}^{(b)})$.
6 $\quad$ Compute $w_i^{(b+1)} = w_i^{(b)} \exp(-\alpha^{(b)} y_i \widehat{y}^{(b)}(\mathbf{x}_i))$, $i = 1, \ldots, n$.
7 $\quad$ Set $w_i^{(b+1)} \leftarrow w_i^{(b+1)}/\sum_{j=1}^n w_j^{(b+1)}$, for $i = 1, \ldots, n$.
8 **end**

Predict with the AdaBoost classifier

Data: B weak classifiers with confidence values $\{\widehat{y}^{(b)}(\mathbf{x}), \alpha^{(b)}\}_{b=1}^B$ and test input $\mathbf{x}_\star$
Result: Prediction $\widehat{y}_{\text{boost}}^{(B)}(\mathbf{x}_\star)$

1 Output $\widehat{y}_{\text{boost}}^{(B)}(\mathbf{x}_\star) = \text{sign}\left\{\sum_{b=1}^B \alpha^{(b)} \widehat{y}^{(b)}(\mathbf{x}_\star)\right\}$.

Method 7.2 AdaBoost

Example 7.6 AdaBoost and bagging for a binary classification example

Consider the same binary classification problem as in Example 7.4. We now compare how AdaBoost and bagging perform on this problem, when using trees of depth one (decision stumps) and three. It should be noted that this comparison is made to illustrate the difference between the methods. In practice, we would typically not use bagging with such shallow trees.

The decision boundaries for each method with $B = 1, 5, 20$, and 100 ensemble members are shown in Figure 7.8. Despite using quite weak ensemble members (a shallow tree has high bias), AdaBoost adapts quite well to the data. This is in contrast to bagging, where the decision boundary does not become much more flexible despite using many ensemble members. In other words, AdaBoost reduces the bias of the base model, whereas bagging only has minor effect on the bias.

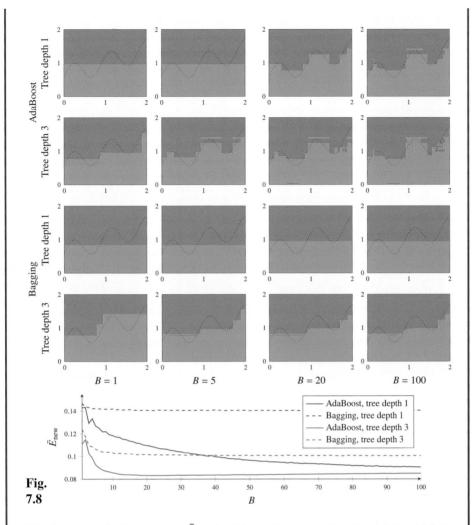

Fig. 7.8

We also numerically compute $\bar{E}_{new}$ for this problem, as a function of B, which is shown at the bottom of Figure 7.8. Remember that $\bar{E}_{new}$ depends on both the bias and the variance. As discussed, the main effect of bagging is variance reduction, but that does not help much since the base model is already quite low-variance (but high-bias). Boosting, on the other hand, reduces bias, which has a much bigger effect in this case. Furthermore, bagging does not overfit as $B \to \infty$, but that is *not* the case for boosting! We can indeed see that for trees of depth 3, the smallest $\bar{E}_{new}$ is obtained for $B \approx 25$, and there is actually a slight increase in $\bar{E}_{new}$ for larger values of B. Hence, AdaBoost with depth-3 trees suffers from a (minor) overfit as $B \gtrsim 25$ in this problem.

Design Choices for AdaBoost

AdaBoost, and in fact any boosting algorithm, has two important design choices: *(i)* which base classifier to use and *(ii)* how many iterations B to run the boosting

181

algorithm for. As previously pointed out, we can use essentially any classification method as the base classifier. However, the most common choice in practice is to use a shallow classification tree, or even a decision stump (a tree of depth one; see Example 7.5). This choice is guided by the fact that boosting reduces bias efficiently and can thereby learn good models despite using a very weak (high-bias) base model. Since shallow trees can be trained quickly, they are a good default choice. Practical experience suggests that trees with a handful of terminal nodes may work well as base models, but trees of depth one (only $M = 2$ terminal nodes in binary classification) are perhaps even more commonly used. In fact, using deep classification trees (high-variance models) as base classifiers typically deteriorates performance.

The base models are trained sequentially in boosting: each iteration introduces a new base model aiming at reducing the errors made by the current model. As a consequence, the boosting model becomes more and more flexible as the number of iterations B increases, and using too many base models can result in overfitting (in contrast to bagging, where increased B cannot lead to overfit). It has been observed in practice, however, that this overfitting often occurs slowly, and the performance tends to be rather insensitive to the choice of B. Nevertheless, it is a good practice to select B in some systematic way, for instance using early stopping during training. Another unfortunate aspect of the sequential nature of boosting is that it is not possible to parallelise the training.

In the method discussed above, we have assumed that each base classifier outputs a class prediction, $\widehat{y}^{(b)}(\mathbf{x}) \in \{-1, 1\}$. However, many classification models output $g(\mathbf{x})$, which is an estimate of the class probability $p(y = 1 \mid \mathbf{x})$. In AdaBoost it is possible to use the predicted probabilities $g(\mathbf{x})$ (instead of the binary prediction $\widehat{y}(\mathbf{x})$) when constructing the prediction; however, this is at the cost of a more complicated expression than (7.4). This extension of Method 7.2 is referred to as Real AdaBoost.

7.4 Gradient Boosting

It has been seen in practice that AdaBoost often performs well if there is little noise in the data. However, as the data becomes more noisy, either due to outliers (mislabelled data) or high uncertainty in the true input–output relationship, the performance of the method can deteriorate. This is not an artefact of the boosting idea but rather of the exponential loss function used in the construction of AdaBoost. As we discussed in Section 5.2, the exponential loss will heavily penalise large negative margins, making it sensitive to noise; see Figure 5.2. To mitigate this issue and construct more robust boosting algorithms, we can consider choosing some other (more robust) loss function. However, this will be at the expense of a more computationally involved training procedure.

To lay the foundation for more general boosting algorithms, we will start by presenting a slightly different view on boosting. In the discussion above, we have described boosting as *learning a sequence of weak classifiers, where each classifier tries to correct the mistakes made by the previous ones*. This is an intuitive interpretation, but from a mathematical perspective, a perhaps more useful interpretation is that boosting is as a way to train an additive model. The fundamental task of supervised learning is to approximate some unknown function, mapping inputs to outputs, based on observed data. A very useful – and indeed common – way of constructing a flexible function approximator is by using an additive model of the form

$$f^{(B)}(\mathbf{x}) = \sum_{b=1}^{B} \alpha^{(b)} f^{(b)}(\mathbf{x}), \tag{7.14}$$

where $\alpha^{(b)}$ are real-valued coefficients and $f^{(b)}(\mathbf{x})$ are some 'basis functions'. For a regression problem, the function $f^{(B)}(\mathbf{x})$ can be used directly as the model's prediction. For a classification problem, it can be thresholded by a sign function to obtain a hard class prediction or transformed into a class probability by passing it through a logistic function.[4]

Comparing (7.14) with (7.4), it is clear that AdaBoost follows this additive form, where the weak learners (ensemble members) are the basis functions, and their confidence scores are the coefficients. However, we have in fact seen other examples of additive models before. To put boosting algorithms in a broader context, we provide a couple of examples:

If the basis functions $f^{(b)}(\mathbf{x})$ are fixed *a priori*, then the only learnable parameters are the coefficients $\alpha^{(b)}$. The model (7.14) is then nothing but a linear regression, or generalised linear model. For instance, in Chapter 3, we discussed polynomial regression, where the basis functions are defined as polynomial transformations of the input. In Chapter 8, we will discuss more systematic ways of constructing (fixed) basis functions for additive models.

A more flexible model can be obtained if we also allow the basis functions themselves to be learnable. This is also something that we have come across before. In Chapter 6, we introduced the neural network model, and writing out the expression for a two-layer regression network, it can be seen that it corresponds to an additive model.

> **Time to reflect 7.3** *If we write a two-layer regression neural network in the form of an additive model, then what do B, $\alpha^{(b)}$, and $f^{(b)}(\mathbf{x})$ correspond to?*

An important consequence of this interpretation of boosting as an additive model is that the individual ensemble members do not necessarily have to correspond to 'weak learners' for the specific problem under study. Put differently, for a classification problem, each ensemble member does not have to correspond to a classifier trained to solve (some modified version of) the original problem. What is important is just that the sum over all ensemble members in (7.14) results in a useful model! We will

---

[4]Similarly, we can use other link functions to turn the additive model $f^{(B)}(\mathbf{x})$ into a likelihood that is suitable for the properties of the data under study, akin to generalised linear models (see Section 3.4).

see an example of this below, when we discuss how regression trees can be used to solve classification problems in the context of gradient boosting. This is also the reason why we use f instead of $\widehat{y}$ in the notation above. Even for a classification problem, the outputs from the ensemble members do not have to correspond to class predictions in general.

Instead, there are two properties that distinguish boosting from other additive models.

(i) The basis functions are learned from data and, specifically, each function (that is ensemble member) corresponds to a machine learning model itself – the base model of the boosting procedure.

(ii) The basis functions and their coefficients are learned sequentially. That is, we add one component to the sum in (7.14) at each iteration, and after B iterations the learning algorithm terminates.

The goal when training an additive model is to select $\{\alpha^{(b)}, f^{(b)}(\mathbf{x})\}_{b=1}^{B}$ such that the final $f^{(B)}(\mathbf{x})$ minimises

$$J(f(\mathbf{X})) = \frac{1}{n} \sum_{i=1}^{n} L(y_i, f(\mathbf{x}_i)) \tag{7.15}$$

for some arbitrary loss function L; see Section 5.2. For instance, in a binary classification setting, choosing the logistic loss (or some other robust loss function) instead of the exponential loss will result in a model which is less sensitive to outliers. Here we define $f(\mathbf{X}) = [f(\mathbf{x}_1) \cdots f(\mathbf{x}_n)]^\mathsf{T}$ as the vector of function values obtained by evaluating the model $f(\mathbf{x})$ at the n training data points. Since we do not have an explicit parametric form for $f(\mathbf{x})$, we consider J to be a function of the model $f(\mathbf{x})$ itself.

A consequence of the first point in the list above – that the basis function themselves are generic machine learning models – is that the objective (7.15) will lack a closed form minimiser, and we thus need to resort to some approximate numerical solution. The sequential learning (second point above) can be viewed as one way of handling this, by using 'greedy' step-wise training. Connecting this back to the AdaBoost algorithm, using the exponential loss function is convenient since it results in tractable expressions for each step of this iterative training procedure. However, this is not strictly necessary. Indeed, by similar arguments as in numerical optimisation, we can improve the model at each iteration as long as we 'move in the right direction'. That is, at iteration b we introduce a new ensemble member with the objective of *reducing the value* of the cost function (7.15) but without requiring that it is (greedily) minimised. This leads us in to the idea of gradient boosting.

Consider the bth iteration of the training procedure. As before, we can use the sequential nature of the method to write

$$f^{(b)}(\mathbf{x}) = f^{(b-1)}(\mathbf{x}) + \alpha^{(b)} f^{(b)}(\mathbf{x}), \tag{7.16}$$

and the goal is to select $\{\alpha^{(b)}, f^{(b)}(\mathbf{x})\}$ to reduce the value of the cost function (7.15). That is, we want to choose the bth ensemble member such that

$$J\left(f^{(b-1)}(\mathbf{X}) + \alpha^{(b)} f^{(b)}(\mathbf{X})\right) < J\left(f^{(b-1)}(\mathbf{X})\right). \tag{7.17}$$

Akin to the gradient descent algorithm (see Section 5.4), we do this by taking a step in the negative direction of the gradient of the cost function.

However, in the context of boosting, we do not assume a specific parametric form for the basis function but rather construct each ensemble member using a learnable base model, such as a tree. What, then, should we compute the gradient of the cost function with respect to? The idea behind gradient boosting, which allows us to address this question, is to take a non-parametric approach and represent the model $c(\mathbf{x})$ by the values it assigns to the n training data points. That is, we compute the gradient of the cost function directly with respect to the (vector of) function values $f(\mathbf{X})$. This gives us an n-dimensional gradient vector

$$\nabla_c J(c^{(b-1)}(\mathbf{X})) \stackrel{\text{def}}{=} \begin{bmatrix} \frac{\partial J(f(\mathbf{X}))}{\partial f(\mathbf{x}_1)} \\ \vdots \\ \frac{\partial J(f(\mathbf{X}))}{\partial f(\mathbf{x}_n)} \end{bmatrix}_{|f(\mathbf{X})=f^{(b-1)}(\mathbf{X})} = \frac{1}{n} \begin{bmatrix} \frac{\partial L(y_1,f)}{\partial f} \Big|_{f=f^{(b-1)}(\mathbf{x}_1)} \\ \vdots \\ \frac{\partial L(y_n,f)}{\partial f} \Big|_{f=f^{(b-1)}(\mathbf{x}_n)} \end{bmatrix}, \tag{7.18}$$

where we have assumed that the loss function L is differentiable. Hence, to satisfy (7.17), we should select $f^{(b)}(\mathbf{X}) = -\nabla_c J(c^{(b-1)}(\mathbf{X}))$ and then pick the coefficient $\alpha^{(b)}$ – which takes the role of the step length in the gradient descent analogy – in some suitable way, for instance by line search.

However, selecting the bth ensemble member $f^{(b)}(\mathbf{X})$ so that it *exactly* matches the negative gradient is typically not possible. The reason is that the ensemble members $f(\mathbf{x})$ are restricted to some specific functional form, for instance the set of functions that can be represented by a tree-based model of a certain depth. Neither would it be desirable in general, since exactly matching the gradient at all training data points could easily lead to overfitting. Indeed, as usual we are not primarily interested in finding a model that fits the training data as well as possible but rather one that generalises to new data. Restricting our attention to a class of functions that generalise beyond the observed training data is therefore a key requirement.

To proceed, we will therefore train the bth ensemble member $f^{(b)}(\mathbf{x})$ as a machine learning model, with the training objective that its predictions on the training data points (that is, the vector $f^{(b)}(\mathbf{X})$) are close to the negative gradient (7.18). Closeness can be evaluated by any suitable distance function, such as the squared distance. This corresponds to solving a *regression problem* where the target values are the elements of the gradient, and the loss function (for example squared loss) determines how we measure closeness. Note that, even when the actual problem under study is classification, the gradient values in (7.18) will be real-valued in general.

Having found the bth ensemble member, it remains to compute the coefficient $\alpha^{(b)}$. As pointed out above, this corresponds to the step size (or learning rate) in gradient descent. In the simplest version of gradient descent, it is considered a tuning parameter left to the user. However, it can also be found by solving a line-search optimisation problem at each iteration. For gradient boosting, it is most often handled in the latter way. If multiplying the optimal $\alpha^{(b)}$ with a constant <1, a regularising effect is obtained which has proven useful in practice. We summarise gradient boosting in Method 7.3.

Learn a simple gradient boosting classifier

Data: Training data $\mathcal{T} = \{\mathbf{x}_i, y_i\}_{i=1}^n$, step size multiplier $\gamma < 1$
Result: A boosted classifier $f^{(B)}(\mathbf{x})$

1   Initialise (as a constant) $f^0(\mathbf{x}) \equiv \arg\min_c \sum_{i=1}^n L(y_i, c)$.
2   **for** $b = 1, \ldots, B$ **do**
3   Compute the negative gradient of the loss function
$$d_i^{(b)} = -\frac{1}{n}\left[\frac{\partial L(y_i, c)}{\partial c}\right]_{c=f^{(b-1)}(\mathbf{x}_i)}.$$
4   Learn a *regression* model $f^{(b)}(\mathbf{x})$ from the input-output training data
$\{\mathbf{x}_i, d_i^{(b)}\}_{i=1}^n$.
5   Compute $\alpha^{(b)} = \arg\min_\alpha \sum_{i=1}^n L(y_i, f^{(b-1)}(\mathbf{x}_i) + \alpha f^{(b)}(\mathbf{x}_i))$.
6   Update the boosted model $f^{(b)}(\mathbf{x}) = f^{(b-1)}(\mathbf{x}) + \gamma\alpha^{(b)} f^{(b)}(\mathbf{x})$.
7   **end**

Predict with the gradient boosting classifier

Data: B weak classifiers and test input $\mathbf{x}_\star$
Result: Prediction $\widehat{y}_{\text{boost}}^{(B)}(\mathbf{x}_\star)$

1   Output $\widehat{y}_{\text{boost}}^{(B)}(\mathbf{x}) = \text{sign}\{f^{(B)}(\mathbf{x})\}$.

Method 7.3 A simple gradient boosting algorithm

When using trees as base models, optimising $\alpha^{(b)}$ can be done jointly with learning $f^{(b)}(\mathbf{x})$. Specifically, instead of first computing constant predictions for all terminal nodes of the tree (see Section 2.3) and then multiplying these by a constant $\alpha^{(b)}$, we can solve one separate line search problem for each terminal node in the tree directly.

> **Time to reflect 7.4** *We have described boosting algorithms as greedy step-wise training of an additive model. Based on this interpretation, another approach for training these models is by coordinate ascent (see Section 5.4). That is, instead of adding a new component at each iteration of the training algorithm and stopping after B iterations, we can fix the number of components and cycle through them (updating one component at a time) until convergence. What are the possible drawbacks and benefits of this alternative training approach?*

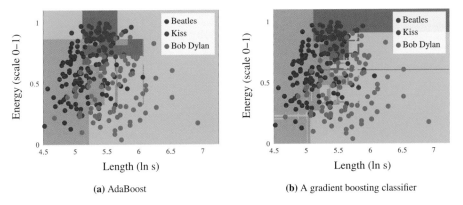

Figure 7.9 Two boosting algorithms applied to the music classification problem from Example 2.1.

While presented for classification in Method 7.3, gradient boosting can also be used for regression, with minor modifications. As mentioned above, gradient boosting requires a certain amount of smoothness in the loss function. A minimal requirement is that it is differentiable almost everywhere, so that it is possible to compute the gradient of the loss function. However, some implementations of gradient boosting require stronger conditions, such as second order differentiability. The logistic loss (see Section 5.2) is in this respect a 'safe choice' as it is infinitely differentiable and strongly convex while still enjoying good statistical properties. As a consequence, the logistic loss is one of the most commonly used loss functions in practice.

We conclude this chapter by applying AdaBoost and gradient boosting to the music classification problem from Example 2.1; see Figure 7.9.

7.5 Further Reading

The general bagging idea was initially proposed by Breiman (1996), whereas the more specific random forest algorithm dates back to Ho (1995), who essentially proposed to limit the set of possible splitting variables for each tree. The idea to also use a bootstraped data set (that is, bagging) is due to Breiman (2001).

Boosting was popularised by the introduction of AdaBoost by Freund and Schapire (1996), who were also awarded the prestigious Gödel Prize in 2003 for their algorithm. Real AdaBoost was proposed by Friedman et al. (2000), and gradient boosting by Friedman (2001) and Mason et al. (1999). Efficient and widely used implementations of gradient boosting include the XGBoost package by T. Chen and Guestrin (2016) and LightGBM by Ke et al. (2017).

8 Non-linear Input Transformations and Kernels

In this chapter, we will continue to develop the idea from Chapter 3 of creating new input features by using non-linear transformations $\boldsymbol{\phi}(\mathbf{x})$. It turns out that by the so-called *kernel trick*, we can have *infinitely* many such non-linear transformations, and we can extend our basic methods, such as linear regression and k-NN, into more versatile and flexible ones. When we also change the loss function of linear regression, we obtain support vector regression and its classification counterpart support vector classification, two powerful off-the-shelf machine learning methods. The concept of kernels is important also to the next chapter (9), where a Bayesian perspective of linear regression and kernels leads us to the Gaussian process model.

8.1 Creating Features by Non-linear Input Transformations

The reason for the word 'linear' in the name 'linear regression' is that the output is modelled as a *linear* combination of the inputs. However, we have not provided a clear definition of what an input is. Recall the car stopping distance problem in Example 2.2. If the speed is an input in that example, then could the kinetic energy – the square of the speed – not also be considered as another input? The answer is: yes, it can. We can in fact make use of arbitrary non-linear transformations of the 'original' input variables in any model, including linear regression. For example, if we only have a one-dimensional input x, the vanilla linear regression model (3.2) is

$$y = \theta_0 + \theta_1 x + \varepsilon. \tag{8.1}$$

Starting from this, we can extend the model with $x^2, x^3, \ldots, x^{d-1}$ as inputs (d is a user-choice) and thus obtain a linear regression model which is a polynomial in x:

$$y = \theta_0 + \theta_1 x + \theta_2 x^2 + \cdots + \theta_{d-1} x^{d-1} + \varepsilon = \boldsymbol{\theta}^\mathsf{T} \boldsymbol{\phi}(x) + \varepsilon. \tag{8.2}$$

Since x is known, we can directly compute $x^2, \ldots, x^{d-1}$. Note that this is still a linear regression model since *the parameters $\boldsymbol{\theta}$ appear in a linear fashion* with $\boldsymbol{\phi}(x) = [1 \ \ x \ \ x^2 \ \ \ldots \ \ x^{d-1}]^\mathsf{T}$ as a new input vector. We refer to a transformation of $\mathbf{x}$

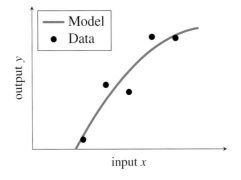
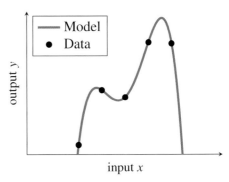

(a) A linear regression model with a 2nd order polynomial, trained with squared error loss. The line is no longer straight (as in Figure 3.1), but this is merely an artifact of the plot: in a three-dimensional plot with each feature (here, x and x^2) on a separate axis, it would still be an affine model.

(b) A linear regression model with a 4th order polynomial, trained with squared error loss. Note that a 4th order polynomial implies five unknown parameters, which roughly means that we can expect the learned model to fit five data points exactly, a typical case of overfitting.

Figure 8.1 A linear regression model with 2nd and 4th order polynomials in the input x, as in (8.2).

as a *feature*[1] and the vector of transformed inputs $\boldsymbol{\phi}(\mathbf{x})$, a vector of dimension $d \times 1$, as a *feature vector*. The parameters $\widehat{\boldsymbol{\theta}}$ are still learned in the same way, but we

$$
\text{replace the original } \mathbf{X} = \underbrace{\begin{bmatrix} \mathbf{x}_1^{\mathsf{T}} \\ \mathbf{x}_2^{\mathsf{T}} \\ \vdots \\ \mathbf{x}_n^{\mathsf{T}} \end{bmatrix}}_{n \times p+1} \text{ with the transformed } \boldsymbol{\Phi}(\mathbf{X}) = \underbrace{\begin{bmatrix} \boldsymbol{\phi}(\mathbf{x}_1)^{\mathsf{T}} \\ \boldsymbol{\phi}(\mathbf{x}_2)^{\mathsf{T}} \\ \vdots \\ \boldsymbol{\phi}(\mathbf{x}_n)^{\mathsf{T}} \end{bmatrix}}_{n \times d} .
$$

(8.3)

For linear regression, this means that we can learn the parameters by making the substitution (8.3) directly in the normal equations (3.13).

The idea of non-linear input transformations is not unique to linear regression, and any choice of non-linear transformation $\boldsymbol{\phi}(\cdot)$ can be used with any supervised machine learning method. The non-linear transformation is first applied to the input, like a pre-processing step, and the transformed input is thereafter used when training, evaluating, and using the model. We illustrated this for regression already in Example 3.5 in Chapter 3 and for classification in Example 8.1.

---

[1] The original input $\mathbf{x}$ is sometimes also referred to as a feature.

> ***Time to reflect 8.1*** *Figure 8.1 shows an example of two linear regression models with transformed (polynomial) inputs. When studying the figure, one may ask how a* linear *regression model can result in a* curved *line? Are linear regression models not restricted to linear (or affine) straight lines?*

Example 8.1 Non-linear feature transformations for classification

Consider the data for a binary classification problem in the left panel of Figure 8.2, with $\mathbf{x} = [x_1 \ x_2]^\mathsf{T}$ and with a blue and a red class. By just looking at the data, we can conclude that a linear classifier would not be able to perform well on this problem.

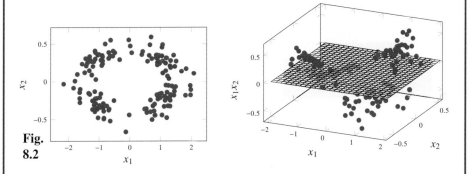

Fig. 8.2

However, by adding the non-linear transformation $x_1 x_2$ as a feature, such that $\boldsymbol{\phi}(\mathbf{x}) = [x_1 \ x_2 \ x_1 x_2]^\mathsf{T}$, we get the situation in the right panel in Figure 8.2. With this relatively simple introduction of an extra feature, the problem now appears to be much better suited to a linear classifier, since the data can be separated relatively well by the sketched plane. The conclusion here is that one strategy for increasing the capability of otherwise relatively simple methods is to introduce non-linear feature transformations.

Polynomials are only one out of (infinitely) many possible choices of features $\boldsymbol{\phi}(\mathbf{x})$. One should take care when using polynomials higher than second order in practice because of their behavior outside the range where the data is observed (recall Figure 8.1b). Instead, there are several alternatives that are often more useful in practice, such as Fourier series, essentially corresponding to (for scalar x) $\boldsymbol{\phi}(x) = [1 \ \sin(x) \ \cos(x) \ \sin(2x) \ \cos(2x) \ \cdots]^\mathsf{T}$, step functions, regression splines, etc. The use of non-linear input transformations $\boldsymbol{\phi}(\mathbf{x})$ arguably makes simple models more flexible and applicable to real-world problems with non-linear characteristics. In order to obtain good performance, it is important to chose $\boldsymbol{\phi}(\mathbf{x})$ such that enough flexibility is obtained but overfitting avoided. With a very careful choice of $\boldsymbol{\phi}(\mathbf{x})$, good performance can be obtained for many problems, but that choice is problem-specific and requires some craftmanship. Let us instead explore the conceptual idea of letting the number of features $d \to \infty$ and combine this with regularisation. In a sense this will automate the choice of features, and it leads us to a family of powerful off-the-shelf machine learning tools called kernel methods.

8.2 Kernel Ridge Regression

A carefully engineered transformation $\phi(x)$ in linear regression, or any other method for that matter, may indeed perform well for a specific machine learning problem. However, we would like $\phi(x)$ to contain a lot of transformations that could possibly be of interest for most problems, in order to obtain a general off-the-shelf method. We will, therefore, explore the idea of choosing d really large, much larger than the number of data points n, and eventually even let $d \to \infty$. The derivation and reasoning will be done using L^2-regularised linear regression, but we will later see that the idea is also applicable to other model types.

Re-formulating Linear Regression

First of all, we have to use some kind of regularisation if we are going to increase d in linear regression, in order to avoid overfitting when $d > n$. For reasons that we will discuss later, we chose to use L^2-regularisation. Recall the equation for L^2-regularised linear regression:

$$\widehat{\theta} = \arg\min_{\theta} \frac{1}{n} \sum_{i=1}^{n} \big(\underbrace{\theta^{\mathsf{T}} \phi(\mathbf{x}_i)}_{\widehat{y}(\mathbf{x}_i)} - y_i \big)^2 + \lambda \|\theta\|_2^2 = (\mathbf{\Phi}(\mathbf{X})^{\mathsf{T}} \mathbf{\Phi}(\mathbf{X}) + n\lambda \mathbf{I})^{-1} \mathbf{\Phi}(\mathbf{X})^{\mathsf{T}} \mathbf{y},$$

$$(8.4a)$$

We have not fixed the non-linear transformations $\phi(\mathbf{x})$ to anything specific yet, but we are preparing for choosing $d \gg n$ in these transformations. The downside of choosing d, the dimension of $\phi(\mathbf{x})$, large is that we also have to learn d parameters when training. In linear regression, we usually first learn and store the d-dimensional vector $\widehat{\theta}$, and thereafter we use it for computing a prediction

$$\widehat{y}(\mathbf{x}_\star) = \widehat{\theta}^{\mathsf{T}} \phi(\mathbf{x}_\star). \tag{8.5}$$

To be able to choose d really large, conceptually even $d \to \infty$, we have to re-formulate the model such that there are no computations or storage demands that scale with d. The first step is to realise that the prediction $\widehat{y}(\mathbf{x}_\star)$ can be rewritten as

$$\widehat{y}(\mathbf{x}_\star) = \underbrace{\widehat{\theta}^{\mathsf{T}}}_{1 \times d} \underbrace{\phi(\mathbf{x}_\star)}_{d \times 1} = (\mathbf{\Phi}(\mathbf{X})^{\mathsf{T}} \mathbf{\Phi}(\mathbf{X}) + n\lambda \mathbf{I})^{-1} \mathbf{\Phi}(\mathbf{X})^{\mathsf{T}} \mathbf{y})^{\mathsf{T}} \phi(\mathbf{x}_\star)$$

$$= \underbrace{\mathbf{y}^{\mathsf{T}}}_{1 \times n} \underbrace{\mathbf{\Phi}(\mathbf{X})}_{n \times d} \underbrace{(\mathbf{\Phi}(\mathbf{X})^{\mathsf{T}} \mathbf{\Phi}(\mathbf{X}) + n\lambda \mathbf{I})^{-1}}_{d \times d} \underbrace{\phi(\mathbf{x}_\star)}_{d \times 1}, \tag{8.6}$$

$$\underbrace{\phantom{\mathbf{y}^{\mathsf{T}} \mathbf{\Phi}(\mathbf{X}) (\mathbf{\Phi}(\mathbf{X})^{\mathsf{T}} \mathbf{\Phi}(\mathbf{X}) + n\lambda \mathbf{I})^{-1} \phi(\mathbf{x}_\star)}}_{n \times 1}$$

where the underbraces give the sizes of the corresponding vectors and matrices. This expression for $\widehat{y}(\mathbf{x}_\star)$ suggests that, instead of computing and storing the d-dimensional $\widehat{\theta}$ once (independently of $\mathbf{x}_\star$), we could, for each test input $\mathbf{x}_\star$, compute the n-dimensional vector $\boldsymbol{\Phi}(\mathbf{X})(\boldsymbol{\Phi}(\mathbf{X})^\mathsf{T}\boldsymbol{\Phi}(\mathbf{X}) + n\lambda\mathbf{I})^{-1}\boldsymbol{\phi}(\mathbf{x}_\star)$. By doing so, we avoid storing a d-dimensional vector. But this would still require the inversion of a $d \times d$ matrix. We therefore have some more work to do before we have a practically useful method where we can select d arbitrarily large.

The push-through matrix identity says that $\mathbf{A}(\mathbf{A}^\mathsf{T}\mathbf{A} + \mathbf{I})^{-1} = (\mathbf{A}\mathbf{A}^\mathsf{T} + \mathbf{I})^{-1}\mathbf{A}$ holds for any matrix $\mathbf{A}$. By using it in (8.6), we can further rewrite $\widehat{y}(\mathbf{x}_\star)$ as

$$\widehat{y}(\mathbf{x}_\star) = \underbrace{\mathbf{y}^\mathsf{T}}_{1\times n} \underbrace{(\boldsymbol{\Phi}(\mathbf{X})\boldsymbol{\Phi}(\mathbf{X})^\mathsf{T} + n\lambda\mathbf{I})^{-1}}_{n\times n} \underbrace{\boldsymbol{\Phi}(\mathbf{X})\boldsymbol{\phi}(\mathbf{x}_\star)}_{n\times 1}. \tag{8.7}$$

It appears in (8.7) as if we can compute $\widehat{y}(\mathbf{x}_\star)$ *without* having to deal with any d-dimensional vectors or matrices, provided that the matrix multiplications $\boldsymbol{\Phi}(\mathbf{X})\boldsymbol{\Phi}(\mathbf{X})^\mathsf{T}$ and $\boldsymbol{\Phi}(\mathbf{X})\boldsymbol{\phi}(\mathbf{x}_\star)$ in (8.7) can somehow be computed. Let us therefore have a closer look at these:

$$\boldsymbol{\Phi}(\mathbf{X})\boldsymbol{\Phi}(\mathbf{X})^\mathsf{T} = \begin{bmatrix} \boldsymbol{\phi}(\mathbf{x}_1)^\mathsf{T}\boldsymbol{\phi}(\mathbf{x}_1) & \boldsymbol{\phi}(\mathbf{x}_1)^\mathsf{T}\boldsymbol{\phi}(\mathbf{x}_2) & \cdots & \boldsymbol{\phi}(\mathbf{x}_1)^\mathsf{T}\boldsymbol{\phi}(\mathbf{x}_n) \\ \boldsymbol{\phi}(\mathbf{x}_2)^\mathsf{T}\boldsymbol{\phi}(\mathbf{x}_1) & \boldsymbol{\phi}(\mathbf{x}_2)^\mathsf{T}\boldsymbol{\phi}(\mathbf{x}_2) & \cdots & \boldsymbol{\phi}(\mathbf{x}_2)^\mathsf{T}\boldsymbol{\phi}(\mathbf{x}_n) \\ \vdots & & \ddots & \vdots \\ \boldsymbol{\phi}(\mathbf{x}_n)^\mathsf{T}\boldsymbol{\phi}(\mathbf{x}_1) & \boldsymbol{\phi}(\mathbf{x}_n)^\mathsf{T}\boldsymbol{\phi}(\mathbf{x}_2) & \cdots & \boldsymbol{\phi}(\mathbf{x}_n)^\mathsf{T}\boldsymbol{\phi}(\mathbf{x}_n) \end{bmatrix} \quad \text{and} \tag{8.8}$$

$$\boldsymbol{\Phi}(\mathbf{X})\boldsymbol{\phi}(\mathbf{x}_\star) = \begin{bmatrix} \boldsymbol{\phi}(\mathbf{x}_1)^\mathsf{T}\boldsymbol{\phi}(\mathbf{x}_\star) \\ \boldsymbol{\phi}(\mathbf{x}_2)^\mathsf{T}\boldsymbol{\phi}(\mathbf{x}_\star) \\ \vdots \\ \boldsymbol{\phi}(\mathbf{x}_n)^\mathsf{T}\boldsymbol{\phi}(\mathbf{x}_\star) \end{bmatrix}. \tag{8.9}$$

Remember that $\boldsymbol{\phi}(\mathbf{x})^\mathsf{T}\boldsymbol{\phi}(\mathbf{x}')$ is an inner product between the two d-dimensional vectors $\boldsymbol{\phi}(\mathbf{x})$ and $\boldsymbol{\phi}(\mathbf{x}')$. The key insight here is to note that the transformed inputs $\boldsymbol{\phi}(\mathbf{x})$ enter into (8.7) only as inner products $\boldsymbol{\phi}(\mathbf{x})^\mathsf{T}\boldsymbol{\phi}(\mathbf{x}')$, where each inner product is a scalar. That is, if we are able to compute the inner product $\boldsymbol{\phi}(\mathbf{x})^\mathsf{T}\boldsymbol{\phi}(\mathbf{x}')$ directly, without first explicitly computing the d-dimensional $\boldsymbol{\phi}(\mathbf{x})$, we have reached our goal.

As a concrete illustration, let us for simplicity consider polynomials. With $p = 1$, meaning $\mathbf{x}$ is a scalar x, and $\boldsymbol{\phi}(x)$ is a third-order polynomial ($d = 4$) with the second and third-term scaled by $\sqrt{3}$,[2] we have

$$\boldsymbol{\phi}(x)^\mathsf{T}\boldsymbol{\phi}(x') = \begin{bmatrix} 1 & \sqrt{3}x & \sqrt{3}x^2 & x^3 \end{bmatrix} \begin{bmatrix} 1 \\ \sqrt{3}x' \\ \sqrt{3}x'^2 \\ x'^3 \end{bmatrix}$$

$$= 1 + 3xx' + 3x^2x'^2 + x^3x'^3 = (1 + xx')^3. \tag{8.10}$$

It can generally be shown that if $\boldsymbol{\phi}(x)$ is a (suitably re-scaled) polynomial of order $d - 1$, then $\boldsymbol{\phi}(x)^\mathsf{T}\boldsymbol{\phi}(x') = (1 + xx')^{d-1}$. The point we want to make is that instead of first computing the two d-dimensional vectors $\boldsymbol{\phi}(x)$ and $\boldsymbol{\phi}(x')$ and thereafter

---

[2] The scaling $\sqrt{3}$ can be compensated for by an inverse scaling of the second and third element in $\boldsymbol{\theta}$.

computing their inner product, we could just evaluate the expression $(1 + xx')^{d-1}$ directly instead. With a second- or third-order polynomial, this might not make much of a difference, but consider the computational scaling in a situation where it is of interest to use d in the hundreds or thousands.

The main point we are getting at is that *if we just make the choice of $\phi(\mathbf{x})$ such that the inner product $\phi(\mathbf{x})^\mathsf{T}\phi(\mathbf{x}')$ can be computed without first computing $\phi(\mathbf{x})$, we can let d be arbitrary big.* Since it is possible to define inner products between infinite-dimensional vectors, there is nothing preventing us from letting $d \to \infty$.

We have now derived a version of L^2-regularised linear regression that we can use in practice with an unbounded number of features d in $\phi(\mathbf{x})$, if we restrict ourselves to $\phi(\mathbf{x})$ such that its inner product $\phi(\mathbf{x})^\mathsf{T}\phi(\mathbf{x}')$ has a closed-form expression (or can, at least, be computed in such a way that it does not scale with d). This might appear to be of rather limited interest for a machine learning engineer, since one still has to come up with a non-linear transformation $\phi(\mathbf{x})$, choose d (possibly ∞), and thereafter make a pen-and-paper derivation (like (8.10)) of $\phi(\mathbf{x})^\mathsf{T}\phi(\mathbf{x}')$. Fortunately it is possible to bypass this by introducing the concept of a *kernel*.

Introducing the Kernel Idea

A kernel $\kappa(\mathbf{x}, \mathbf{x}')$ is (in this book) any function that takes two arguments $\mathbf{x}$ and $\mathbf{x}'$ from the same space and returns a scalar. Throughout this book, we will limit ourselves to kernels that are real-valued and symmetric, that is, $\kappa(\mathbf{x}, \mathbf{x}') = \kappa(\mathbf{x}', \mathbf{x}) \in \mathbb{R}$ for all $\mathbf{x}$ and $\mathbf{x}'$. Equation (8.10), for example, is such a kernel. And more generally, the inner product of two non-linear input transformations is an example of a kernel:

$$\kappa(\mathbf{x}, \mathbf{x}') = \phi(\mathbf{x})^\mathsf{T}\phi(\mathbf{x}'). \tag{8.11}$$

The important point at this stage is that since $\phi(\mathbf{x})$ only appears in the linear regression model (8.7) via inner products, we do not have to design a d-dimensional vector $\phi(\mathbf{x})$ and derive its inner product. Instead, we can just choose a kernel $\kappa(\mathbf{x}, \mathbf{x}')$ directly. This is known as the *kernel trick*:

> If $\mathbf{x}$ enters the model as $\phi(\mathbf{x})^\mathsf{T}\phi(\mathbf{x}')$ only, we can choose a kernel $\kappa(\mathbf{x}, \mathbf{x}')$ instead of chosing $\phi(\mathbf{x})$.

To be clear on what this means in practice, we rewrite (8.7) using the kernel (8.11):

$$\widehat{y}(\mathbf{x}_\star) = \underbrace{\mathbf{y}^\mathsf{T}}_{1 \times n} \underbrace{(K(\mathbf{X}, \mathbf{X}) + n\lambda\mathbf{I})^{-1}}_{n \times n} \underbrace{K(\mathbf{X}, \mathbf{x}_\star)}_{n \times 1}, \tag{8.12a}$$

$$\text{where } K(\mathbf{X}, \mathbf{X}) = \begin{bmatrix} \kappa(\mathbf{x}_1, \mathbf{x}_1) & \kappa(\mathbf{x}_1, \mathbf{x}_2) & \cdots & \kappa(\mathbf{x}_1, \mathbf{x}_n) \\ \kappa(\mathbf{x}_2, \mathbf{x}_1) & \kappa(\mathbf{x}_2, \mathbf{x}_2) & \cdots & \kappa(\mathbf{x}_2, \mathbf{x}_n) \\ \vdots & & \ddots & \vdots \\ \kappa(\mathbf{x}_n, \mathbf{x}_1) & \kappa(\mathbf{x}_n, \mathbf{x}_2) & \cdots & \kappa(\mathbf{x}_n, \mathbf{x}_n) \end{bmatrix} \text{ and} \tag{8.12b}$$

$$K(\mathbf{X}, \mathbf{x}_\star) = \begin{bmatrix} \kappa(\mathbf{x}_1, \mathbf{x}_\star) \\ \kappa(\mathbf{x}_2, \mathbf{x}_\star) \\ \vdots \\ \kappa(\mathbf{x}_n, \mathbf{x}_\star) \end{bmatrix}. \tag{8.12c}$$

These equations describe linear regression with L^2-regularisation using a kernel $\kappa(\mathbf{x}, \mathbf{x}')$. Since L^2-regularisation is also called ridge regression, we refer to (8.12) as kernel ridge regression. The $n \times n$ matrix $K(\mathbf{X}, \mathbf{X})$ is obtained by evaluating the kernel at all pairs of training inputs and is called the *Gram matrix*. We initially argued that linear regression with a possibly infinite-dimensional non-linear transformation vector $\boldsymbol{\phi}(\mathbf{x})$ could be an interesting model, and (8.12) is (for certain choices of $\boldsymbol{\phi}(\mathbf{x})$ and $\kappa(\mathbf{x}, \mathbf{x}')$) equivalent to this. The design choice for the user is now to select a kernel $\kappa(\mathbf{x}, \mathbf{x}')$ instead of $\boldsymbol{\phi}(\mathbf{x})$. In practice, choosing $\kappa(\mathbf{x}, \mathbf{x}')$ is a much less tedious problem than choosing $\boldsymbol{\phi}(\mathbf{x})$.

As users, we may in principle choose the kernel $\kappa(\mathbf{x}, \mathbf{x}')$ arbitrarily, as long as we can compute (8.12a). This requires that the inverse of $K(\mathbf{X}, \mathbf{X}) + n\lambda\mathbf{I}$ exists. We are, therefore, on the safe side if we restrict ourselves to kernels for which the Gram matrix $K(\mathbf{X}, \mathbf{X})$ is always positive semidefinite. Such kernels are called positive semidefinite kernels.[3] Hence, the user of kernel ridge regression chooses a positive semidefinite kernel $\kappa(\mathbf{x}, \mathbf{x}')$ and neither has to select nor compute $\boldsymbol{\phi}(\mathbf{x})$. However, a corresponding $\boldsymbol{\phi}(\mathbf{x})$ always exists for a positive semidefinite kernel, as we will discuss in Section 8.4.

There is a number of positive semidefinite kernels commonly used in practice. One positive semidefinite kernel is the squared exponential kernel (also known as the RBF, exponentiated quadratic or Gaussian kernel),

$$\kappa(\mathbf{x}, \mathbf{x}') = \exp\left(-\frac{\|\mathbf{x} - \mathbf{x}'\|_2^2}{2\ell^2}\right), \tag{8.13}$$

where the hyperparameter $\ell > 0$ is a design choice left to the user, for example to be chosen using cross validation. Another example of a positive semidefinite kernel mentioned earlier is the polynomial kernel $\kappa(\mathbf{x}, \mathbf{x}') = (c + \mathbf{x}^\mathsf{T}\mathbf{x}')^{d-1}$. A special case thereof is the linear kernel $\kappa(\mathbf{x}, \mathbf{x}') = \mathbf{x}^\mathsf{T}\mathbf{x}'$. We will give more examples later.

From the formulation (8.12), it may seem as if we have to compute the inverse of $K(\mathbf{X}, \mathbf{X}) + n\lambda\mathbf{I}$ every time we want to make a prediction. That is, however, not necessary since it does not depend on the test input $\mathbf{x}_\star$. It is, therefore, wise to introduce the n-dimensional vector

$$\widehat{\boldsymbol{\alpha}} = \begin{bmatrix} \widehat{\alpha}_1 \\ \widehat{\alpha}_2 \\ \vdots \\ \widehat{\alpha}_n \end{bmatrix} = \mathbf{y}^\mathsf{T}(K(\mathbf{X}, \mathbf{X}) + n\lambda\mathbf{I})^{-1}, \tag{8.14a}$$

---

[3] Confusingly enough, such kernels are called positive definite in some texts.

which allows us to rewrite kernel ridge regression (8.12) as

$$\widehat{y}(\mathbf{x}_\star) = \widehat{\alpha}^\mathsf{T} K(\mathbf{X}, \mathbf{x}_\star). \tag{8.14b}$$

That is, instead of computing and storing a d-dimensional vector $\widehat{\theta}$ as in standard linear regression, we now compute and store an n-dimensional vector $\widehat{\alpha}$. However, we also need to store $\mathbf{X}$, since we have to compute $K(\mathbf{X}, \mathbf{x}_\star)$ for every prediction.

We summarise kernel ridge regression in Method 8.1 and illustrate it by Example 8.2. Kernel ridge regression is in itself a practically useful method. That being said, we will next take a step back and discuss what we have derived, in order to prepare for more kernel methods. We will also come back to kernel ridge regression in Chapter 9, where it is used as a stepping stone in deriving the Gaussian process regression model.

Example 8.2 Linear regression with kernels

We consider again the car stopping distance problem from Example 2.2 and apply kernel ridge regression to it. We use $\lambda = 0.01$ here and explore what happens when using different kernels.

We start, in the left panel in Figure 8.3, using the squared exponential kernel with $\ell = 1$ (blue line). We see that it does not really interpolate well between the data points, whereas $\ell = 3$ (green line) gives a more sensible behavior. (We could select ℓ using cross validation, but we do not pursue that any further here.)

It is interesting to note that prediction reverts to zero when extrapolating beyond the range of the training data. This is, in fact, a general property of the squared exponential kernel as well as many other commonly used kernels. The reason for this behavior is that, by construction, the kernel $\kappa(\mathbf{x}, \mathbf{x}')$ drops to zero as the distance between $\mathbf{x}$ and $\mathbf{x}'$ increases. Intuitively, this means that the resulting predictions are based on local interpolation, and as we extrapolate far beyond the range of the training data, the method will revert to a 'default prediction' of zero. This can be seen from (8.14b) – if $\mathbf{x}_\star$ is far from the training data points, then all elements of the vector $K(\mathbf{X}, \mathbf{x}_\star)$ will be close to zero (for a kernel with the aforementioned property) and so will the resulting prediction.

We have previously seen that this data, to some extent, follows a quadratic function. As we will discuss in Section 8.4, the sum of two kernels is another kernel. In the right panel in Figure 8.3, we therefore try using the sum of the squared exponential kernel (with $\ell = 3$) *and* the polynomial kernel of degree 2 ($d = 3$) (red line). As a reference, we also include kernel ridge regression with only the polynomial kernel of degree 2 ($d = 3$) (dashed blue line; equivalent to L^2-regularised polynomial regression). The combined kernel gives a more flexible model than only a quadratic function, but it also (for this example) seems to extrapolate better than only using the squared exponential kernel.

This can be understood by noting that the polynomial kernel is *not local* (in the sense discussed above). That is, it does not drop to zero for test data points that are far from the training data. Instead it corresponds to a polynomial trend, and the predictions will follow this trend when extrapolating. Note that the two kernels considered here result in very similar extrapolations. The reason for this is that the

---

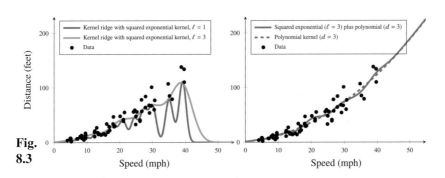

Fig. 8.3

squared exponential component of the combined kernel will only 'be active' when interpolating. For extrapolation, the combined kernel will thus revert to using only the polynomial component.

By studying Figure 8.3, we can see that kernel ridge regression is a very flexible model, and the result is highly dependent on the choice of kernel. As we will stress throughout this (and the next) chapter, the kernel is indeed a crucial choice for the machine learning engineer when using kernel methods.

Time to reflect 8.2 *Verify that you retrieve L^2-regularised linear regression, without any non-linear transformations, by using the linear kernel $\kappa(\mathbf{x}, \mathbf{x}') = \mathbf{x}^\mathsf{T}\mathbf{x}$ in (8.12).*

Learn Kernel ridge regression

Data: Training data $\mathcal{T} = \{\mathbf{x}_i, y_i\}_{i=1}^n$ and a kernel κ
Result: Learned dual parameters $\widehat{\alpha}$

1 Compute $\widehat{\alpha}$ as per (8.14a)

Predict with Kernel ridge regression

Data: Learned dual parameters $\widehat{\alpha}$ and test input $\mathbf{x}_\star$
Result: Prediction $\widehat{y}(\mathbf{x}_\star)$

1 Compute $\widehat{y}(\mathbf{x}_\star)$ as (8.14b).

Method 8.1 Kernel ridge regression.

8.3 Support Vector Regression

Kernel ridge regression, as we just derived, is our fist kernel method for regression, which is a useful method on its own. We will now extend kernel ridge regression into support vector regression by replacing the loss function. First, however, we

197

take a step back and make an interesting observation that suggests the so-called representer theorem, which will be useful later in this chapter.

Preparing for More Kernel Methods: The Representer Theorem

The formulation (8.14) is not only practical for implementation; it is also important for theoretical understanding. We can interpret (8.14) as a *dual formulation* of linear regression, where we have the *dual parameters* α instead of the primal formulation (8.4) with primal parameters θ. Remember that d, the (possibly infinite) number of primal parameters in θ, is a user design choice, whereas n, the number of dual parameters in α, is the number of data points.

By comparing (8.14b) and (8.5), we have that

$$\widehat{y}(\mathbf{x}_\star) = \widehat{\boldsymbol{\theta}}^\mathsf{T} \boldsymbol{\phi}(\mathbf{x}_\star) = \widehat{\boldsymbol{\alpha}}^\mathsf{T} \underbrace{\boldsymbol{\Phi}(\mathbf{X})\boldsymbol{\phi}(\mathbf{x}_\star)}_{K(\mathbf{X},\mathbf{x}_\star)} \tag{8.15}$$

for all $\mathbf{x}_\star$, which suggests that

$$\widehat{\boldsymbol{\theta}} = \boldsymbol{\Phi}(\mathbf{X})^\mathsf{T}\widehat{\boldsymbol{\alpha}}. \tag{8.16}$$

This relationship between the primal parameters θ and the dual parameters α is not specific for kernel ridge regression, but (8.16) is the consequence of a general result called *the representer theorem*.

In essence, the representer theorem states that if $\widehat{y}(\mathbf{x}) = \boldsymbol{\theta}^\mathsf{T}\boldsymbol{\phi}(\mathbf{x})$, the equation (8.16) holds when θ is learned using (almost) any loss function and L^2-regularisation. A full treatment is beyond the scope of this chapter, but we give a complete statement of the theorem in Section 8.A. An implication of the representer theorem is that L^2-regularisation is crucial in order to obtain kernel ridge regression (8.14), and we could not have achieved it using, say, L^1 regularisation instead. The representer theorem is a cornerstone of most kernel methods, since it tells us that *we can express some models in terms of dual parameters α (of finite length n) and a kernel $\kappa(\mathbf{x}, \mathbf{x}')$, instead of the primal parameters θ (possibly of infinite length d) and a non-linear feature transformation $\boldsymbol{\phi}(\mathbf{x})$*, just like we did with linear regression in (8.14).

Support Vector Regression

We will now look at support vector regression, another off-the-shelf kernel method for regression. From a model perspective, the only difference to kernel ridge regression is a change of loss function. This new loss function has an interesting effect in that the dual parameter vector $\widehat{\boldsymbol{\alpha}}$ in support vector regression becomes *sparse*, meaning that several elements of $\widehat{\boldsymbol{\alpha}}$ are exactly zero. Recall that we can associate each element in $\widehat{\boldsymbol{\alpha}}$ with one training data point. The training data points corresponding to the non-zero elements of $\widehat{\boldsymbol{\alpha}}$ are referred to as *support vectors*, and the prediction $\widehat{y}(\mathbf{x}_\star)$

will depend only on these (in contrast to kernel ridge regression (8.14b), where all training data points are needed to compute $\widehat{y}(\mathbf{x}_\star)$). This makes support vector regression an example of a so-called *support vector machine* (SVM), a family of methods with sparse dual parameter vectors.

The loss function we will use for support vector regression is the ϵ-insensitive loss,

$$L(y,\widehat{y}) = \begin{cases} 0 & \text{if } |y - \widehat{y}| < \epsilon, \\ |y - \widehat{y}| - \epsilon & \text{otherwise,} \end{cases} \tag{8.17}$$

or equivalently $L(y,\widehat{y}) = \max 0, |y - \widehat{y}| - \epsilon$, which was introduced in (5.9) in Chapter 5. The parameter ϵ is a user design choice. In its primal formulation, support vector regression also makes use of the linear regression model

$$\widehat{y}(\mathbf{x}_\star) = \boldsymbol{\theta}^\mathsf{T}\boldsymbol{\phi}(\mathbf{x}_\star), \tag{8.18a}$$

but instead of the least square cost function in (8.4), we now have

$$\widehat{\boldsymbol{\theta}} = \arg\min_{\boldsymbol{\theta}} \frac{1}{n}\sum_{i=1}^{n} \max\{0, \underbrace{|y_i - \boldsymbol{\theta}^\mathsf{T}\boldsymbol{\phi}(\mathbf{x}_i)|}_{\widehat{y}(\mathbf{x}_i)} - \epsilon\} + \lambda\|\boldsymbol{\theta}\|_2^2. \tag{8.18b}$$

As with kernel ridge regression, we reformulate the primal formulation (8.18) into a dual formulation with α instead of $\boldsymbol{\theta}$ and use the kernel trick. For the dual formulation, we cannot repeat the convenient closed-form derivation along the lines of (8.4–8.14) since there is no closed-form solution for $\widehat{\boldsymbol{\theta}}$. Instead we have to use optimisation theory, introduce slack variables, and construct the Lagrangian of (8.18b). We do not give the full derivation here (it is similar to the derivation of support vector classification in Appendix 8.B), but as it turns out, the dual formulation becomes

$$\widehat{y}(\mathbf{x}_\star) = \widehat{\boldsymbol{\alpha}}^\mathsf{T}K(\mathbf{X},\mathbf{x}_\star), \tag{8.19a}$$

where $\widehat{\boldsymbol{\alpha}}$ is the solution to the optimisation problem

$$\widehat{\boldsymbol{\alpha}} = \arg\min_{\boldsymbol{\alpha}} \frac{1}{2}\boldsymbol{\alpha}^\mathsf{T}K(\mathbf{X},\mathbf{X})\boldsymbol{\alpha} - \boldsymbol{\alpha}^\mathsf{T}\mathbf{y} + \epsilon\|\boldsymbol{\alpha}\|_1, \tag{8.19b}$$

$$\text{subject to } |\alpha_i| \leq \frac{1}{2n\lambda}. \tag{8.19c}$$

Note that (8.19a) is identical to the corresponding expression for kernel ridge regression (8.14b). This is a consequence of the representer theorem. The only difference to kernel ridge regression is how the dual parameters α are learned: by numerically solving the optimisation problem (8.19b) instead of using the closed-form solution in (8.14a).

The ϵ-insensitive loss function could be used for any regression model, but it is particularly interesting in this kernel context since the dual parameter vector α becomes sparse (meaning that only some elements are non-zero). Remember that α has one entry per training data point. This implies that the prediction (8.19a) depends only on *some* of the training data points, namely those whose corresponding α_i is non-zero, the so-called *support vectors*. In fact it can be shown that the support vectors are the data points for which the loss function is non-zero, that is, the data points for which $|\widehat{y}(\mathbf{x}_i) - y_i| \geq \epsilon$. That is, a larger ϵ results in fewer support vectors, and vice versa. This effect can also be understood by interpreting ϵ as a regularisation parameter in an L^1 penalty in the dual formulation (8.19b). (The number of support vectors is, however, also affected by λ, since λ influences the shape of $\widehat{y}(\mathbf{x})$.) We illustrate this in Example 8.3.

All training data is indeed used at training time (that is, solving (8.19b)), but when making predictions (using (8.19a)), only the support vectors contribute. This can significantly reduce the computational burden. The larger ϵ chosen by the user, the fewer support vectors and the fewer computations needed when making predictions. It can, therefore, be said that ϵ has a regularising effect, in the sense that the more/fewer support vectors that are used, the more/less complicated model. We summarise support vector regression in Method 8.2.

Learn support vector regression

Data: Training data $\mathcal{T} = \{\mathbf{x}_i, y_i\}_{i=1}^n$
Result: Learned parameters $\widehat{\alpha}$

1 Compute $\widehat{\alpha}$ by numerically solving (8.19b–8.19c)

Predict with kernel ridge regression

Data: Learned parameters $\widehat{\alpha}$ and test input $\mathbf{x}_\star$
Result: Prediction $\widehat{y}(\mathbf{x}_\star)$

1 Compute $\widehat{y}(\mathbf{x}_\star)$ as per (8.19a).

Method 8.2 Support vector regression.

Example 8.3 Support vector regression and kernel ridge regression

We consider yet again the car stopping distance problem from Example 2.2 in Figure 8.4. With the combined squared exponential and polynomial kernel from Example 8.2, $\lambda = 0.01$ and $\epsilon = 15$, we apply support vector regression to the data (red line). As a reference, we also show the corresponding kernel ridge regression (blue line).

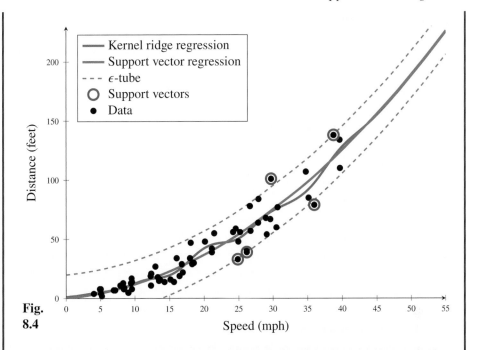

Fig. 8.4

In Figure 8.4, we have circled (in red) all data points for which $\alpha_i \neq 0$, the so-called support vectors. We have also included the 'ϵ-tube' ($\widehat{y}(\mathbf{x}) \pm \epsilon$; dotted lines), and we can confirm that all support vectors are located outside the 'ϵ-tube'. This is a direct effect of using the ϵ-insensitive loss, which explicitly encodes that the loss function for data points within ϵ from $\widehat{y}(\mathbf{x})$ is exactly zero. If choosing a smaller ϵ, we would have more support vectors, and vice versa. Another consequence of the sparsity of α is that when computing a prediction (8.19a) with support vector regression, it is sufficient to do the computation using (in this case) only five data points. For kernel ridge regression, which does not have a sparse α, the prediction (8.14b) depends on all 62 data points.

The ϵ-insensitive loss makes the dual parameter vector α sparse. Note, however, that this does *not* mean that the corresponding primal parameter vector θ is sparse (their relationship is given by (8.16)). Also note that (8.19b) is a *constrained* optimisation problem (there is a constraint given by (8.19c)), and more theory than we presented in Section 5.4 is needed to derive a good solver.

The feature vector $\mathbf{\Phi}(\mathbf{x})$ corresponding to some kernels, such as the squared exponential kernel (8.13), does not have a constant offset term. Therefore, an additional θ_0 is sometimes included in (8.19a) for support vector regression, which adds the constraint $\sum_i \alpha_i = 0$ to the optimisation problem in (8.19b). The same addition could also be made to kernel ridge regression (8.14b), but that would break the closed-form calculation of α (8.14b).

Conclusions on Using Kernels for Regression

With kernel ridge regression and support vector regression, we have been dealing with the interplay between three different concepts, each of them interesting on its own. To clarify this, we repeat them in an ordered list:

(i) We have considered the **primal and dual formulations** of a model. The primal formulation expresses the model in terms of θ (fixed size d), whereas the dual formulation uses α (one α_i per data point i, hence α has size is n no matter what d happens to be). Both formulations are mathematically equivalent but more or less useful in practice depending on whether $d > n$ or $n > d$.

(ii) We have introduced **kernels** $\kappa(\mathbf{x}, \mathbf{x}')$, which allows us to let $d \to \infty$ without explicitly formulating an infinite vector of non-linear transformations $\boldsymbol{\phi}(\mathbf{x})$. This idea is practically useful only when using the dual formulation with α, since d is the dimension of θ.

(iii) We have used **different loss functions**. Kernel ridge regression makes use of squared error loss, whereas support vector regression uses the ϵ-insensitive loss. The ϵ-insensitive loss is particularly interesting in the dual formulation, since it gives *sparse* α. (We will later also use the hinge loss for support vector classification in Section 8.5, which has a similar effect.)

We will now spend some additional effort on understanding the kernel concept in Section 8.4 and thereafter introduce support vector classification in Section 8.5.

8.4 Kernel Theory

We have defined a kernel as being any function taking two arguments from the same space and returning a scalar. We have also suggested that we can often restrict ourselves to positive semidefinite kernels, and presented two practically useful algorithms – kernel ridge regression and support vector regression. Before we continue and introduce support vector classification, we will discuss the kernel concept further and also give a flavour of the available theory behind it. To make the discussion more concrete, let us start by introducing another kernel method, namely a kernel version of k-NN.

Introducing Kernel k-NN

As you know from Chapter 2, k-NN constructs the prediction for $\mathbf{x}_\star$ by taking the average or a majority vote among the k nearest neighbours to $\mathbf{x}_\star$. In its standard formulation, 'nearest' is defined by the Euclidean distance. Since the Euclidean distance is always positive, we can equivalently consider the squared Euclidean distance instead, which can be written in terms of the linear kernel $\kappa(\mathbf{x}, \mathbf{x}') = \mathbf{x}^\mathsf{T}\mathbf{x}'$ as

$$\|\mathbf{x} - \mathbf{x}'\|_2^2 = (\mathbf{x} - \mathbf{x}')^\mathsf{T}(\mathbf{x} - \mathbf{x}') = \mathbf{x}^\mathsf{T}\mathbf{x} + \mathbf{x}'^\mathsf{T}\mathbf{x}' - 2\mathbf{x}^\mathsf{T}\mathbf{x}'$$
$$= \kappa(\mathbf{x}, \mathbf{x}) + \kappa(\mathbf{x}', \mathbf{x}') - 2\kappa(\mathbf{x}, \mathbf{x}'). \tag{8.20}$$

To generalise the k-NN algorithm to use kernels, we allow the linear kernel to be replaced by any, say, positive semidefinite kernel $\kappa(\mathbf{x}, \mathbf{x}')$ in (8.20). *Kernel k-NN* thus works the same as standard k-NN but determines proximity between the data points using the right hand side of (8.20) with a user-chosen kernel $\kappa(\mathbf{x}, \mathbf{x}')$ instead of the left hand side of (8.20).

For many (but not all) kernels, it holds that $\kappa(\mathbf{x}, \mathbf{x}) = \kappa(\mathbf{x}', \mathbf{x}') = $ constant for all $\mathbf{x}$ and $\mathbf{x}'$, suggesting that the most interesting part of the right hand side of (8.20) is the term $-2\kappa(\mathbf{x}, \mathbf{x}')$. Thus, if $\kappa(\mathbf{x}, \mathbf{x}')$ takes a large value, the two data points $\mathbf{x}$ and $\mathbf{x}'$ are considered to be close, and vice versa. That is, *the kernel determines how close any two data points are*.

Furthermore, kernel k-NN allows us to also use k-NN for data where the Euclidean distance has no natural meaning. As long as we have a kernel which acts on the input space, we can apply kernel k-NN even if the Euclidean distance is not defined for that input type. We can thereby apply kernel k-NN to input data that is neither numerical nor categorical, such as text snippets, as illustrated by Example 8.4.

Example 8.4 Kernel k-NN for interpreting words

This example illustrates how kernel k-NN can be applied to text data, where the Euclidean distance has no meaning, and standard k-NN therefore cannot be applied. In this example, the input is single words (or more technically, character strings), and we use the so-called Levenshtein distance to construct a kernel. The Levenshtein distance is the number of single-character edits needed to transform one word (string) into another. It takes two strings and returns a non-negative integer, which is zero only if the two strings are equivalent. It fulfills the properties of being a metric on the space of character strings, and we can thereby use it, for example, in the squared exponential to construct a kernel as $\kappa(x, x') = \exp\left(-\frac{(\mathrm{LD}(x, x'))^2}{2\ell^2}\right)$ (where LD is the Levenshtein distance) with, say, $\ell = 5$.

In this very small example, we consider a training dataset of 10 adjectives shown below (x_i), each labelled (y_i) `Positive` or `Negative`, according to their meaning. We will now use kernel k-NN (with the kernel defined above) to predict whether the word 'horrendous' $(x_\star)$ is a positive or negative word. In the third column below, we have therefore computed the Levenshtein distance (LD) between each labelled word (x_i) and 'horrendous' $(x_\star)$. The rightmost column shows the value of the right hand side of (8.20), which is the value that kernel k-NN uses to determine how close two data points are.

Word, x_i	Meaning, y_i	Levenshtein dist. from x_i to $x_\star$	$\kappa(x_i, x_i) + \kappa(x_\star, x_\star) - 2\kappa(x_i, x_\star)$
Awesome	`Positive`	8	1.44
Excellent	`Positive`	10	1.73
Spotless	`Positive`	9	1.60
Terrific	`Positive`	8	1.44
Tremendous	`Positive`	4	0.55
Awful	`Negative`	9	1.60
Dreadful	`Negative`	6	1.03
Horrific	`Negative`	6	1.03
Outrageous	`Negative`	6	1.03
Terrible	`Negative`	8	1.44

Inspecting the rightmost column, the closest word to horrendous is the positive word tremendous. Thus, if we use $k = 1$, the conclusion would be that horrendous is a positive word. However, the second, third, and fourth closest words are all negative (dreadful, horrific, outrageous), and with $k = 3$ or $k = 4$, the conclusion thereby becomes that horrendous is a negative word (which also happens to be correct in this case).

The purpose of this example is to illustrate how a kernel allows a basic method such as k-NN to be used for a problem where the input has a more intricate structure than just being numerical. For the particular application of predicting word semantics, the character-by-character similarity is clearly an oversimplified approach, and more elaborate machine learning methods exist.

The Meaning of a Kernel

From kernel k-NN we got (at least) two lessons about kernels that are generally applicable to all supervised machine learning methods that use kernels:

- The kernel defines how close/similar any two data points are. If, say, $\kappa(\mathbf{x}_i, \mathbf{x}_\star) > \kappa(\mathbf{x}_j, \mathbf{x}_\star)$, then $\mathbf{x}_\star$ is considered to be more similar to $\mathbf{x}_i$ than $\mathbf{x}_j$. Intuitively speaking, for most methods, the prediction $\widehat{y}(\mathbf{x}_\star)$ is most influenced by the training data points that are closest/most similar to $\mathbf{x}_\star$. The kernel thereby plays an important role in determining the individual influence of each training data point when making a prediction.

- Even though we started by introducing kernels via the inner product $\boldsymbol{\phi}(\mathbf{x})^\mathsf{T}\boldsymbol{\phi}(\mathbf{x}')$, we do not have to bother about inner product for the space in which $\mathbf{x}$ itself lives. As we saw in Example 8.4, we can also apply a positive semidefinite kernel method to text strings without worrying about inner products of strings, as long as we have a kernel for that type of data.

In addition to this, the kernel also plays a somewhat more subtle role in methods that build on the representer theorem (such as kernel ridge regression, support vector regression, and support vector classification, but not kernel k-NN). Remember that the primal formulation of those methods, by virtue of the representer theorem, contains the L^2-regularisation term $\lambda\|\boldsymbol{\theta}\|_2^2$. Even though we do not solve the primal formulation explicitly when using kernels (we solve the dual instead), it is nevertheless an equivalent representation, and we may ask what impact the regularisation $\lambda\|\boldsymbol{\theta}\|_2^2$ has on the solution?

The L^2-regularisation means that primal parameter values $\boldsymbol{\theta}$ close to zero are favoured. Besides the regularisation term, $\boldsymbol{\theta}$ only appears in the expression $\boldsymbol{\theta}^\mathsf{T}\boldsymbol{\phi}(\mathbf{x})$. The solution $\widehat{\boldsymbol{\theta}}$ to the primal problem is therefore an interplay between the feature vector $\boldsymbol{\phi}(\mathbf{x})$ and the L^2-regularisation term. Consider two different choices of feature vectors, $\boldsymbol{\phi}_1(\mathbf{x})$ and $\boldsymbol{\phi}_2(\mathbf{x})$. If they both span the same space of functions, there exist $\boldsymbol{\theta}_1$ and $\boldsymbol{\theta}_2$ such that $\boldsymbol{\theta}_1^\mathsf{T}\boldsymbol{\phi}_1(\mathbf{x}) = \boldsymbol{\theta}_2^\mathsf{T}\boldsymbol{\phi}_2(\mathbf{x})$ for all $\mathbf{x}$, and it might appear irrelevant which feature vector that is used. However, the L^2-regularisation complicates the situation because it acts directly on $\boldsymbol{\theta}$, and it therefore matters whether we use $\boldsymbol{\phi}_1(\mathbf{x})$ or $\boldsymbol{\phi}_2(\mathbf{x})$. In the dual formulation, we choose the kernel $\kappa(\mathbf{x}, \mathbf{x}')$ instead of feature vector $\boldsymbol{\phi}(\mathbf{x})$, but since that choice implicitly corresponds to a feature vector, the effect is still present, and we may add one more bullet point about the meaning of a kernel:

- The choice of kernel corresponds to a choice of a regularisation functional. That is, the kernel implies a preference for certain functions in the space of all functions that are spanned by the feature vector. For example, the squared exponential kernel implies a preference for smooth functions.

Using a kernel makes a method quite flexible, and one could perhaps expect it to suffer heavily from overfitting. However, the regularising role of the kernel explains why that rarely is the case in practice.

All three bullet points above are central to understanding the usefulness and versatility of kernel methods. They also highlight the importance for the machine learning engineer of choosing the kernel wisely and not simply resorting to 'default' choices.

Valid Choices of Kernels

We introduced kernels as a way to compactly work with non-linear feature transformations like (8.11). A direct consequence of this is that it is now sufficient to consider $\kappa(\mathbf{x}, \mathbf{x}')$, and not $\boldsymbol{\phi}(\mathbf{x})$. A natural question to ask is whether an arbitrary kernel $\kappa(\mathbf{x}, \mathbf{x}')$ always corresponds to a feature transformation $\boldsymbol{\phi}(\mathbf{x})$, such that it can be written as the inner product

$$\kappa(\mathbf{x}, \mathbf{x}') = \boldsymbol{\phi}(\mathbf{x})^\mathsf{T}\boldsymbol{\phi}(\mathbf{x}')? \tag{8.21}$$

Before answering the question, we have to be aware that this question is primarily of theoretical nature. As long as we can use $\kappa(\mathbf{x}, \mathbf{x}')$ when computing predictions, it serves its purpose, no matter whether it admits the factorisation (8.21) or not. The specific requirements on $\kappa(\mathbf{x}, \mathbf{x}')$ are different for different methods – for example, the inverse $(\boldsymbol{K}(\mathbf{X}, \mathbf{X}) + n\lambda\mathbf{I})^{-1}$ is needed for kernel ridge regression but not for support vector regression. Furthermore, whether a kernel admits the factorisation (8.21) or not has no direct correspondence to how well it performs in terms of E_{new}. For any practical machine learning problem, the performance still has to be evaluated using cross-validation or similarly.

That being said, we will now have a closer look at the important family of positive semidefinite kernels. A kernel is said to be positive semidefinite if the Gram matrix $K(\mathbf{X}, \mathbf{X})$ as defined in (8.12b) is positive semidefinite (has no negative eigenvalues) for any choice of $\mathbf{X}$.

First, it holds that any kernel $\kappa(\mathbf{x}, \mathbf{x}')$ that is defined as an inner product between feature vectors $\boldsymbol{\phi}(\mathbf{x})$, as in (8.21), is always positive semidefinite. It can, for example, be shown from the equivalent definition of positive semidefinite that $\mathbf{v}^{\mathsf{T}} K(\mathbf{X}, \mathbf{X})\mathbf{v} \geq 0$ holds for any vector $\mathbf{v} = [v_1 \ \ldots \ v_n]^{\mathsf{T}}$. By using (8.12b), the definition of matrix multiplication (first equality below), and properties of the inner product (second equality below), we can indeed conclude that

$$\mathbf{v}^{\mathsf{T}} K(\mathbf{X}, \mathbf{X})\mathbf{v} = \sum_{i=1}^{n} \sum_{j=1}^{n} v_i (\boldsymbol{\phi}(\mathbf{x}_i))^{\mathsf{T}} \boldsymbol{\phi}(\mathbf{x}_j) v_j = \left(\sum_{i=1}^{n} v_i \boldsymbol{\phi}(\mathbf{x}_i) \right)^{\mathsf{T}} \left(\sum_{j=1}^{n} v_j \boldsymbol{\phi}(\mathbf{x}_j) \right) \geq 0.$$

(8.22)

Less trivially, the other direction also holds – that is, for any positive semidefinite kernel $\kappa(\mathbf{x}, \mathbf{x}')$, there always exists a feature vector $\boldsymbol{\phi}(\mathbf{x})$ such that $\kappa(\mathbf{x}, \mathbf{x}')$ can be written as an inner product (8.21). Technically it can be shown that for any positive semidefinite kernel $\kappa(\mathbf{x}, \mathbf{x}')$, it is possible to construct a function space, more specifically a Hilbert space, that is spanned by a feature vector $\boldsymbol{\phi}(\mathbf{x})$ for which (8.21) holds. The dimensionality of the Hilbert space, and thereby also the dimension of $\boldsymbol{\phi}(\mathbf{x})$, can, however, be infinite.

Give a kernel $\kappa(\mathbf{x}, \mathbf{x}')$, there are multiple ways to construct a Hilbert space spanned by $\boldsymbol{\phi}(\mathbf{x})$, and we will only mention some directions here. One alternative is to consider the so-called reproducing kernel map. The reproducing kernel map is obtained by consider one argument, say the latter, to $\kappa(\mathbf{x}, \mathbf{x}')$ fixed and let $\kappa(\cdot, \mathbf{x}')$ span the Hilbert space with an inner product $\langle \cdot, \cdot \rangle$ such that $\langle \kappa(\cdot, \mathbf{x}), \kappa(\cdot, \mathbf{x}') \rangle = \kappa(\mathbf{x}, \mathbf{x}')$. This inner product has a so-called reproducing property, and it is the main building block for the so-called reproducing kernel Hilbert space. Another alternative is to use the so-called Mercer kernel map, which constructs the Hilbert space using eigenfunctions to an integral operator which is related to the kernel.

A given Hilbert space uniquely defines a kernel, but for a given kernel, there exist multiple Hilbert spaces which correspond to it. In practice this means that given a kernel $\kappa(\mathbf{x}, \mathbf{x}')$, the corresponding feature vector $\boldsymbol{\phi}(\mathbf{x})$ is not unique; in fact not even its dimensionality is unique. As a simple example, consider the linear kernel $\kappa(\mathbf{x}, \mathbf{x}') = \mathbf{x}^{\mathsf{T}} \mathbf{x}'$, which can either be expressed as an inner product between $\boldsymbol{\phi}(\mathbf{x}) = \mathbf{x}$ (one-dimensional $\boldsymbol{\phi}(\mathbf{x})$) or as an inner product between $\boldsymbol{\phi}(\mathbf{x}) = \left[\frac{1}{\sqrt{2}}\mathbf{x} \ \ \frac{1}{\sqrt{2}}\mathbf{x} \right]^{\mathsf{T}}$ (two-dimensional $\boldsymbol{\phi}(\mathbf{x})$).

Examples of Kernels

We will now give a list of some commonly used kernels, of which we have already introduced some. These examples are only for the case where $\mathbf{x}$ is a numeric variable. For other types of input variables (such as in Example 8.4), we have to resort to the more application-specific literature. We start with some positive semidefinite kernels, where the *linear kernel* might be the simplest one:

$$\kappa(\mathbf{x}, \mathbf{x}') = \mathbf{x}^\mathsf{T}\mathbf{x}'. \tag{8.23}$$

A generalisation thereof, still positive semidefinite, is the *polynomial kernel*,

$$\kappa(\mathbf{x}, \mathbf{x}') = (c + \mathbf{x}^\mathsf{T}\mathbf{x}')^{d-1}, \tag{8.24}$$

with hyperparameter $c \geq 0$ and polynomial order $d - 1$ (integer). The polynomial kernel corresponds to a finite-dimensional feature vector $\boldsymbol{\phi}(\mathbf{x})$ of monomials up to order $d - 1$. The polynomial kernel does not therefore conceptually enable anything that could not be achieved by instead implementing the primal formulation and the finite-dimensional $\boldsymbol{\phi}(\mathbf{x})$ explicitly. The other positive semidefinite kernels below, on the other hand, all correspond to infinite-dimensional feature vectors $\boldsymbol{\phi}(\mathbf{x})$.

We have previously mentioned the *squared exponential kernel*,

$$\kappa(\mathbf{x}, \mathbf{x}') = \exp\left(-\frac{\|\mathbf{x} - \mathbf{x}'\|_2^2}{2\ell^2}\right), \tag{8.25}$$

with hyperparameter $\ell > 0$ (usually called lengthscale). As we saw in Example 8.2, this kernel has more of a 'local' nature compared to the polynomial since $\kappa(\mathbf{x}, \mathbf{x}') \to 0$ as $\|\mathbf{x} - \mathbf{x}'\| \to \infty$. This property makes sense in many problems and is perhaps the reason why this might be the most commonly used kernel.

Somewhat related to the squared exponential, we have the family of *Matérn kernels*,

$$\kappa(\mathbf{x}, \mathbf{x}') = \frac{2^{1-\nu}}{\Gamma(\nu)}\left(\frac{\sqrt{2\nu}\|\mathbf{x} - \mathbf{x}'\|_2}{\ell}\right)^\nu k_\nu\left(\frac{\sqrt{2\nu}\|\mathbf{x} - \mathbf{x}'\|}{\ell}\right), \tag{8.26}$$

with hyperparameters $\ell > 0$ and $\nu > 0$, where the latter is a type of smoothness parameter. Here, Γ is the Gamma function and k_ν is a modified Bessel function of the second kind. All Matérn kernels are positive semidefinite. Of particular interest are the cases $\nu = \frac{1}{2}, \frac{3}{2}$, and $\frac{5}{2}$, when (8.26) simplifies to

$$\nu = \frac{1}{2} \implies \kappa(\mathbf{x}, \mathbf{x}') = \exp\left(-\frac{\|\mathbf{x} - \mathbf{x}'\|_2}{\ell}\right), \tag{8.27}$$

$$\nu = \frac{3}{2} \implies \kappa(\mathbf{x}, \mathbf{x}') = \left(1 + \frac{\sqrt{3}\|\mathbf{x} - \mathbf{x}'\|_2}{\ell}\right)\exp\left(-\frac{\sqrt{3}\|\mathbf{x} - \mathbf{x}'\|_2}{\ell}\right), \tag{8.28}$$

$$\nu = \frac{5}{2} \implies \kappa(\mathbf{x}, \mathbf{x}') = \left(1 + \frac{\sqrt{5}\|\mathbf{x} - \mathbf{x}'\|_2}{\ell} + \frac{5\|\mathbf{x} - \mathbf{x}'\|_2^2}{3\ell^2}\right)\exp\left(-\frac{\sqrt{5}\|\mathbf{x} - \mathbf{x}'\|_2}{\ell}\right). \tag{8.29}$$

The Matérn kernel with $v = \frac{1}{2}$ is also called the *exponential kernel*. It can furthermore be shown that the Matérn kernel (8.26) equals the squared exponential (8.25) when $v \to \infty$.

As a final example of a positive semidefinite kernel, we mention the *rational quadratic kernel*,

$$\kappa(\mathbf{x}, \mathbf{x}') = \left(1 + \frac{\|\mathbf{x} - \mathbf{x}'\|_2^2}{2a\ell^2} \right)^{-a}, \tag{8.30}$$

with hyperparameters $\ell > 0$ and $a > 0$. The squared exponential, Matérn, and rational quadratic kernel are all examples of *stationary* kernels, since they are functions of only $\mathbf{x} - \mathbf{x}'$. In fact they are also *isotropic* kernels, since they are only functions of $\|\mathbf{x} - \mathbf{x}'\|_2$. The linear kernel is neither isotropic nor stationary.

Going back to the discussion in connection to (8.21), positive semidefinite kernels are a subset of all kernels, for which we know that certain theoretical properties hold. In practice, however, a kernel is potentially useful as long as we can compute a prediction using it, regardless of its theoretical properties. One (at least historically) popular kernel for SVMs which is not positive semidefinite is the *sigmoid kernel*

$$\kappa(\mathbf{x}, \mathbf{x}') = \tanh\left(a\mathbf{x}^\mathsf{T}\mathbf{x}' + b \right), \tag{8.31}$$

where $a > 0$ and $b < 0$ are hyperparameters. The fact that it is not positive semidefinite can, for example, be seen by computing the eigenvalues of $K(\mathbf{X}, \mathbf{X})$ with $a = 1$, $b = -1$, and $\mathbf{X} = [1\ 2]^\mathsf{T}$. Since this kernel is not positive semidefinite, the inverse $(K(\mathbf{X}, \mathbf{X}) + n\lambda\mathbf{I})^{-1}$ does not always exists, and it is therefore not suitable for kernel ridge regression. It can, however, be used in support vector regression and classification, where that inverse is not needed. For certain values of b, it can be shown to be a so-called conditional positive semidefinite kernel (a weaker property than positive semidefinite).

It is possible to construct 'new' kernels by modifying or combining existing ones. In particular there is a set of operations that preserve the positive semidefinite property: If $\kappa(\mathbf{x}, \mathbf{x}')$ is a positive semidefinite kernel, then so is $a\kappa(\mathbf{x}, \mathbf{x}')$ if $a > 0$ (scaling). Furthermore, if both $\kappa_1(\mathbf{x}, \mathbf{x}')$ and $\kappa_2(\mathbf{x}, \mathbf{x}')$ are positive semidefinite kernels, then so are $\kappa_1(\mathbf{x}, \mathbf{x}') + \kappa_2(\mathbf{x}, \mathbf{x}')$ (addition) and $\kappa_1(\mathbf{x}, \mathbf{x}')\kappa_2(\mathbf{x}, \mathbf{x}')$ (multiplication).

Most kernels contain a few hyperparameters that are left for the user to choose. Much as cross-validation can provide valuable help in choosing between different kernels, it can also help in choosing hyperparameters with grid search, as discussed in Chapter 5.

8.5 Support Vector Classification

We have spent most of our time so far deriving two kernel versions of linear regression: kernel ridge regression and support vector regression. We will now focus on classification. Unfortunately the derivations become more technically involved than for kernel ridge regression, and we have placed the details in the chapter appendix. However, the intuition carries over from regression, as well as the main ideas of the dual formulation, the kernel trick, and the change of loss function.

It is possible to derive a kernel version of logistic regression with L^2-regularisation. The derivation can be made by first replacing $\mathbf{x}$ with $\boldsymbol{\phi}(\mathbf{x})$, and then using the representer theorem to derive its dual formulation and applying the kernel trick. However, since kernel logistic regression is rarely used in practice, we will instead go straight to support vector classification. As the name suggests, support vector classification is the classification counterpart of support vector regression. Both support vector regression and classification are SVMs since they both have sparse dual parameter vectors.

We consider the binary classification problem $y \in \{-1, 1\}$ and start with the margin formulation (see (5.12) in Chapter 5) of the logistic regression classifier

$$\widehat{y}(\mathbf{x}_\star) = \text{sign} \left\{ \boldsymbol{\theta}^\mathsf{T} \boldsymbol{\phi}(\mathbf{x}_\star) \right\}. \tag{8.32}$$

If we now were to learn $\boldsymbol{\theta}$ using the logistic loss (5.13), we would obtain logistic regression with a non-linear feature transformation $\boldsymbol{\phi}(\mathbf{x})$, from which kernel logistic regression eventually would follow. However, inspired by support vector regression, we will instead make use of the hinge loss function (5.16),

$$L(\mathbf{x}, y, \boldsymbol{\theta}) = \max \left\{ 0, 1 - y_i \boldsymbol{\theta}^\mathsf{T} \boldsymbol{\phi}(\mathbf{x}_i) \right\} = \begin{cases} 1 - y \boldsymbol{\theta}^\mathsf{T} \boldsymbol{\phi}(\mathbf{x}) & \text{if } y \boldsymbol{\theta}^\mathsf{T} \boldsymbol{\phi}(\mathbf{x}) < 1 \\ 0, & \text{otherwise} \end{cases}. \tag{8.33}$$

From Figure 5.2, it is not immediately clear what advantages the hinge loss has over the logistic loss. Analogously to the ϵ-insensitive loss, the main advantage of the hinge loss comes when we look at the dual formulation using α instead of the primal formulation with $\boldsymbol{\theta}$. But before introducing a dual formulation, we first have to consider the primal one. Since the representer theorem is behind all this, we have to use L^2-regularisation, which together with (8.33) gives the primal formulation

$$\widehat{\boldsymbol{\theta}} = \arg\min_{\boldsymbol{\theta}} \frac{1}{n} \sum_{i=1}^{n} \max \left\{ 0, 1 - y_i \boldsymbol{\theta}^\mathsf{T} \boldsymbol{\phi}(\mathbf{x}_i) \right\} + \lambda \|\boldsymbol{\theta}\|_2^2. \tag{8.34}$$

The primal formulation does not allow for the kernel trick, since the feature vector does not appear as $\boldsymbol{\phi}(\mathbf{x})^\mathsf{T} \boldsymbol{\phi}(\mathbf{x})$. By using optimisation theory and constructing the Lagrangian (the details can be found in Appendix 8.B), we can arrive at the dual formulation of (8.34),[4]

$$\widehat{\alpha} = \arg\min_{\alpha} \frac{1}{2} \alpha^\mathsf{T} K(\mathbf{X}, \mathbf{X}) \alpha - \alpha^\mathsf{T} \mathbf{y} \tag{8.35a}$$

---

[4]In other texts, it is common to let the Lagrange multipliers (see Appendix 8.B) also be the dual variables. It is mathematically equivalent, but we have instead chosen this formulation to highlight the similarities to the other kernel methods and the importance of the representer theorem.

$$\text{subject to } |\alpha_i| \leq \frac{1}{2n\lambda} \text{ and } 0 \leq \alpha_i y_i \tag{8.35b}$$

with

$$\widehat{y}(\mathbf{x}_\star) = \text{sign}\left(\widehat{\alpha}^\mathsf{T} K(\mathbf{X}, \mathbf{x}_\star)\right) \tag{8.35c}$$

instead of (8.32). Note that we have also made use of the kernel trick here by replacing $\boldsymbol{\phi}(\mathbf{x})^\mathsf{T}\boldsymbol{\phi}(\mathbf{x}')$ with $\kappa(\mathbf{x}, \mathbf{x}')$, which gives $K(\mathbf{X}, \mathbf{X})$ in (8.35a) and $K(\mathbf{X}, \mathbf{x}_\star)$ in (8.35c). As for support vector regression, adding an offset term θ_0 to (8.32) corresponds to enforcing an additional constraint $\sum_{i=1}^{n} \alpha_i = 0$ in (8.35).

Because of the representer theorem, the formulation (8.35c) should come as no surprise to us, since it simply corresponds to inserting (8.16) into (8.32). However, the representer theorem only tells us that this dual formulation exists; the solution (8.35a)–(8.35b) does not follow automatically from the representer theorem but requires its own derivation.

Perhaps the most interesting property of the constrained optimisation problem (8.35) is that its solution $\widehat{\alpha}$ turns out to be sparse. This is exactly the same phenomenon as with support vector regression, and it explains why (8.35) is also an SVM. More specifically, (8.35) is called support vector classification. The strength of this method, like support vector regression, is that the model has the full flexibility of being a kernel method, and yet the prediction (8.35c) only explicitly depends on a subset of the training data points (the support vectors). It is, however, important to realise that all training data points are needed when solving (8.35a). We summarise as Method 8.3.

The support vector property is due to the fact that the loss function is exactly equal to zero when the margin (see Chapter 5) is ≥ 1. In the dual formulation, the parameter α_i becomes nonzero only if the margin for data point i is ≤ 1, which makes $\widehat{\alpha}$ sparse. It can be shown that this corresponds to data points being either on the 'wrong side' of the decision boundary or within $\frac{1}{\|\boldsymbol{\theta}\|_2} = \frac{1}{\|\boldsymbol{\Phi}(\mathbf{X})^\mathsf{T}\boldsymbol{\alpha}\|_2}$ of the decision boundary in the feature space $\boldsymbol{\phi}(\mathbf{x})$. We illustrate this by Example 8.5.

Example 8.5 Support vector classification

We consider the binary classification problem with the data given in Figure 8.5 and apply support vector classification with linear and squared exponential kernels, respectively, in Figure 8.6. We mark the support vectors with yellow circles. For the linear kernel, the locations of the support vectors are either on the 'wrong side' of the decision boundary or within $\frac{1}{\|\boldsymbol{\theta}\|_2}$ of it, marked with dashed white lines. As we decrease, λ we allow for larger $\boldsymbol{\theta}$ and thereby a smaller band $\frac{1}{\|\boldsymbol{\theta}\|_2}$ and consequently fewer support vectors.

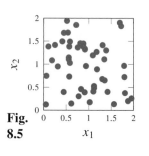

Fig. 8.5

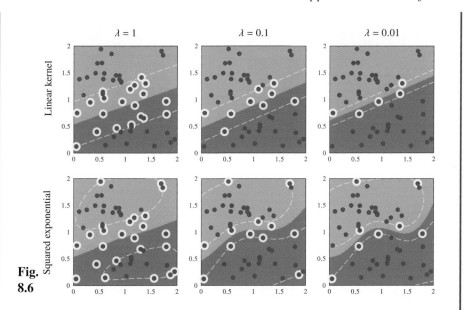

Fig. 8.6

When using the (indeed non-linear) squared exponential kernel, the situation becomes somewhat harder to interpret. It still holds that the support vectors are either on the 'wrong side' of the decision boundary or within $\frac{1}{\|\theta\|_2}$ of it, but the distance is measured in infinite dimensional $\phi(\mathbf{x})$-space. Mapping this back to the original input space, we observe this heavily non-linear behavior. The meaning of the dashed white lines is the same as above. This also serves as a good illustration of the power of using kernels.

Learn Support vector classification

Data: Training data $\mathcal{T} = \{\mathbf{x}_i, y_i\}_{i=1}^{n}$
Result: Learned parameters $\widehat{\alpha}$

1 Compute $\widehat{\alpha}$ by numerically solving (8.35a)–(8.35b)

Predict with Support vector classification

Data: Learned parameters $\widehat{\alpha}$ and test input $\mathbf{x}_\star$
Result: Prediction $\widehat{y}(\mathbf{x}_\star)$

1 Compute $\widehat{y}(\mathbf{x}_\star)$ as per (8.35c).

Method 8.3 Support vector classification.

In the SVM literature, it is common to use an equivalent formulation with $C = \frac{1}{2\lambda}$ or $C = \frac{1}{2n\lambda}$ as the regularisation hyperparameter. There also exists a slightly different formulation using another hyperparameter called ν as, effectively, a regularisation hyperparameter. Those primal and dual problems become slightly more involved, and we do not include them here, but ν has a somewhat more natural interpretation

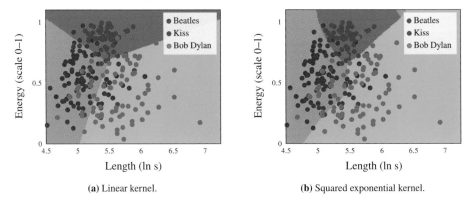

(a) Linear kernel.   (b) Squared exponential kernel.

Figure 8.7 The decision boundaries for support vector classification with linear and squared exponential kernels, respectively. In this multiclass problem, the one-versus-one strategy has been used. It is clear from this figure that the support vector classification is a linear classifier when using a linear kernel and otherwise is a non-linear classifier.

as it bounds the number of support vectors. To distinguish between the different versions, (8.35) is commonly referred to as *C*-support vector classification and the other version as *v*-support vector classification. A corresponding '*v*-version' also exists for support vector regression.

As a consequence of using the hinge loss, as we discussed in Chapter 5, support vector classification does not provide probability estimates $g(\mathbf{x})$ but only a 'hard' classification $\widehat{y}(\mathbf{x}_\star)$. The predicted margin, which is $\widehat{\alpha}K(\mathbf{X}, \mathbf{x}_\star)$ for support vector classification, is not possible to interpret as a class probability estimate, because of the asymptotic minimiser of the hinge loss. As an alternative, it is instead possible to use the squared hinge loss or the Huberised squared hinge loss, which allows for a probability interpretation of the margin. Since all these loss functions are exactly zero for margins ≥ 1, they retain the support vector property with a sparse $\widehat{\alpha}$. However, by using a different loss function than the hinge loss, we will obtain a different optimisation problem and a different solution to the one discussed above.

The support vector classifier is most often formulated as a solution to the binary classification problem. The generalisation to the multiclass problem is, unfortunately, not straightforward, since it requires a multiclass generalisation of the loss function, as discussed in Chapter 5. In practice, it is common to construct a multiclass classifier from multiple binary ones using either the one-versus-rest or the one-versus-one strategy (see page 102). The latter is used when we apply it to the music classification problem in Figure 8.7.

It is not *necessary* to make use of kernels in support vector classification. It is perfectly possible to use the linear kernel $\kappa(\mathbf{x}, \mathbf{x}') = \mathbf{x}^\mathsf{T}\mathbf{x}'$ or any other kernel corresponding to a finite dimensional $\boldsymbol{\phi}(\mathbf{x})$ in (8.35). That would indeed limit the flexibility of the classifier; the linear kernel limits the classifier to linear decision boundaries, as was illustrated in Example 8.5. The possible benefit of not making full use of kernels, however, is that it suffices to implement and solve the primal (and not the dual) formulation (8.34), since $\boldsymbol{\theta}$ is of finite dimension. The support vector property would still be present but much less visible since α is not explicitly computed. If only using the primal formulation, the representer theorem is not needed, and one could therefore also replace the L^2-regularisation with any other regularisation method.

8.6 Further Reading

A comprehensive textbook on kernel methods is Schölkopf and Smola (2002), which includes a thorough discussion on SVM and kernel theory as well as several references to original work which we do not repeat here. A commonly used software package for solving SVM problems is Chang and Lin (2011). Kernel k-NN is described by Yu et al. (2002) (and the specific kernel based on the Levenshtein distance in example Example 8.4 is found in Xu and X. Zhang (2004)) and kernel logistic regression by Zhu and Hastie (2005). Some more discussion related to the comment about the presence or absence of the offset term in the SVM formulation on page 201 is found in Poggio et al. (2001) and Steinwart et al. (2011).

8.A The Representer Theorem

We give a slightly simplified version of the representer theorem by Schölkopf et al. (2001) adapted to our notation and terminology, without using the reproducing kernel Hilbert space formalism. It is stated in a regression-like setting, since $\widehat{y}(\mathbf{x}) = \boldsymbol{\theta}^{\mathsf{T}}\boldsymbol{\phi}(\mathbf{x})$, and we discuss how it also applies to classification below.

Theorem 8.1 (The representer theorem) *Let* $\widehat{y}(\mathbf{x}) = \boldsymbol{\theta}^{\mathsf{T}}\boldsymbol{\phi}(\mathbf{x})$ *with fixed non-linear feature transformations* $\boldsymbol{\phi}(\mathbf{x})$ *and* $\boldsymbol{\theta}$ *to be learned from training data* $\{\mathbf{x}_i, y_i\}_{i=1}^n$. *(The dimensionality of* $\boldsymbol{\theta}$ *and* $\boldsymbol{\phi}(\mathbf{x})$ *does not have to be finite.) Furthermore, let* $L(y, \widehat{y})$ *be any arbitrary loss function and* $h : [0, \infty] \mapsto \mathbb{R}$ *a strictly monotonically increasing function. Then each minimiser* $\boldsymbol{\theta}$ *to the regularised cost function*

$$\frac{1}{n} \sum_{i=1}^n L(y_i, \underbrace{\boldsymbol{\theta}^{\mathsf{T}}\boldsymbol{\phi}(\mathbf{x}_i)}_{\widehat{y}(\mathbf{x}_i)}) + h(\|\boldsymbol{\theta}\|_2^2) \tag{8.36}$$

can be written as $\boldsymbol{\theta} = \boldsymbol{\Phi}(\mathbf{X})^{\mathsf{T}}\boldsymbol{\alpha}$ *(or, equivalently,* $\widehat{y}(\mathbf{x}) = \boldsymbol{\alpha}K(\mathbf{X}, \mathbf{x}_\star)$*) with some* n-*dimensional vector* $\boldsymbol{\alpha}$.

Proof: For a given $\mathbf{X}$, any $\boldsymbol{\theta}$ can be decomposed into one part $\boldsymbol{\Phi}(\mathbf{X})^{\mathsf{T}}\boldsymbol{\alpha}$ (with some $\boldsymbol{\alpha}$) that lives in the row span of $\boldsymbol{\Phi}(\mathbf{X})$ and one part $\mathbf{v}$ orthogonal to it, that is, $\boldsymbol{\theta} = \boldsymbol{\Phi}(\mathbf{X})^{\mathsf{T}}\boldsymbol{\alpha} + \mathbf{v}$ with $\mathbf{v}$ being orthogonal to all rows $\boldsymbol{\phi}(\mathbf{x}_i)$ of $\boldsymbol{\Phi}(\mathbf{X})$.

For any $\mathbf{x}_i$ in $\{\mathbf{x}_i, y_i\}_{i=1}^n$, it therefore holds that

$$\widehat{y}(\mathbf{x}_i) = \boldsymbol{\theta}^{\mathsf{T}}\boldsymbol{\phi}(\mathbf{x}_i) = (\boldsymbol{\Phi}(\mathbf{X})^{\mathsf{T}}\boldsymbol{\alpha} + \mathbf{v})^{\mathsf{T}}\boldsymbol{\phi}(\mathbf{x}_i)$$
$$= \boldsymbol{\alpha}^{\mathsf{T}}\boldsymbol{\Phi}(\mathbf{X})\boldsymbol{\phi}(\mathbf{x}_i) + \underbrace{\mathbf{v}^{\mathsf{T}}\boldsymbol{\phi}(\mathbf{x}_i)}_{= 0} = \boldsymbol{\alpha}^{\mathsf{T}}\boldsymbol{\Phi}(\mathbf{X})\boldsymbol{\phi}(\mathbf{x}_i). \tag{8.37}$$

The first term in (8.36) is therefore independent of $\mathbf{v}$. Concerning the second term in (8.36), we have

$$h\left(\|\boldsymbol{\theta}\|_2^2\right) = h\left(\|\boldsymbol{\Phi}(\mathbf{X})^{\mathsf{T}}\boldsymbol{\alpha} + \mathbf{v}\|_2^2\right) = h\left(\|\boldsymbol{\Phi}(\mathbf{X})^{\mathsf{T}}\boldsymbol{\alpha}\|_2^2 + \|\mathbf{v}\|_2^2\right) \geq h\left(\|\boldsymbol{\Phi}(\mathbf{X})^{\mathsf{T}}\boldsymbol{\alpha}\|_2^2\right),$$
(8.38)

where the second inequality follows from the fact that $\mathbf{v}$ is orthogonal to $\boldsymbol{\Phi}(\mathbf{X})^{\mathsf{T}}\boldsymbol{\alpha}$, and equality in the last step only holds if $\mathbf{v} = 0$. The equation (8.38) therefore implies that the minimum of (8.36) is found for $\mathbf{v} = 0$, from which the theorem follows. $\blacksquare$

The assumption that the model is linear in both parameters and features, $\boldsymbol{\theta}^{\mathsf{T}}\boldsymbol{\phi}(\mathbf{x})$, is indeed crucial for Theorem 8.1. That is not an issue when we consider models of linear regression type, but in order to apply it to, for example, logistic regression, we have to find a linear formulation of that model. Not all models are possible to formulate as linear, but logistic regression can (instead of (3.29a)) be understood as a linear model predicting the so-called log-odds, $\boldsymbol{\theta}^{\mathsf{T}}\boldsymbol{\phi}(\mathbf{x}) = \ln\left(\frac{p(y=1\,|\,\mathbf{x})}{p(y=-1\,|\,\mathbf{x})}\right)$, and the representer theorem is therefore applicable to it. Furthermore, support vector classification is also a linear model if we consider the function $c(\mathbf{x}) = \boldsymbol{\theta}^{\mathsf{T}}\boldsymbol{\phi}(\mathbf{x})$ rather than the predicted class $\widehat{y}(\mathbf{x}_\star) = \text{sign}\left\{\boldsymbol{\theta}^{\mathsf{T}}\boldsymbol{\phi}(\mathbf{x})\right\}$.

8.B Derivation of Support Vector Classification

We will derive (8.35) from (8.34),

$$\underset{\boldsymbol{\theta}}{\text{minimise}} \; \frac{1}{n} \sum_{i=1}^{n} \max\left\{0, 1 - y_i\boldsymbol{\theta}^{\mathsf{T}}\boldsymbol{\phi}(\mathbf{x}_i)\right\} + \lambda\|\boldsymbol{\theta}\|_2^2,$$

by first re-formulating it into an equivalent formulation using slack variables $\boldsymbol{\xi} = [\xi_1 \ldots \xi_n]^{\mathsf{T}}$:

$$\underset{\boldsymbol{\theta},\boldsymbol{\xi}}{\text{minimise}} \quad \frac{1}{n} \sum_{i=1}^{n} \xi_i + \lambda\|\boldsymbol{\theta}\|_2^2, \tag{8.39a}$$

$$\text{subject to} \quad \xi_i \geq 1 - y_i\boldsymbol{\theta}^{\mathsf{T}}\boldsymbol{\phi}(\mathbf{x}_i), \tag{8.39b}$$

$$(i = 1, \ldots, n) \quad \xi_i \geq 0. \tag{8.39c}$$

The Lagrangian for (8.39) is then

$$L(\boldsymbol{\theta},\boldsymbol{\xi},\boldsymbol{\beta},\boldsymbol{\gamma}) = \frac{1}{n} \sum_{i=1}^{n} \xi_i + \lambda\|\boldsymbol{\theta}\|_2^2 - \sum_{i=1}^{n} \beta_i(\xi_i + y_i\boldsymbol{\theta}^{\mathsf{T}}\boldsymbol{\phi}(\mathbf{x}_i) - 1) - \sum_{i=1}^{n} \gamma_i\xi_i, \tag{8.40}$$

with Lagrange multipliers $\beta_i \geq 0$ and $\gamma_i \geq 0$. According to Lagrange duality theory, instead of solving (8.34), we can minimise (8.40) with respect to $\boldsymbol{\theta}$ and $\boldsymbol{\xi}$ and maximise it with respect to $\boldsymbol{\beta}$ and $\boldsymbol{\gamma}$. Two necessary conditions for optimality of (8.40) are

$$\frac{\partial}{\partial\boldsymbol{\theta}}L(\boldsymbol{\theta},\boldsymbol{\xi},\boldsymbol{\beta},\boldsymbol{\gamma}) = 0, \tag{8.41a}$$

$$\frac{\partial}{\partial \xi} L(\boldsymbol{\theta}, \boldsymbol{\xi}, \boldsymbol{\beta}, \boldsymbol{\gamma}) = 0. \tag{8.41b}$$

In more detail, and using the fact that $\|\boldsymbol{\theta}\|_2^2 = \boldsymbol{\theta}^\mathsf{T}\boldsymbol{\theta}$, and hence $\frac{\partial}{\partial \boldsymbol{\theta}}\|\boldsymbol{\theta}\|_2^2 = 2\boldsymbol{\theta}$, (8.41a) gives

$$\boldsymbol{\theta} = \frac{1}{2\lambda} \sum_{i=1}^{n} y_i \beta_i \boldsymbol{\phi}(\mathbf{x}_i), \tag{8.41c}$$

and (8.41b) gives

$$\gamma_i = \frac{1}{n} - \beta_i. \tag{8.41d}$$

Inserting (8.41c) and (8.41d) into (8.40) and scaling it with $\frac{1}{2\lambda}$ (assuming $\lambda > 0$), we now seek to maximise

$$\tilde{L}(\boldsymbol{\beta}) = \sum_{i=1}^{n} \frac{\beta_i}{2\lambda} - \frac{1}{2} \sum_{i=1}^{n} \sum_{j=1}^{n} y_i y_j \frac{\beta_i \beta_j}{4\lambda^2} \boldsymbol{\phi}^\mathsf{T}(\mathbf{x}_i) \boldsymbol{\phi}(\mathbf{x}_j). \tag{8.42}$$

For (8.42), we have the constraint $0 \le \beta_i \le \frac{1}{n}$, where the upper bound on b_i comes from (8.41d) and the fact that $\gamma_i \ge 0$. With $\alpha_i = \frac{y_i \beta_i}{2\lambda}$, we see (noting that $y_i = 1/y_i$ since $y_i \in -1, 1$) that maximising (8.42) is equivalent to solving

$$\underset{\alpha}{\text{minimise}} \ \frac{1}{2} \sum_{i=1}^{n} \sum_{j=1}^{n} \alpha_i \alpha_j \boldsymbol{\phi}^\mathsf{T}(\mathbf{x}_i) \boldsymbol{\phi}(\mathbf{x}_j) - \sum_{i=1}^{n} y_i \alpha_i \tag{8.43}$$

or, using matrix notation,

$$\underset{\alpha}{\text{minimise}} \ \frac{1}{2} \boldsymbol{\alpha}^\mathsf{T} \mathbf{K}(\mathbf{X}, \mathbf{X})\boldsymbol{\alpha} - \boldsymbol{\alpha}^\mathsf{T}\mathbf{y}. \tag{8.44}$$

Finally, we note that by (8.41c) we have

$$\text{sign}(\boldsymbol{\theta}^\mathsf{T}\boldsymbol{\phi}(\mathbf{x}_\star)) = \text{sign}\left(\frac{1}{2\lambda} \sum_{i=1}^{n} y_i \beta_i \boldsymbol{\phi}^\mathsf{T}(\mathbf{x}_i)\boldsymbol{\phi}(\mathbf{x}_\star)\right) = \text{sign}\left(\boldsymbol{\alpha}^\mathsf{T}\mathbf{K}(\mathbf{X}, \mathbf{x}_\star)\right), \tag{8.45}$$

and we have arrived at (8.35).

9 The Bayesian Approach and Gaussian Processes

So far, learning a parametric model has amounted to somehow finding a parameter value $\widehat{\theta}$ that best fits the training data. With the *Bayesian approach* (also called the *probabilistic approach*), learning amounts to instead finding the *distribution* of parameter values θ conditioned on the observed training data $\mathcal{T}$, that is, $p(\theta \,|\, \mathcal{T})$. Furthermore, with the Bayesian approach, the prediction is a distribution $p(y_\star \,|\, \mathbf{x}_\star, \mathcal{T})$ instead of a single value. Before we get into the details, let us just say that on a theoretical (or even philosophical) level, the Bayesian approach is rather different to what we have previously seen in this book. However, it opens up for a family of new, versatile, and practically useful methods, and the extra effort required to understand this somewhat different approach pays off well and provides another interesting perspective on supervised machine learning. As the Bayesian approach makes repeated use of probability distributions, it is also natural that this chapter will be heavier on the probability theory side compared to the rest of the book.

We will start this chapter by first giving a general introduction to the Bayesian idea. We thereafter go back to basics and apply the Bayesian approach to linear regression, which we thereafter extend to the non-parametric Gaussian process model.

9.1 The Bayesian Idea

In the Bayesian approach, the parameters θ of any model are consistently treated as being random variables. As a consequence, in this chapter we will use the term *model* with a very specific meaning. A model, in this chapter, refers to the *joint* distribution over all outputs $\mathbf{y}$ and the parameters θ given all inputs $\mathbf{X}$, that is, $p(\mathbf{y}, \theta \,|\, \mathbf{X})$. To ease the notation, we will, however, consistently omit $\mathbf{X}$ in the conditioning (mathematically we motivate this by the fact that we only consider $\mathbf{y}$, and not $\mathbf{X}$, to be a random variable) and simply write $p(\mathbf{y}, \theta)$.

Learning in the Bayesian setting amounts to computing the distribution of θ *conditional on* training data $\mathcal{T} = \{\mathbf{x}_i, y_i\}_{i=1}^n = \{\mathbf{X}, \mathbf{y}\}$. Since we omit $\mathbf{X}$, we denote this distribution as $p(\theta \,|\, \mathbf{y})$. The computation of $p(\theta \,|\, \mathbf{y})$ is done using the laws of probabilities. First, we use the rule of conditioning to factorise the joint distribution into two factors: $p(\mathbf{y}, \theta) = p(\mathbf{y} \,|\, \theta)p(\theta)$. By using the rule of conditioning once more, now conditioning on $\mathbf{y}$, we arrive at Bayes' theorem,

$$p(\theta \,|\, \mathbf{y}) = \frac{p(\mathbf{y} \,|\, \theta)p(\theta)}{p(\mathbf{y})}, \tag{9.1}$$

which is the reason why it is called the Bayesian approach. The left hand side of (9.1) is the sought-after distribution $p(\boldsymbol{\theta} \mid \mathbf{y})$. The right hand side of (9.1) contains some important elements: $p(\mathbf{y} \mid \boldsymbol{\theta})$ is the distribution of the observations in view of the parameters, and $p(\boldsymbol{\theta})$ is the distribution of $\boldsymbol{\theta}$ before any observations are made (that is, not conditional on training data). By definition $p(\boldsymbol{\theta})$ cannot be computed but has to be postulated by the user. Finally $p(\mathbf{y})$ can, by the laws of probabilities, be rewritten as

$$p(\mathbf{y}) = \int p(\mathbf{y}, \boldsymbol{\theta})d\boldsymbol{\theta} = \int p(\mathbf{y} \mid \boldsymbol{\theta})p(\boldsymbol{\theta})d\boldsymbol{\theta}, \tag{9.2}$$

which is an integral that, at least in theory, can be computed. In other words, training a parametric model (in the Bayesian fashion) amounts to conditioning $\boldsymbol{\theta}$ on $\mathbf{y}$, that is, computing $p(\boldsymbol{\theta} \mid \mathbf{y})$. After being trained, a model can be used to compute predictions. Again this is a matter of computing a distribution $p(y_\star \mid \mathbf{y})$ (rather than a point prediction $\widehat{y}$) for a test input $\mathbf{x}_\star$, which, since $\boldsymbol{\theta}$ is a random variable, connects to $p(\boldsymbol{\theta} \mid \mathbf{y})$ via the marginalisation

$$p(y_\star \mid \mathbf{y}) = \int p(y_\star \mid \boldsymbol{\theta})p(\boldsymbol{\theta} \mid \mathbf{y})d\boldsymbol{\theta}. \tag{9.3}$$

Here $p(y_\star \mid \boldsymbol{\theta})$ encodes the distribution of the test data output $y_\star$ (again the corresponding input $\mathbf{x}_\star$ is omitted in the notation).

Often $p(\mathbf{y} \mid \boldsymbol{\theta})$ is referred to as the likelihood.[1] The other elements involved in the Bayesian approach are traditionally given the names

- $p(\boldsymbol{\theta})$ *prior,*

- $p(\boldsymbol{\theta} \mid \mathbf{y})$ *posterior,*

- $p(y_\star \mid \mathbf{y})$ *posterior predictive.*

These names are useful when talking about the various component of the Bayesian approach, but it is important to remember that they are nothing but different probability distributions connected to each other via the likelihood $p(\mathbf{y} \mid \boldsymbol{\theta})$. In addition, $p(\mathbf{y})$ is often called the *marginal likelihood* or *evidence*.

A Representation of Beliefs

The main feature of the Bayesian approach is its use of probability distributions. It is possible to interpret those distributions as representing *beliefs* in the following

---

[1] Remember that $p(\mathbf{y} \mid \boldsymbol{\theta})$ was also used for the maximum likelihood perspective; one example of $p(\mathbf{y} \mid \boldsymbol{\theta})$ is linear regression (3.17)–(3.18).

sense: The prior $p(\theta)$ represents our beliefs about θ *a priori*, that is, before any data has been observed. The likelihood, encoded as $p(\mathbf{y} \mid \theta)$, defines how data $\mathbf{y}$ relates to the parameter θ. Using Bayes' theorem (9.1), we *update* the belief about θ to the posterior $p(\theta \mid \mathbf{y})$ which also takes the observed data $\mathbf{y}$ into account. In everyday language, these distributions could be said to represent the uncertainty about θ before and after observing the data $\mathbf{y}$, respectively.

An interesting and practically relevant consequence is that the Bayesian approach is less prone to overfitting, compared to using a maximum-likelihood based method. In maximum-likelihood, we obtain a single value $\widehat{\theta}$ and use that value to make our prediction according to $p(y_\star \mid \widehat{\theta})$. In the Bayesian approach, we instead obtained an entire distribution $p(\theta \mid \mathbf{y})$ representing different hypotheses of the value for our model parameters. We account for all of these hypotheses we do the marginalisation in (9.3) to compute the posterior predictive. In the regime of small datasets in particular, the 'uncertainty' seen in the posterior $p(\theta \mid \mathbf{y})$ reflects how much (or little) can be said about θ from the (presumably) limited information in $\mathbf{y}$, under the assumed conditions.

The posterior $p(\theta \mid \mathbf{y})$ is a combination of the prior belief $p(\theta)$ and the information about θ carried by $\mathbf{y}$ through the likelihood. Without a meaningful prior $p(\theta)$, the posterior $p(\theta \mid \mathbf{y})$ is not meaningful either. In some applications it can be hard to make a choice of $p(\theta)$ that is not influenced by the personal experience of the machine learning engineer, which is sometimes emphasised by saying that $p(\theta)$, and thereby also $p(\theta \mid \mathbf{y})$, represents a *subjective* belief. This notion is meant to reflect that the result is not independent of the human that designed the solution. However, no matter whether or not the Bayesian approach is used, the likelihood is often chosen based on the personal experience of the machine learning engineer, meaning that most machine learning results are in that sense subjective anyway.

An interesting situation for the Bayesian approach is when data arrives in a sequential fashion, that is, one data point after the other. Say that we have two sets of data, $\mathbf{y}_1$ and $\mathbf{y}_2$. Starting with a prior $p(\theta)$, we can condition on $\mathbf{y}_1$ by computing $p(\theta \mid \mathbf{y}_1)$ using Bayes' theorem (9.1). However, if we thereafter want to condition on all data, $\mathbf{y}_1$ and $\mathbf{y}_2$ as $p(\theta \mid \mathbf{y}_1, \mathbf{y}_2)$, we do not have to start over again. We can instead replace the prior $p(\theta)$ with $p(\theta \mid \mathbf{y}_1)$ in Bayes' theorem to compute $p(\theta \mid \mathbf{y}_1, \mathbf{y}_2)$. In a sense, the 'old posterior' becomes the 'new prior' when data arrives sequentially.

The Marginal Likelihood as a Model Selection Tool

When using the Bayesian approach, there are often some hyperparameters in the likelihood or the prior, say η, that need to be chosen. It is an option to assume a 'hyper'-prior $p(\eta)$ and compute the posterior also for the hyperparameters, $p(\eta \mid \mathbf{y})$. That would be the fully Bayesian solution, but sometimes this is too computationally challenging.

A more pragmatic solution is to select a value $\widehat{\eta}$ using cross-validation instead. It is perfectly possible to use cross-validation, but the Bayesian approach also comes with an alternative for selecting hyperparameters η by maximising the marginal likelihood (9.2):

$$\widehat{\eta} = \arg\max_{\eta} p_{\eta}(\mathbf{y}), \tag{9.4}$$

where we have added an index η to emphasise the fact that $p(\mathbf{y})$ depends on η. This approach is sometimes referred to as *empirical Bayes*. Choosing hyperparameter η is, in a sense, a selection of a likelihood (and/or prior), and we can therefore understand the marginal likelihood as a tool for selecting a likelihood. Maximising the marginal likelihood is, however, not equivalent to using cross-validation (the obtained hyperparameter value might differ), and unlike cross-validation, the marginal likelihood does not give an estimate of E_{new}. In many situations, however, it is relatively easy to compute (and maximise) the marginal likelihood, compared to employing a full cross-validation procedure.

In the previous section we argued that the Bayesian approach was less prone to overfitting compared to the maximum likelihood approach. However, maximising the marginal likelihood is, in a sense, a kind of a maximum likelihood approach, and one may ask if there is a risk of overfitting when maximising the marginal likelihood. To some extent that might be the case, but the key point is that handling one (or, at most, a few) hyperparameters η with maximum (marginal) likelihood typically does not cause any severe overfitting, much like there rarely are overfitting issues when learning a straight line with plain linear regression. In other words, we can usually 'afford' to learn one or a few (hyper)parameters by maximising the (marginal) likelihood; overfitting typically only becomes a potential issue when learning a larger number of (hyper)parameters.

9.2 Bayesian Linear Regression

As a first example of the Bayesian approach, we will apply it to linear regression. In itself Bayesian linear regression is perhaps not the most versatile method, but just like ordinary linear regression, it is a good starting point and illustrates the main concepts well. Just like ordinary linear regression, it is possible to extend it in various directions. It also opens the way for the perhaps more interesting Gaussian process model. Before we work out the details of the Bayesian approach applied to linear regression, we will repeat some facts about the multivariate Gaussian distribution that will be useful.

The Multivariate Gaussian Distribution

A central mathematical object for Bayesian linear regression (and later also the Gaussian process) is the multivariate Gaussian distribution. We assume that the reader already has some familiarity with multivariate random variables, or equivalently random vectors, and repeat only the most important properties of the multivariate Gaussian distribution here.

Let $\mathbf{z}$ denote a q-dimensional multivariate Gaussian random vector $\mathbf{z} = [z_1 \ z_2 \ \dots \ z_q]^\mathsf{T}$. The multivariate Gaussian distribution is parametrised by a q-dimensional mean vector $\boldsymbol{\mu}$ and a $q \times q$ covariance matrix $\boldsymbol{\Sigma}$,

$$
\boldsymbol{\mu} = \begin{bmatrix} \mu_1 \\ \mu_2 \\ \vdots \\ \mu_q \end{bmatrix}, \quad \boldsymbol{\Sigma} = \begin{bmatrix} \sigma_1^2 & \sigma_{12} & \cdots & \sigma_{1q} \\ \sigma_{21} & \sigma_2^2 & & \sigma_{2q} \\ \vdots & & & \vdots \\ \sigma_{q1} & \sigma_{q2} & \cdots & \sigma_q^2 \end{bmatrix}.
$$

The covariance matrix is a real-valued positive semidefinite matrix, that is, a symmetric matrix with nonnegative eigenvalues. As a shorthand notation, we write $\mathbf{z} \sim \mathcal{N}(\boldsymbol{\mu}, \boldsymbol{\Sigma})$ or $p(\mathbf{z}) = \mathcal{N}(\mathbf{z}; \boldsymbol{\mu}, \boldsymbol{\Sigma})$. Note that we use the same symbol $\mathcal{N}$ to denote the univariate as well as the multivariate Gaussian distribution. The reason is that the former is just a special case of the latter.

The expected value of $\mathbf{z}$ is $\mathbb{E}[\mathbf{z}] = \boldsymbol{\mu}$, and the variance of z_1 is $\mathrm{var}(z_1) = \mathbb{E}\left[(z_1 - \mathbb{E}[z_1])^2\right] = \sigma_1^2$, and similarly for $z_2, \dots, z_q$. Moreover, the covariance between z_1 and z_2 is $\mathrm{cov}(z_1, z_2) = \mathbb{E}[(z_1 - \mathbb{E}[z_1])(z_2 - \mathbb{E}[z_2])] = \sigma_{12} = \sigma_{21}$, and similarly for any other pair of z_i, z_j. All these properties can be derived from the probability density function of the multivariate Gaussian distribution, which is

$$
\mathcal{N}(\mathbf{z}; \boldsymbol{\mu}, \boldsymbol{\Sigma}) = (2\pi)^{-\frac{q}{2}} \det(\boldsymbol{\Sigma})^{-\frac{1}{2}} \exp\left(-\frac{1}{2}(\mathbf{z} - \boldsymbol{\mu})^\mathsf{T} \boldsymbol{\Sigma}^{-1}(\mathbf{z} - \boldsymbol{\mu})\right). \tag{9.5}
$$

If all off-diagonal elements of $\boldsymbol{\Sigma}$ are 0, the elements of $\mathbf{z}$ are just independent univariate Gaussian random variables. However, if some off-diagonal element, say σ_{ij} ($i \neq j$), is nonzero, then there is a correlation between z_i and z_j. Intuitively, the correlation means that z_i carries information also about z_j, and vice versa. Some important results on how the multivariate Gaussian distribution can be manipulated are summarised in Appendix 9.A.

Linear Regression with the Bayesian Approach

We will now apply the Bayesian approach to the linear regression model. We will first spend some effort on mapping the elements of linear regression from Chapter 3 to the Bayesian terminology, and thereafter we will derive the solution.

From Chapter 3, we have that the linear regression model is

$$
y = f(\mathbf{x}) + \varepsilon, \quad f(\mathbf{x}) = \boldsymbol{\theta}^\mathsf{T}\mathbf{x}, \quad \varepsilon \sim \mathcal{N}(0, \sigma^2), \tag{9.6}
$$

which can be written equivalently as

$$
p(y \mid \boldsymbol{\theta}) = \mathcal{N}(y; \boldsymbol{\theta}^\mathsf{T}\mathbf{x}, \sigma^2). \tag{9.7}
$$

This is an expression for one output data point y, and for the entire vector of all training data outputs $\mathbf{y}$, we can write

$$p(\mathbf{y} \mid \boldsymbol{\theta}) = \prod_{i=1}^{n} p(y_i \mid \boldsymbol{\theta}) = \prod_{i=1}^{n} \mathcal{N}(y_i; \boldsymbol{\theta}^{\mathsf{T}} \mathbf{x}_i, \sigma^2) = \mathcal{N}(\mathbf{y}; \mathbf{X}\boldsymbol{\theta}, \sigma^2 \mathbf{I}), \qquad (9.8)$$

where in the last step, we used the notation $\mathbf{X}$ from (3.5) and the fact that an n-dimensional Gaussian random vector with a diagonal covariance matrix is equivalent to n scalar Gaussian random variables.

In the Bayesian approach, there is also a need for a prior $p(\boldsymbol{\theta})$ for the unknown parameters $\boldsymbol{\theta}$. In Bayesian linear regression, the prior distribution is most often chosen as a Gaussian with mean $\boldsymbol{\mu}_0$ and covariance $\boldsymbol{\Sigma}_0$,

$$p(\boldsymbol{\theta}) = \mathcal{N}(\boldsymbol{\theta}; \boldsymbol{\mu}_0, \boldsymbol{\Sigma}_0), \qquad (9.9)$$

with, for example, $\boldsymbol{\Sigma}_0 = \mathbf{I}\sigma_0^2$. The reason for this choice is frankly that it simplifies the calculations, much like the squared error loss simplifies the computations for plain linear regression.

The next step is now to compute the posterior. It is possible to derive it using Bayes' theorem, but since $p(\mathbf{y} \mid \boldsymbol{\theta})$ as well as $p(\boldsymbol{\theta})$ are multivariate Gaussian distributions, Corollary 9.1 in Appendix 9.A directly gives us that

$$p(\boldsymbol{\theta} \mid \mathbf{y}) = \mathcal{N}(\boldsymbol{\theta}; \boldsymbol{\mu}_n, \boldsymbol{\Sigma}_n), \qquad (9.10\text{a})$$

$$\boldsymbol{\mu}_n = \boldsymbol{\Sigma}_n \left(\tfrac{1}{\sigma_0^2} \boldsymbol{\mu}_0 + \tfrac{1}{\sigma^2} \mathbf{X}^{\mathsf{T}} \mathbf{y} \right), \qquad (9.10\text{b})$$

$$\boldsymbol{\Sigma}_n = \left(\tfrac{1}{\sigma_0^2} \mathbf{I} + \tfrac{1}{\sigma^2} \mathbf{X}^{\mathsf{T}} \mathbf{X} \right)^{-1}. \qquad (9.10\text{c})$$

From (9.10), we can also derive the posterior predictive for $f(\mathbf{x}_\star)$ by Corollary 9.2 in Appendix 9.A:

$$p(f(\mathbf{x}_\star) \mid \mathbf{y}) = \mathcal{N}(f(\mathbf{x}_\star); m_\star, s_\star), \qquad (9.11\text{a})$$

$$m_\star = \mathbf{x}_\star^{\mathsf{T}} \boldsymbol{\mu}_n, \qquad (9.11\text{b})$$

$$s_\star = \mathbf{x}_\star^{\mathsf{T}} \boldsymbol{\Sigma}_n \mathbf{x}_\star. \qquad (9.11\text{c})$$

We have so far only derived the posterior predictive for $f(\mathbf{x}_\star)$. Since we have $y_\star = f(\mathbf{x}_\star) + \varepsilon$ according to the linear regression model (9.10), where ε is assumed to be independent of f with variance σ^2, we can also compute the posterior predictive for $\mathbf{y}_\star$

$$p(y_\star \mid \mathbf{y}) = \mathcal{N}(y_\star; m_\star, s_\star + \sigma^2). \qquad (9.11\text{d})$$

Note, that only difference from $p(f(\mathbf{x}_\star) \mid \mathbf{y})$ is that we add the variance of the measurement noise σ^2, which reflects the the additional uncertainty we expect to get from the test data output. In both $p(f(\mathbf{x}_\star)\,|\,\mathbf{y})$ and $p(y_\star\,|\,\mathbf{y})$, the measurement noise of the training data output is reflected via the posterior.

We now have all the pieces of Bayesian linear regression in place. The main difference to plain linear regression is that we compute a posterior distribution $p(\boldsymbol{\theta}\,|\,\mathbf{y})$ (instead of a single value $\widehat{\boldsymbol{\theta}}$) and a posterior predictive distribution $p(y_\star\,|\,\mathbf{y})$ instead of a prediction $\widehat{y}$. We summarise it as Method 9.1 and illustrate it with Example 9.1.

Learn Bayesian linear regression

Data: Training data $\mathcal{T} = \{\mathbf{x}_i, y_i\}_{i=1}^n$
Result: Posterior $p(\boldsymbol{\theta}\,|\,\mathbf{y}) = \mathcal{N}\big(\boldsymbol{\theta}; \boldsymbol{\mu}_n, \boldsymbol{\Sigma}_n\big)$

1 Compute $\boldsymbol{\mu}_n$ and $\boldsymbol{\Sigma}_n$ as (9.10).

Predict with Bayesian linear regression

Data: Posterior $p(\boldsymbol{\theta}\,|\,\mathbf{y}) = \mathcal{N}\big(\boldsymbol{\theta}; \boldsymbol{\mu}_n, \boldsymbol{\Sigma}_n\big)$ and test input $\mathbf{x}_\star$
Result: Posterior predictive $p(f(\mathbf{x}_\star)\,|\,\mathbf{y}) = \mathcal{N}(f(\mathbf{x}_\star); m_\star, s_\star)$

1 Compute $m_\star$ and $s_\star$ as (9.11).

Method 9.1 Bayesian linear regression.

We have so far assumed that the noise variance σ^2 is fixed. Most often σ^2 is also a parameter the user has to decide, which can be done by maximising the marginal likelihood. Corollary 9.2 gives us the marginal likelihood:

$$p(\mathbf{y}) = \mathcal{N}\Big(\mathbf{y}; \mathbf{X}\boldsymbol{\mu}_0, \sigma^2\mathbf{I} + \mathbf{X}\boldsymbol{\Sigma}_0\mathbf{X}^\mathsf{T}\Big). \tag{9.12}$$

It is also possible to chose the prior variance σ_0^2 by maximising (9.12).

Just as for plain linear regression, it is possible to use non-linear input transformations, such as polynomials, in Bayesian linear regression. We give an example of that in Example 9.2, where we return to the running regression example of car stopping distances. We can, however, go one step further and also use the kernel trick from Chapter 8. That will lead us to the Gaussian process, which is the topic of Section 9.3.

Example 9.1 Bayesian linear regression

To illustrate the inner workings of Bayesian linear regression, we consider a one-dimensional example with $y = \theta_1 + \theta_2 x + \varepsilon$. In the first row of Figure 9.1, the left panel shows the prior $p(\boldsymbol{\theta})$ (blue surface; a two-dimensional Gaussian distribution over θ_1 and θ_2) from which 10 samples are drawn (blue dots). Each of these samples correspond to a straight line in the plot to the right (blue lines).

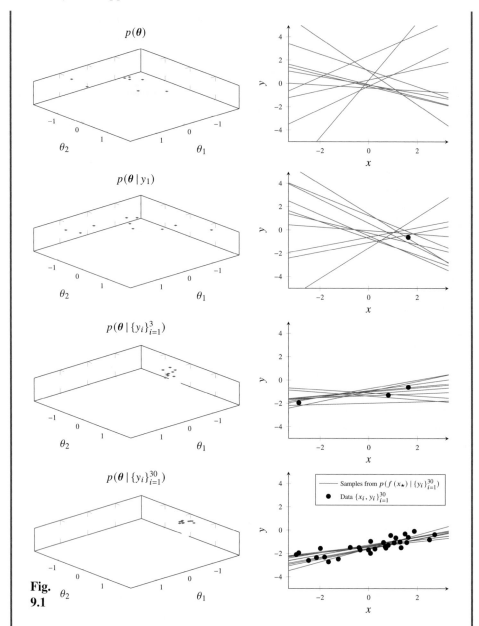

Fig. 9.1

In the second row of Figure 9.1 one ($n = 1$) data point $\{x_1, y_1\}$ is introduced. Its value is shown in the right panel (black dot), and the posterior for $\boldsymbol{\theta}$ in the left panel (a Gaussian; blue surface). In addition, 10 samples are drawn from the posterior (blue dots), each corresponding to a straight line in the right panel (blue lines). In the Bayesian formulation, the sampled lines can be thought of as equally likely posterior hypotheses about $f(x_\star)$. This is repeated also with $n = 3$ and $n = 30$ data points in Figure 9.1. We can in particular see how the posterior contracts ('less uncertainty') as more data arrives, in terms of the blue surface being more peaked as well as the blue lines being more concentrated.

Example 9.2 Car stopping distances

We consider the car stopping distance problem from Example 2.2 and apply probabilistic linear regression with $y = 1 + \theta_1 x + \varepsilon$ and $y = 1 + \theta_1 x + \theta_2 x^2 + \varepsilon$, respectively. We set σ^2 and σ_0^2 by maximising the marginal likelihood, which gives us $\sigma^2 = 12.0^2$ and $\sigma_0^2 = 14.1^2$ for the linear model, and $\sigma^2 = 10.1^2$ and $\sigma_0^2 = 0.3^2$ for the quadratic model.

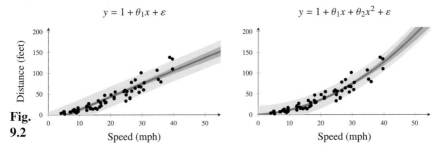

Fig. 9.2

In Figure 9.2 we illustrate $p(f(\mathbf{x}_\star) \mid \mathbf{y})$ and $p(y_\star \mid \mathbf{y})$ (9.11) using the somewhat darker blue line for the mean (they both have the same mean) and the shaded blue areas of different intensities to visualise two standard deviations of $p(f(\mathbf{x}_\star) \mid \mathbf{y})$ and $p(y_\star \mid \mathbf{y})$, respectively.

Connection to Regularised Linear Regression

The main feature of the Bayesian approach is that it provides a full distribution $p(\theta \mid \mathbf{y})$ over the parameters θ, rather than a single point estimate $\widehat{\theta}$. There is, however, also an interesting connection between the Bayesian approach and regularisation. We will make this concrete by considering the posterior $p(\theta \mid \mathbf{y})$ from Bayesian linear regression and the point estimate $\widehat{\theta}_{L^2}$ obtained from L^2-regularised linear regression with squared error loss. Let us extract the so called *maximum a posteriori (MAP)* point estimate $\widehat{\theta}_{\text{MAP}}$ from the posterior $p(\theta \mid \mathbf{y})$. The MAP estimate is the value of θ for which the posterior reaches its maximum,

$$\widehat{\theta}_{\text{MAP}} = \arg\max_{\theta} p(\theta \mid \mathbf{y}) = \arg\max_{\theta} p(\mathbf{y} \mid \theta)p(\theta) = \arg\max_{\theta} \left[\ln p(\mathbf{y} \mid \theta) + \ln p(\theta)\right], \tag{9.13}$$

where the second equality follows from the fact that $p(\theta \mid \mathbf{y}) = \frac{p(\mathbf{y}\mid\theta)p(\theta)}{p(\mathbf{y})}$ and that $p(\mathbf{y})$ does not depend on θ. Remember that L^2-regularised linear regression can be understood as using the cost function (3.48),

$$\widehat{\theta}_{L^2} = \arg\max_{\theta} \left[\ln p(\mathbf{y} \mid \theta) + \lambda\|\theta\|_2^2\right], \tag{9.14}$$

with some regularisation parameter λ. When comparing (9.14) to (9.13), we realise that if $\ln p(\theta) \propto \|\theta\|_2^2$, the MAP estimate and the L^2 regularised estimate of θ are identical for some value of λ. With the prior $p(\boldsymbol{\theta})$ in (9.9), that is indeed the case, and the MAP estimate is in that case identical to $\widehat{\boldsymbol{\theta}}_{L^2}$.

This connection between MAP estimates and regularised maximum likelihood estimates holds as long as the regularisation is proportional to the logarithm of the prior. If, for example, we instead chose a Laplace prior for $\boldsymbol{\theta}$, the MAP estimate would be identical to L^1 regularisation. In general there are many regularisation methods that can be interpreted as implicitly choosing a certain prior. This connection to regularisation gives another perspective as to why the Bayesian approach is less prone to overfitting.

It is, however, important to note that the connection between the Bayesian approach and the use of regularisation does *not* imply that the two approaches are equivalent. The main point with the Bayesian approach is still that a posterior *distribution* is computed for $\boldsymbol{\theta}$, instead of just a point estimate $\widehat{\boldsymbol{\theta}}$.

9.3 The Gaussian Process

We introduced the Bayesian approach as the idea of considering unknown parameters $\boldsymbol{\theta}$ as random variables and consequently learning a posterior distribution $p(\boldsymbol{\theta} \mid \mathbf{y})$ instead of a single value $\widehat{\boldsymbol{\theta}}$. However, the Bayesian idea does not only apply to models with parameters but also to nonparametric models. We will now introduce the Gaussian process, where instead of considering parameters $\boldsymbol{\theta}$ as being random variables, we effectively consider an entire function $f(\mathbf{x})$ to be a stochastic process and compute the posterior $p(f(\mathbf{x}) \mid \mathbf{y})$. The Gaussian process is an interesting and commonly used Bayesian nonparametric model. In a nutshell, it is the Bayesian approach applied to kernel ridge regression (Chapter 8). We will present the Gaussian process as a method for handling regression problems, but it is possible to use it for classification problems as well (similarly to how linear regression can be modified into logistic regression).

In this section we will introduce the fundamentals of the Gaussian process, and thereafter, in Section 9.4, we describe how it can be used as a supervised machine learning method. We will first discuss what a Gaussian process is and thereafter see how we can construct a Gaussian process that connects closely to kernel ridge regression from Section 8.2.

What Is a Gaussian Process?

A Gaussian process is a specific type of stochastic process. A stochastic process, in turn, is a generalisation of a random variable. Most commonly we think about a stochastic process as some random quantity that evolves over time. Mathematically this corresponds to a collection of random variables $\{z(t) : t \in \mathbb{R}\}$ indexed by time t. That is, for each time point t, the value of the process $z(t)$ is a random variable. Furthermore, most often, we assume that values at different time points, say $z(t)$ and $z(s)$, are correlated and that the correlation depends on the time difference. More abstractly, however, we can view $z(t)$ as a random function, where the input to the function is the index variable (time) t. With this interpretation it, is possible to generalise the concept of a stochastic process to random functions with arbitrary inputs, $\{f(\mathbf{x}) : \mathbf{x} \in \mathcal{X}\}$, where $\mathcal{X}$ denotes the (possibly high-dimensional) input space. Similarly to above, this means that we view the *function value* $f(\mathbf{x})$ for any input $\mathbf{x}$ as a random variable and that the function values $f(\mathbf{x})$ and $f(\mathbf{x}')$ for inputs $\mathbf{x}$ and $\mathbf{x}'$ are dependent. As we will see below, the dependencies can be used to control certain properties of the function. For instance, if we expect the function to be smooth (varies slowly), then the function values $f(\mathbf{x})$ and $f(\mathbf{x}')$ should be highly correlated if $\mathbf{x}$ is close to $\mathbf{x}'$. This generalisation opens the way for using random functions as priors for unknown functions (such as a regression function) in a Bayesian setting.

To introduce the Gaussian process as a random function, we will start by making the simplifying assumption that the input variable $\mathbf{x}$ is discrete and can take only q different values, $\mathbf{x}_1, \ldots, \mathbf{x}_q$. Hence, the function $f(\mathbf{x})$ is completely characterised by the q-dimensional vector $\mathbf{f} = [f_1 \; \cdots \; f_q]^\mathsf{T} = [f(\mathbf{x}_1) \; \cdots \; f(\mathbf{x}_q)]^\mathsf{T}$. We can then model $f(\mathbf{x})$ as a random function by assigning a joint probability distribution to this vector $\mathbf{f}$. In the Gaussian process model, this distribution is the multivariate Gaussian distribution,

$$p(\mathbf{f}) = \mathcal{N}(\mathbf{f}; \boldsymbol{\mu}, \boldsymbol{\Sigma}), \tag{9.15}$$

with mean vector $\boldsymbol{\mu}$ and covariance matrix $\boldsymbol{\Sigma}$. Let us partition $\mathbf{f}$ into two vectors $\mathbf{f}_1$ and $\mathbf{f}_2$ such that $\mathbf{f} = \begin{bmatrix} \mathbf{f}_1^\mathsf{T} & \mathbf{f}_2^\mathsf{T} \end{bmatrix}^\mathsf{T}$, and $\boldsymbol{\mu}$ and $\boldsymbol{\Sigma}$ similarly, allowing us to write

$$p\left(\begin{bmatrix} \mathbf{f}_1 \\ \mathbf{f}_2 \end{bmatrix}\right) = \mathcal{N}\left(\begin{bmatrix} \mathbf{f}_1 \\ \mathbf{f}_2 \end{bmatrix}; \begin{bmatrix} \boldsymbol{\mu}_1 \\ \boldsymbol{\mu}_2 \end{bmatrix}, \begin{bmatrix} \boldsymbol{\Sigma}_{11} & \boldsymbol{\Sigma}_{12} \\ \boldsymbol{\Sigma}_{21} & \boldsymbol{\Sigma}_{22} \end{bmatrix}\right). \tag{9.16}$$

If some elements of $\mathbf{f}$, let us say the ones in $\mathbf{f}_1$, are observed, the conditional distribution for $\mathbf{f}_2$ given the observation of $\mathbf{f}_1$ is, by Theorem 9.2 in Appendix 9.A,

$$p(\mathbf{f}_2 \mid \mathbf{f}_1) = \mathcal{N}\left(\mathbf{f}_2; \boldsymbol{\mu}_2 + \boldsymbol{\Sigma}_{21}\boldsymbol{\Sigma}_{11}^{-1}(\mathbf{f}_1 - \boldsymbol{\mu}_1), \boldsymbol{\Sigma}_{22} - \boldsymbol{\Sigma}_{21}\boldsymbol{\Sigma}_{11}^{-1}\boldsymbol{\Sigma}_{12}\right). \tag{9.17}$$

The conditional distribution is nothing but another Gaussian distribution with closed-form expressions for the mean and covariance.

Figure 9.3a shows a two-dimensional example ($\mathbf{f}_1$ is a scalar f_1, and $\mathbf{f}_2$ is a scalar f_2). For this model we choose the prior where the prior mean and variances for f_1 and f_2 are the same, that is $\mu_1 = \mu_2$ and $\Sigma_1 = \Sigma_2$. We also assume a positive prior correlation between $\mathbf{f}_1$ and $\mathbf{f}_2$ before any observations have been received, reflecting the smoothness assumption we have about the underlying random function $f(x)$. That is why the multivariate Gaussian distribution in Figure 9.3a is skewed in the diagonal direction. This multivariate Gaussian distribution is now conditioned on an observation of f_1, which is reflected in Figure 9.3b. In Figure 9.4, we have plotted the marginal distributions from Figure 9.3. Since $\mathbf{f}_1$ and $\mathbf{f}_2$ are correlated according to the prior, the marginal distribution of f_2 is also affected by this observation.

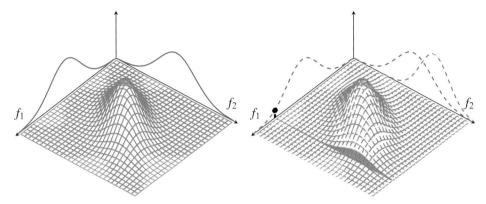

(a) A two-dimensional Gaussian distribution for the random variables f_1 and f_2, with a blue surface plot for the density, and the marginal distribution for each component sketched using blue lines along each axis. Note that the marginal distributions do *not* contain all information about the distribution of f_1 and f_2, since the covariance information is lacking in that representation.

(b) The conditional distribution of f_2 (red line) when f_1 is observed (black dot). The conditional distribution of f_2 is given by (9.17), which (apart from a normalising constant) in this graphical representation is the red 'slice' of the joint distribution (blue surface). The marginals of the joint distribution from Figure 9.3a are kept for reference (blue dashed lines).

Figure 9.3 A two-dimensional multivariate Gaussian distribution for f_1 and f_2 in (a), and the conditional distribution for f_2, when a particular value of f_1 is observed, in (b).

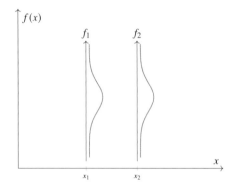
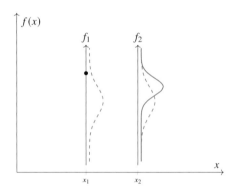

(a) The marginal distributions for f_1 and f_2 from Figure 9.3a.

(b) The distribution for f_2 (red line) when f_1 is observed (black dot), as in Figure 9.3b.

Figure 9.4 The marginals of the distributions in Figure 9.3, here plotted slightly differently. Note that this more compact plot comes at the cost of missing the information about the covariance between f_1 and f_2.

In a similar fashion to Figure 9.4, we can plot a six-dimensional multivariate Gaussian distribution by its marginal distributions in Figure 9.5. Also in this model we assume a positive prior correlation between all elements f_i and f_j which decays with the distance between their corresponding inputs x_i and x_j. Bear in mind that to fully illustrate the joint distribution for $f_1, \ldots, f_6$, a six-dimensional surface plot would be needed, whereas Figure 9.5a only contains the marginal distributions for each component. We may also condition the six-dimensional distribution underlying

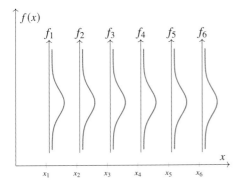
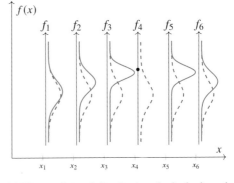

(a) A six-dimensional Gaussian distribution, plotted in the same way as Figure 9.4a, that is, only its marginals are illustrated.

(b) The conditional distribution f_1, f_2, f_3, f_5, and f_6 when f_4 is observed (black dot), illustrated by its marginals (red lines) similarly to Figure 9.4b.

Figure 9.5 A six-dimensional Gaussian distribution, illustrated in the same fashion as Figure 9.4.

Figure 9.5a on an observation of, say, f_4. Once again, the conditional distribution is another Gaussian distribution, and the marginal distributions of the five-dimensional random variable $[f_1, f_2, f_3, f_5, f_6]^\mathsf{T}$ are plotted in Figure 9.5b.

In Figures 9.4 and 9.5, we illustrated the marginal distributions for a finite-dimensional multivariate Gaussian random variable. However, we are aiming for the Gaussian process, which is a stochastic process on a continuous space.

The extension of the Gaussian distribution (defined on a finite set) to the Gaussian process (defined on a continuous space) is achieved by replacing the discrete index set $\{1, 2, 3, 4, 5, 6\}$ in Figure 9.5 by a variable $\mathbf{x}$ taking values on a continuous space, for example the real line. We then also have to replace the random variables $f_1, f_2, \ldots, f_6$ with a random function (that is, a stochastic process) f which can be evaluated at any $\mathbf{x}$ as $f(\mathbf{x})$. Furthermore, in the Gaussian multivariate distribution, $\boldsymbol{\mu}$ is a vector with q components, and Σ is a $q \times q$ matrix. Instead of having a separate hyperparameter for each element in this mean vector and covariance matrix, in the Gaussian process we replace $\boldsymbol{\mu}$ by a mean *function* $\mu(\mathbf{x})$ into which we can insert any $\mathbf{x}$, and the covariance matrix Σ is replaced by a covariance *function* $\kappa(\mathbf{x}, \mathbf{x}')$ into which we can insert any pair $\mathbf{x}$ and $\mathbf{x}'$. This mean function and covariance function we can then parametrise with a few hyperparameters. In these functions we can also encode certain properties that we want the Gaussian process to obey, for example that two function values $f(\mathbf{x}_1)$ and $f(\mathbf{x}_2)$ should be more correlated if $\mathbf{x}_1$ and $\mathbf{x}_2$ are closer to each other than if they are further apart.

From this we can define the Gaussian process. If, for any arbitrary finite set of points $\{\mathbf{x}_1, \ldots, \mathbf{x}_n\}$, it holds that

$$
p\left(\begin{bmatrix} f(\mathbf{x}_1) \\ \vdots \\ f(\mathbf{x}_n) \end{bmatrix}\right) = \mathcal{N}\left(\begin{bmatrix} f(\mathbf{x}_1) \\ \vdots \\ f(\mathbf{x}_n) \end{bmatrix}; \begin{bmatrix} \mu(\mathbf{x}_1) \\ \vdots \\ \mu(\mathbf{x}_n) \end{bmatrix}, \begin{bmatrix} \kappa(\mathbf{x}_1, \mathbf{x}_1) & \cdots & \kappa(\mathbf{x}_1, \mathbf{x}_n) \\ \vdots & & \vdots \\ \kappa(\mathbf{x}_n, \mathbf{x}_1) & \cdots & \kappa(\mathbf{x}_n, \mathbf{x}_n) \end{bmatrix}\right), \tag{9.18}
$$

then f is a Gaussian process.

That is, with a Gaussian process f and any choice of $\{x_1, \ldots, x_n\}$, the vector of function values $[f(x_1), \ldots, f(x_n)]$ has a multivariate Gaussian distribution, just like the one in Figure 9.5. Since $\{x_1, \ldots, x_n\}$ can be chosen arbitrarily from the continuous space on which it lives, the Gaussian process defines a distribution for *all* points in that space. For this definition to make sense, $\kappa(x, x')$ has to be such that a positive semidefinite covariance matrix is obtained for any choice of $\{x_1, \ldots, x_n\}$.

We will use the notation

$$f \sim \mathcal{GP}(\mu, \kappa) \tag{9.19}$$

to express that the function $f(x)$ is distributed according to a Gaussian process with mean function $\mu(x)$ and covariance function $\kappa(x, x')$. If we want to illustrate a Gaussian process, which we do in Figure 9.6, we can choose $\{x_1, \ldots, x_n\}$ to correspond to the pixels on the screen or the printer dots on the paper and print the marginal distributions for each $\{x_1, \ldots, x_n\}$ so that it appears as a continuous line to the eye (despite the fact that we can only actually access the distribution in a finite, but arbitrary, set of points).

It is no coincidence that we use the same symbol κ for covariance functions as we used for kernels in Chapter 8. As we will soon discuss, applying the Bayesian approach to kernel ridge regression will result in a Gaussian process where the covariance function is the kernel.

We can also condition the Gaussian process on some observations $\{f(x_i), x_i\}_{i=1}^n$, the Gaussian process counterpart to Figures 9.3b, 9.4b, and 9.5b. As usual we stack the observed inputs in X and let $f(X)$ denote the vector of observed outputs (we assume for now that the observations are made without any noise). We use the notations $K(X, X)$ and $K(X, x_\star)$ as defined by (8.12b) and (8.12c) to write the joint distribution between the observed values $f(X)$ and the test value $f(x_\star)$ as

$$p\left(\begin{bmatrix} f(x_\star) \\ f(X) \end{bmatrix}\right) = \mathcal{N}\left(\begin{bmatrix} f(x_\star) \\ f(X) \end{bmatrix}; \begin{bmatrix} \mu(x_\star) \\ \mu(X) \end{bmatrix}, \begin{bmatrix} \kappa(x_\star, x_\star) & K(X, x_\star)^\mathsf{T} \\ K(X, x_\star) & K(X, X) \end{bmatrix}\right). \tag{9.20}$$

Now, as we have observed $f(X)$, we use the expressions for the Gaussian distribution to write the distribution for $f(x_\star)$ conditional on the observations of $f(X)$ as

$$p(f(x_\star) \mid f(X)) = \mathcal{N}(f(x_\star); \mu(x_\star) + K(X, x_\star)^\mathsf{T} K(X, X)^{-1} \tag{9.21}$$
$$\times (f(X) - \mu(X)), \kappa(x_\star, x_\star) - K(X, x_\star)^\mathsf{T} K(X, X)^{-1} K(X, x_\star)),$$

which is another Gaussian distribution for any test input $x_\star$. We illustrate this in Figure 9.6.

We have now introduced the somewhat abstract concept of a Gaussian process. In some subjects, such as signal processing, so-called white Gaussian processes are common. A white Gaussian process has a white covariance function

$$\kappa(x, x') = \mathbb{I}\{x = x'\} = \begin{cases} 1 & \text{if } x = x', \\ 0 & \text{otherwise,} \end{cases} \tag{9.22}$$

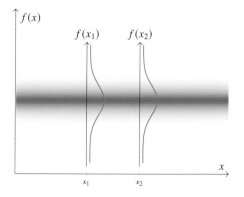 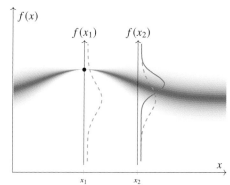

(a) A Gaussian process defined on the real line, parameterised by x, not conditioned on any observations. The intensity of the blue colour is proportional to the (marginal) density, and the marginal distributions for two test inputs x_1 and x_2 are shown in red. Similarly to Figure 9.5, we only plot the marginal distribution for each test input, but the Gaussian process defines a full joint distribution for all points on the x-axis.

(b) The conditional Gaussian process given the observation of $f(x_1)$ in the point x_1. The prior distribution from Figure (a) is shown in dashed grey. Note how the conditional distribution adjusts to the observation, both in terms of mean (closer to the observation) and (marginal) variance (smaller in the proximity of the observation, but it remains more or less unchanged in areas far from it).

Figure 9.6 A Gaussian process. Figure (a) shows the prior distribution, whereas (b) shows the posterior distribution after conditioning on one observation (black dot).

which implies that $f(\mathbf{x})$ is uncorrelated to $f(\mathbf{x}')$ unless $\mathbf{x} = \mathbf{x}'$. White Gaussian processes are of less use in supervised machine learning, but we will instead have a look at how kernel ridge regression can be turned into a Gaussian process, where the mean function becomes zero, and the covariance function becomes the kernel from Chapter 8.

Extending Kernel Ridge Regression into a Gaussian Process

An alternative way to obtain the Gaussian process construction is to apply the kernel trick from Section 8.2 to Bayesian linear regression from (9.11). The connection between linear regression, Bayesian linear regression, kernel ridge regression, and the Gaussian process is summarised in Figure 9.7. This will essentially lead us back to (9.21), with the kernel being the covariance function $\kappa(\mathbf{x}, \mathbf{x}')$, and the mean function being $\mu(\mathbf{x}) = 0$.

Let us now repeat the posterior predictive for Bayesian linear regression (9.11), but with two changes. The first change is that we assume the prior mean and covariance for $\boldsymbol{\theta}$ are $\boldsymbol{\mu}_0 = \mathbf{0}$ and $\boldsymbol{\Sigma}_0 = \mathbf{I}$, respectively. This assumption is not strictly needed for our purposes but simplifies the expressions. The second change is that, as in Section 8.1, we introduce non-linear feature transformations $\boldsymbol{\phi}(\mathbf{x})$ of the input variable $\mathbf{x}$ in the linear regression model. We therefore replace $\mathbf{X}$ with $\boldsymbol{\Phi}(\mathbf{X})$ in the notation. Altogether, (9.11) becomes

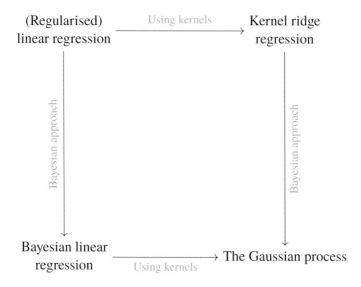

Figure 9.7 A graphical summary of the connections between linear regression, Bayesian linear regression, kernel ridge regression, and the Gaussian process.

$$p(f(\mathbf{x}_\star) \,|\, \mathbf{y}) = \mathcal{N}(f(\mathbf{x}_\star); m_\star, s_\star), \tag{9.23a}$$

$$m_\star = \boldsymbol{\phi}(\mathbf{x}_\star)^\mathsf{T} \left(\sigma^2 \mathbf{I} + \boldsymbol{\Phi}(\mathbf{X})^\mathsf{T}\boldsymbol{\Phi}(\mathbf{X})\right)^{-1} \boldsymbol{\Phi}(\mathbf{X})^\mathsf{T}\mathbf{y}, \tag{9.23b}$$

$$s_\star = \boldsymbol{\phi}(\mathbf{x}_\star)^\mathsf{T} \left(\mathbf{I} + \tfrac{1}{\sigma^2}\boldsymbol{\Phi}(\mathbf{X})^\mathsf{T}\boldsymbol{\Phi}(\mathbf{X})\right)^{-1} \boldsymbol{\phi}(\mathbf{x}_\star). \tag{9.23c}$$

In a similar fashion to the derivation of kernel ridge regression, we use the push-through matrix identity $\mathbf{A}(\mathbf{A}^\mathsf{T}\mathbf{A} + \mathbf{I})^{-1} = (\mathbf{A}\mathbf{A}^\mathsf{T} + \mathbf{I})^{-1}\mathbf{A}$ to re-write $m_\star$ with the aim of having $\boldsymbol{\phi}(\mathbf{x})$ only appearing through inner products:

$$m_\star = \boldsymbol{\phi}(\mathbf{x}_\star)^\mathsf{T}\boldsymbol{\Phi}(\mathbf{X})^\mathsf{T} \left(\sigma^2 \mathbf{I} + \boldsymbol{\Phi}(\mathbf{X})\boldsymbol{\Phi}(\mathbf{X})^\mathsf{T}\right)^{-1} \mathbf{y}. \tag{9.24a}$$

To re-write $s_\star$ in a similar fashion, we have to use the matrix inversion lemma $(\mathbf{I} - \mathbf{U}\mathbf{V})^{-1} = \mathbf{I} - \mathbf{U}(\mathbf{I} + \mathbf{V}\mathbf{U})^{-1}\mathbf{V}$ (which holds for any matrices $\mathbf{U}, \mathbf{V}$ of compatible dimensions):

$$s_\star = \boldsymbol{\phi}(\mathbf{x}_\star)^\mathsf{T}\boldsymbol{\phi}(\mathbf{x}_\star) - \boldsymbol{\phi}(\mathbf{x}_\star)^\mathsf{T}\boldsymbol{\Phi}(\mathbf{X})^\mathsf{T} \left(\sigma^2 \mathbf{I} + \boldsymbol{\Phi}(\mathbf{X})\boldsymbol{\Phi}(\mathbf{X})^\mathsf{T}\right)^{-1} \boldsymbol{\Phi}(\mathbf{X})\boldsymbol{\phi}(\mathbf{x}_\star). \tag{9.24b}$$

Analogously to the derivation of kernel ridge regression as in (8.12), we are now ready to apply the kernel trick and replace all instances of $\boldsymbol{\phi}(\mathbf{x})^\mathsf{T}\boldsymbol{\phi}(\mathbf{x}')$ with a kernel $\kappa(\mathbf{x}, \mathbf{x}')$. With the same notation as in (8.12), we get

$$m_\star = K(\mathbf{X}, \mathbf{x}_\star)^\mathsf{T} \left(\sigma^2 \mathbf{I} + K(\mathbf{X}, \mathbf{X})\right)^{-1} \mathbf{y}, \tag{9.25a}$$

$$s_\star = \kappa(\mathbf{x}_\star, \mathbf{x}_\star) - K(\mathbf{X}, \mathbf{x}_\star)^\mathsf{T} \left(\sigma^2 \mathbf{I} + K(\mathbf{X}, \mathbf{X})\right)^{-1} K(\mathbf{X}, \mathbf{x}_\star). \tag{9.25b}$$

The posterior predictive that is defined by (9.23a) and (9.25) is the Gaussian process model again, identical to (9.21) if $\mu(\mathbf{x}_\star) = 0$ and $\sigma^2 = 0$. The reason for $\mu(\mathbf{x}_\star) = 0$ is that we made this derivation starting with $\mu_0 = 0$. When we derived (9.21), we assumed that we observed $f(\mathbf{x}_\star)$ (rather than $y_\star = f(\mathbf{x}_\star) + \varepsilon$), which is the reason why $\sigma^2 = 0$ in (9.21). The Gaussian process is thus a kernel version of Bayesian linear regression, much like kernel ridge regression is a kernel version of (regularised) linear regression, as illustrated in Figure 9.7. In order to see the connection to kernel ridge regression, note that (9.25a) is identical to (8.14) with $\sigma^2 = n\lambda$. It is, however, also important to note the difference in that there is no counterpart to (9.25b) for kernel ridge regression, simply because kernel ridge regression does not predict a probability distribution.

The fact that the kernel plays the role of a covariance function in the Gaussian process gives us another interpretation of the kernel in addition to the ones in Section 8.4, namely that the kernel $\kappa(\mathbf{x}, \mathbf{x}')$ determines how strong the correlation between $f(\mathbf{x})$ and $f(\mathbf{x}')$ is assumed to be.

> **Time to reflect 9.1** *Verify that you retrieve Bayesian linear regression when using the linear kernel (8.23) in the Gaussian process. Why is that?*

It is common not to write out the addition of $\sigma^2 \mathbf{I}$ to the Gram matrix $K(\mathbf{X}, \mathbf{X})$ but instead to add a white noise kernel (9.22) multiplied by σ^2 to the original kernel: as $\tilde{\kappa}(\mathbf{x}, \mathbf{x}') = \kappa(\mathbf{x}, \mathbf{x}') + \sigma^2 \mathbb{I}\{\mathbf{x}, \mathbf{x}'\}$. We can then replace $\sigma^2 \mathbf{I} + K(\mathbf{X}, \mathbf{X})$ with $\tilde{K}(\mathbf{X}, \mathbf{X})$, where $\tilde{K}$ is built up using $\tilde{\kappa}(\mathbf{x}, \mathbf{x}')$ rather than $\kappa(\mathbf{x}, \mathbf{x}')$. In this notation, (9.25) simplifies to

$$m_\star = \tilde{K}(\mathbf{X}, \mathbf{x}_\star)^\mathsf{T} \tilde{K}(\mathbf{X}, \mathbf{X})^{-1} \mathbf{y}, \tag{9.26a}$$

$$s_\star = \tilde{\kappa}(\mathbf{x}_\star, \mathbf{x}_\star) - \tilde{K}(\mathbf{X}, \mathbf{x}_\star)^\mathsf{T} \tilde{K}(\mathbf{X}, \mathbf{X})^{-1} \tilde{K}(\mathbf{X}, \mathbf{x}_\star) - \sigma^2. \tag{9.26b}$$

As in Bayesian linear regression, if we are interested in the posterior predictive $p(y_\star \mid \mathbf{y})$ instead of $p(f(\mathbf{x}_\star) \mid \mathbf{y})$, we add σ^2 to the variance of the prediction; see (9.11d). We summarise the Gaussian process as Method 9.2.

Data: Training data $\mathcal{T} = \{\mathbf{x}_i, y_i\}_{i=1}^n$, kernel $\kappa(\mathbf{x}, \mathbf{x}')$, noise variance σ^2 and test input $\mathbf{x}_\star$

Result: Posterior predictive $p(f(\mathbf{x}_\star) \mid \mathbf{y}) = \mathcal{N}(f(\mathbf{x}_\star); m_\star, s_\star)$

1 Compute $m_\star$ and $s_\star$ according to (9.25)

Method 9.2 Gaussian process regression.

A Nonparametric Distribution over Functions

As a supervised machine learning tool, we use the Gaussian process for making predictions, that is, computing the posterior predictive $p(f(\mathbf{x}_\star) \mid \mathbf{y})$ (or $p(y_\star \mid \mathbf{y})$).

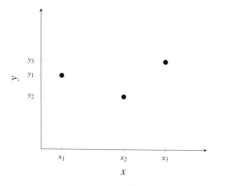

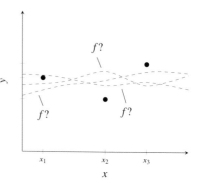

(a) The training data $\{x_i, y_i\}_{i=1}^3$ of a regression problem is given to us.

(b) The underlying assumption when we do regression is that there exists *some* function f, which describes the data as $y_i = f(x_i) + \varepsilon$. It is unknown to us, but the purpose of regression (no matter which method is used) is to determine f.

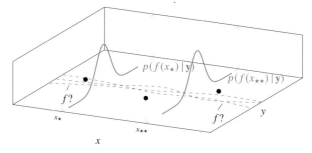

(c) The Gaussian process defines a distribution over f. We can condition that distribution on training data (that is, learning) and access it for any input, say $x_\star$ and $x_{\star\star}$. That is, we make a prediction for $x_\star$ and $x_{\star\star}$. The Gaussian process gives us a Gaussian distribution for $f(x_\star)$ and $f(x_{\star\star})$, illustrated by solid red lines. That distribution is heavily influenced by the choice of kernel, which is a design choice in the Gaussian process.

Figure 9.8 The Gaussian process defines a distribution over functions, which we can condition on training data and access at arbitrary points (such as $x_\star$ and $x_{\star\star}$) in order to compute predictions.

However, unlike most other methods, which only deliver a point prediction $\widehat{y}(\mathbf{x}_\star)$, the posterior predictive is a distribution. Since we can compute the posterior predictive for any $\mathbf{x}_\star$, the Gaussian process actually defines a *distribution over functions*, as we illustrate in Figure 9.8.

Much like we could derive a connection between Bayesian linear regression and L^2 regularised linear regression, we have also seen a similar connection between the Gaussian process and kernel ridge regression. If we only consider the mean $m_\star$ of the posterior predictive, we recover kernel ridge regression. To take full advantage of the Bayesian perspective, we also have to consider the posterior predictive variance $s_\star$. With most kernels, the predictive variance is smaller if there is a training data point nearby and larger if the closest training data point is distant. Hence, the predictive variance provides a quantification of the 'uncertainty' in the prediction.

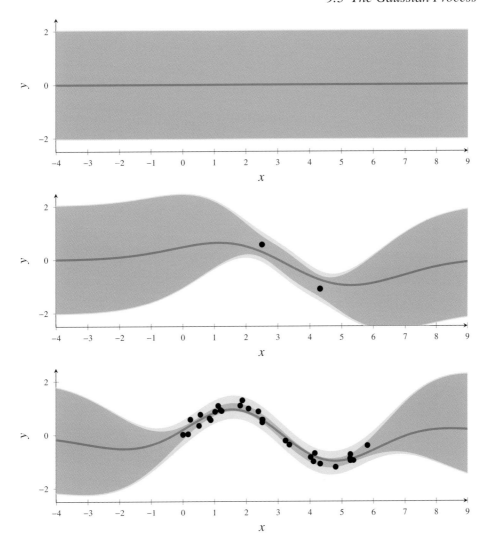

Figure 9.9 The Gaussian process as a supervised machine learning method: we can learn (that is, compute (9.23a) and (9.25)) the posterior predictive for $f(x_\star)$ and $y_\star$ (shaded blue; darker blue for two standard deviations for $p(y_\star \mid y)$, lighter blue for two standard deviations for $p(f(x_\star) \mid y)$, and solid blue line for the mean) learned from 0 (upper), 2 (middle), and 30 (bottom) observations (black dots). We see how the model adapts to training data, and note in particular that the variance shrinks in the regions where observations are made but remains larger in regions where no observations are made.

Altogether, the Gaussian process is another useful tool for regression problems, as we illustrate in Figure 9.9.

Drawing Samples from a Gaussian Process

When computing a prediction of $f(x_\star)$ for a single input point $x_\star$, the posterior predictive $p(f(x_\star) \mid y)$ captures all information the Gaussian process has about

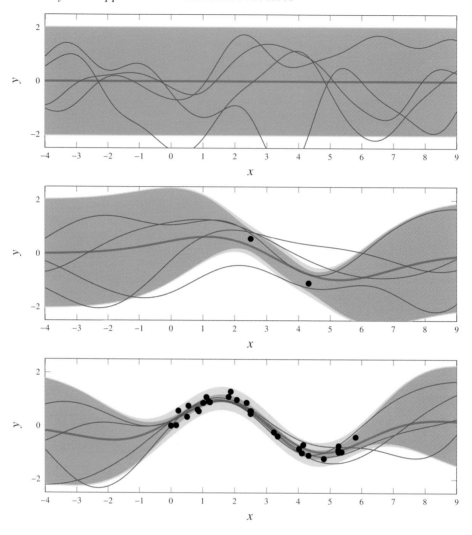

Figure 9.10 Figure 9.9 again, this time appended also with samples from $p(f(x_\star) \mid \mathbf{y})$.

$f(\mathbf{x}_\star)$. However, if we are interested not only in predicting $f(\mathbf{x}_\star)$, but also $f(\mathbf{x}_\star + \boldsymbol{\delta})$, the Gaussian process contains more information than is present in the two posterior predictive distributions $p(f(\mathbf{x}_\star) \mid \mathbf{y})$ and $p(f(\mathbf{x}_\star + \boldsymbol{\delta}) \mid \mathbf{y})$ separately. This is because the Gaussian process also contains information about the correlation between the function values $f(\mathbf{x}_\star)$ and $f(\mathbf{x}_\star + \boldsymbol{\delta})$, and the pitfall is that $p(f(\mathbf{x}_\star) \mid \mathbf{y})$ and $p(f(\mathbf{x}_\star + \boldsymbol{\delta}) \mid \mathbf{y})$ are only the marginal distributions of the joint distribution $p(f(\mathbf{x}_\star), f(\mathbf{x}_\star + \boldsymbol{\delta}) \mid \mathbf{y})$, just as the joint distribution in Figure 9.3 contains more information than only the marginal distributions in Figure 9.4.

If we are interested in computing predictions for a larger set of input values, it can be rather cumbersome to grasp and visualise the resulting high-dimensional posterior predictive distribution. An useful alternative can therefore be to visualise the Gaussian process posterior by samples from it. Technically this simply amounts to drawing a sample from the posterior predictive distribution, which we illustrate in Figure 9.10.

9.4 Practical Aspects of the Gaussian Process

When using the Gaussian process as a method for supervised machine learning, there are a few important design choices left to the user. Like the methods presented in Chapter 8, the Gaussian process is a kernel method, and the choice of kernel is very important. Most kernels contain a few hyperparameters, which also have to be chosen. That choice can be done by maximising the marginal likelihood, which we will discuss now.

Kernel Choice

Since the Gaussian process can be understood as the Bayesian version of kernel ridge regression, the Gaussian process also requires a positive semidefinite kernel. Any of the positive semidefinite kernels presented in Section 8.4 can also be used for Gaussian processes.

Among all kernel methods presented in this book, the Gaussian process could be the method where the exact choice of kernel has the biggest impact since the Gaussian posterior predictive $p(f(\mathbf{x}_\star \mid \mathbf{y}))$ has a mean and a variance, both of which are heavily affected by the choice of kernel. It is therefore important to make a good choice, and besides the discussion in Section 8.4, it can also be instructive to visually compare different kernel choices as in Figure 9.11, at least when working with one-dimensional problems where that visualisation is possible. For example, as can be seen from Figure 9.11, the squared exponential and the Matérn kernel with $\nu = \frac{1}{2}$ correspond to drastically different assumptions about the smoothness of $f(\mathbf{x})$.

A positive semidefinite kernel $\kappa(\mathbf{x}, \mathbf{x}')$ remains a positive semidefinite kernel when multiplied with a positive constant ς^2, $\varsigma^2 \kappa(\mathbf{x}, \mathbf{x}')$. For the kernel methods in Chapter 8, such a scaling has effectively no impact beyond what can be achieved by tuning the regularisation parameter λ. However, for the Gaussian process, it is important to choose a constant ς^2 wisely since it becomes an important factor in the predicted variance.

In the end, the kernel, with all its hyperparameters including ς^2 and σ^2, is a design choice left to the machine leraing engineer. In the Bayesian perspective, the kernel is an important part of the prior that implements crucial assumptions about the function f.

Hyperparameter Tuning

Most kernels $\kappa(\mathbf{x}, \mathbf{x}')$ contain a few hyperparameters, such as ℓ and α and some possible scaling ς^2, in addition to the noise variance σ^2. Some of the hyperparameters might be possible to set manually, for example if they have a natural interpretation, but most often some hyperparameters are left as tuning parameters for the user. We jointly refer to all those hyperparameters that need to be chosen as η, meaning that η could be a vector. Cross-validation can indeed be used for this purpose,

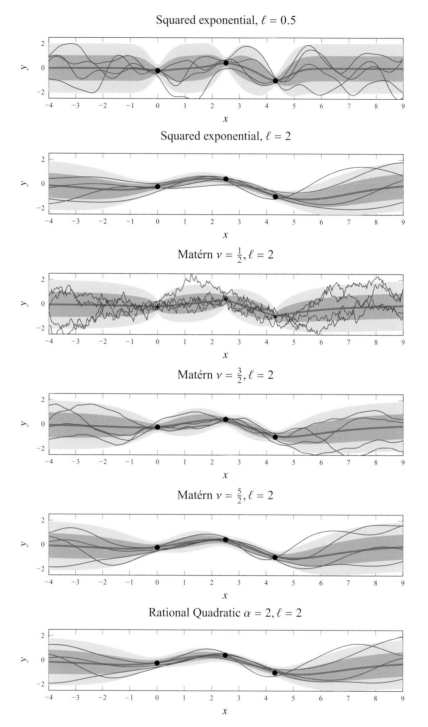

Figure 9.11 The Gaussian process applied to the same data with different kernels and hyperparameters, in order to illustrate what assumptions are made by the different kernels. The data is marked with black dots, and the Gaussian process is illustrated by its mean (blue thick line), variance (blue areas; darker for one standard deviation and lighter for two standard deviations), and samples (thin lines).

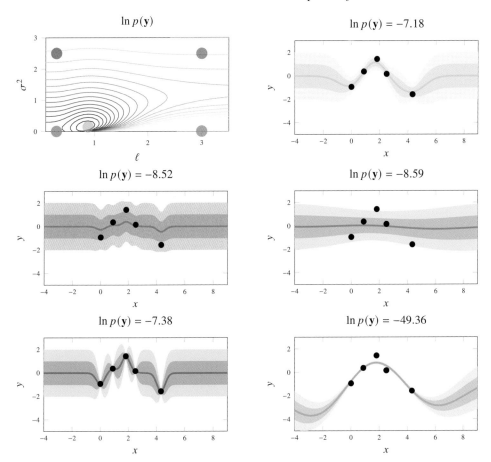

Figure 9.12 To choose hyperparameters $\eta = (\ell, \sigma^2)$ for the Gaussian process kernel, the marginal likelihood $p_\eta(\mathbf{y})$ can be maximised. For a given dataset of five points (black dots) and the squared exponential kernel, the landscape of the logarithm of the marginal likelihood (as a function of the hyperparameters lengthscale ℓ and noise variance σ^2) is shown as a contour plot in the upper left panel. Each point in that plot corresponds to a certain selection of the hyperparameters ℓ, σ^2. For five such points (grey, purple, blue, green, and orange dots), the corresponding Gaussian process is shown in separate panels with the same colour. Note that the orange dot is located at the maximum of $p_\eta(\mathbf{y})$. The orange upper right plot therefore corresponds to a Gaussian process where the hyperparameters have been maximised using marginal likelihood. It is clear that optimising $p_\eta(\mathbf{y})$ does *not* mean selecting hyperparameters such that the Gaussian process follows the data as closely as possible (as the blue one does).

but the Bayesian approach also comes with the option to maximise the marginal likelihood $p(\mathbf{y})$ as a method for selecting hyperparameters, as in (9.4). To emphasise how η enters into the marginal likelihood, we add the subscript η to all terms that depends on it. From the construction of the Gaussian process, we have that $p_\eta(\mathbf{y}) = \mathcal{N}\left(\mathbf{y}; 0, \tilde{\boldsymbol{K}}_\eta(\mathbf{X}, \mathbf{X})\right)$, and consequently

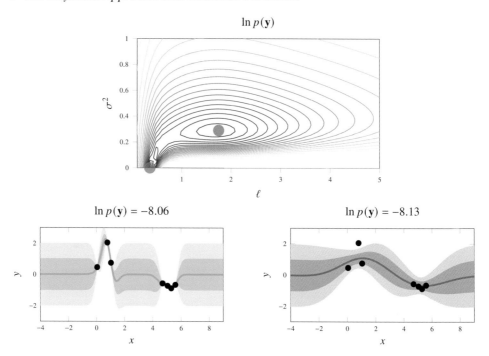

Figure 9.13 The landscape of $p(\mathbf{y})$ may have several local maxima. In this case there is one local maximum at the blue dot, with relatively large noise variance and length scale. There is also another local maximum, which also is the global one, at the green dot, with much less noise variance and a shorter lengthscale. There is also a third local maximum in between (not shown). It is not uncommon that the different maxima provide different 'interpretations' of the data. As a machine learning engineer, it is important to be aware that this can happen; the green one does indeed optimise the marginal likelihood, but the blue one can also be practically useful.

$$\ln p_\eta(\mathbf{y}) = -\frac{1}{2}\mathbf{y}^\top \tilde{K}_\eta(\mathbf{X},\mathbf{X})^{-1}\mathbf{y} - \frac{1}{2}\ln\det\left(\tilde{K}_\eta(\mathbf{X},\mathbf{X})\right) - \frac{n}{2}\log 2\pi. \qquad (9.27)$$

In other words, the hyperparameters of the Gaussian process kernel can be chosen by solving the optimisation problem of maximising (9.27) with respect to η. If using this approach, solving the optimisation problem can be seen as a part of learning the Gaussian process, which is illustrated in Figure 9.12.

When selecting hyperarameters η of a kernel, it is important to be aware that (9.27) (as a function of the hyperparameters) may have multiple local maxima, as we illustrate in Figure 9.13. It is therefore important to carefully choose the initialisation of the optimisation procedure. The challenge with local maxima is not unique to using the marginal likelihood approach but can also arise when cross-validation is used to choose hyperparameters.

We conclude this part about the Gaussian process by applying it to the car stopping distance problem in Example 9.3.

Example 9.3 Car stopping distances

We again consider the car stopping distance problem from Example 2.2. We have already discussed the application of the other kernel methods, kernel ridge regression, and support vector regression in Examples 8.2 and 8.3, respectively, both in Chapter 8. Since the results in the previous examples looked reasonable, we use the same kernel and hyperparameters again, meaning that we have

$$\tilde{\kappa}(x, x') = \exp\left(-\frac{|x - x'|^2}{2\ell^2}\right) + (1 + xx')^2 + \sigma^2 \mathbb{I}\{x = x'\},$$

with $\ell = 3$ and $\sigma^2 = \lambda n$ (with $\lambda = 0.01$ and $n = 62$ data points). However, we also have the option to introduce yet another hyperparameter ς^2 as $\varsigma^2 \tilde{\kappa}(\mathbf{x}, \mathbf{x}')$. In the top part of Figure 9.14, we use $\varsigma^2 = 2^2$ and $\varsigma^2 = 40^2$ to illustrate the fundamental impact that ς^2 has on the posterior predictive. (Note that only the variance, and not the mean, is affected by ς^2. This can be confirmed by the fact that ς^2 cancels algebraically in (9.26a) but not in (9.26b).)

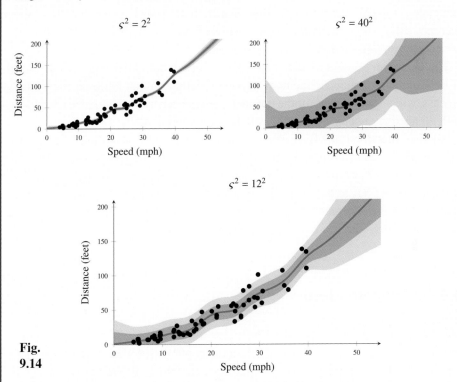

Fig. 9.14

To select ς^2, we therefore maximise the marginal likelihood with respect to it, which gives us $\varsigma^2 = 12^2$, as shown in the bottom panel of Figure 9.14. Indeed, it seems to have a very reasonable variance ('uncertainty') in the posterior predictive distribution.

9.5 Other Bayesian Methods in Machine Learning

Besides introducing the Bayesian approach in general, this chapter contains the Bayesian treatment of linear regression (Bayesian linear regression, Section 9.2) and kernel ridge regression (Gaussian processes, Section 9.3–9.4). The Bayesian approach is, however, applicable to all methods that somehow learn a model from training data. The reason for the selection of methods in this chapter is frankly that Bayesian linear regression and Gaussian process regression are among the few Bayesian supervised machine learning methods where the posterior and/or the posterior predictive are easy to compute.

Most often, the Bayesian approach requires numerical integration routines as well as numerical methods for representing the posterior distribution (the posterior does not have to be a Gaussian or any other standard distribution) when applied to various models. There are two major families of such numerical methods, called variational inference and Monte Carlo methods. The idea of variational inference is to approximate probability distributions in such a way that the problem becomes sufficiently tractable, whereas Monte Carlo methods represent probability distributions using random samples from them.

The Gaussian process model is an example of a method belonging to the family of Bayesian nonparametric methods. Another method in that family is the Dirichlet process, which can be used for the unsupervised clustering problem (see Chapter 10), with no need to specify the number of clusters beforehand.

Another direction is the Bayesian approach applied to deep learning, often referred to as Bayesian deep learning. In short, Bayesian deep learning amounts to computing the posterior $p(\theta \mid \mathbf{y})$, instead of only parameter values $\widehat{\theta}$. In doing so, stochastic gradient descent has to be replaced with either some version of variational inference or some Monte Carlo method. Due to the massive number of parameters often used in deep learning, that is a computationally challenging problem.

9.6 Further Reading

The Bayesian approach has a long history within statistics. The name originates from Thomas Bayes and his 1763 posthumously published work 'An Essay towards solving a Problem in the Doctrine of Chances', but Pierre-Simon Laplace also made significant contributions to the idea in the late 18th and early 19th century. For an overview of its use in statistics and its historical controversies, we refer to Efron and Hastie (2016, Part I).

A relatively short review article on modern Bayesian machine learning with many suggestions for further reading is Ghahramani (2015). There are also several textbooks on the modern use of the Bayesian approach in machine learning, including Barber (2012), Gelman et al. (2014), and Rogers and Girolami (2017), and for some aspects also Bishop (2006) and Murphy (2012).

Gaussian processes are covered in depth by the textbook Rasmussen and Williams (2006). Other Bayesian nonparametric models in general and the Dirichlet process in particular are introduced in Gershman and Blei (2012), Ghahramani (2013), and Hjort et al. (2010).

As mentioned above, the Bayesian approach often requires more advanced computational methods not discussed in this chapter. Two entry points for further studies of variational inference are Bishop (2006, Chapter 10) and Blei et al. (2017). Introductions to Monte Carlo methods are found in Owen (2013), Robert and Casella (2004), and Gelman et al. (2014, Part III).

Although a very recent research topic, the idea of Bayesian learning of neural networks was laid out already in the 90s (R. M. Neal 1996). Some more recent contributions include Blundell et al. (2015), Dusenberry et al. (2020), Fort et al. (2019), Kendall and Gal (2017), and R. Zhang et al. (2020).

9.A The Multivariate Gaussian Distribution

This appendix contains some results on the multivariate Gaussian distribution that are essential for Bayesian linear regression and the Gaussian process. Figure 9.15 summarises how they relate to each other.

Theorem 9.1 (Marginalisation) *Partition the Gaussian random vector $\mathbf{z} \sim \mathcal{N}(\boldsymbol{\mu}, \boldsymbol{\Sigma})$ according to*

$$\mathbf{z} = \begin{pmatrix} \mathbf{z}_a \\ \mathbf{z}_b \end{pmatrix}, \qquad \boldsymbol{\mu} = \begin{pmatrix} \boldsymbol{\mu}_a \\ \boldsymbol{\mu}_b \end{pmatrix}, \qquad \boldsymbol{\Sigma} = \begin{pmatrix} \boldsymbol{\Sigma}_{aa} & \boldsymbol{\Sigma}_{ab} \\ \boldsymbol{\Sigma}_{ba} & \boldsymbol{\Sigma}_{bb} \end{pmatrix}. \tag{9.28}$$

The marginal distribution $p(\mathbf{z}_a)$ is then given by

$$p(\mathbf{z}_a) = \mathcal{N}(\mathbf{z}_a; \boldsymbol{\mu}_a, \boldsymbol{\Sigma}_{aa}). \tag{9.29}$$

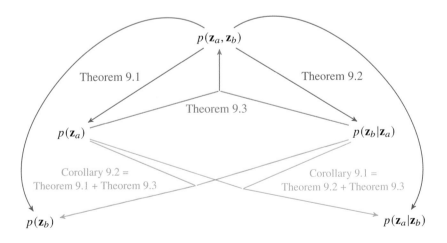

Figure 9.15 A graphical summary of how Theorems 9.1–9.3 and Corollaries 9.1–9.2 relate to each other. In all results, $\mathbf{z}_a$ and $\mathbf{z}_b$ are dependent multivariate Gaussian random variables.

Theorem 9.2 (Conditioning) *Partition the Gaussian random vector* $\mathbf{z} \sim N(\boldsymbol{\mu}, \boldsymbol{\Sigma})$ *according to*

$$\mathbf{z} = \begin{pmatrix} \mathbf{z}_a \\ \mathbf{z}_b \end{pmatrix}, \qquad \boldsymbol{\mu} = \begin{pmatrix} \boldsymbol{\mu}_a \\ \boldsymbol{\mu}_b \end{pmatrix}, \qquad \boldsymbol{\Sigma} = \begin{pmatrix} \boldsymbol{\Sigma}_{aa} & \boldsymbol{\Sigma}_{ab} \\ \boldsymbol{\Sigma}_{ba} & \boldsymbol{\Sigma}_{bb} \end{pmatrix}. \tag{9.30}$$

The conditional distribution $p(\mathbf{z}_a \mid \mathbf{z}_b)$ *is then given by*

$$p(\mathbf{z}_a \mid \mathbf{z}_b) = N\left(\mathbf{z}_a; \boldsymbol{\mu}_{a|b}, \boldsymbol{\Sigma}_{a|b}\right), \tag{9.31a}$$

where

$$\boldsymbol{\mu}_{a|b} = \boldsymbol{\mu}_a + \boldsymbol{\Sigma}_{ab}\boldsymbol{\Sigma}_{bb}^{-1}(\mathbf{z}_b - \boldsymbol{\mu}_b), \tag{9.31b}$$

$$\boldsymbol{\Sigma}_{a|b} = \boldsymbol{\Sigma}_{aa} - \boldsymbol{\Sigma}_{ab}\boldsymbol{\Sigma}_{bb}^{-1}\boldsymbol{\Sigma}_{ba}. \tag{9.31c}$$

Theorem 9.3 (Affine transformation) *Assume that* $\mathbf{z}_a$ *as well as* $\mathbf{z}_b \mid \mathbf{z}_a$ *are both Gaussian distributed according to*

$$p(\mathbf{z}_a) = N\left(\mathbf{z}_a; \boldsymbol{\mu}_a, \boldsymbol{\Sigma}_a\right), \tag{9.32a}$$

$$p(\mathbf{z}_b \mid \mathbf{z}_a) = N\left(\mathbf{z}_b; \mathbf{A}\mathbf{z}_a + \mathbf{b}, \boldsymbol{\Sigma}_{b|a}\right). \tag{9.32b}$$

Then the joint distribution of $\mathbf{z}_a$ *and* $\mathbf{z}_b$ *is*

$$p(\mathbf{z}_a, \mathbf{z}_b) = N\left(\begin{bmatrix} \mathbf{z}_a \\ \mathbf{z}_b \end{bmatrix}; \begin{bmatrix} \boldsymbol{\mu}_a \\ \mathbf{A}\boldsymbol{\mu}_a + \mathbf{b} \end{bmatrix}, \mathbf{R}\right) \tag{9.33a}$$

with

$$\mathbf{R} = \begin{bmatrix} \boldsymbol{\Sigma}_a & \boldsymbol{\Sigma}_a \mathbf{A}^\mathsf{T} \\ \mathbf{A}\boldsymbol{\Sigma}_a & \boldsymbol{\Sigma}_{b|a} + \mathbf{A}\boldsymbol{\Sigma}_a \mathbf{A}^\mathsf{T} \end{bmatrix}. \tag{9.33b}$$

Corollary 9.1 (Affine transformation – conditional) *Assume that* $\mathbf{z}_a$ *as well as* $\mathbf{z}_b \mid \mathbf{z}_a$ *are both Gaussian distributed according to*

$$p(\mathbf{z}_a) = N\left(\mathbf{z}_a; \boldsymbol{\mu}_a, \boldsymbol{\Sigma}_a\right), \tag{9.34a}$$

$$p(\mathbf{z}_b \mid \mathbf{z}_a) = N\left(\mathbf{z}_b; \mathbf{A}\mathbf{z}_a + \mathbf{b}, \boldsymbol{\Sigma}_{b|a}\right). \tag{9.34b}$$

Then the conditional distribution of $\mathbf{z}_a$ *given* $\mathbf{z}_b$ *is*

$$p(\mathbf{z}_a \mid \mathbf{z}_b) = N\left(\mathbf{z}_a; \boldsymbol{\mu}_{a|b}, \boldsymbol{\Sigma}_{a|b}\right), \tag{9.35a}$$

with

$$\boldsymbol{\mu}_{a|b} = \boldsymbol{\Sigma}_{a|b}\left(\boldsymbol{\Sigma}_a^{-1}\boldsymbol{\mu}_a + \mathbf{A}^\mathsf{T}\boldsymbol{\Sigma}_{b|a}^{-1}(\mathbf{z}_b - \mathbf{b})\right), \tag{9.35b}$$

$$\boldsymbol{\Sigma}_{a|b} = \left(\boldsymbol{\Sigma}_a^{-1} + \mathbf{A}^\mathsf{T}\boldsymbol{\Sigma}_{b|a}^{-1}\mathbf{A}\right)^{-1}. \tag{9.35c}$$

Corollary 9.2 (Affine transformation – Marginalisation) *Assume that $\mathbf{z}_a$ as well as $\mathbf{z}_b \mid \mathbf{z}_a$ are both Gaussian distributed according to*

$$p(\mathbf{z}_a) = \mathcal{N}\left(\mathbf{z}_a; \boldsymbol{\mu}_a, \boldsymbol{\Sigma}_a\right), \tag{9.36a}$$

$$p(\mathbf{z}_b \mid \mathbf{z}_a) = \mathcal{N}\left(\mathbf{z}_b; \mathbf{A}\mathbf{z}_a + \mathbf{b}, \boldsymbol{\Sigma}_{b\mid a}\right). \tag{9.36b}$$

Then the marginal distribution of $\mathbf{z}_b$ is given by

$$p(\mathbf{z}_b) = \mathcal{N}\left(\mathbf{z}_b; \boldsymbol{\mu}_b, \boldsymbol{\Sigma}_b\right), \tag{9.37a}$$

where

$$\boldsymbol{\mu}_b = \mathbf{A}\boldsymbol{\mu}_a + \mathbf{b}, \tag{9.37b}$$

$$\boldsymbol{\Sigma}_b = \boldsymbol{\Sigma}_{b\mid a} + \mathbf{A}\boldsymbol{\Sigma}_a\mathbf{A}^{\mathsf{T}}. \tag{9.37c}$$

10 Generative Models and Learning from Unlabelled Data

The models introduced so far in this book are so-called *discriminative* models, also referred to as *conditional* models. These models are designed to learn from data how to predict the output conditionally on a given input. Hence, they distinguish (or discriminate between) different inputs only in terms of their corresponding outputs. In the first half of this chapter, we will introduce another modelling paradigm, so-called *generative* modelling. Generative models are also learned from data, but their scope is wider. In contrast to discriminative models, which only describe the conditional distribution of the output for a given input, a generative model describes the *joint* distribution of both inputs and outputs. Also having access to a probabilistic model for the input variables allows synthetic data to be simulated from the model, for instance. However, perhaps more interestingly, it can be argued that a generative model has a 'deeper understanding' of the data. For instance, it can be used to reason about whether or not a certain input variable is typical, and it can be used to find patterns among input variables even in the absence of corresponding output values. Generative modelling is therefore a natural way to take us beyond supervised learning, which we will do in the second half of this chapter.

Specifically, a generative model aims to describe the distribution $p(\mathbf{x}, y)$. That is, it provides a probabilistic description of how both the input and the output data is generated. Perhaps we should write $p(\mathbf{x}, y \mid \boldsymbol{\theta})$ to emphasise that generative models also contain some parameters that we will learn from data, but to ease the notation, we settle for $p(\mathbf{x}, y)$. To use a generative model for predicting the value of y for a given input $\mathbf{x}$, the expression for the conditional distribution $p(y \mid \mathbf{x})$ has to be derived from $p(\mathbf{x}, y)$ using probability theory. We will make this idea concrete by considering the rather simple, yet useful, generative Gaussian mixture model (GMM). The GMM can be used for different purposes. When trained in a supervised way, from fully labelled data, it results in methods traditionally called linear or quadratic discriminant analysis. We will then see how the generative nature of the GMM naturally opens up for *semi-supervised learning* (where labels y are partly missing) and *unsupervised learning* (where no labels at all are present; there are only $\mathbf{x}$ and no y) as well. In the latter case, the GMM can be used for solving the so-called *clustering* problem, which amounts to grouping similar $\mathbf{x}$-values together in clusters.

We will then extend the idea of generative models beyond the Gaussian case, by describing deep generative models that make use of deep neural networks (see Chapter 6) for modelling $p(\mathbf{x})$. Specifically, we will discuss two such models:

normalising flows and generative adversarial networks. Both types are capable of learning the distribution of high-dimensional data with complicated dependencies in an unsupervised way, that is, based only on observed **x**-values.

Generative models bridge the gap between supervised and unsupervised machine learning, but not all methods for unsupervised learning come from generative models. We therefore end this chapter by introducing (non-generative) methods for unsupervised representation learning. Specifically, we introduce the nonlinear auto-encoder and its linear counterpart, principal component analysis (PCA), both of which are useful for learning a low-dimensional representation of high-dimensional data.

10.1 The Gaussian Mixture Model and Discriminant Analysis

We will now introduce a generative model, the GMM, from which we will derive several methods for different purposes. We assume that **x** is numerical and y is a categorical variable, that is, we are considering a situation similar to classification. The GMM attempts to model $p(\mathbf{x}, y)$, that is, the *joint* distribution between inputs **x** and outputs y. This is a more ambitious goal than the discriminative classifiers encountered in previous chapters, which only attempt to model the conditional distribution $p(y \mid \mathbf{x})$, since $p(y \mid \mathbf{x})$ can be derived from $p(\mathbf{x}, y)$ but not vice versa.

The Gaussian Mixture Model

The GMM makes use of the factorisation

$$p(\mathbf{x}, y) = p(\mathbf{x} \mid y)p(y) \tag{10.1a}$$

of the joint probability density function. The second factor is the marginal distribution of y. Since y is categorical, and thereby takes values in the set $\{1, \dots, M\}$, this is given by a categorical distribution with M parameters $\{\pi_m\}_{m=1}^{M}$:

$$p(y = 1) = \pi_1,$$

$$\vdots \tag{10.1b}$$

$$p(y = M) = \pi_M.$$

The first factor in (10.1a) is the class-conditional distribution of the input **x** for a certain class y. In a classification setting, it is natural to assume that these distributions are different for different classes y. Indeed, if it is possible to predict the class y based on the information contained in **x**, then the characteristics (that is, the distribution) of **x** should depend on y. However, to complete the model, we need to make additional assumptions on these class-conditional distributions. The basic assumption for a GMM is that each $p(\mathbf{x} \mid y)$ is a Gaussian distribution

$$p(\mathbf{x} \mid y) = \mathcal{N}(\mathbf{x} \mid \boldsymbol{\mu}_y, \boldsymbol{\Sigma}_y), \tag{10.1c}$$

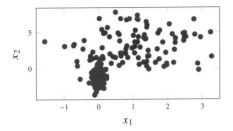 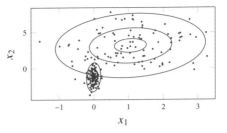

Figure 10.1 The GMM is a generative model, and we think about the input variables **x** as random and *assume* that they have a certain distribution. The GMM assumes that $p(\mathbf{x} \mid y)$ has a Gaussian distribution for each y. In this figure, **x** is two-dimensional, and there are two classes y (red and blue). The left panel shows some data with this nature. The right panel shows, for each value of y, the contour lines of the Gaussians $p(\mathbf{x} \mid y)$ that are learned from the data using (10.3).

with class-dependent mean vector $\boldsymbol{\mu}_y$ and covariance matrix $\boldsymbol{\Sigma}_y$. In words, the model (10.1) starts from a categorical distribution over y, and, for each possible value of y, it *assumes* a Gaussian distribution for **x**. Considering the marginal distribution $p(\mathbf{x})$, as we do in Figure 10.1, the model corresponds to a mixture of Gaussians (one component for each value of y), hence the name. Altogether, (10.1) is a generative model for how data $(\mathbf{x}, y)$ is generated. As always, the model builds on some simplifying assumptions, and most central to the GMM is the Gaussian assumption for the class-conditional distributions over **x** in (10.1c).

In the supervised setting, the GMM will lead us to classifiers that are easy to learn (no numerical optimisation is needed) and that turn out to be useful in practice even when the data does not obey the Gaussian assumption (10.1c) perfectly. These classifiers are (for historical reasons) called linear and quadratic discriminant analysis, LDA[1] and QDA, respectively. However, the GMM can also be used for clustering in an *unsupervised* setting, as well as learning from partially labelled data (the output label y is missing for some of the training data points) in a *semi-supervised* setting.

Supervised Learning of the Gaussian Mixture Model

Like any machine learning model, the GMM (10.1) is learned from training data. The unknown parameters to be learned are $\boldsymbol{\theta} = \{\boldsymbol{\mu}_m, \boldsymbol{\Sigma}_m, \pi_m\}_{m=1}^M$. We start with the supervised case, meaning that the training data contains inputs **x** and corresponding outputs (labels) y, that is $\mathcal{T} = \{\mathbf{x}_i, y_i\}_{i=1}^n$ (which has been the case for all other methods in this book so far).

---

[1] Note to be confused with Latent Dirichlet Allocation, also abbreviated LDA, which is a completely different method.

Mathematically, we learn the GMM by maximising the log-likelihood of the training data[2]

$$\widehat{\boldsymbol{\theta}} = \arg\max_{\boldsymbol{\theta}} \underbrace{\ln p(\{\mathbf{x}_i, y_i\}_{i=1}^{n} \mid \boldsymbol{\theta})}_{\mathcal{T}}. \tag{10.2a}$$

Note that, due to the generative nature of the model, this is based on the joint likelihood of both the inputs and the outputs. It follows from the model definition (10.1) that the log-likelihood is given by

$$\ln p(\{\mathbf{x}_i, y_i\}_{i=1}^{n} \mid \boldsymbol{\theta}) = \sum_{i=1}^{n} \{\ln p(\mathbf{x}_i \mid y_i, \boldsymbol{\theta}) + \ln p(y_i \mid \boldsymbol{\theta})\}$$

$$= \sum_{i=1}^{n} \sum_{m=1}^{M} \mathbb{I}\{y_i = m\} \left\{ \ln \mathcal{N}\left(\mathbf{x}_i \mid \boldsymbol{\mu}_m, \boldsymbol{\Sigma}_m\right) + \ln \pi_m \right\}, \tag{10.2b}$$

where the indicator function $\mathbb{I}\{y_i = m\}$ effectively separates the log-likelihood into M independent sums, one for each class, depending on the class labels of the training data points.

The optimisation problem (10.2) turns out to have a closed-form solution. Starting with the marginal class probabilities $\{\pi_m\}_{m=1}^{M}$, we get

$$\widehat{\pi}_m = \frac{n_m}{n}, \tag{10.3a}$$

where n_m is the number of training data points in class m. Consequently, $\sum_m n_m = n$ and thus $\sum_m \widehat{\pi}_m = 1$. This simply states that the probability of a certain class $y = m$, without having any additional information, is estimated as the proportion of this class in the training data.

Furthermore, the mean vector $\boldsymbol{\mu}_m$ of each class is estimated as

$$\widehat{\boldsymbol{\mu}}_m = \frac{1}{n_m} \sum_{i:y_i=m} \mathbf{x}_i, \tag{10.3b}$$

the empirical mean among all training data points of class m. Similarly, the covariance matrix $\boldsymbol{\Sigma}_m$ for each class $m = 1, \ldots, M$, is estimated as[3]

$$\widehat{\boldsymbol{\Sigma}}_m = \frac{1}{n_m} \sum_{i:y_i=m} (\mathbf{x}_i - \widehat{\boldsymbol{\mu}}_m)(\mathbf{x}_i - \widehat{\boldsymbol{\mu}}_m)^{\mathsf{T}}. \tag{10.3c}$$

The expressions (10.3b)–(10.3c) learns a Gaussian distribution for $\mathbf{x}$ for each class such that the mean and covariance fit the data – so-called moment-matching. Note that we can compute the parameters $\widehat{\boldsymbol{\theta}}$ no matter if whether the data actually comes from a Gaussian distribution or not.

---

[2] Alternatively, it is possible to learn the GMM by following the Bayesian approach, but we do not pursue that any further here. See Section 10.5 for suggestions for further reading.

[3] A common alternative is to normalise the estimate by $n_m - 1$ instead of n_m, resulting in an unbiased estimate of the covariance matrix, but that is in fact not the maximum likelihood solution. The two options are not mathematically equivalent, but for machine learning purposes, the practical difference is often minor.

Predicting Output Labels for New Inputs: Discriminant Analysis

We have so far described the generative GMM $p(\mathbf{x}, y)$, where $\mathbf{x}$ is numerical and y categorical, and how to learn the unknown parameters in $p(\mathbf{x}, y)$ from training data. We will now see how this can be used as a classifier for supervised machine learning.

The key insight for using a generative model $p(\mathbf{x}, y)$ to make predictions is to realise that predicting the output y for a known value $\mathbf{x}$ amounts to computing the conditional distribution $p(y \mid \mathbf{x})$. From probability theory, we have

$$p(y \mid \mathbf{x}) = \frac{p(\mathbf{x}, y)}{p(\mathbf{x})} = \frac{p(\mathbf{x}, y)}{\sum_{j=1}^{M} p(\mathbf{x}, y = j)}. \tag{10.4}$$

The left hand side $p(y \mid \mathbf{x})$ is the predictive distribution, whereas all expressions on the right hand side are defined by the generative GMM (10.1). We therefore get the classifier

$$p(y = m \mid \mathbf{x}_\star) = \frac{\widehat{\pi}_m \mathcal{N}\left(\mathbf{x}_\star \mid \widehat{\boldsymbol{\mu}}_m, \widehat{\boldsymbol{\Sigma}}_m\right)}{\sum_{j=1}^{M} \widehat{\pi}_j \mathcal{N}\left(\mathbf{x}_\star \mid \widehat{\boldsymbol{\mu}}_j, \widehat{\boldsymbol{\Sigma}}_j\right)}. \tag{10.5}$$

As usual, we can obtain 'hard' predictions $\widehat{y}_\star$ by selecting the class which is predicted to be the most probable,

$$\widehat{y}_\star = \arg\max_{m} p(y = m \mid \mathbf{x}_\star), \tag{10.6}$$

and compute corresponding decision boundaries. Taking the logarithm (which does not change the maximising argument) and noting that only the numerator in (10.5) depends on m, we can equivalently write this as

$$\widehat{y}_\star = \arg\max_{m} \left\{ \ln \widehat{\pi}_m + \ln \mathcal{N}\left(\mathbf{x}_\star \mid \widehat{\boldsymbol{\mu}}_m, \widehat{\boldsymbol{\Sigma}}_m\right) \right\}. \tag{10.7}$$

Since the logarithm of the Gaussian probability density function is a quadratic function in $\mathbf{x}$, the decision boundary for this classifier is also quadratic, and the method is therefore referred to as quadratic discriminant analysis (QDA). We summarise this by Method 10.1 and Figure 10.3, and in Figure 10.2, we show the decision boundary when the GMM from Figure 10.1 is turned into a QDA classifier.

The QDA method arises naturally from the GMM. However, if we make an additional simplifying assumption about the model, we instead obtain an even more well-known and commonly used classifier, referred to as linear discriminant analysis (LDA), The additional assumption is that the covariance matrix is equal for all classes, that is, $\boldsymbol{\Sigma}_1 = \boldsymbol{\Sigma}_2 = \cdots = \boldsymbol{\Sigma}_M = \boldsymbol{\Sigma}$ in (10.1c). With this restriction, we only have a single covariance matrix to learn, and (10.3c) is replaced by[4]

$$\widehat{\boldsymbol{\Sigma}} = \frac{1}{n} \sum_{m=1}^{M} \sum_{i:y_i=m} (\mathbf{x}_i - \widehat{\boldsymbol{\mu}}_m)(\mathbf{x}_i - \widehat{\boldsymbol{\mu}}_m)^\mathsf{T}. \tag{10.8}$$

---

[4]Similarly to the comment about (10.3c), the sum can alternatively be normalised by $n - M$, instead of n.

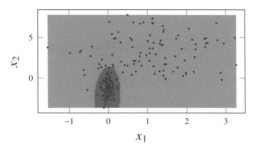

Figure 10.2 The decision boundary for the QDA classifier (obtained by (10.5) and (10.7)) corresponding to the learned GMM in the right panel of Figure 10.1.

Learn the Gaussian mixture model

Data: Training data $\mathcal{T} = \{\mathbf{x}_i, y_i\}_{i=1}^n$

Result: Gaussian mixture model

1 **for** $m = 1, \ldots, M$ **do**
2 $\quad$ Compute $\widehat{\pi}_m$ (10.3a), $\widehat{\boldsymbol{\mu}}_m$ (10.3b) and $\widehat{\boldsymbol{\Sigma}}_m$ (10.3c)
3 **end**

Predict with Gaussian mixture model

Data: Gaussian mixture model and test input $\mathbf{x}_\star$

Result: Prediction $\widehat{y}_\star$

1 **for** $m = 1, \ldots, M$ **do**
2 $\quad$ Compute $\delta_m \overset{\text{def}}{=} \ln \widehat{\pi}_m + \ln \mathcal{N}\left(\mathbf{x}_\star \mid \widehat{\boldsymbol{\mu}}_m, \widehat{\boldsymbol{\Sigma}}_m\right)$
3 **end**
4 Set $\widehat{y}_\star = \arg\max_m \delta_m$.

Method 10.1 Quadratic Discriminant Analysis, QDA.

Using this assumption in (10.5) results in a convenient cancellation of all quadratic terms when computing the class predictions in (10.7), and the LDA classifier will therefore have linear decision boundaries. Consequently, LDA is a linear classifier, just like logistic regression, and the two methods will often perform similarly. They are not equivalent, however, since the parameters are learned in different ways. This usually results in small differences in their respective decision boundaries. Note that LDA is obtained by replacing (10.3c) with (10.8) in Method 10.1. We compare LDA and QDA in Figure 10.4 by applying both of them to the music classification problem from Example 2.1.

> ***Time to reflect 10.1*** *In the GMM, it was assumed that $p(\mathbf{x} \mid y)$ is Gaussian. When applying LDA or QDA 'off the shelf' for a classification problem, is there any check that the Gaussian assumption actually holds? If yes, what? If no, is that a problem?*

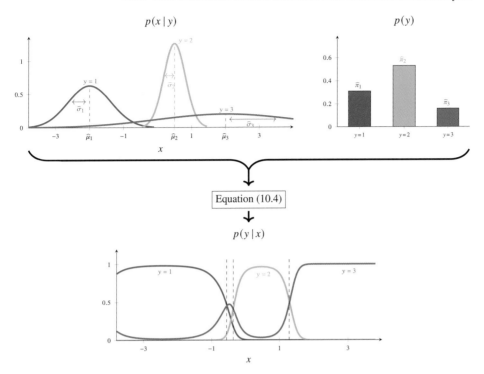

Figure 10.3 An illustration of QDA for $M = 3$ classes, with dimension $p = 1$ of the input x. At the top, the generative GMM is shown. To the left is the Gaussian model of $p(x \mid y = m)$, parameterised by $\widehat{\mu}_m$ and $\widehat{\sigma}_m^2$ (since $p = 1$, we only have a scalar variance σ_m^2, instead of a covariance matrix Σ_m). To the right the model of $p(y)$ is shown, parameterised by $\widehat{\pi}_m$. All parameters are learned from training data, not shown in the figure. By computing the conditional distribution (10.4) the generative model is 'warped' into $p(y = m \mid x)$, shown in the bottom. The decision boundaries are shown as vertical dotted lines in the bottom plot (assuming that we classify x based on the most probable class).

We have now derived a classifier, QDA, from a generative model. In practice, the QDA classifier can be employed just like any discriminative classifier. It can be argued that a generative model contains more assumptions than a discriminative model, and if the assumptions are fulfilled, we could possibly expect QDA to be slightly more data efficient (requiring fewer data points to reach a certain performance) than a discriminative model. However, in most practical cases this will not make a big difference. The difference between using a generative and a discriminative model will, however, become more evident when we next look at the semi-supervised learning problem.

Semi-supervised Learning of the Gaussian Mixture Model

We have so far discussed how the GMM can be learned in the supervised setting, that is, from training data that contains both input and corresponding output values

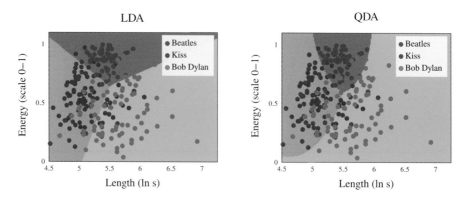

(a) Decision boundaries for the music classifi-cation problem for an LDA classifier.

(b) Decision boundaries for the music classifi-cation problem for a QDA classifier.

Figure 10.4 We apply LDA and QDA classifiers to the music classification problem from Example 2.1 and plot the resulting decision boundaries. Note that the LDA classifier gives linear decision boundaries, whereas the QDA classifier has decision boundaries with quadratic shapes.

(that is, class labels). We will now have a look at the so-called *semi-supervised* problem where some output values y_i are missing in the training data. The input values $\mathbf{x}_i$ for which the corresponding y_i are missing are called *unlabelled* data points. As before, we denote the total number of training data points as n, out of which now only n_l are labelled input-output pairs $\{\mathbf{x}_i, y_i\}_{i=1}^{n_l}$ and the remaining n_u unlabelled data points $\{\mathbf{x}_i\}_{i=n_l+1}^{n}$, where $n = n_l + n_u$. All in all we have the training data $\mathcal{T} = \{\{\mathbf{x}_i, y_i\}_{i=1}^{n_l}, \{\mathbf{x}_i\}_{i=n_l+1}^{n}\}$. For notational purposes we have, without loss of generality, ordered the data points so that the first n_l are labelled and the remaining n_u are unlabelled.

Semi-supervised learning is of high practical relevance. Indeed, in many applications it is easy to obtain large amounts of unlabelled data, but annotating this data (that is, assigning labels y_i to the training data points) can be a very costly and time consuming procedure. This is particularly true when the labeling is done manually by a domain expert. For instance, consider learning a model for classifying images of skin lesions as either benign or malignant, to be used in a medical diagnosis support system. The training inputs $\mathbf{x}_i$ will then correspond to images of the skin lesions, and it is easy to acquire a large number of such images. To annotate the training data with labels y_i, however, we need to determine whether or not each lesion is benign or malignant, which requires a (possibly expensive) medical examination by a dermatologist.

The simplest solution to the semi-supervised problem would be to discard the n_u unlabelled data points and thereby turn the problem into a standard supervised machine learning problem. This is a pragmatic solution, but possibly very wasteful if the number of labelled data points n_l is only a small fraction of the total number

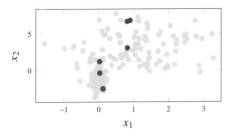 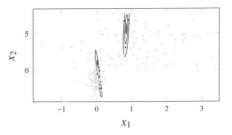

Figure 10.5 We consider the same situation as in Figure 10.1, except for the fact that we have 'lost' the output y_i for most of the data points. The problem is now semi-supervised. The unlabelled data points $\{\mathbf{x}_i\}_{i=n_l+1}^n$ are illustrated in the left panel as grey dots, whereas the $n_l = 6$ labelled data points $\{\mathbf{x}_i, y_i\}_{i=1}^{n_l}$ are red or blue. In the right panel, we have learned a GMM using only the labelled data points, as if the problem were supervised with only n_l data points. Clearly the unlabelled data points have made the problem harder, compared to Figure 10.1. We will, however, continue this story in Figure 10.6 where we instead use this as an initialisation to a semi-supervised procedure.

of data points n. We illustrate this with Figure 10.5, which depicts a semi-supervised problem where we have learned a (poor) GMM by only using the few n_l labelled data points.

The idea behind semi-supervised learning is to exploit the information available in the unlabelled data points to, hopefully, end up with a better model in the end. There are different ways in which the semi-supervised problem can be approached, but one principled way is to make use of a generative model. Remember that a generative model is a model of the joint distribution $p(\mathbf{x}, y)$, which can be factorised as $p(\mathbf{x}, y) = p(\mathbf{x})p(y \mid \mathbf{x})$. Since the marginal distribution of the inputs $p(\mathbf{x})$ is a part of the model, it seems plausible that the unlabelled data points $\{\mathbf{x}_i\}_{i=n_l+1}^n$ can also be useful when learning the model. Intuitively, the unlabelled inputs can be used to find groups (or *clusters*) of input values with similar properties, which can then be assumed to belong to the same class. Looking at Figure 10.5 again, by considering the unlabelled data points (grey dots), it is reasonable to assume that the two apparent clusters of points correspond to the two classes (red and blue, respectively). As we will see below, by exploiting this information, we can thus obtain better estimates of the class-conditional distributions $p(\mathbf{x} \mid y)$ and thereby also obtain a better classifier.

We will now turn to the technical details of how to learn the GMM in this semi-supervised setting. Similarly to above, we take the maximum likelihood approach, meaning that we seek the model parameters that maximise the likelihood of the observed data. Contrary to the supervised case, however, the observed data now contains both labelled and unlabelled instances. That is, we would like to solve

$$\widehat{\boldsymbol{\theta}} = \arg\max_{\boldsymbol{\theta}} \ln p(\underbrace{\{\{\mathbf{x}_i, y_i\}_{i=1}^{n_l}, \{\mathbf{x}_i\}_{i=n_l+1}^n\}}_{\mathcal{T}} \mid \boldsymbol{\theta}). \tag{10.9}$$

Unfortunately this problem has no closed-form solution for the GMM. We will discuss the reason for this intractability in more detail in Section 10.2, where we revisit the same problem in the fully unsupervised setting. Intuitively, however, we can conclude that it is not possible to compute the model parameters as in (10.3), because we do not know which classes the unlabelled data points belong to. Hence, when computing the mean vector for the mth class as in (10.3b), for instance, we do not know which data points should be included in the sum.

However, a possible way around this issue is to first learn an initial GMM, which is then used to predict the missing values $\{y_i\}_{i=1}^{n_u}$, and thereafter these predictions are used to update the model. Doing this iteratively results in the following algorithm:

(i) Learn the GMM from the n_l labelled input-output pairs $\{\mathbf{x}_i, y_i\}_{i=1}^{n_l}$,

(ii) Use the GMM to predict (as a QDA classifier) the missing outputs to $\{\mathbf{x}_i\}_{i=n_l+1}^{n}$,

(iii) Update the GMM including the predicted outputs from step (ii),

and then repeat step (ii) and (iii) until convergence.

At first this might look like an *ad hoc* procedure, and it is far from obvious that it will converge to anything sensible. However, it turns out that it is an instance of a widely used statistical tool referred to as the expectation-maximisation (EM) algorithm. We will study the EM algorithm and discuss its validity in more detail in Section 10.2. For now we simply note that the algorithm, when applied to the maximum likelihood problem (10.9), indeed boils down to the procedure outlined above, as long as we pay attention to a few important details: From step (ii) we should return the predicted class probabilities $p(y = m \mid \mathbf{x}, \widehat{\boldsymbol{\theta}})$ (and not the class prediction $\widehat{y}(\mathbf{x}_\star)$) computed using the current parameter estimates $\widehat{\boldsymbol{\theta}}$, and in step (iii) we make use of the predicted class probabilities by introducing the notation

$$w_i(m) = \begin{cases} p(y = m \mid \mathbf{x}_i, \widehat{\boldsymbol{\theta}}) & \text{if } y_i \text{ is missing} \\ 1 & \text{if } y_i = m \\ 0 & \text{otherwise} \end{cases} \tag{10.10a}$$

and update the parameters as follows:

$$\widehat{\pi}_m = \frac{1}{n} \sum_{i=1}^{n} w_i(m), \tag{10.10b}$$

$$\widehat{\boldsymbol{\mu}}_m = \frac{1}{\sum_{i=1}^{n} w_i(m)} \sum_{i=1}^{n} w_i(m)\mathbf{x}_i, \tag{10.10c}$$

$$\widehat{\boldsymbol{\Sigma}}_m = \frac{1}{\sum_{i=1}^{n} w_i(m)} \sum_{i=1}^{n} w_i(m)(\mathbf{x}_i - \widehat{\boldsymbol{\mu}}_m)(\mathbf{x}_i - \widehat{\boldsymbol{\mu}}_m)^{\mathsf{T}}. \tag{10.10d}$$

Note that we use the current parameter estimate $\widehat{\boldsymbol{\theta}}$ in step (ii), which is then updated in step (iii), so when we go back to step (ii) for the next iteration, the class probabilities will be computed using a new value of $\widehat{\boldsymbol{\theta}}$.

When computing the parameters for class m according to (10.10), the unlabelled data points contribute proportionally to the current estimates of the probabilities that they belong to this class. Note that this is a generalisation of the supervised case, as (10.3) is a special case of (10.10) when no labels y_i are missing. With these modifications, it can be shown (see Section 10.2) that the procedure discussed above converges to a stationary point of (10.9) even in the semi-supervised setting. We summarise the procedure as Method 10.2 and illustrate it in Figure 10.6 by applying it to the semi-supervised data introduced in Figure 10.5.

Learn the GMM

Data: Partially labelled training data $\mathcal{T} = \{\{\mathbf{x}_i, y_i\}_{i=1}^{n_l}, \{\mathbf{x}_i\}_{i=n_l+1}^{n}\}$ (with output classes $m = 1, \ldots, M$)
Result: Gaussian mixture model

1 Compute $\boldsymbol{\theta} = \{\widehat{\pi}_m, \widehat{\boldsymbol{\mu}}_m, \widehat{\boldsymbol{\Sigma}}_m\}_{m=1}^{M}$ according to (10.3), using only the labelled data $\{\mathbf{x}_i, y_i\}_{i=1}^{n_l}$
2 **repeat**
3   For each $\mathbf{x}_i$ in $\{\mathbf{x}_i\}_{i=n_l+1}^{n}$, compute the prediction $p(y \mid \mathbf{x}_i, \widehat{\boldsymbol{\theta}})$ according to (10.5) using the current parameter estimates $\widehat{\boldsymbol{\theta}}$
4   Update the parameter estimates $\widehat{\boldsymbol{\theta}} \leftarrow \{\widehat{\pi}_m, \widehat{\boldsymbol{\mu}}_m, \widehat{\boldsymbol{\Sigma}}_m\}_{m=1}^{M}$ according to (10.10)
5 **until** *convergence*

Predict as QDA, Method 10.1

Method 10.2 Semi-supervised learning of the GMM

We have now devised a way to handle semi-supervised classification problems using the GMM and thereby extended the QDA classifier such that it can also be used in the semi-supervised setting, when some output values y_i are missing from the training data.

It is perhaps not clear why we have chosen to introduce the semi-supervised problem in connection to generative models. Alternatively, we could think of using any discriminative model (instead of the GMM) for iteratively predicting the missing y_i and updating the model using these predictions. This is indeed possible, and such discriminative label-imputation methods can be made to work well in many challenging semi-supervised cases. However, the generative modelling paradigm provides us with a more principled and coherent framework for reasoning about missing labels. Indeed, we have derived a method for the semi-supervised setting which is a direct generalisation of the corresponding supervised method. In the next section, we will take this one step further and apply the same procedure to the fully unsupervised case (by simply assuming that *all* labels are missing). In all cases, the method is numerically solving the corresponding maximum likelihood problem.

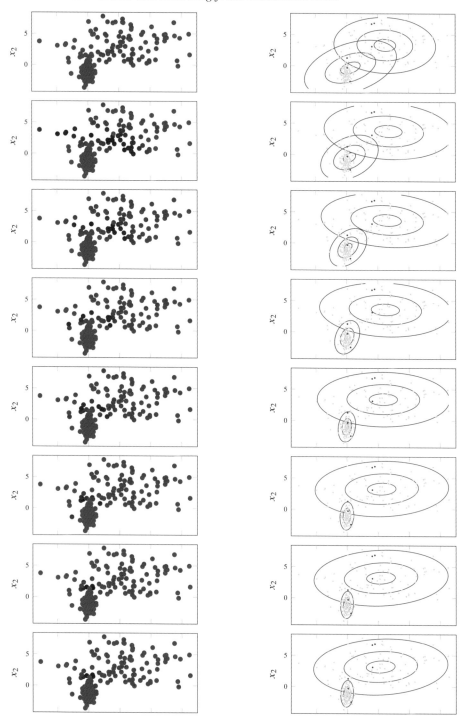

Figure 10.6 The iterative Method 10.2 applied to the problem from Figure 10.5. For each iteration, the left panel shows the predicted class probabilities from the previously learned model (using colour coding; purple is in the middle between red and blue). The new models learned using (10.10) (based in the predictions from the left panel) are shown in the right panel for each row. The iteration is initialised using the model shown in Figure 10.5.

Another explanation for why generative models can be useful in the semi-supervised setting is that they provide a richer description of the data generating process than a discriminative model, making it easier to leverage the information contained in the unlabelled data points. A discriminative model of $p(y \mid \mathbf{x})$ encodes information like 'if $\mathbf{x}$, then y ... ', but it does not contain any explicit model for the inputs themselves. The generative model, on the other hand, contains additional assumptions on $p(\mathbf{x} \mid y)$, that can be useful when handling the semi-supervised problem. For instance, the GMM encodes the information that all inputs $\mathbf{x}$ that belong to a certain class y should have the same Gaussian distribution and thereby belong to a *cluster*. The model parameters are then inferred from these clusters as in (10.10), where both labelled and unlabelled data points contribute. This assumption is the key enabler for Method 10.2 to work in practice, even in such a challenging situation as in Figures 10.5 and 10.6 where the vast majority of the data points are unlabelled.

The generative modelling paradigm thus provides a principled approach for modelling both labelled and unlabelled data. The downside, however, is that it requires additional assumptions on the data distribution, and the result can possibly be misleading if these assumptions are not fulfilled. Furthermore, in many contemporary machine learning problems, the input $\mathbf{x}$ is extremely high-dimensional, and it can then be difficult to design and/or learn a suitable model for its distribution. For instance, assume that $\mathbf{x}$ is an image (as we discussed in the context of convolutional neural networks, Section 6.3); then modelling the pixel values in $\mathbf{x}$ using a (very high-dimensional) Gaussian distribution is not going to capture the characteristics of natural images in a good way. We will return to this in Section 10.3 where we discuss how generative models of such high-dimensional and complex data can be constructed using neural networks.

10.2 Cluster Analysis

In supervised learning, the objective is to learn a model for some input–output relationship based on examples, that is training data consisting of both inputs and corresponding (labelled) outputs. However, we saw above that it is possible to relax the assumption that all inputs are labelled. In semi-supervised learning, we mix labelled and unlabelled data and learn a model which makes use of both sources of information. In *unsupervised learning*, we take this one step further and assume that *all* data points are unlabelled. Hence, given some training data $\mathcal{T} = \{\mathbf{x}_i\}_{i=1}^n$, the objective is to build a model that can be used to reason about key properties of the data (or rather, the data generating process). From the perspective of generative modelling, this means building a model of the distribution $p(\mathbf{x})$.

In this section, we will build on the classification setting considered above and study the so-called *clustering* problem. Clustering is one example of unsupervised learning. It amounts to finding groups of similar $\mathbf{x}$ values in the data space and associating these with a discrete set of clusters. From a mathematical and methodological point of view, clustering is intimately related to classification. Indeed, we assign a discrete index to each cluster and say that all **x** values in the *m*th cluster are of class $y = m$. The difference between classification and clustering is then that we wish to train a model for the clusters based solely on the **x** values, without any corresponding labels. Still, as we show below, one way to address this problem is to use the same GMM model and EM algorithm as was found useful in the context of semi-supervised learning above.

From a more conceptual point of view, there are some differences between classification and clustering though. In classification we usually know what the different classes correspond to. They are typically specified as part of the problem formulation, and the objective is to build a predictive classifier. Clustering, on the other hand, is often applied in a more exploratory way. We might expect that there are groups of data points with similar properties, and the objective is to group them together into clusters, to obtain a better understanding of the data. However, the clusters might not correspond to any *interpretable* classes. Moreover, the number of clusters is typically unknown and left to the user to decide.

We start this section by adapting the GMM to the unsupervised setting, thereby turning it into a clustering method. We will also discuss the EM algorithm introduced above in bit more detail, as well as highlighting some technical subtleties that differ between the semi-supervised and unsupervised setting. Next, we present the *k*-means algorithm, which is an alternative clustering method, and discuss similarities between this method and the GMM.

Unsupervised Learning of the Gaussian Mixture Model

The GMM (10.1) is a joint model for **x** and y, given by

$$p(\mathbf{x}, y) = p(\mathbf{x} \mid y)p(y) = \mathcal{N}\left(\mathbf{x} \mid \boldsymbol{\mu}_y, \boldsymbol{\Sigma}_y\right) \pi_y. \tag{10.11}$$

To obtain a model only for **x**, we can marginalise out y as $p(\mathbf{x}) = \sum_y p(\mathbf{x}, y)$ from it. The marginalisation implies that we consider y as being a latent random variable, that is, a random variable that exists in the model but which is not observed in the data. In practice, we still learn the joint model $p(\mathbf{x}, y)$, but from data containing only $\{\mathbf{x}_i\}_{i=1}^n$. Intuitively, learning the GMM from such unlabelled training data amounts to figuring out which $\mathbf{x}_i$ values come from the same class-conditional distribution $p(\mathbf{x} \mid y)$, based on their similarity. That is, we need to infer the latent variables $\{y_i\}_{i=1}^n$ from the data and then use this inferred knowledge to fit the model parameters. Once this is done, the learned class-conditional distributions $p(\mathbf{x} \mid y = m)$ for $m = 1, \ldots, M$ define M different clusters in data space.

Conveniently, we already have a tool for learning the GMM from unlabelled data. Method 10.2, which we devised for the semi-supervised case, also works for completely unlabelled data $\{\mathbf{x}_i\}_{i=1}^n$. We just need to replace the initialisation (line 1) with some pragmatic choice of initial $\{\widehat{\pi}_m, \widehat{\boldsymbol{\mu}}_m, \widehat{\boldsymbol{\Sigma}}_m\}_{m=1}^M$. We repeat the algorithm with these minor modifications in Method 10.3 for convenience.

Learn the GMM

Data: Unlabelled training data $\mathcal{T} = \{\mathbf{x}_i\}_{i=1}^n$, number of clusters M
Result: Gaussian mixture model

1   Initialise $\widehat{\boldsymbol{\theta}} = \{\widehat{\pi}_m, \widehat{\boldsymbol{\mu}}_m, \widehat{\boldsymbol{\Sigma}}_m\}_{m=1}^M$
2   **repeat**
3   For each $\mathbf{x}_i$ in $\{\mathbf{x}_i\}_{i=1}^n$, compute the prediction $p(y \mid \mathbf{x}_i, \widehat{\boldsymbol{\theta}})$ according to
         (10.5) using the current parameter estimates $\widehat{\boldsymbol{\theta}}$.
4   Update the parameter estimates $\widehat{\boldsymbol{\theta}} \leftarrow \{\widehat{\pi}_m, \widehat{\boldsymbol{\mu}}_m, \widehat{\boldsymbol{\Sigma}}_m\}_{m=1}^M$ according to
         (10.16)
5   **until** *convergence*

Method 10.3 Unsupervised learning of the GMM

Method 10.3 corresponds to the EM algorithm applied to solve the unsupervised maximum likelihood problem

$$\widehat{\boldsymbol{\theta}} = \arg\max_{\boldsymbol{\theta}} \ln p(\{\mathbf{x}_i\}_{i=1}^n \mid \boldsymbol{\theta}). \tag{10.12}$$

To show that this is indeed the case, and that the suggested procedure is a well-grounded way of addressing the maximum likelihood problem (10.12), we will now take a closer look at the EM algorithm itself.

The EM algorithm is a general tool for solving maximum likelihood problems in probabilistic models with latent variables, that is, models containing both observed and unobserved random variables. In the current setting, the latent variables are $\{y_i\}_{i=1}^n$, where $y_i \in \{1, \ldots, M\}$ is the cluster index for data point $\mathbf{x}_i$. For notational brevity, we stack these latent cluster indices into an n-dimensional vector $\mathbf{y}$. Similarly, we stack the observed data points $\{\mathbf{x}_i\}_{i=1}^n$ into an $n \times p$ matrix $\mathbf{X}$. The task is thus to maximise the *observed data log-likelihood* $\ln p(\mathbf{X} \mid \boldsymbol{\theta})$ with respect to the model parameters $\boldsymbol{\theta} = \{\boldsymbol{\mu}_m, \boldsymbol{\Sigma}_m, \pi_m\}_{m=1}^M$.

The challenge we face is that the observed data likelihood is not readily available, due to the presence of the latent variables $\mathbf{y}$ in the model specification. Thus, evaluating the log-likelihood requires marginalising out these variables. In the EM algorithm, we address this challenge by alternating between computing an *expected* log-likelihood and then *maximising* this expected value to update the model parameters.

Let $\widehat{\boldsymbol{\theta}}$ denote the current estimate of $\boldsymbol{\theta}$ at some intermediate iteration of Method 10.3. This can be some arbitrary parameter configuration (for instance corresponding to the initialisation at the first iteration). Then, one iteration of the EM algorithm consists of the following two steps:

(E)   Compute $Q(\boldsymbol{\theta}) \stackrel{\text{def}}{=} \mathbb{E}\left[\ln p(\mathbf{X}, \mathbf{y} \mid \boldsymbol{\theta}) \mid \mathbf{X}, \widehat{\boldsymbol{\theta}}\right]$,

(M)   Update $\widehat{\boldsymbol{\theta}} \leftarrow \arg\max_{\boldsymbol{\theta}} Q(\boldsymbol{\theta})$.

The algorithm alternates between these two steps until convergence. It can be shown that the value of the observed data log-likelihood increases at each iteration of the procedure, unless it has reached a stationary point (where the gradient of the log-likelihood is zero). Hence, it is a valid numerical optimisation algorithm for solving (10.12).

To see that this procedure boils down to Method 10.3 for the GMM model, we start by expanding the E-step. The expected value is computed with respect to the conditional distribution $p(\mathbf{y} \mid \mathbf{X}, \widehat{\boldsymbol{\theta}})$. This represents the probabilistic belief regarding the cluster assignment for all data points, given the current parameter configuration $\widehat{\boldsymbol{\theta}}$. In Bayesian language, it is the posterior distribution over the latent variables $\mathbf{y}$, conditionally on the observed data $\mathbf{X}$. We thus have

$$Q(\boldsymbol{\theta}) = \mathbb{E}\left[\ln p(\mathbf{X}, \mathbf{y} \mid \boldsymbol{\theta}) \mid \mathbf{X}, \widehat{\boldsymbol{\theta}}\right] = \sum_{\mathbf{y}} \ln\left(p(\mathbf{X}, \mathbf{y} \mid \boldsymbol{\theta})\right) p(\mathbf{y} \mid \mathbf{X}, \widehat{\boldsymbol{\theta}}). \tag{10.13}$$

The first expression in the sum is referred to as the *complete data log-likelihood*. It is the log-likelihood that we would have, if the latent variables were known. Since it involves both the observed data and the latent variables (that is, the 'complete data'), it is readily available from the model:

$$\ln p(\mathbf{X}, \mathbf{y} \mid \boldsymbol{\theta}) = \sum_{i=1}^{n} \ln p(\mathbf{x}_i, y_i \mid \boldsymbol{\theta}) = \sum_{i=1}^{n} \left\{\ln \mathcal{N}\left(\mathbf{x}_i \mid \boldsymbol{\mu}_{y_i}, \boldsymbol{\Sigma}_{y_i}\right) + \ln \pi_{y_i}\right\}. \tag{10.14}$$

Each term in this expression depends only on one of the latent variables. Hence, when we plug this expression for the complete data log-likelihood into (10.13), we get

$$Q(\boldsymbol{\theta}) = \sum_{i=1}^{n} \sum_{m=1}^{M} w_i(m) \left\{\ln \mathcal{N}\left(\mathbf{x}_i \mid \boldsymbol{\mu}_{y_i}, \boldsymbol{\Sigma}_{y_i}\right) + \ln \pi_{y_i}\right\}, \tag{10.15}$$

where $w_i(m) = p(y_i = m \mid \mathbf{x}_i, \widehat{\boldsymbol{\theta}})$ is the probability that the data point $\mathbf{x}_i$ belongs to cluster m, computed based on the current parameter estimates $\widehat{\boldsymbol{\theta}}$.

Comparing this with the log-likelihood in the supervised setting (10.2b), when all labels $\{y_i\}_{i=1}^{n}$ are known, we note that the two expressions are very similar. The only difference is that the indicator function $\mathbb{I}\{y_i = m\}$ in (10.2b) is replaced by the weight $w_i(m)$ in (10.15). In words, instead of making a hard cluster assignment of each data point based on a given class label, we make a soft cluster assignment based on the probabilities that this data point belongs to the different clusters.

We will not go into the details, but it is hopefully not hard to believe that maximising (10.15) with respect to $\boldsymbol{\theta}$ – which is what we do in the M-step of the algorithm – gives a solution similar to the supervised setting but where the training data points are weighted by $w_i(m)$. That is, analogously to (10.10), the M-step becomes:

$$\widehat{\pi}_m = \frac{1}{n} \sum_{i=1}^{n} w_i(m), \qquad (10.16\text{a})$$

$$\widehat{\mu}_m = \frac{1}{\sum_{i=1}^{n} w_i(m)} \sum_{i=1}^{n} w_i(m)\mathbf{x}_i, \qquad (10.16\text{b})$$

$$\widehat{\Sigma}_m = \frac{1}{\sum_{i=1}^{n} w_i(m)} \sum_{i=1}^{n} w_i(m)(\mathbf{x}_i - \widehat{\mu}_m)(\mathbf{x}_i - \widehat{\mu}_m)^\mathsf{T}. \qquad (10.16\text{c})$$

Putting this together, we conclude that one iteration of the EM algorithm indeed corresponds to one iteration of Method 10.3. We illustrate the method in Figure 10.7.

There are a few important details when learning the GMM in the unsupervised setting which deserve some attention. First, the number of clusters (that is, the number of Gaussian components in the mixture) M has to be specified in order to run the algorithm. We discuss this hyperparameter choice in more detail below. Second, since there are only unlabelled data points, the indexation of the M Gaussian components becomes arbitrary. Put differently, all possible permutations of the cluster labels will have the same likelihood. In Figure 10.7 this means that the colours (red and blue) are interchangeable, and the only reason for why we ended up with this particular solution is that we initialised the blue cluster in the upper part and the red in the lower part of the data space.

Related to this is that the maximum likelihood problem (10.12) is a non-convex optimisation problem. The EM algorithm is only guaranteed to converge to a stationary point, which means that a poor initialisation can result in a convergence to a poor local optimum. In the semi-supervised setting, we could use the labelled training data point as a way to initialise the method, but this is not possible in a fully unsupervised setting. Hence, the initialisation becomes an important detail to consider. A pragmatic approach is to run Method 10.3 multiple times with different random initialisations.

Finally, there is a subtle issue with the maximum likelihood problem (10.12) itself, that we have so far swept under the rug. Without any constraints on the parameters $\boldsymbol{\theta}$, the unsupervised maximum likelihood problem for a GMM is in fact ill-posed, in the sense that the likelihood is unbounded. The problem is that the peak value of the Gaussian probability density function becomes larger and larger as the (co-)variance approaches zero. For any $M \geq 2$, the GMM is in principle able to exploit this fact to attain an infinite likelihood. This is possible by focusing one of the clusters on a single data point; by centering the cluster on the data point and then shrinking the (co-)variance towards zero, the likelihood of this particular data point goes to infinity. The remaining $M - 1$ clusters then just have to cover the remaining $n - 1$ data points so that their likelihoods are bounded away from zero.[5] In practice, the EM algorithm will often get stuck in a local optimum before this 'degeneracy' shows itself, but it is nevertheless a good idea to regularise or constrain the model to make

---

[5]This degeneracy can happen in the semi-supervised setting as well, but only if there are p or fewer labelled data points of each class.

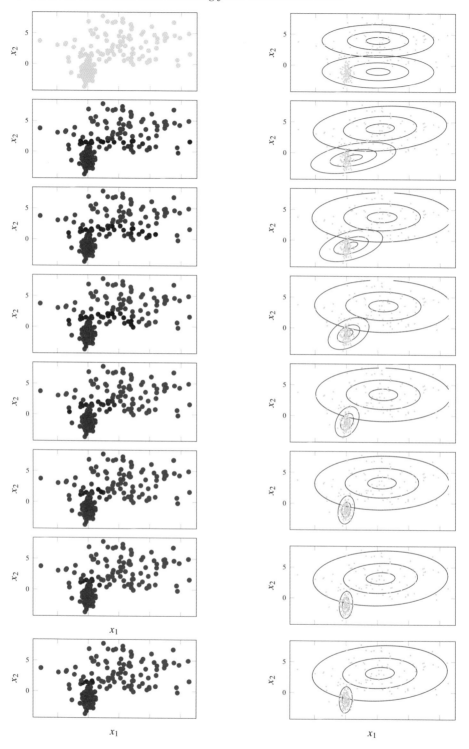

Figure 10.7 The Method 10.3 applied to an unsupervised clustering problem, where all training data points are unlabelled. In practice, the only difference from Figure 10.6 is the initialisation (in the upper row), which here is done arbitrarily instead of using the labelled data points.

it more robust to this potential issue. One simple solution is to add small constant value to all diagonal elements of the covariance matrices Σ_m, thereby preventing them from degenerating to zero.

k-Means Clustering

Before leaving this section, we will introduce an alternative clustering method known as *k*-means. This algorithm is in many ways similar to the GMM model for clustering discussed above but is derived from a different objective and lacks the generative interpretation of the GMM. The *k* in *k*-means refers to the number of clusters, so to agree with our notation, we should perhaps refer to it as *M*-means. However, the term *k*-means is so well established that will we keep it as the name of the method but to agree with the mathematical notation above, we nevertheless let *M* denote the number of clusters.

The key difference between the GMM and *k*-means is that in the former we model cluster assignments probabilistically, whereas in the latter we make 'hard' cluster assignments. That is, we can partition the training data points $\{\mathbf{x}_i\}_{i=1}^{n}$ into *M* distinct clusters $R_1, R_2, \ldots, R_M$, where each data point $\mathbf{x}_i$ should be a member of exactly one cluster R_m. *k*-means clustering then amounts to selecting the clusters so that the sum of pairwise squared Euclidean distances *within each cluster* is minimised,

$$\arg\min_{R_1, R_2, \ldots, R_M} \sum_{m=1}^{M} \frac{1}{|R_m|} \sum_{\mathbf{x}, \mathbf{x}' \in R_m} \|\mathbf{x} - \mathbf{x}'\|_2^2, \tag{10.17}$$

where $|R_m|$ is the number of data points in cluster R_m. The intention of (10.17) is to select the clusters such that all points within each cluster are as similar as possible. It can be shown that the problem (10.17) is equivalent to selecting the clusters such that the distances to the cluster centres, summed over all data points, is minimised,

$$\arg\min_{R_1, R_2, \ldots, R_M} \sum_{m=1}^{M} \sum_{\mathbf{x} \in R_m} \|\mathbf{x} - \widehat{\boldsymbol{\mu}}_m\|_2^2. \tag{10.18}$$

Here $\widehat{\boldsymbol{\mu}}_m$ is the centre of cluster *m*, that is the mean of all data points $\mathbf{x}_i \in R_m$.

Unfortunately both (10.17) and (10.18) are combinatorial problems, meaning that we cannot expect to solve them exactly if the number of data points *n* is large. However, an approximate solution can be found as follows:

(i) Set the cluster centers $\widehat{\boldsymbol{\mu}}_1, \widehat{\boldsymbol{\mu}}_2, \ldots, \widehat{\boldsymbol{\mu}}_M$ to some initial values;

(ii) Determine which cluster R_m each $\mathbf{x}_i$ belongs to, that is, find the cluster center $\widehat{\boldsymbol{\mu}}_m$ that is closest to $\mathbf{x}_i$ for all $i = 1, \ldots, n$;

(iii) Update the cluster centers $\widehat{\boldsymbol{\mu}}_m$ as the average of all $\mathbf{x}_i$ that belongs to R_m;

and then iterate steps (ii) and (iii) until convergence.

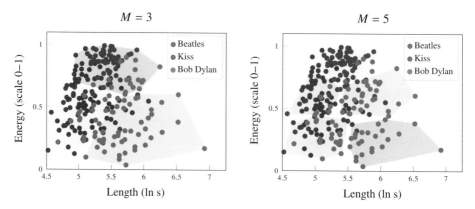

Figure 10.8 k-means applied to the music classification data Example 2.1. In this example, we actually have labelled data, so the purpose of applying a clustering algorithm to the inputs (without considering the corresponding labels) is purely for illustrative purposes. We try $M = 3$ (left) and $M = 5$ (right). It is worth noting that it so happens that for $M = 3$, there is almost one artist per cluster.

This procedure is an instance of Lloyd's algorithm, but it is often simply called 'the k-means algorithm'. Comparing this with the EM algorithm in Method 10.3, we see a clear resemblance. As pointed out above, the key difference is that the EM algorithm uses a soft cluster assignment based on the estimated cluster probabilities, whereas k-means makes a hard cluster assignment in step (ii). Another difference is that k-means measures similarity between data points using Euclidean distance, whereas the EM algorithm applied to the GMM model takes the covariance of the clusters into account.[6]

Similarly to the EM algorithm, Lloyd's algorithm will converge to a stationary point of the objective (10.18), but it is not guaranteed to find the global optimum. In practice it is common to run it multiple times, each with a different initialisation in step (i), and pick the result of the run for which the objective in (10.17)/(10.18) attains the smallest value. As an illustration of k-means, we apply it to the input data from the music classification problem in Example 2.1; see Figure 10.8.

The name of the algorithm, k-means, is reminiscent of another method studied in this book, namely k-NN. The two methods do have some similarities, in particular that they both use Euclidean distance to define similarities in the input space. This implies that k-means, just as k-NN, is sensitive to the normalisation of the input values. That being said, the two methods should not be confused. While k-NN is a supervised learning method (applicable to classification and regression problems), k-means is a method for solving the (unsupervised) clustering problem. Note in particular that the 'k' in the name has a different meaning for the two methods.

---

[6]Put differently, the EM algorithm for the GMM model uses the Mahalanobis distance instead of Euclidean distance.

Choosing the Number of Clusters

In both the GMM model and the k-means algorithm for clustering, we need to select the number of clusters M before running the corresponding algorithm. Hence, unless there is some application-specific prior knowledge regarding how to select M, this becomes a design choice. Like many other model selection problems, it is not possible to optimise M simply by taking the value that gives the smallest training cost (negative of (10.12) for GMM, or (10.18) for k-means). The reason is that increasing M to $M + 1$ will give more flexibility to the model, and this increased flexibility can only decrease the value of the cost function. Intuitively, in the extreme case when $M = n$, we would end up with the trivial (but uninteresting) solution where each data point is assigned to its own cluster. This is a type of overfitting.

Validation techniques such as hold-out and cross-validation (see Chapter 4) can be used to guide the model selection, but they need to be adapted to the unsupervised setting (specifically, there is no new data error E_{new} for the clustering model). For instance, for the GMM, which is a probabilistic generative model, it is possible to use the likelihood of a held-out validation data set to find a suitable value for M. That is, we set aside some validation data $\{\mathbf{x}'_j\}_{j=1}^{n_v}$ which is not used to learn the clustering model. We then train different models for different values of M on the remaining data and evaluate the held-out likelihood $p(\{\mathbf{x}'_j\}_{j=1}^{n_v} \mid \widehat{\boldsymbol{\theta}}, M)$ for each candidate model. The model with the largest held-out likelihood is then selected as the final clustering model.

This provides us with a systematic way of selecting M; however, in the unsupervised setting, such validation methods should be used with care. In the context of supervised learning of a predictive model, minimising the new data (prediction) error is often the ultimate goal of the model, so it makes sense to base the evaluation on this. In the context of clustering, however, it is not necessarily the case that minimising the 'clustering loss' on new data is what we are really after. Instead, clustering is often applied to gain insights regarding the data, by finding a *small number* of clusters where data points within each cluster have similar characteristics. Thus, as long as the model results in a coherent and meaningful grouping of the data points, we might favour a smaller model over a larger one, even if the latter results in a better validation loss.

One heuristic approach to handling this is to fit models of different orders, $M = 1$ to $M = M_{\text{max}}$. We then plot the loss (either the training loss, the validation loss, or both) as a function of M. Based on this plot, the user can make a subjective decision about when the decrease in the objective appears to level off, so that it is unjustified to increase the model complexity further. That is, we select M such that the gain in going from M to $M + 1$ clusters is insignificant. If the dataset indeed has a few distinct clusters, this graph will typically look like an elbow, and this method for selecting M in thus sometimes called the *elbow method*. We illustrate it for the k-means method in Figure 10.9.

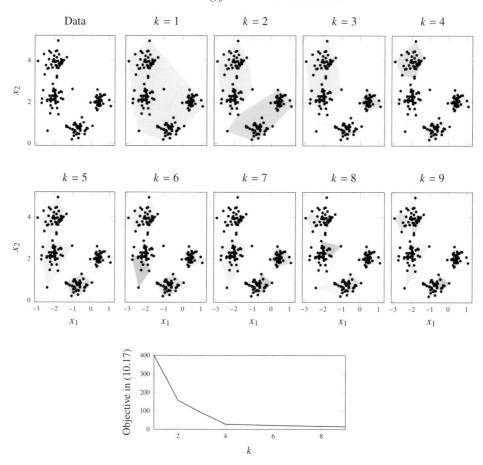

Figure 10.9 For selecting M in k-means, we can use the so-called elbow method, which amounts to trying different values of M (the upper panels) and recording the objective in (10.17) (the bottom panel). To select M, we look for a 'bend' in the bottom panel. In the ideal case, there is a very distinct kink, but for this particular data, we could either draw the conclusion that $M = 2$ or $M = 4$, and it is up to the user to decide. Note that in this example the data has only two dimensions, and we can therefore show the clusters themselves and compare them visually. If the data has more than two dimensions, however, we have to select M based only on the 'elbow plot' in the bottom panel.

10.3 Deep Generative Models

Key to the generative modelling paradigm is that we model **x** as a random variable, and it thus requires making some assumptions regarding its distribution. In the GMM discussed above, we used a Gaussian to model the (class-conditional) distribution of **x**. It is important to note that this assumption does not mean that we truly believe that the data is Gaussian, but rather that it is close enough to being Gaussian so that we can obtain a useful model (whether for clustering or classification). That being said, however, in many situations the Gaussian assumption is an oversimplification, which can limit the performance of the resulting model.

One way to relax the assumption is to manually design some alternative distribution that is believed to better correspond to the properties of the data. However, in many situations it is very challenging to come up with a suitable distribution 'by hand', not least when $\mathbf{x}$ is high-dimensional and with complex dependencies between the individual coordinates x_i, $i = 1, \ldots, p$. In this section, we will consider an alternative approach, which is to view $\mathbf{x}$ as a transformation of some simple random variable $\mathbf{z}$. With a high degree of flexibility in the transformation, we can model very complex distributions over $\mathbf{x}$ in this way. Specifically, we will discuss how deep neural networks (see Chapter 6) can be used in this context, resulting in so-called *deep generative models*.

Since the key challenge in developing such a flexible non-Gaussian generative model is to construct the distribution over $\mathbf{x}$, we will throughout this section (and for the remainder of this chapter) drop the class, or cluster, label y from the model. That is, we will try to learn the distribution $p(\mathbf{x})$ in an unsupervised way, without assuming that there are any clusters in the data (or, put differently, that there is only a single cluster). The purpose of this is twofold. First, learning generative models for high-dimensional data can be useful even in the absence of distinct clusters in the distribution. Second, it simplifies the notation in the presentation below. If we *do expect* that the data contains clusters, then the methods presented below can easily be generalised to model the class-conditional distribution $p(\mathbf{x} \mid y)$ instead.

The problem that we are concerned with in this section can thus be formulated as: given a training data set $\{\mathbf{x}_i\}_{i=1}^n$ of n independent samples from some distribution $p(\mathbf{x})$, learn a parametric model of this distribution.

Invertible non-Gaussian Models and Normalising Flows

To lay the foundation for non-Gaussian deep generative models, let us stick with a simple Gaussian model for the time being:

$$p(\mathbf{x}) = \mathcal{N}(\mathbf{x} \mid \mu, \Sigma). \tag{10.19}$$

The parameters of this model are the mean vector and the covariance matrix, $\theta = \{\mu, \Sigma\}$, which can be learned from the training data $\{\mathbf{x}_i\}_{i=1}^n$ by maximum likelihood. As we discussed above, this boils down to estimating μ by the sample mean and Σ by the sample covariance (analogously to (10.3), but with a single class).

Since a linear transformation of a Gaussian random vector is also Gaussian, an equivalent representation of (10.19) is to introduce a random variable $\mathbf{z}$ of the same dimension p as $\mathbf{x}$, following a standard Gaussian distribution,[7]

$$p_{\mathbf{z}}(\mathbf{z}) = \mathcal{N}(\mathbf{z} \mid 0, I) \tag{10.20a}$$

and then expressing $\mathbf{x}$ by a linear change of variables,

$$\mathbf{x} = \mu + L\mathbf{z}. \tag{10.20b}$$

---

[7] We use a subscript on $p_{\mathbf{z}}(\mathbf{z})$ to emphasise that this is the distribution of $\mathbf{z}$, and to distinguish it from $p(\mathbf{x})$.

Here L is any matrix[8] such that $LL^\mathsf{T} = \Sigma$. Note that, in this representation, the distribution $p_{\mathbf{z}}(\mathbf{z}) = \mathcal{N}(\mathbf{z} \mid 0, I)$ takes a very simple and generic form, which is independent of the model parameters. Instead, the parameters are shifted to the transformation (10.20b). Specifically, we can use the alternative re-parameterisation $\theta = \{\mu, L\}$, which directly defines the linear transformation.

The models (10.19) and (10.20) are equivalent, so we have not yet accomplished anything with this reformulation. However, the latter form suggests a non-linear generalisation. Specifically, we can model the *distribution* of $\mathbf{x}$ indirectly as the transformation of a Gaussian random variable,

$$p_{\mathbf{z}}(\mathbf{z}) = \mathcal{N}(\mathbf{z} \mid 0, I), \tag{10.21a}$$

$$\mathbf{x} = f_{\theta}(\mathbf{z}), \tag{10.21b}$$

for some arbitrary parametric function f_{θ}. Note that, even though we start from a Gaussian, the implied distribution of $\mathbf{x}$ is going to be non-Gaussian due to the non-linear transformation. Indeed, we can model arbitrarily complex distributions in this way by considering complex and flexible non-linear transformations.

The challenge with this approach is how to learn the model parameters from data. Following the maximum likelihood approach, we would like to solve

$$\widehat{\theta} = \arg\max_{\theta} p(\{\mathbf{x}_i\}_{i=1}^{n} \mid \theta) = \arg\max_{\theta} \sum_{i=1}^{n} \ln p(\mathbf{x}_i \mid \theta). \tag{10.22}$$

Hence, we still need to *evaluate* the likelihood of $\mathbf{x}$ to learn the model parameters, but this likelihood is not explicitly given in the model specification (10.21).

To make progress, we will start by making the assumption that $f_{\theta} : \mathbb{R}^P \to \mathbb{R}^P$ is an *invertible* function, with inverse $h_{\theta}(\mathbf{x}) = f_{\theta}^{-1}(\mathbf{x}) = \mathbf{z}$. Note that this implies that $\mathbf{z}$ is of the same dimension as $\mathbf{x}$. Under this assumption, we can make use of the change of variables formula for probability density functions to write

$$p(\mathbf{x} \mid \theta) = |\nabla h_{\theta}(\mathbf{x})| \, p_{\mathbf{z}}(h_{\theta}(\mathbf{x})), \tag{10.23a}$$

where

$$\nabla h_{\theta}(\mathbf{x}) = \begin{pmatrix} \dfrac{\partial h_{\theta,1}(\mathbf{x})}{\partial x_1} & \cdots & \dfrac{\partial h_{\theta,1}(\mathbf{x})}{\partial x_p} \\ \vdots & \ddots & \vdots \\ \dfrac{\partial h_{\theta,p}(\mathbf{x})}{\partial x_1} & \cdots & \dfrac{\partial h_{\theta,p}(\mathbf{x})}{\partial x_p} \end{pmatrix} \tag{10.23b}$$

is the $p \times p$ matrix of all partial derivatives of $h_{\theta}(\mathbf{x})$, referred to as the Jacobian matrix, and $|\nabla h_{\theta}(\mathbf{x})|$ is the absolute value of its determinant.

---

[8]For a positive definite covariance matrix Σ, such a factorisation always exists. For instance, we can take L to be the lower triangular matrix obtained from a Cholesky factorisation of Σ. However, for our purposes it is not important how the matrix L is obtained, just that it exists.

Plugging this expression into the maximum likelihood problem (10.22), we can thus learn the model as:

$$\widehat{\theta} = \arg\max_{\theta} \sum_{i=1}^{n} \ln |\nabla h_{\theta}(\mathbf{x}_i)| + \ln p_{\mathbf{z}}(h_{\theta}(\mathbf{x}_i)), \qquad (10.24)$$

where both terms of the loss function are now given by the model specification (10.21). This provides us with a practical approach for learning the transformation-based generative model from data, although we make the following observations:

(i) The inverse mapping $h_{\theta}(\mathbf{x}) = f_{\theta}^{-1}(\mathbf{x})$ needs to be explicitly available, since it is part of the loss function.

(ii) The Jacobian determinant $|\nabla h_{\theta}(\mathbf{x}_i)|$ needs to be tractable. In the general case, the computational cost associated with (practical algorithms for) computing the determinant of a $p \times p$ matrix scales cubically with p. For high-dimensional problems, this easily results in a prohibitively large computational bottleneck, unless the Jacobian has some special structure that can be exploited for faster computation.

(iii) The forward mapping $f_{\theta}(\mathbf{z})$ *does not* enter the loss function, so in principle we can learn the model without explicitly evaluating this function (it is enough to know that it exists). However, if we want to use the model to generate samples from $p(\mathbf{x})$, then explicit evaluation of the forward mapping is also needed. Indeed, the way to sample from the model (10.21) is to first sample a standard Gaussian vector $\mathbf{z}$ and then propogate this sample through the mapping to obtain a sample $\mathbf{x} = f_{\theta}(\mathbf{z})$.

Designing parametric functions that satisfy these conditions while still being flexible enough to accurately describe complex high-dimensional probability distributions is non-trivial. Models based on neural networks are often used, but to satisfy the requirements on invertibility and computational tractability, special-purpose network architectures are needed. This involves, for instance, restricting the mapping f_{θ} so that the Jacobian of its inverse becomes a triangular matrix, in which case the determinant is easily computable.

An interesting observation when designing this type of transform-based generative model using neural networks is that it is enough to ensure invertibility and tractability of each layer of the network independently. Assume that $f_{\theta}(\mathbf{z})$ is a network with L layers, where the lth layer corresponds to a function $f_{\theta}^{(l)} : \mathbb{R}^p \to \mathbb{R}^p$. We can then write $f_{\theta}(\mathbf{z}) = f_{\theta}^{(L)} \circ f_{\theta}^{(L-1)} \circ \cdots \circ f_{\theta}^{(1)}(\mathbf{z})$, where $\circ$ denotes the composition of functions. This is just a mathematical shorthand for saying that the output of an L-layer neural network is obtained by first feeding the input to the first layer, then propagating the result through the second layer, and so on, until we obtain the final output after L layers. The inverse of f_{θ} is then obtained by applying the layer-wise inverse functions in reverse order, $h_{\theta}(\mathbf{x}) = h_{\theta}^{(1)} \circ h_{\theta}^{(2)} \circ \cdots \circ h_{\theta}^{(L)}(\mathbf{x})$, where $h_\theta^{(l)}$ is the inverse of $f_\theta^{(l)}$. Furthermore, by the chain rule of differentiation and the multiplicativity of determinants, we can express the Jacobian determinant as a product:

$$|\nabla h_\theta(\mathbf{x})| = \prod_{l=1}^{L} \left| \nabla h_\theta^{(l)}(\mathbf{x}^{(l)}) \right|, \quad \text{where} \quad \mathbf{x}^{(l)} = h_\theta^{(l+1)} \circ h_\theta^{(l+2)} \circ \cdots \circ h_\theta^{(L)}(\mathbf{x}).$$

This means that it is enough to design each $f_\theta^{(l)}$ so that it is invertible and has a computationally tractable Jacobian determinant. While this still puts restrictions on the architecture and activation functions used in $f_\theta^{(l)}$, there are many ways in which this can be accomplished. We can then build more complex models by stacking multiple such layers after each other, with a computational cost growing only linearly with the number of layers. Models exploiting this property are referred to as *normalising flows*. The idea is that a data point $\mathbf{x}$ 'flows' through a sequence of transformations, $h_\theta^{(L)}, h_\theta^{(L-1)}, \ldots, h_\theta^{(1)}$, and after L such transformations, the data point has been 'normalised'. That is, the result of the sequence of mappings is that the data point has been transformed into a standard Gaussian vector $\mathbf{z}$.

Many practical network architectures for normalising flows have been proposed in the literature, with different properties. We shall not pursue these specific architectures further, however, but instead turn to an alternative way of learning deep generative models that circumvents the architectural restrictions of normalising flows, resulting in so-called *generative adversarial networks*.

Generative Adversarial Networks

The idea of transforming a Gaussian vector $\mathbf{z}$ by a deep generative model (10.21) to parameterise a complex distribution over data $\mathbf{x}$ is very powerful. However, we noted above that evaluating the data likelihood $p(\mathbf{x} \mid \theta)$ implied by the model is non-trivial and imposes certain restrictions on the mapping f_θ. Hence, without these restrictions, learning the model by explicit likelihood maximisation is not possible. However, motivated by this limitation, we can ask ourselves: Is there some other way of learning the model, which *does not* require evaluating the likelihood?

To answer this question, we note that one useful property of the deep generative model is that *sampling* from the distribution $p(\mathbf{x} \mid \theta)$ is trivial, as long as the forward mapping $f_\theta(\mathbf{z})$ is available. This is true even in situations when we are unable to evaluate the corresponding probability density function. That is, we can generate 'synthetic' data points from the model, simply by sampling a Gaussian vector $\mathbf{z} \sim \mathcal{N}(0, I)$ and then feeding the obtained sample through the parametric function, $f_\theta(\mathbf{z})$. This does not impose any specific requirements on the mapping, such as invertibility. In fact, we do not even require that the dimension of $\mathbf{z}$ is the same as that of $\mathbf{x}$!

Generative adversarial networks (GANs) make use of this property for training the model, by comparing synthetic samples (generated by the model) with real samples from the training data set $\{\mathbf{x}_i\}_{i=1}^{n}$. The basic idea is to iteratively update the model parameters $\boldsymbol{\theta}$ with the objective of making the synthetic samples resemble the real data points as much as possible. If it is difficult to tell them apart, then we can conclude that the learned distribution is a good approximation of the true data distribution. To illustrate the idea, assume that the data we are working with consists of natural images of some type, say pictures of human faces. This is indeed a typical example where these models have shown remarkable capabilities. A data point $\mathbf{x}$ is thus an image of dimension $p = w \times h \times 3$ (width in pixels $\times$ height in pixels $\times$ three colour channels), $\mathbf{z}$ is a Gaussian vector of dimension q, and the mapping $f_{\boldsymbol{\theta}} : \mathbb{R}^q \rightarrow \mathbb{R}^{w \times h \times 3}$ takes this Gaussian vector and transforms it into the shape of an image. Without going into details, such mappings can be constructed using deep neural networks in various ways, for instance using upsampling layers and deconvolutions (inverse convolutions). Such networks are reminiscent of convolutional neural networks (see Section 6.3) but go in the other direction – instead of taking an image as input and transforming this to a vector of class probabilities, say, we now take a vector as input and transform this into the shape of an image.

To learn a model $p(\mathbf{x} | \boldsymbol{\theta})$ for the distribution of the observed data, we will play a type of game, which goes as follows. At each iteration of the learning algorithm:

(i) 'Flip a coin', that is, set $y = 1$ with probability 0.5 and $y = -1$ with probability 0.5:

    (a) If $y = 1$, then generate a synthetic sample from the model $\mathbf{x}' \sim p(\mathbf{x} | \boldsymbol{\theta})$. That is, we sample $\mathbf{z}' \sim \mathcal{N}(0, I)$ and compute $\mathbf{x}' = f_{\boldsymbol{\theta}}(\mathbf{z}')$.

    (b) If $y = -1$, then pick a random sample from the training data set instead. That is, we set $\mathbf{x}' = \mathbf{x}_i$ for some index i sampled uniformly at random from $\{1, \ldots, n\}$.

(ii) Ask a critic to determine if the sample is real or fake. For instance, in the example with pictures of faces, we would ask the question: does $\mathbf{x}'$ look like a real face, or is it synthetically generated?

(iii) Use the critic's reply as a signal for updating the model parameters $\boldsymbol{\theta}$. Specifically, update the parameters with the goal of making the critic as 'confused as possible', regarding whether or not the sample that is presented is real or fake.

The first point is easy to implement, but when we get to the second point, the procedure becomes more abstract. What do we mean by 'critic'? In a practical learning algorithm, using a human-in-the-loop to judge the authenticity of the sample $\mathbf{x}'$ is of course, not feasible. Instead, the idea behind generative adversarial networks is to *learn an auxiliary classifier* alongside the generative model, which plays the role of the critic in the game. Specifically, we design a binary classifier $g_{\boldsymbol{\eta}}(\mathbf{x})$ which takes a data point (for example an image of a face) as input and estimates the probability that this is synthetically generated, that is,

$$g_{\boldsymbol{\eta}}(\mathbf{x}) \approx p(y = 1 | \mathbf{x}). \qquad (10.25)$$

273

Here, η denotes the parameters of the auxiliary classifier, which are distinct from the parameters θ of the generative model.

The classifier is learned as usual to minimise some classification loss L,

$$\hat{\eta} = \arg\min_{\eta} \mathbb{E}\left[L(y, g_\eta(\mathbf{x}'))\right], \tag{10.26}$$

where the expected value is with respect to the random variables y and $\mathbf{x}'$ generated by the process described above. Note that this becomes a *supervised* binary classification problem, but where the labels y are automatically generated as part of the 'game'. Indeed, since these labels correspond to the flip of a fair coin, we can express the optimisation problem as

$$\min_{\eta} \left\{ \tfrac{1}{2}\mathbb{E}\left[L(1, g_\eta(f_\theta(\mathbf{z}')))\right] + \tfrac{1}{2}\mathbb{E}\left[L(-1, g_\eta(\mathbf{x}_i))\right] \right\}. \tag{10.27}$$

Moving on to the third step of the procedure, we wish to update the mapping $f_\theta(\mathbf{z})$, defining the generative model, to make the generated samples as difficult as possible for the critic to reject as being fake. This is in some sense the most important step of the procedure, since this is where we learn the generative model. This is done in a competition with the auxiliary classifier, where the objective for the generative model is to *maximise* the classification loss (10.27) with respect to θ,

$$\max_{\theta}\min_{\eta} \left\{ \tfrac{1}{2}\mathbb{E}\left[L(1, g_\eta(f_\theta(\mathbf{z}')))\right] + \tfrac{1}{2}\mathbb{E}\left[L(-1, g_\eta(\mathbf{x}_i))\right] \right\}. \tag{10.28}$$

This results in a so-called minimax problem, where two adversaries compete for the same objective, one trying to minimise it and the other trying to maximise it. Typically, the problem is approached by alternating between updating θ and updating η using stochastic gradient optimisation. We provide pseudo-code for one such algorithm in Method 10.4.

From an optimisation point-of-view, solving the minimax problem is more challenging than solving a pure minimisation problem, due to the competing forces that can result in oscillative behavior. However, many modifications and variations of the procedure outlined above have been developed, among other things to stabilise the optimisation and obtain efficient learning algorithms. Still, this is one of the drawbacks with generative adversarial networks compared to, for instance, normalising flows that can be learned by direct likelihood maximisation. Related to this is that, even if we successfully learn the generative model $f_\theta(\mathbf{z})$, which implicitly defines the distribution $p(\mathbf{x}\,|\,\theta)$, it can still not be used to evaluate the likelihood $p(\mathbf{x}_\star\,|\,\theta)$ for some newly observed data point $\mathbf{x}_\star$. Having access to an explicit likelihood can be useful in certain applications, for instance to reason about the plausibility of the observed $\mathbf{x}_\star$ under the learnt model of $p(\mathbf{x})$.[9]

---

[9] Although using the probability density function to reason about plausibility can itself be challenging and potentially misleading in very high-dimensional spaces.

Learn a generative adversarial network

Data: Training data $\mathcal{T} = \{\mathbf{x}_i\}_{i=1}^n$, initial parameters θ and η, learning rate γ
and batch size n_b, critic iterations per generator iteration T_{critic}
Result: Deep generative model $f_\theta(\mathbf{z})$

1 **repeat**
2   **for** $t = 0, \ldots, T_{\text{critic}}$ **do**
3   Sample mini-batch $\{\mathbf{x}_i\}_{i=1}^{n_b}$ from training data
4   Sample mini-batch $\{\mathbf{z}_i\}_{i=1}^{n_b}$ independently from $\mathcal{N}(0, I)$
5   Compute gradient
$$\widehat{\mathbf{d}}_{\text{critic}} = \tfrac{1}{2n_b} \sum_{i=1}^{n_b} \nabla_\eta \left\{ L(1, g_\eta(f_\theta(\mathbf{z}_i))) + L(-1, g_\eta(\mathbf{x}_i)) \right\}$$
6   Update critic: $\eta \leftarrow \eta - \gamma \widehat{\mathbf{d}}_{\text{critic}}$
7   **end**
8   Sample mini-batch $\{\mathbf{z}_i\}_{i=1}^{n_b}$ independently from $\mathcal{N}(0, I)$
9   Compute gradient $\widehat{\mathbf{d}}_{\text{gen.}} = \tfrac{1}{2n_b} \sum_{i=1}^{n_b} \nabla_\theta L(1, g_\eta(f_\theta(\mathbf{z}_i)))$
10   Update generator: $\theta \leftarrow \theta + \gamma \widehat{\mathbf{d}}_{\text{gen.}}$
11 **until** *convergence*

Sample from a generative adversarial network

Data: Generator model f_θ
Result: Synthetic sample $\mathbf{x}'$

1 Sample $\mathbf{z}' \sim \mathcal{N}(0, I)$
2 Output $\mathbf{x}' = f_\theta(\mathbf{z}')$

Method 10.4 Training a generative adversarial network.

10.4 Representation Learning and Dimensionality Reduction

A deep generative model $\mathbf{x} = f_\theta(\mathbf{z})$ defines a relationship between the observed data point $\mathbf{x}$ and some *latent representation* $\mathbf{z}$ of the same data point. The word *latent* (hidden), here, refers to the fact that $\mathbf{z}$ is not observed directly, but it nevertheless carries useful information about the data. Indeed, given the mapping f_θ (that is, once it has been learned), knowing the latent variable $\mathbf{z}$ is enough to *reconstruct* the data point $\mathbf{x}$, simply by computing $\mathbf{x} = f_\theta(\mathbf{z})$. The variable $\mathbf{z}$ is also commonly referred to as a (latent) *code*, and the mapping f_θ as a *decoder*, which uses the code to reconstruct the data.

Much of contemporary machine learning, and in particular deep learning, concerns learning from very high-dimensional data $\mathbf{x}$ with intricate dependencies between the coordinates x_i, $i = 1, \ldots, p$. Put differently, in the 'raw data space', each coordinate x_i individually might not carry much useful information, but when we put them together, we obtain meaningful patterns across **x** that we wish to learn from. The typical example is (once again) when **x** corresponds to an image, and the coordinates x_i the individual pixel values. One-by-one, the pixel values are not very informative about the contents of the image, but when processed jointly (as an image), deep neural networks can learn to recognise faces, classify objects, diagnose diseases, and solve many other highly non-trivial tasks. Similar examples are found, for instance, in natural language processing, where each x_i might correspond to a character in a text, but it is not until we put all the characters together into **x** that the semantic meaning of the text can be understood.

With these examples in mind, it can be argued that much of the success of deep learning is due to its capability of

> learning a useful representation of high-dimensional data.

For supervised learning of neural networks, as we discussed in Chapter 6, the representation learning is often implicit and takes place alongside the learning of a specific classification or regression model. There is no clear-cut definition of what we mean by a latent representation in such cases. However, intuitively we can think about the first chunk of layers in a deep network as being responsible for learning an informative representation of the raw data,[10] which is then used by the latter part of the network to solve the specific (for example, regression or classification) task at hand.

This is in contrast to deep generative models where, as pointed out above, the latent representation is an explicit part of the model. However, the possibility of learning a representation directly from data is not unique to generative models. In this section, we will introduce a method for unsupervised representation learning referred to as an *auto-encoder*. The auto-encoder can be used for dimensionality reduction by mapping the data to a lower-dimensional latent code. We will then derive a classical statistical method known as *principal component analysis* and show how this can be viewed as a special case of an auto-encoder which is restricted to be linear.

Auto-encoders

For many high-dimensional problems, it is reasonable to assume that the *effective dimension* of the data is smaller than the observed dimension. That is, most of the information contained in the p-dimensional variable **x** can be retained even if we compress the data into a q-dimensional representation **z** with $q < p$. For instance, in the context of generative adversarial networks (see Section 10.3), we argued that the latent variable **z** can be of (much) lower dimension than the final output **x**, say, if the model is trained to generate high-resolution images. In such a case, the effective

---

[10]That is, the representation in this case would correspond to the hidden units somewhere in the middle of the network.

dimension of the generatcd samples for a fixed model f_θ is q, irrespective of the observed dimension (or resolution) of $\mathbf{x}$.[11]

Training a generative adversarial network amounts to learning the decoder mapping $\mathbf{x} = f_\theta(\mathbf{z})$, which takes a latent representation $\mathbf{z}$ and maps this to a (higher-dimensional) output $\mathbf{x}$. However, a natural question is: Can we learn a mapping that goes in the other direction? That is, an *encoder* mapping $\mathbf{z} = h_\theta(\mathbf{z})$ which takes a data point $\mathbf{x}$ and computes its (lower-dimensional) latent representation.

For generative adversarial networks, this is far from trivial, since f_θ in general is a very complicated non-invertible function, and there is no simple way of reversing this mapping. For normalising flows, which we also discussed in Section 10.3, reversing the decoder mapping *is in fact* possible, since for these models we assumed that f_θ has an inverse $h_\theta = f_\theta^{-1}$. However, this requires certain restrictions on the model, in particular that the dimensions of $\mathbf{x}$ and $\mathbf{z}$ are the same. Hence, such mappings are not useful for dimensionality reduction.

In an *auto-encoder*, we tackle this issue by relaxing the requirement that h_θ is an exact inverse of f_θ. Instead, we jointly learn the encoder and decoder mappings via the objective that $f_\theta(h_\theta(\mathbf{x})) \approx \mathbf{x}$, while enforcing the dimensionality reduction through the model architecture. Specifically, we assume that the:

Encoder $h_\theta : \mathbb{R}^p \to \mathbb{R}^q$ maps a data point to a latent representation,

Decoder $f_\theta : \mathbb{R}^q \to \mathbb{R}^p$ maps a latent representation to a point in data space.

Importantly, the dimension q of the latent representation is selected to be smaller than p. Often, the encoder and decoder mappings are parameterised as neural networks. Contrary to normalising flows, the two functions are constructed separately, and they are allowed to depend on different parameters. However, for brevity we group both the encoder and decoder parameters into the joint parameter vector $\boldsymbol{\theta}$.

If we take a data point $\mathbf{x}$, we can compute its latent representation using the encoder as $\mathbf{z} = h_\theta(\mathbf{x})$. If we then feed this representation through the decoder, we obtain a *reconstruction* $\widehat{\mathbf{x}} = f_\theta(\mathbf{z})$ of the data point. In general, this will not be identical to $\mathbf{x}$, because we have forced the encoder to compress the data into a lower-dimensional representation in the first step. This will typically result in a loss of information that the decoder is unable to compensate for. However, we can nevertheless train the model to approximate the identity mapping as closely as possible by minimising the reconstruction error over the training data. For instance, using the squared error loss, we obtain the training objective,

$$\widehat{\theta} = \arg\min_{\theta} \sum_{i=1}^{n} \|\mathbf{x}_i - f_\theta(h_\theta(\mathbf{x}_i))\|^2. \tag{10.29}$$

---

[11] We say that the model defines a q-dimensional *manifold* in the p-dimensional data space. We can think of a manifold as a non-linear subspace. For instance, a two-dimensional manifold in three-dimensional space is a curved surface. If $\mathbf{z} \in \mathbb{R}^2$ and $\mathbf{x} = f_\theta(\mathbf{z}) \in \mathbb{R}^3$, then all points $\mathbf{x}$ generated in this way will be constrained to lie on such a surface.

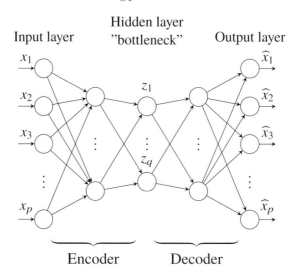

Figure 10.10 The auto-encoder can be viewed as a neural network with a bottleneck layer in the middle. The first part of the network corresponds to the encoder, the second part to the decoder, and the latent representation is given by the hidden variables at the bottleneck.

It is important that $q < p$ for this problem to be interesting, otherwise we would just end up learning an identity mapping. However, when q is indeed smaller than p, then the objective will encourage the encoder to compress the data into a lower dimensional vector while retaining as much of the actual information content as possible to enable accurate reconstruction. In other words, the encoder is forced to learn a useful representation of the data.

When using neural networks to parameterise the encoder and decoder mappings, the complete auto-encoder can also be viewed a neural network but with a 'bottleneck layer' in the middle corresponding to the latent code. We illustrate this in Figure 10.10.

One possible issue when using auto-encoders is the risk of learning a memorisation of the training data. To illustrate the point, assume that $q = 1$ so that we have a scalar latent code z. For any realistic problem, this should be insufficient to represent the actual information content in some complex data $\mathbf{x}$. However, conceptually, the auto-encoder could learn to map any training data point $\mathbf{x}_i$ to the value $z_i = i$, and then learn to reconstruct the data point exactly based on this unique identifier. This will never happen exactly in practice, but we can still suffer to some extent from this memorisation effect. Put differently, the model might learn to store information about the *training data* in the parameter vector $\boldsymbol{\theta}$, which helps it so minimise the reconstruction error, instead of learning a useful and generalisable representation. This is a potential issue in particular when the model is very flexible (very high-dimensional $\boldsymbol{\theta}$) so that it has the capacity of memorising the data.

Various extensions to the basic auto-encoder have been proposed in the literature to combat this memorisation effect, among other things. Regularisation is one useful approach. For instance, it is possible to add a probabilistic prior on the distribution of the latent representation, effectively bridging the gap between auto-encoders and deep generative models. Another approach is to limit the capacity of the encoder and decoder mappings. Taking this to the extreme, we can restrict both mappings to be linear functions. As it turns out, this results in a well-known dimensionality reduction method referred to as principal component analysis, which we will discuss next.

Principal Component Analysis

Principal component analysis (PCA) is similar to an auto-encoder, in the sense that the objective is to learn a low-dimensional representation $\mathbf{z} \in \mathbb{R}^q$ of the data $\mathbf{x} \in \mathbb{R}^p$, where $q < p$. This is done by projecting $\mathbf{x}$ onto a q-dimensional (linear) subspace of $\mathbb{R}^p$ by applying a linear transformation. Traditionally, the transformation is derived based on the objective of retaining as much information as possible, where information is measured in terms of variance. We will briefly discuss this view on PCA below. However, an alternative approach is to consider PCA as an auto-encoder that is restricted to be linear. That is, the encoder is a linear mapping that transforms $\mathbf{x}$ into the latent representation $\mathbf{z}$, the decoder is another linear mapping that tries to reconstruct $\mathbf{x}$ from $\mathbf{z}$, and both mappings are learned simultaneously by minimising the reconstruction error with respect to the training data. This means that we can write

$$\mathbf{z} = \underbrace{W_e}_{q \times p} \mathbf{x} + \underbrace{b_e}_{q \times 1} \qquad \text{and} \qquad \mathbf{x} = \underbrace{W_d}_{p \times q} \mathbf{z} + \underbrace{b_d}_{p \times 1} \qquad (10.30)$$

for the encoder and decoder mappings, respectively. The parameters of the model are the weight matrices and offset vectors, $\theta = \{W_e, b_e, W_d, b_d\}$. In light of Figure 10.10, this can be viewed as a two-layer neural network with a bottleneck layer and linear activation functions. Note that the complete auto-encoder is also given by a linear transformation, and the reconstruction of $\mathbf{x}$ is

$$\widehat{\mathbf{x}} = W_d \mathbf{z} + b_d \qquad (10.31a)$$
$$= W_d (W_e \mathbf{x} + b_e) + b_d \qquad (10.31b)$$
$$= \underbrace{W_d W_e}_{p \times p} \mathbf{x} + \underbrace{W_d b_e + b_d}_{p \times 1}. \qquad (10.31c)$$

To learn the model parameters, we minimise the squared reconstruction error of the training data points $\{\mathbf{x}_i\}_{i=1}^n$:

$$\widehat{\theta} = \arg\min_{\theta} \sum_{i=1}^n \|\mathbf{x}_i - (W_d W_e \mathbf{x}_i + W_d b_e + b_d)\|^2. \qquad (10.32)$$

Before proceeding, let us pause for a minute and consider this expression. The reconstruction $\widehat{\mathbf{x}}$ of a data point $\mathbf{x}$ is, according to (10.31c), a linear transformation of $\mathbf{x}$. However, this transformation depends on the model parameters only through the matrix $W_d W_e$ and the vector $W_d b_e + b_d$. Consequently, there is no hope of uniquely determining all model parameters based on (10.32). For instance, we can replace $W_d W_e$ with $W_d TT^{-1} W_e$, for any invertible $q \times q$ matrix T, and obtain an equivalent model. At best we can hope to learn the product $W_d W_e$ and the vector $W_d b_e + b_d$, but it is not possible to uniquely identifying W_e, b_e, W_d, and b_d from these expressions. Therefore, when performing PCA, we wish to find *one* solution to (10.32), without necessarily characterising all possible solutions. As we will see below, however, we will not just find *any* solution but one which has a nice geometrical interpretation.

Based on this observation, we start by noting that there is redundancy in the 'combined offset' vector $W_d b_e + b_d$. Since b_d is a free parameter, we can without loss of generality set $b_e = 0$. This means that the encoder mapping simplifies to $\mathbf{z} = W_e \mathbf{x}$. Next, plugging this into (10.32), it is possible to solve for b_d. Indeed, it follows from a standard least squares argument[12] that, for any $W_d W_e$, the optimal value for b_d is

$$b_d = \frac{1}{n} \sum_{i=1}^{n} (\mathbf{x}_i - W_d W_e \mathbf{x}_i) = (I - W_d W_e)\bar{\mathbf{x}}, \tag{10.33}$$

where $\bar{\mathbf{x}} = \frac{1}{n} \sum_{i=1}^{n} \mathbf{x}_i$ is the mean of the training data. For notational brevity, we define the *centred* data $\mathbf{x}_{0,i} = \mathbf{x}_i - \bar{\mathbf{x}}$ for $i = 1, \ldots, n$ by subtracting the mean value from each data point. The objective (10.32) thus simplifies to

$$\widehat{W}_e, \widehat{W}_d = \arg\min_{W_e, W_d} \sum_{i=1}^{n} \|\mathbf{x}_{0,i} - W_d W_e \mathbf{x}_{0,i}\|^2. \tag{10.34}$$

We note that the role of the offset vectors in the auto-encoder is to centre the data around its mean. In practice, we handle this as a pre-processing step and

> centre the data manually by subtracting the mean value from each data point.

We can then focus on how to solve the problem (10.34) for the matrices W_e and W_d.

As we have seen previously in this book, when working with linear models, it is often convenient to stack the data vectors into matrices and make use of tools from matrix algebra. This is true also when deriving the PCA solution to (10.34). We thus define the matrices of centred data points and reconstructions as

$$\mathbf{X}_0 = \begin{bmatrix} \mathbf{x}_{0,1}^\mathsf{T} \\ \mathbf{x}_{0,2}^\mathsf{T} \\ \vdots \\ \mathbf{x}_{0,n}^\mathsf{T} \end{bmatrix} \quad \text{and} \quad \widehat{\mathbf{X}}_0 = \begin{bmatrix} \widehat{\mathbf{x}}_{0,1}^\mathsf{T} \\ \widehat{\mathbf{x}}_{0,2}^\mathsf{T} \\ \vdots \\ \widehat{\mathbf{x}}_{0,n}^\mathsf{T} \end{bmatrix}, \tag{10.35}$$

---

[12] It is easy to verify this by differentiating the expression and setting the gradient to zero.

respectively, where both matrices are of size $n \times p$. Here $\widehat{\mathbf{x}}_{0,i} = W_d W_e \mathbf{x}_{0,i}$ is the centred reconstruction of the ith data point. With this notation, we can write the training objective (10.34) as

$$\widehat{W}_e, \widehat{W}_d = \arg\min_{W_e, W_d} \|\mathbf{X}_0 - \widehat{\mathbf{X}}_0\|_F^2, \tag{10.36}$$

where $\|\cdot\|_F$ denotes the Frobenius norm[13] of a matrix, and the dependence on W_e and W_d is implicit in the notation $\widehat{\mathbf{X}}_0$.

By the definition of the reconstructed data points, it follows that $\widehat{\mathbf{X}}_0 = \mathbf{X}_0 W_e^\mathsf{T} W_d^\mathsf{T}$. An important implication of this is that *the rank of the matrix $\widehat{\mathbf{X}}_0$ is at most q.* The rank of a matrix is defined as the number of linearly independent rows (or, equivalently, columns) of the matrix. Hence, the rank is always bounded by the smallest dimension of the matrix. Assuming that all matrices in the expression for $\widehat{\mathbf{X}}_0$ are *full rank*, this means that $\mathbf{X}_0$ is of rank p, whereas W_e and W_d are both of rank $q < p$. (We assume that $n > p$.) Furthermore, it holds that the rank of a matrix product is bounded by the smallest rank of the involved factors. It follows that the rank of $\widehat{\mathbf{X}}_0$ is (at most) q.

Based on this observation and the learning objective (10.36), the PCA problem can be formulated as:

> Find the best rank q approximation $\widehat{\mathbf{X}}_0$ of the centred data matrix $\mathbf{X}_0$.

It turns out that this matrix approximation problem has a well-known solution, given by the Eckart–Young–Mirsky theorem. The theorem is based on a powerful tool from matrix algebra, a matrix factorisation technique known as singular value decomposition (SVD). Applying SVD to the centred data matrix $\mathbf{X}_0$ results in the factorisation

$$\mathbf{X}_0 = \mathbf{U}\boldsymbol{\Sigma}\mathbf{V}^\mathsf{T}. \tag{10.37}$$

Here, $\boldsymbol{\Sigma}$ is an $n \times p$ rectangular diagonal matrix of the form

$$\boldsymbol{\Sigma} = \begin{pmatrix} \sigma_1 & 0 & \cdots & 0 \\ 0 & \sigma_2 & \cdots & 0 \\ \vdots & \vdots & \ddots & \vdots \\ 0 & 0 & \cdots & \sigma_p \\ 0 & 0 & \cdots & 0 \\ \vdots & \vdots & \ddots & \vdots \\ 0 & 0 & \cdots & 0 \end{pmatrix}. \tag{10.38}$$

The values σ_j are positive real numbers, referred to as the *singular values* of the matrix. They are ordered so that $\sigma_1 \geq \sigma_2 \geq \cdots \geq \sigma_p > 0$. In general, the number of

---

[13] The Frobenius norm of matrix A is defined as $\|A\|_F = \sqrt{\sum_{ij} A_{ij}^2}$.

non-zero singular values of a matrix is equal to its rank, but since we have assumed that $\mathbf{X}_0$ is of full rank p, all singular values are positive. The matrix $\mathbf{U}$ is an $n \times n$ orthogonal matrix, meaning that its columns are orthogonal unit vectors of length n. Similarly, $\mathbf{V}$ is an orthogonal matrix of size $p \times p$.

Using the SVD, the Eckart–Young–Mirsky theorem states that the best[14] rank q approximation of the matrix $\mathbf{X}_0$ is obtained by truncating the SVD to keep only the q largest singular values. Specifically, using a block matrix notation, we can write

$$\mathbf{U} = \begin{bmatrix} \mathbf{U}_1 & \mathbf{U}_2 \end{bmatrix}, \qquad \Sigma = \begin{bmatrix} \Sigma_1 & 0 \\ 0 & \Sigma_2 \end{bmatrix}, \qquad \mathbf{V} = \begin{bmatrix} \mathbf{V}_1 & \mathbf{V}_2 \end{bmatrix}, \tag{10.39}$$

where $\mathbf{U}_1$ is $n \times q$ (corresponding to the first q columns of $\mathbf{U}$), $\mathbf{V}_1$ is $p \times q$ (first q columns of $\mathbf{V}$), and Σ_1 is $q \times q$ (with the q largest singular values on the diagonal). The best rank q approximation of $\mathbf{X}_0$ is then obtained by replacing Σ_2 by zeros in the SVD, resulting in

$$\widehat{\mathbf{X}}_0 = \mathbf{U}_1 \Sigma_1 \mathbf{V}_1^{\mathsf{T}}. \tag{10.40}$$

It remains to connect this expression to the matrices W_e and W_d defining the linear auto-encoder. Specifically, from the definition of reconstructed data points, it must hold that $\widehat{\mathbf{X}}_0 = \mathbf{X}_0 W_e^{\mathsf{T}} W_d^{\mathsf{T}}$, and we thus need to find matrices W_e and W_d so that this expression agrees with (10.40), the best possible approximation according to the Eckart–Young–Mirsky theorem. It turns out that this connection is readily available from the SVD. Indeed, choosing $W_e = \mathbf{V}_1^{\mathsf{T}}$ and $W_d = \mathbf{V}_1$ attains the desired result:

$$\mathbf{X}_0 W_e^{\mathsf{T}} W_d^{\mathsf{T}} = \begin{bmatrix} \mathbf{U}_1 & \mathbf{U}_2 \end{bmatrix} \begin{bmatrix} \Sigma_1 & 0 \\ 0 & \Sigma_2 \end{bmatrix} \begin{bmatrix} \mathbf{V}_1^{\mathsf{T}} \\ \mathbf{V}_2^{\mathsf{T}} \end{bmatrix} \mathbf{V}_1 \mathbf{V}_1^{\mathsf{T}} = \mathbf{U}_1 \Sigma_1 \mathbf{V}_1^{\mathsf{T}}, \tag{10.41}$$

where we have used the fact that $\mathbf{V}$ is orthogonal, so that $\mathbf{V}_1^{\mathsf{T}} \mathbf{V}_1 = I$ and $\mathbf{V}_2^{\mathsf{T}} \mathbf{V}_1 = 0$.

This completes the derivation of PCA. We summarise the procedure in Method 10.5.

Learn the PCA model

Data: Training data $\mathcal{T} = \{\mathbf{x}_i\}_{i=1}^{n}$
Result: Principal axes $\mathbf{V}$ and scores $\mathbf{Z}_0$

1 Compute the mean vector $\bar{\mathbf{x}} = \frac{1}{n} \sum_{i=1}^{n} \mathbf{x}_i$
2 Centre the data, $\mathbf{x}_{0,i} = \mathbf{x}_i - \bar{\mathbf{x}}$, for $i = 1, \ldots, n$
3 Construct the data matrix $\mathbf{X}_0$ according to (10.35)
4 Perform SVD on $\mathbf{X}_0$ to obtain the factorisation $\mathbf{X}_0 = \mathbf{U}\Sigma\mathbf{V}^{\mathsf{T}}$
5 Compute principal components $\mathbf{Z}_0 = \mathbf{U}\Sigma$

Method 10.5 Principal component analysis

---

[14]In the sense of minimising the Frobenius norm of the difference.

It is interesting to note that the algorithm boils down to simply applying SVD to the centred data matrix $\mathbf{X}_0$, and this operation is independent of the choice of q. Hence, in contrast with non-linear auto-encoders,[15] we do not have to decide on the dimension q of the latent representation beforehand. Instead, we obtain the solution for *all possible values* of q from a single SVD factorisation. In fact, the orthogonal matrix $\mathbf{V}$ corresponds to a change-of-basis in $\mathbb{R}^p$. By defining a transformed data matrix

$$\underbrace{\mathbf{Z}_0}_{n \times p} = \underbrace{\mathbf{X}_0}_{n \times p} \underbrace{\mathbf{V}}_{p \times p} , \tag{10.42}$$

we obtain an alternative representation of the data. Note that this data matrix is also of size $n \times p$, and we have not lost any information in this transformation since $\mathbf{V}$ is invertible.

The columns of $\mathbf{V}$ correspond to the basis vectors of the new basis. From the derivation above, we also know that the columns of $\mathbf{V}$ are ordered in terms of relevance, that is, the best auto-encoder of dimension q is given by the first q columns, or basis vectors. We refer to these vectors as the *principal axes* of $\mathbf{X}_0$. Furthermore, this means that we can obtain the best low-dimensional representation of $\mathbf{X}_0$, for arbitrary dimension $q < p$, simply by keeping only the first q columns of the transformed data matrix $\mathbf{Z}_0$. The coordinates of the data in the new basis, that is, the values in $\mathbf{Z}_0$, are referred to as the principal components (or scores). An interesting observation is that we can obtain the principal components directly from the SVD since $\mathbf{Z}_0 = \mathbf{X}_0 \mathbf{V} = \mathbf{U\Sigma V}^\mathsf{T}\mathbf{V} = \mathbf{U\Sigma}$. We illustrate the PCA method in Figure 10.11 (left and middle panels).

> **Time to reflect 10.2** *We have defined the principal components in terms of the centred data. However, we can also compute the non-centred principal components in the same way,* $\mathbf{Z} = \mathbf{XV}$ *(note that $\mathbf{V}$ is still computed from the SVD of the centred data matrix). How is $\mathbf{Z}$ related to $\mathbf{Z}_0$? How does this relate to the encoder mapping* $\mathbf{z} = W_e\mathbf{x}$ *that we started the derivation from?*

At the beginning of this section, we mentioned that there is a tight link between PCA and the covariance of the data. Indeed, an alternative view of PCA is that it finds the directions in $\mathbb{R}^p$ along which the data varies the most. Specifically, the first principal axis is the direction with the largest variance; the second principal axis is the direction with the largest variance, but under the constraint that it should be orthogonal to the first principal axis; and so on. This can be seen in Figure 10.11, where the principal axes are indeed aligned with the directions of largest variation of the data.

---

[15] This refers to the basic non-linear auto-encoder presented above. There are extensions to auto-encoders than enable learning a suitable value for q on the fly.

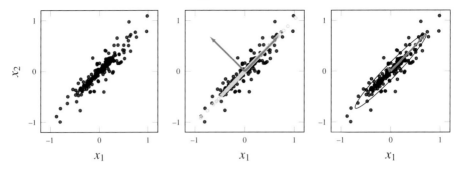

Figure 10.11 An illustration of PCA in $\mathbb{R}^2$. In the left panel, some data $\{\mathbf{x}_i\}_{i=1}^n$ is shown. The middle columns shows the first (red) and second (green) principal axes. These vectors are given by the first and second columns of $\mathbf{V}$, respectively. The plot also shows the data points when projected onto the first principal axis (pink), which are the same as the reconstructed data points obtained by a linear auto-encoder with $q = 1$ latent dimensions. The right panel show an ellipse fitted to the covariance matrix $\frac{1}{n}\mathbf{X}_0^\mathsf{T}\mathbf{X}_0$ of the data. The principal axes of the ellipse agree with the ones from the middle panel, but the width of the ellipse along each principal axis is scaled by the standard deviation in the corresponding direction. This illustrates that PCA finds a new basis for $\mathbb{R}^p$ which is rotated to align with the covariance of the data.

To formalise this, note that the (sample) covariance matrix of the data is given by

$$\frac{1}{n}\sum_{i=1}^n (\mathbf{x}_i - \bar{\mathbf{x}})(\mathbf{x}_i - \bar{\mathbf{x}})^\mathsf{T} = \frac{1}{n}\mathbf{X}_0^\mathsf{T}\mathbf{X}_0 = \frac{1}{n}\mathbf{V}\mathbf{\Sigma}^\mathsf{T}\mathbf{U}^\mathsf{T}\mathbf{U}\mathbf{\Sigma}\mathbf{V}^\mathsf{T} = \mathbf{V}\mathbf{\Lambda}\mathbf{V}^\mathsf{T}, \qquad (10.43)$$

where $\mathbf{\Lambda}$ is a $p \times p$ diagonal matrix with the values $\mathbf{\Lambda}_{ii} = \sigma_i^2/n$ on the diagonal. This can be recognised as an eigenvalue decomposition of the covariance matrix. Consequently, the principal axes (columns of $\mathbf{V}$) are the same as the eigenvectors of the covariance matrix. Furthermore, the eigenvalues are given by the squared singular values, normalised by n. The eigenvectors and eigenvalues of a covariance matrix can be said to define its 'geometry'. If we think about fitting a Gaussian distribution to the data and then drawing a level curve of the corresponding probability density function, then this will take the form of an ellipse. The shape of the ellipse can be identified with the covariance matrix of the distribution. Specifically, the principal axes of the ellipse correspond to the eigenvectors of the covariance matrix (which are the same as the principal axes of the data). Furthermore, the variances of the data in the directions of the principal axes are given by the corresponding eigenvalues. The width of the ellipse along each principal axis is proportional to the standard deviation of the data along this direction, which thus corresponds to the singular values of the data matrix! We illustrate this in the right panel of Figure 10.11.

As a final comment, we note that it can often be a good idea to standardise the data before applying PCA, in particular if the different variables $x_j, j = 1, \ldots, p$ have very different scales. Otherwise, the principal directions can be heavily biased towards certain variables simply because they are expressed in a unit with a dominant scale.

However, if the units and scales of the variables are meaningful for the problem at hand, it can also be argued that standardising counteracts the purpose of PCA since the intention is to find the directions with maximum variance. Thus, what is most appropriate needs to be decided on a case-by-case basis.

10.5 Further Reading

Many textbooks on machine learning contain more discussions and methods for unsupervised learning, including Bishop (2006), Hastie et al. (2009, Chapter 14), and Murphy (2012). A longer discussion on the GMM, and the related k-means, is found in Bishop (2006, Chapter 9). For a more detailed discussion on the LDA and QDA classifiers in particular, see Hastie et al. (2009, Section 4.3) or Mardia et al. (1979, Chapter 10).

For more discussion on the fundamental choice between generative and discriminative models, see Bishop and Lasserre (2007), Liang and Jordan (2008), Ng and Jordan (2001), and Xue and Titterington (2008) and also the textbook by Jebara (2004).

The book by Goodfellow, Bengio, et al. (2016) has more in-depth discussions about deep generative models (Chapter 20), auto-encoders (Chapter 14), and other approaches for representation learning (Chapter 15). Generative adversarial networks were introduced by Goodfellow, Pouget-Abadie, et al. (2014) and are reviewed by, among others, Creswell et al. (2018). Kobyzev et al. (2020) provide an overview of normalising flows.

Among the deep generative models that we have not discussed in this chapter, perhaps the most famous is the variational autoencoder (Diederik P. Kingma and Welling 2014, Diederik P. Kingma and Welling 2019, Rezende et al. 2014), which provides a way of connecting deep generative models with auto-encoders. This model has also been used for semi-supervised learning (Diederik P. Kingma, Rezende, et al. 2014) in a way which is similar to how we used the GMM in the semi-supervised setting.

11 User Aspects of Machine Learning

Dealing with supervised machine learning problems in practice is to a great extent an engineering discipline where many practical issues have to be considered and where the available amount of work-hours to undertake the development is often the limiting resource. To use this resource efficiently, we need to have a well-structured procedure for how to develop and improve the model. Multiple actions can potentially be taken. How do we know which action to take and if it is really worth spending the time implementing it? Is it, for example, worth spending an extra week collecting and labelling more training data, or should we do something else? These issues will be addressed in this chapter. Note that the layout of this chapter is thematic and does not necessarily represent the sequential order in which the different issues should be addressed.

11.1 Defining the Machine Learning Problem

Solving a machine learning problem in practice is an iterative process. We train the model, evaluate the model, and from there suggest an action for improvement and then train the model again, and so on. To do this efficiently, we need to be able to tell whether a new model is an improvement over the previous one or not. One way to evaluate the model after each iteration would be to put it into production (for example running a traffic-sign classifier in a self-driving car for a few hours). Besides the obvious safety issues, this evaluation procedure would be very time consuming and cumbersome. It would most likely also be inaccurate since it could still be hard to tell whether the proposed change was an actual improvement or not.

A better strategy is to automate this evaluation procedure without the need to put the model into production each time we want to evaluate its performance. We do this by putting aside a *validation* dataset and a *test* dataset and evaluate the performance using a scalar *evaluation metric*. The validation and test datasets together with the evaluation metric will define the machine learning problem that we are solving.

Training, Validation, and Test Data

In Chapter 4, we introduced the strategy of splitting the available data into training data, validation data, and test data, as repeated in Figure 11.1.

All available data

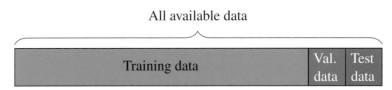

Figure 11.1 Splitting the data into training data, hold-out validation data, and test data.

- **Training data** is used for training the model.

- **Hold-out validation data** is used for comparing different model structures, choosing hyperparameters of the model, feature selection, and so on.

- **Test data** is used to evaluate the performance of the final model.

If the amount of available data is small, it is possible to perform k-fold cross-validation instead of putting aside hold-out validation data; the idea of how to use it in the iterative procedure is unchanged. To get a final estimate of the performance, test data is used.

In the iterative procedure, the hold-out validation data (or k-fold cross-validation) is used to judge if the new model is an improvement over the previous model. During this validation stage, we can also choose to train several new models. For example, if we have a neural network model and are interested in the number of hidden units to use in a certain layer, we can train several models, each with a different choice of hidden units. Afterwards, we pick the one that performs best on the validation data. The number of hidden units in a certain layer is one example of a hyperparameter. If we have more hyperparmeteters that we want to evaluate, we can perform a grid search over these parameters. In Section 5.6, we discuss hyper-parameter optimisation in more detail.

Eventually, we will effectively have used the validation data to compare many models. Depending on the size of the validation data, we might risk picking a model that does particularly well on the validation data in comparison to completely unseen data. To detect this and to get a fair estimate of the actual performance of a model, we use the test data, which has been used neither during training nor validation. If the performance on the validation data is substantially better than the performance on the test data, we have overfitted on the validation data. The easiest solution in that case would be to extend the size of the validation data. The test data should not be used repeatedly as a part of the training and model selection procedure. If we start making major decisions based on our test data, then the model will be adapted to the test data, and we can no longer trust that the test performance is an objective measure of the actual performance of our model.

It is important that both the validation data and the test data always come from the same data distribution, namely the data distribution that we are expecting to see when we put the model into production. If they do not stem from the same distribution, we are validating and improving our model towards something that is not represented in the test data and hence are 'aiming for the wrong target'. Usually, the training data is also expected to come from the same data distribution as the test and validation data, but this requirement can be relaxed if we have good reasons to do so. We will discuss this further in Section 11.2.

When splitting the data into training, validation, and test, *group leakage* could be a potential problem. Group leakage can occur if the data points are not really stochastically independent but are ordered into different groups. For example, in the medical domain many, X-ray images may belong to the same patient. In this case, if we do a random split over the images, different images belonging to the same patient will most likely end up both in the training and the validation set. If the model learns the properties of a certain patient, then the performance on the validation data might be better than what we could expect in production.

The solution to the group leakage problem is to do group partitioning. Instead of doing a random split over the data points, we do the split over the groups that the data points belong to. In the medical example above, that would mean that we do a random split of the patients rather than of the medical images. By this, we make sure that the images for a certain patient only end up in one of the datasets, and the leakage of unintentional information from the training data to the validation and test data is avoided.

Even though we advocate the use of validation and test data to improve and assess the performance of the model, we should eventually also evaluate the performance of the model in production. If we realise that the model is performing systematically worse in production than on the test data, we should try to find the reason for why this is the case. If possible, the best way of improving the model is to update the test data and validation data such they actually represent what we expect to see in production.

Size of Validation and Test Datasets

How much data should we set aside as hold-out validation data and test data, or should we even avoid setting aside hold-out validation data and use k-fold cross-validation instead? This depends on how much data we have available, what performance difference we plan to detect, and how many models we plan to compare. For example, if we have a classification model with a 99.8% accuracy and want to know if a new model is even better, a validation dataset of 100 data points will not be able to tell that difference. Also, if we plan to compare many (say, hundreds or more) different hyperparameter values and model structures using 100 validation data points, we will most likely overfit to that validation data.

If we have, say, 500 data points, one reasonable split could be 60%–20%–20% (that is 300–100–100 data points) for training–validation–test. With such a small validation dataset, we cannot afford to compare several hyperparameter values and model structures or to detect an improvement in accuracy of 0.1%. In this situation, we are probably better off using k-fold cross-validation to decrease the risk of overfitting to the validation data. Be aware, however, that the risk of overfitting the training data still exists even with k-fold cross-validation. We also still need to set aside test data if we want a final unbiased estimate of the performance.

Many machine learning problems have substantially larger datasets. Assume we have a dataset of 1 000 000 data points. In this scenario, one possible split could be 98%–1%–1%, that is, leaving 10 000 data points for validation and test, respectively, unless we really care about the very last decimals in performance. Here, k-fold cross-validation is of less use in comparison to the scenario with just 500 data points, since having all 99% = 98% + 1% (training + validation) available for training would make a small difference in comparison to using 'only' 98%. Also, the price for training k models (instead of only one) with this amount of data would be much higher.

Another advantage of having a separate validation dataset is that we can allow the training data to come from a slightly different distribution than the validation and test dataset, for example if that would enable us to find a much larger training dataset. We will discuss this more in Section 11.2.

Single Number Evaluation Metric

In Section 4.5, we introduced additional metrics besides the misclassification rate, such as precision, recall, and F1-score for evaluating binary classifiers. There is no unique answer to which metric is the most appropriate. What metric to pick is rather a part of the problem definition. To improve the model quickly and in a more automated fashion, it is advisable to agree on a single number evaluation metric, especially if a larger team of engineers is working on the problem.

The single number evaluation metric together with the validation data are what defines the supervised machine learning problem. Having an efficient procedure in place where we can evaluate the model on the hold-out validation data (or by k-fold cross-validation) using the metric allows us to speed up the iterations since we can quickly see if a proposed change to the model improves the performance or not. This is important in order to manage an efficient workflow of trying out and accepting or rejecting new models.

That being said, beside the single number evaluation metric, it is useful to monitor other metrics as well to reveal the tradeoffs being made. For example, we might develop the model with different end users in mind who care more or less about different metrics, but for practical reasons, we only train one model to accommodate them all. If we, based on these tradeoffs, realise that the single number evaluation metric we have chosen does not favour the properties we want a good model to have, we can always change that metric.

Baseline and Achievable Performance Level

Before working with the machine learning problem, it is a good idea to establish some reference points for the performance level of the model. A baseline is a very simple model that serves as a lower expected performance level. A baseline can, for example, bc to randomly pick an output value y_i from the training data and use that as the prediction. Another baseline for the regression problem is to take the mean of all output values in the training data and use that as the prediction. A corresponding baseline for a classification problem is to pick the most common class among class labels in the training data and use that for the prediction. For example, if we have a binary classification problem with 70% of the training data belonging to one class and 30% belonging to the other class, and we have chosen the accuracy as our performance metric, the accuracy for that baseline is 70%. The baseline is a lower threshold on the performance. We know that the model has to be better than this baseline.

Hopefully, the model will perform well beyond the naive baselines stated above. In addition, it is also good to define an achievable performance which is on par with the maximum performance we can expect from the model. For a regression problem, this performance is in theory limited by the irreducible error presented in Chapter 4, and for classification problems, the analogous concept is the so-called Bayes error rate. In practice, we might not have access to these theoretical bounds, but there are a few strategies for estimating them. For supervised problems that that are easily solved by human annotators, the human-level performance can serve as the achievable performance. Consider for example an image classification problem. If humans can identify the correct class with an accuracy of 99%, that serves as a reference point for what we can expect to achieve from our model. The achievable performance can also be based on what other state-of-the-art models on the same or a similar problem achieve. To compare the performance with the achievable performance gives us a reference point to assess the quality of the model. Also, if the model is close to the achievable performance, we might not be able to improve our model further.

11.2 Improving a Machine Learning Model

As already mentioned, solving a machine learning problem is an iterative procedure where we train, evaluate, and suggest actions for improvement, for instance by changing some hyperparameters or trying another model. How do we start this iterative procedure?

Try Simple Things First

A good strategy is to try simple things first. This could, for example, be to start with basic methods like k-NN or linear/logistic regression. Also, do not add extra adds-on like regularisation for the first model – this will come at a later stage when the basic model is up and running. A simple thing can also be to start with an already existing solution to the same or a similar problem, which you trust. For example, when building an image classifier, it can be simpler to start with an existing pretrained neural network and fine-tune one rather than handcrafting features from these images to be used with k-NN. Starting simple can also mean to consider only a subset of the available training data for the first model and then retrain the model on all the data if it looks promising. Also, avoid doing more data pre-processing than necessary for your first model, since we want to minimise the risk of introducing bugs early in the process. This first step not only involves writing code for learning your first simple model but also code for evaluating it on your validation data using your single number evaluation metric.

Trying simple things first allows us to start early with the iterative procedure of finding a good model. This is important since it might reveal important aspects of the problem formulation that we need to re-think before it makes sense to proceed with more complicated models. Also, if we start with a low-complexity model, it also reduces the risk of ending up with a too-complicated model, when a much simpler model would have been just as good (or even better).

Debugging your Model

Before proceeding, we should make sure that the code we have is producing what we are expecting it to do. The first obvious check is to make sure that the code runs without any errors or warnings. If it does not, use a debugging tool to spot the error. These are the easy bugs to spot.

The trickier bugs are those where the code is syntactically correct and runs without warnings but is still not doing what we expect it to do. The procedure of how to debug this depends on the model you have picked, but there are a few general tips:

- *Compare with baseline.* Compare you model performance on validation data with the baselines you have stated (see Section 11.1). If we do not manage to beat these baselines or are even worse than them, the code for training and evaluating the model might not be working as expected.

- *Overfit a small subset.* Try to overfit the model on a very small subset (e.g. as small as two data points) of the training data and make sure that we can achieve the best possible performance evaluated on that training data subset. If it is a parametric model, also aim for the lowest possible training cost.

When we have verified to the best of our ability that the code is bug-free and does what it is expected to do, we are ready to proceed. There are many actions that could be taken to improve the model – for example, changing the type of model, increasing/decreasing model complexity, changing input variables, collecting more data, correcting mislabelled data (if there is any), etc. What should we do next? Two possible strategies for guiding us to meaningful actions to improve the solution are by trading *training error and generalisation gap* or by applying *error analysis*.

Training Error vs. Generalisation Gap

With the notation from Chapter 4, the training error E_{train} is the performance of the model on training data, and the validation error $E_{\text{hold-out}}$ is the performance on hold-out validation data. In the validation step, we are interested in changing the model such that $E_{\text{hold-out}}$ is minimised. We can write the validation error as a sum of the training error and the generalisation gap:

$$E_{\text{hold-out}} = E_{\text{train}} + \underbrace{(E_{\text{hold-out}} - E_{\text{train}})}_{\approx \text{ generalisation gap}}. \qquad (11.1)$$

In words, the generalisation gap is approximated by the difference between the validation error $E_{\text{hold-out}}$ and the training error E_{train}.[1]

We can easily compute the training error E_{train} and the generalisation gap $E_{\text{hold-out}} - E_{\text{train}}$; we just have to evaluate the error on the training data and validation data, respectively. By computing these quantities, we can get good guidance for what changes we may consider for the next iteration.

As we discussed in Chapter 4, if the training error is small and the generalisation gap is big (E_{train} small, $E_{\text{hold-out}}$ big), we have typically overfitted the model. The opposite situation, big training error and small generalisation gap (both E_{train} and $E_{\text{hold-out}}$ big), typically indicates underfitting.

If we want to reduce the generalisation gap $E_{\text{hold-out}} - E_{\text{train}}$ (reduce overfitting), the following actions can be explored:

- *Use a less flexible model.* If we have a very flexible model, we might start overfitting to the training data, that is, E_{train} is much smaller than $E_{\text{hold-out}}$. If we use a less flexible model, we also reduce this gap.

- *Use more regularisation.* Using more regularisation will reduce the flexibility of the model and hence also reduce the generalisation gap. Read more about regularisation in Section 5.3

- *Early stopping* For models that are trained iteratively, we can stop the training before reaching the minimum. One good practice is to monitor $E_{\text{hold-out}}$ during training and stop if it starts increasing; see Example 5.7.

- *Use bagging*, or use more ensemble members if we already are using it. Bagging is a method for reducing the variance of the model, which typically also means that we reduce the generalisation gap; see more in Section 7.1.

- *Collect more training data.* If we collect more training data, the model is less prone to overfit that extended training dataset and is forced to only focus on aspects which generalise to the validation data.

---

[1] This can be related to (4.11), if approximating $\bar{E}_{\text{train}} \approx E_{\text{train}}$ and $\bar{E}_{\text{new}} \approx E_{\text{hold-out}}$. If we use k-fold cross validation instead of hold-out validation data, we use $\bar{E}_{\text{new}} \approx E_{k\text{-fold}}$ when computing the generalisation gap.

If we want to reduce the training error E_{train} (reduce underfitting), the following actions can be considered:

- *Use a more flexible model* that is able to fit the training data better. This can be changing a hyperparameter in the model we are considering – for example decreasing k in k-NN– or changing the model to a more flexible one – for example by replacing a linear regression model by a deep neural network.

- *Extend the set of input variables.* If we suspect that there are more input variables that carry information, we might want to extend the data with these input variables.

- *Use less regularisation.* This can, of course, only be applied if regularisation is used at all.

- *Train the model for longer.* For models that are trained iteratively, we can reduce E_{train} by training for longer.

It is usually a balancing act between reducing the training error and the generalisation gap, and measures to decrease one of them might result in an increase of the other. This balancing act is also related to the bias–variance tradeoff discussed in Example 4.3.

We summarise the above discussion in Figure 11.2. Fortunately, evaluating E_{train} and $E_{\text{hold-out}}$ is cheap. We only have to evaluate the model on the training data and the validation data, respectively. Yet, it gives us good advice on what actions to take next. Besides suggesting what action to explore next, this procedure also tells us what *not* to do: If $E_{\text{train}} \gg E_{\text{hold-out}} - E_{\text{train}}$, collecting more training data will most likely not help. Furthermore, if $E_{\text{train}} \ll E_{\text{hold-out}} - E_{\text{train}}$, a more flexible model will most likely not help.

Learning Curves

Of the different methods mentioned to reduce the generalisation gap, collecting more training data is often the simplest and most reliable strategy. However, in contrast to the other techniques, collecting and labelling more data is often significantly more time consuming. Before collecting more data, we would like to tell how much improvement we can expect. By plotting learning curves, we can get such an indication.

In a learning curve, we train models and evaluate E_{train} and $E_{\text{hold-out}}$ using different sizes of training dataset. For example, we can train different models with 10%, 20%, 30%, ... of the available training data and plot how E_{train} and $E_{\text{hold-out}}$ vary with the amount of training data. By extrapolating these plots, we can get an indication of the improvement on the generalisation gap that we can expect by collecting more data.

In Figure 11.3, two sets of learning curves for two different scenarios are depicted. First, note that previously we evaluated E_{train} and $E_{\text{hold-out}}$ only for the rightmost

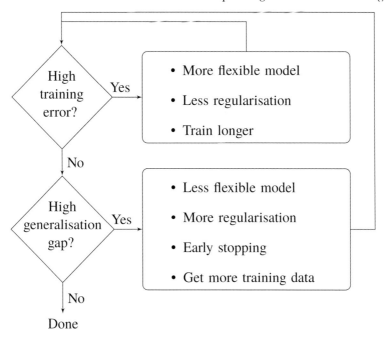

Figure 11.2 The iterative procedure of improving a model based on the decomposition of the validation error into the training error and generalisation gap.

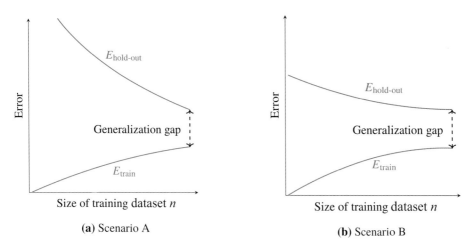

(a) Scenario A   **(b)** Scenario B

Figure 11.3 Learning curve for two different scenarios. In Scenario A, we can expect an improvement in the generalisation gap by collecting more training data, whereas in Scenario B, we are less likely to see an immediate improvement by adding more data.

point in these graphs using all our available data. However, these plots reveal more information about the impact of the training dataset size on the performance of the model. In the two scenarios depicted in Figure 11.3, we have the same values for E_{train} and $E_{\text{hold-out}}$ if we train the model using all the available training data. However, by extrapolating the learning curves for E_{train} and $E_{\text{hold-out}}$ in these two scenarios, it is likely that in Scenario A, we can reduce the generalisation gap much more than we can in Scenario B. Hence, in Scenario A, collecting more training data is more beneficial than in Scenario B. By extrapolating the learning curves, you can also answer the question of how much extra data is needed to reach some desired performance. Plotting these learning curves does not require much extra effort we only have to train a few more models on subsets of our training data. However, it can provide valuable insight on whether it is worth the extra effort of collecting more training data and how much extra data you should collect.

Error Analysis

Another strategy to identify actions that can improve the model is to perform *error analysis*. Below we only describe error analysis for classification problems, but the same strategy can be applied to regression problems as well.

In error analysis, we manually look at a subset, say 100 data points, of the validation data that the model classified incorrectly. Such an analysis does not take much time but might give valuable clues as to what type of data the model is struggling with and how much improvement we can expect by fixing these issues. We illustrate the procedure with an example.

Example 11.1 Error analysis applied to vehicle detection

Consider a classification problem of detecting cars, bicycles, and pedestrians in an image. The model takes an image as input and outputs one of the four classes `car`, `bike`, `pedestrian`, or `other`. Assume that the model has a classification accuracy of 90% on validation data.

When looking at a subset of 100 images that were misclassified in the validation data, we make the following observations:

- All 10 images of class `pedestrian` that were incorrectly classified as `bike` where taken in dark conditions with the pedestrian being equipped with safety reflectors.

- 30 images were substantially tilted.

- 15 images were mislabelled.

From this observation we can conclude:

- If we launch a project for improving the model to classify pedestrians with safety reflectors as `pedestrian` and not incorrectly as `bike`, an improvement of at most a ~1% (a tenth of the 10% classification error rate) can be expected.

- If we improve the performance on tilted images, an improvement of at most ~3% can be expected.

- If we correct all mislabelled data, an improvement of at most ~1.5% can be expected.

Following the example, we get an indication on what improvement we can expect by tackling these three issues. These numbers should be considered as the maximal possible improvement. To prioritise which aspect to focus on, we should also consider what strategies are available for improving them, how much progress we expect to make applying these strategies, and how much effort we would have to invest fixing these issues.

For example, to improve the performance on tilted images, we could try to extend the training data by augmenting it with more tilted images. This strategy could be investigated without too much extra effort by augmenting the training data with tilted versions of the training data points that we already have. Since this could be applied fairly quickly and has a maximal performance increase of 3%, it seems to be a good thing to try out.

To improve the performance on the images of pedestrians with safety reflectors, one approach would be to collect more images in dark conditions of pedestrians with safety reflector. This obviously requires some more manual work, and it can be questioned if it is worth the effort since it would only give a performance improvement of at most 1%. However, for this application, you could also argue that this 1% is of extra importance.

Regarding the mislabelled data, the obvious action to take to improve on this issue is to manually go through the data and correct these labels. In the example above, we may say it is not quite worth the effort to get an improvement of 1.5%. However, assume that we have improved the model with other actions to an accuracy of 98.0% on validation data and that still 1.5% of the total error is due to mislabelled data; this issue is now quite relevant to address if we want to improve the model further. Remember, the purpose of the validation data is to choose between different models. This purpose is degraded when the majority of the reported error on validation is due to incorrectly labelled data rather than the actual performance of the model.

There are two levels of ambition for correcting the labels:

(i) Go through all data points in the validation/test data and correct the labels.

(ii) Go through all data points, including the training data, and correct the labels.

The advantage of approach (i), in comparison to approach (ii), is the lower amount of work it requires. Assume, for example, that we have made a 98%–1%–1% split of training-validation-test data. Then there is 50 times less data to process in comparison to approach (ii). Unless the mislabeling is systematic, correcting the labels in the training data will not necessarily pay off. Also, note that correcting labels in only test and validation data does not necessarily increase the performance of a model in production, but it will give us a fairer estimate of the actual performance of the model.

Applying the data cleaning to validation and test data only, as suggested in approach (i), will result in the training data coming from a slightly different distribution than the validation and test data. However, if we are eager to correct the mislabelled data in the training data as well, a good recommendation would still be to start correcting validation and test data only, and then use the techniques in the following section to see how much extra performance we can expect by cleaning the training data as well before launching that substantially more labor-intensive data cleaning project.

In some domains, for example medical imaging, the labelling can be difficult, and two different lablers might not agree on the label for the very same data point. This agreement between labellers is also called inter-rater reliability. It can be wise to check this metric on a subset of your data by assigning multiple labellers for that data. If the inter-rater reliability is low, you might want to consider addressing this issue. This can, for example, be done by assigning multiple labellers to all data points in the validation and test data and, if you can afford the extra labelling cost, also to the training data. For the samples where labellers do not agree, the majority vote can be used for these labels.

Mismatched Training and Validation/Test Data

As already pointed out in Chapter 4, we should strive to let the training data come from the same distribution as the validation and test data. However, there are situations where, for different reasons, we can accept the training data coming from a slightly different distribution than the validation and test data. One reason was presented in the previous section where we chose to correct mislabelled data in the validation and test data but not necessarily to invest the time to do the same correction to the training data.

Another reason for mismatched training and validation/test data is that we might have access to another, substantially larger dataset which comes from a slightly different distribution than the data we care about but is similar enough that the advantage of having a larger training data outweighs the disadvantage of that data mismatch. This scenario is further described in Section 11.3.

If we have a mismatch between training data and validation/test data, that mismatch contributes to yet another error source of the final validation error $E_{\text{hold-out}}$ that we care about. We want to estimate the magnitude of that error source. This can be done by revising the training–validation–test data split. From the training data, we can carve out a separate *training-validation* dataset, see Figure 11.4. That dataset is neither used for training nor for validation. However, we do evaluate the performance of our model on that dataset as well. As before, the remaining part of the training data is used for training, the validation data is used for comparing different model structures, and test data is used for evaluating the final performance of the model.

This modified data split also allows us to revise the decomposition in (11.1) to include this new error source:

$$E_{\text{hold-out}} = E_{\text{train}} + \underbrace{(E_{\text{train-val}} - E_{\text{train}})}_{\approx \text{ generalisation gap}} + \underbrace{(E_{\text{hold-out}} - E_{\text{train-val}})}_{\approx \text{ train-val mismatch}}, \qquad (11.2)$$

where $E_{\text{train-val}}$ is the performance of the model on the new training-validation data and where, as before, $E_{\text{hold-out}}$ and E_{train} are the performances on the validation and

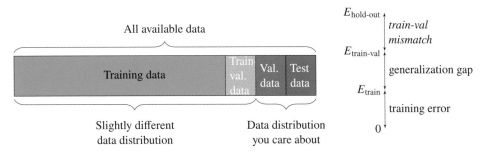

Figure 11.4 Revising the training–validation–test data split by carving out a separate training-validation dataset from the training data.

training data, respectively. With this new decomposition, the term $E_{\text{train-val}} - E_{\text{train}}$ is an approximation of the generalisation gap, that is, how well the model generalises to unseen data *of the same distribution* as the training data, whereas the term $E_{\text{hold-out}} - E_{\text{train-val}}$ is the error related to the training-validation data mismatch. If the term $E_{\text{hold-out}} - E_{\text{train-val}}$ is small in comparison to the other two terms, it seems likely that the training-validation data mismatch is not a big problem and that it is better to focus on techniques reducing the other training error and the generalisation gap as we talked about earlier. On the other hand, if $E_{\text{hold-out}} - E_{\text{train-val}}$ is significant, the data mismatch does have an impact, and it might be worth investing time reducing that term. For example, if the mismatch is caused by the fact that we only corrected labels in the validation and test data, we might want to consider correcting labels for the training data as well.

11.3 What If We Cannot Collect More Data?

We have seen in Section 11.2 that collecting more data is a good strategy to reduce the generalisation gap and hence reduce overfitting. However, collecting labelled data is usually expensive and sometimes not even possible. What can we do if we cannot afford to collect more data but still want to benefit from the advantages that a larger dataset would give? In this section, a few approaches are presented.

Extending the Training Data with Slightly Different Data

As already mentioned, there are situations where we can accept the training data coming from a slightly different distribution than the validation and test data. One reason to accept this is if we then would have access to a substantially larger training dataset.

Consider a problem with 10 000 data points, representing the data that we would also expect to get when the model is deployed in production. We call this Dataset A. We also have another dataset with 200 000 data points that come from a slightly different distribution but which is similar enough that we think exploiting information from that data can improve the model. We call this Dataset B. Some options to proceed would be the following:

- **Option 1** Use only Dataset A and split it into training, validation, and test data.

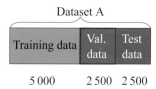

The advantage of this option is that we only train, validate, and evaluate on Dataset A, which is also the type of data that we want our model to perform well on. The disadvantage is that we have quite few data points, and we do not exploit potentially useful information in the larger Dataset B.

- **Option 2** Use both Dataset A and Dataset B. Randomly shuffle the data and split it into training, validation, and test data.

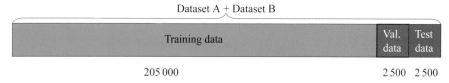

The advantage over option 1 is that we have a lot more data available for training. However, the disadvantage is that we mainly evaluate the model on data from Dataset B, whereas we want our model to perform well on data from Dataset A.

- **Option 3** Use both Dataset A and Dataset B. Use data points from Dataset A for validation data and test data and some in the training data. Dataset B only goes into the training data.

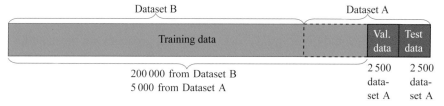

Similar to option 2, the advantage is that we have more training data in comparison to option 1, and in contrast to option 2, we now evaluate the model on data from Dataset A, which is the data we want our model to perform well on. However, one disadvantage is that the training data no longer has the same distribution as the validation and test data.

From these three options, we would recommend either option 1 or 3. In option 3, we exploit the information available in the much larger Dataset B but evaluate only on the data we want the model to perform well on (Dataset A). The main disadvantage with option 3 is that the training data no longer comes from the same distribution as the validation data and test data. In order to quantify how big an impact this mismatch has on the final performance, the techniques described in Section 11.2 can be used. To push the model to do better on data from Dataset A during training, we can also consider giving data from Dataset A a higher weight in the cost function than data from Dataset B, or simply upsample the data points in Dataset A that belong to the training data.

There is no guarantee that adding Dataset B to the training data will improve the model. If that data is very different from Dataset A, it can also do harm, and we might be better off just using Dataset A as suggested in option 1. Using option 2 is generally not recommended since we would then (in contrast to option 1 and 3) evaluate our model on data which is different from that which we want it to perform well on. Hence, if the data in Dataset A is scarce, prioritise putting it into the validation and test datasets and, if we can afford it, some of it in the training data.

Data Augmentation

Data augmentation is another approach to extending the training data without the need to collect more data. In data augmentation, we construct new data points by duplicating the existing data with invariant transformations. This is especially common for images, where such invariant transformations can be cropping, rotation, vertical flipping, noise addition, colour shift, and contrast change. For example, if we vertically flip an image of a cat, it still displays a cat; see the examples Figure 11.5. One should be aware that some objects are not invariant to some of these operations. For example, a flipped image of a digit is not a valid transformation. In some cases such operations can even make the object resemble an object from another class. If we were to flip an image of a '6' both vertically and horizontally, that image would resemble a '9'. Hence, before applying data augmentation, we need to know and understand the problem and the data. Based on that knowledge we can identify valid invariants and suggest which transformations that can be applied to augment the data that we already have.

To apply data augmentation offline before the training would increase the required amount of storage and is hence only recommended for small datasets. For many models and training procedures, we can instead apply it online during training. For example, if we train a parametric model using stochastic gradient descent (see Section 5.5), we can apply the transformation directly on the data that goes into the current mini-batch without the need to store the transformed data.

Transfer Learning

Transfer learning is yet another technique that allows us to exploit information from more data than the dataset we have. In transfer learning we use the

Figure 11.5 Example of data augmentation applied to images. An image of a cat has been reproduced by tilting, vertical flipping, and cropping.
source: Image of cat is reprinted from `https://commons.wikimedia.org/wiki/File:Stray_Cat,_Nafplio.jpg` and is in the public domain.

knowledge from a model that has been trained on a different task with a different dataset and then apply that model in solving a different, but slightly related, problem.

Transfer learning is especially common for sequential model structures such as the neural network models introduced in Chapter 6. Consider an application where we want to detect whether a certain type of skin cancer is malignant or benign, and for this task we have $100\,000$ labelled images of skin cancer. We call this Task A. Instead of training the full neural network from scratch on this data, we can reuse an already pretrained network from another image classification task (Task B), which preferably has been trained on a much larger dataset, not necessarily containing images even resembling skin cancer tumors. By using the weights from the model trained for Task B and only train the last few layers on the data for Task A, we can get a better model than if the whole model would had been trained on only the data for Task A. The procedure is also displayed in Figure 11.6. The intuition is that the layers closer to the input accomplish tasks that are generic for all types of images, such as extracting lines, edges and corners in the image, whereas the layers closer to the output are more specific to the particular problem.

In order for transfer learning to be applicable, we need the two tasks to have the same type of input (in the example above, images of the same dimension). Further, for transfer learning to be an attractive option, the task that we transfer from should have been trained on substantially more data than the task we transfer to.

Learning from Unlabelled Data

We can also improve our model by learning from an additional (typically much larger) dataset without outputs, so called unlabelled data. Two families of such methods are semi-supervised learning and self-supervised learning. In our description below, we call our original dataset with both inputs and output Dataset A and our unlabelled dataset Dataset B.

In semi-supervised learning, we formulate and train a generative model for the inputs in both Dataset A and Dataset B. The generative model of the inputs and the

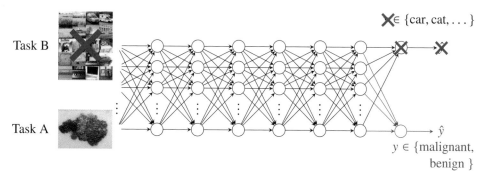

Figure 11.6 In transfer learning, we reuse models that have been trained on a different task than the one we are interested in. Here we reuse a model which has been trained on images displaying all sorts of classes, such as cars, cats, and computers, and later train only the last few layers on the skin cancer data which is the task we are interested in.

source: Skin cancer sample is reprinted from `https://visualsonline.cancer.gov/details.cfm?imageid=9186` and is in the public domain.

supervised model for Dataset A are then trained jointly. The idea is that the generative model on the inputs, which is trained on the much larger dataset, improves the performance of the supervised task. Semi-supervised learning is further described in Chapter 10.

In self-supervised learning, we instead use Dataset B in a very similar way as we do in transfer learning described previously. Hence, we pretrain the model based on Dataset B and then fine-tune that model using Dataset A. Since Dataset B does not contain any outputs, we automatically generate outputs for Dataset B and pretrain our model with these generated outputs. The automatically generated outputs can, for example, be a subset of the input variables or a transformation thereof. As in transfer learning, the idea is that the pretrained model learns to extract features from the input data which then can be used to improve the training of the supervised task that we are interested in. Also, if we don't have an additional unlabelled Dataset B, we can also use self-supervised learning on the inputs in Dataset A as the pretraining before training on the supervised task on that dataset.

11.4 Practical Data Issues

Besides the amount and distribution of data, a machine learning engineer may also face other data issues. In this section, we will discuss some of the most common ones; outliers, missing data, and if some features can be removed.

Outliers

In some applications, a common issue is *outliers*, meaning data points whose outputs do not follow the overall pattern. Two typical examples of outliers are sketched in Figure 11.7. Even though the situation in Figure 11.7 looks simple, it can be quite hard to find outliers when the data has more dimensions and is harder to

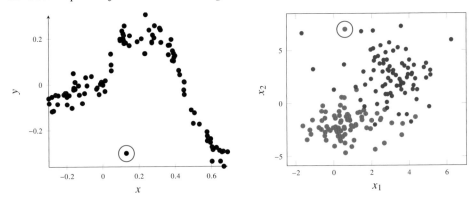

Figure 11.7 Two typical examples of outliers (marked with red circle) in regression (left) and classification (right), respectively.

visualise. The error analysis discussed in Section 11.2, which amounts to inspecting misclassified data points in the validation data, is a systematic way to discover outliers.

When facing a problem with outliers, the first question to ask is whether the outliers are meant to be captured by the model or not. Do the encircled data points in Figure 11.7 describe an interesting phenomenon that we would like to predict, or are they irrelevant noise (possibly originating from a poor data collection process)? The answer to this question depends on the actual problem and ambition. Since outliers by definition (no matter their origin) do not follow the overall pattern, they are typically hard to predict.

If the outliers are not of any interest, the first thing we should do is to consult the data provider and identify the reason for the outliers and if something could be changed in the data collection process to avoid these outliers, for example replacing a malfunctioning sensor. If the outliers are unavoidable, there are basically two approaches one could take. The first approach is to simply delete (or replace) the outliers in the data. Unfortunately this means that one has to first find the outliers, which can be hard, but sometimes some thresholding and manual inspection (that is, look at all data points whose output value is smaller/larger than some value) can help. Once the outliers are removed from the data, one can proceed as usual. The second approach is to instead make sure that the learning algorithm is robust against outliers, for example by using a robust loss function such as absolute error instead of squared error loss (see Chapter 5 for more details). Making a model more robust amounts, to some extent, to making it less flexible. However, robustness amounts to making the model less flexible in a particular way, namely by putting less emphasis on the data points whose predictions are severely wrong.

If the outliers are of interest to the prediction, they are not really an issue but rather a challenge. We have to use a model that is flexible enough to capture the behavior (small bias). This has to be done with care since very flexible models have a high risk of also overfitting to noise. If it turns out that the outliers in a classification problem are indeed interesting and in fact are from an underrepresented class, we are rather facing an imbalanced problem; see Section 4.5.

Missing Data

A common practical issue is that certain values are sporadically missing in the data. Throughout this book so far, the data has always consisted of complete input-output pairs $\{\mathbf{x}_i, y_i\}_{i=1}^n$, and *missing data* refers to the situation where some (or a few) values from either the input $\mathbf{x}_i$ or the output y_i, for some i, are missing. If the output y_i is missing, we can also refer to it as *unlabelled* data. It is a common practice to denote missing data in a computer with NaN (not a number), but less obvious codings also exists, such as 0. Reasons for missing data could, for instance, be a malfunctioning sensor or similar issues at data collection time, or that certain values for some reason have been discarded during the data processing.

As for outliers, a sensible first option is to figure out the reason for the missing data. By going back to the data provider, this issue could potentially be fixed and the missing data recovered. If this is not possible, there is no universal solution for how to handle missing data. There is, however, some common practice which can serve as a guideline. First of all, if the output y_i is missing, the data point is useless for supervised machine learning[2] and can be discarded. In the following, we assume that the missing values are only in the input $\mathbf{x}_i$.

The easiest way to handle missing data is to discard the entire data points ('rows in $\mathbf{X}$') where data is missing. That is, if some feature is missing in $\mathbf{x}_i$, the entire input $\mathbf{x}_i$ and its corresponding output value y_i are discarded from the data, and we are left with a smaller dataset. If the dataset that remains after this procedure still contains enough data, this approach can work well. However, if this would lead to too small a dataset, it is of course problematic. More subtle, but also important, is the situation when the data is missing in a systematic fashion, for example that missing data is more common for a certain class. In such a situation, discarding data points with missing data would lead to a mismatch between reality and training data, which may degrade the performance of the learned model further.

If missing data is common, but only for certain features, another easy option is to not use those features ('column of $\mathbf{X}$') which are suffering from missing data. Whether or not this is a fruitful approach depends on the situation.

Instead of discarding the missing data, it is possible to impute (fill in) the missing values using some heuristics. Say, for example, that the jth feature x_j is missing from data point $\mathbf{x}_i$. A simple imputation strategy would be to take the mean or median of x_j for all other data points (where it is not missing) or the mean or median of x_j for all data points of the same class (if it is a classification problem). It is also possible to come up with more complicated imputation strategies, but each imputation strategy implies some assumptions about the problem. Those assumptions might or might

---

[2]The 'partly labelled data' problem is a semi-supervised problem, which is introduced in Chapter 10 but not covered in depth by this book.

not be fulfilled, and it is hard to guarantee that imputation will help the performance in the end. A poor imputation can even degrade the performance compared to just discarding the missing data.

Some methods are actually able to handle missing data to some extent (which we have not discussed in this book), but under rather restrictive assumptions. Such an example is that the data is 'completely missing at random', meaning that which data is missing is completely uncorrelated to what value it, and other features and the output, would have had, had it not been missing. Assumptions like these are very strong and rarely met in practice, and the performance can be severely degraded if those assumptions are not fulfilled.

Feature Selection

When working with a supervised machine learning problem, the question of whether all available input variables/features contribute to the performance is often relevant. Removing the right feature is indeed a type of regularisation which can possibly reduce overfitting and improve the performance, and the data collection might be simplified if a certain variable does not even have to be collected. Selecting between the available features is an important task for the machine learning engineer.

The connection between regularisation and feature selection becomes clear by considering L^1 regularisation. Since the main feature of L^1 regularisation is that the learned parameter vector $\widehat{\boldsymbol{\theta}}$ is sparse, it effectively removes the influence of certain features. If using a model where L^1 regularisation is possible, we can study $\widehat{\boldsymbol{\theta}}$ to see which features we simply can remove from the dataset. However, if we cannot or prefer not to use L^1 regularisation, we can alternatively use a more manual approach to feature selection.

Remember that our overall goal is to obtain a small new data error E_{new}, which we for most methods estimate using cross-validation. We can therefore always use cross-validation to tell whether we gain or lose by including a certain feature in **x**. Depending on the amount of data, evaluating all possible combinations of removed features might not be a good idea, either due to computational aspects or the risk of overfitting. There are, however, some rules of thumb that can possibly give us some guidance on which features we should investigate more closely for whether they contribute to the performance or not.

To get a feeling for the different features, we can look at the correlation between each feature and the output and thereby get a clue about which features might be more informative about the output. If there is little correlation between a feature and the output, it is possibly a useless feature, and we could investigate further if we can remove it. However, looking one feature at a time can be misleading, and there are cases where this would lead to the wrong conclusion – for example the case in Example 8.1.

Another approach is to explore whether there are redundant features, with the reasoning that having two features that (essentially) contain the same information will lead to an increased variance compared to having only one feature with the same information. Based on this argument, one may look at the pairwise correlation between the features and investigate removing features that have a high correlation to other features. This approach is somewhat related to PCA (Chapter 10).

11.5 Can I Trust my Machine Learning Model?

Supervised machine learning presents a powerful family of all-purpose general black-box methods and has demonstrated impressive performance in many applications. The main argument for supervised machine learning is, frankly, that it works well empirically. However, depending on the requirements of the application, supervised machine learning also has a potential shortcoming, in that it relies on 'repeating patterns seen in training data' rather than 'deduction from a set of carefully written rules'.

Understanding Why a Certain Prediction was Made

In some applications, there might be an interest in 'understanding' why a certain prediction was made by a supervised machine learning model, for example in medicine or law. Unfortunately, the underlying design philosophy in machine learning is to deliver good predictions rather than to explain them.

With a simpler model, like the ones in Chapters 2–3, it can to some degree be possible for an engineer to inspect the learned model and explain the 'reasoning' behind it for a non-expert. For more complicated models, however, it can be a rather hard task.

There are, however, methods at the forefront of research, and the situation may look different in the future. A related topic is that of so-called adversarial examples, which essentially amounts to finding an input $\mathbf{x}'$ which is as close as possible to $\mathbf{x}$ but gives a different prediction. In the image classification setting, it can, for example, be the problem of having a picture of a car being predicted as a dog by only changing a few pixel values.

Worst Case Guarantees

In the view of this book, a supervised machine learning model is good if it attains a small E_{new}. It is, however, important to remember that E_{new} is a *statistical* claim, under the assumption that the training and/or test data resembles the reality which the model will face once it is put into production. And even if that non-trivial assumption is satisfied, there are no claims about how badly the model will predict in the worst individual cases. This is indeed a shortcoming of supervised machine learning and potentially also a show-stopper for some applications.

Simpler and more interpretable models, like logistic regression and trees, for example, can be inspected manually in order to deduce the 'worst case' that could happen. By looking at the leaf nodes in a regression tree, as an example, it is possible to give an interval within which all predictions will lie. With more complicated models, like random forests and deep learning, it is very hard to give any worst case guarantees about how inaccurate the model can be in its predictions when faced with some particular input. However, an extensive testing scheme might reveal some of the potential issues.

11.6 Further Reading

The user aspects of machine learning is a fairly under-explored area, both in academic research publications and in standard textbooks on machine learning. Two exceptions are Ng (2019) and Burkov (2020), from which parts of this chapter have been inspired. Regarding data augmentation, see Shorten and Khoshgoftaar (2019) for a review of different techniques for images.

Some of the research on 'understanding' why a certain prediction was made by a machine learning method is summarised by Guidotti et al. (2018).

12 Ethics in Machine Learning

by David Sumpter[1]

In this chapter, we give three examples of ethical challenges that arise in connection to machine learning applications. These are all examples where an apparently 'neutral' design choice in how we implement or measure the performance of a machine learning model leads to an unexpected consequence for its users or for society. For each case study, we give concrete application examples. In general, we will emphasise an *ethics through awareness* approach, where instead of attempting a technical solution to ethical dilemmas, we explain how they impact our role as machine learning engineers.

There are many more ethical issues that arise from applications of machine learning than are covered in this chapter. These range from legal issues of privacy of medical and social data collected on individuals (Pasquale 2015); through on-line advertising which, for example, identifies the most vulnerable people in society and targets them with adverts for gambling, unnecessary health services, and high interest loans (O'Neil 2016); to the use of machine learning to develop weapons and oppressive technology (Russell et al. 2015). In addition to this, there is significant evidence of gender and racial discrimination in the tech industry (Alfrey and Twine 2017).

These issues are important (in many cases more important to society than the issues we cover here), and the qualified data scientist should have become aware of them. But they are largely beyond the scope of this book. Instead, here we look specifically at examples where the technical properties of the machine learning techniques we have learnt so far become unexpectedly intertwined with ethical issues. It turns out that just this narrow subset of challenges is still substantial in size.

12.1 Fairness and Error Functions

At first sight, the choice of an error function (4.1) might appear an entirely technical issue, without any ethical ramifications. After all, the aim of the error function is to find out how well a model has performed on test data. It should be chosen so that we can tell whether our method works as we want it to. We might (naively) assume that

---

[1]Please cite this chapter as Sumpter (2021) **Ethics in machine learning**, In: *Machine Learning: A First Course for Engineers and Scientists*, Cambridge University Press

Table 12.1 Proportion of people shown and/or interested in a course for an imagined machine learning algorithm. The top table is for non-Swedes (in this case we can think of them as citizens of another country, but who are eligible to study in Sweden); the bottom table is for Swedes.

Non-Swedes	Not Interested $(y = -1)$	Interested $(y = 1)$
Not recommended course $(\widehat{y}(\mathbf{x}) = -1)$	TN = 300	FN = 100
Recommended course $(\widehat{y}(\mathbf{x}) = 1)$	FP = 100	TP = 100

Swedes	Not Interested $(y = -1)$	Interested $(y = 1)$
Not recommended course $(\widehat{y}(\mathbf{x}) = -1)$	TN = 400	FN = 50
Recommended course $(\widehat{y}(\mathbf{x}) = 1)$	FP = 350	TP = 400

a technical decision of this nature is neutral. To investigate how such an assumption plays out, let's look at an example.

Fairness Through Awareness

Imagine your colleagues have created a supervised machine learning model to find people who might be interested in studying at a university in Sweden, based on their activity on a social networking site. Their algorithm either recommends or doesn't recommend the course to users. They have tested it on two different groups of people (600 non-Swedes and 1 200 Swedes), all of whom would be eligible for the course and have given permission for their data to be used. As a test, your colleagues first applied the method, then asked the potential students whether or not they would be interested in the course. To illustrate their results, they produced the confusion matrices shown in Table 12.1 for non-Swedes and Swedes.

Let's focus on the question of whether the algorithm performs equally well on both groups, non-Swedes and Swedes. We might call this property 'fairness'. Does the method treat the two groups fairly? To answer this question, we first need to quantify fairness. One suggestion here would be ask if the method performs equally well for both groups. Referring to Table 4.1, and Chapter 4 in general, we see that one way of measuring performance is to use misclassification error. For Table 12.1, the misclassification error is $(100 + 100)/600 = 1/3$ for non-Swedes and $(50 + 350)/1\,200 = 1/3$ for Swedes. It has the same performance for both categories.

It is now that alarm bells should start to ring about equating fairness with performance. If we look at the false negatives (FN) for both cases, we see that there are twice as many non-Swede FN cases as Swedish cases (100 vs. 50), despite their being twice as many Swedes as non-Swedes. This can be made more precise by calculating the false negative rate (or miss rate), i.e. FN/(TP+FN) (again see Table 4.1). This is $100/(100 + 100) = 1/2$ for non-Swedes and $50/(400 + 50) = 1/9$

for Swedes. This new result can be put in context by noting that Swedes have a slightly greater tendency to be interested in the course (450 out of 1 200 vs. 200 out of 600). However, an interested non-Swede is 4.5 times more likely *not* to be recommended the course than an interested Swede. A much larger difference than that observed in the original data.

There are other fairness calculations we can do. Imagine we are concerned with intrusive advertising, where people are shown adverts that are uninteresting for them. The probability of experiencing a recommendation that is uninteresting is the false positive rate, FP/(TN+FP). This is $100/(300 + 100) = 1/4$ for non-Swedes and $350/(350 + 400) = 7/15$ for Swedes. Swedes receive almost twice as many unwanted recommendations as non-Swedes. Now it is the Swedes who are discriminated against!

This is a fictitious example, but it serves to illustrate the first point we now want to make: *There is no single function for measuring fairness.* In some applications, fairness is perceived as misclassification; in others it is false negative rates, and in others it is expressed in terms of false positives. It depends strongly on the application. If the data above had been for a criminal sentencing application, where 'positives' are sentenced to longer jail terms, then problems with the false positive rate would have serious consequences for those sentenced on the basis of it. If it was for a medical test, where those individuals not picked up by the test had a high probability of dying, then the false negative rate is most important for judging fairness.

As a machine learning engineer, you should never tell a client that your algorithm is fair. You should instead explain how your model performs in various aspects related to their conception of fairness. This insight is well captured by Dwork and colleagues' article, 'Fairness Through Awareness' (Dwork et al. 2012), which is recommended further reading. Being fair is about being aware of the decisions we make both in the design and in reporting the outcome of our model.

Complete Fairness Is Mathematically Impossible

We now come to an even more subtle point: *It is mathematically impossible to create models that fulfil all desirable fairness criteria.* Let's demonstrate this point with another example, this time using a real application. The Compas algorithm was developed by a private company, Northpointe, to help with criminal sentencing decisions. The model used logistic regression with input variables including age at first arrest, years of education, and questionnaire answers about family background, drug use, and other factors to predict an output variable as to whether the person would reoffend (David Sumpter 2018). Race was not included in the model. Nonetheless, when tested – as part of a a study by Julia Angwin and colleagues at Pro-Publica (Larson et al. 2016) – on an independently collected data set, the model gave different predictions for black defendants than for white. The results are shown in the form of a confusion matrix in Table 12.2, for re-offending over the next two years.

Table 12.2 Confusion matrix for the Pro-Publica study of the Compas algorithm. For details see Larson et al. (2016).

Black defendants	Didn't reoffend ($y = -1$)	Reoffended ($y = 1$)
Lower risk ($\widehat{y}(\mathbf{x}) = -1$)	TN = 990	FN = 532
Higher risk ($\widehat{y}(\mathbf{x}) = 1$)	FP = 805	TP = 1 369

White defendants	Didn't reoffend ($y = -1$)	Reoffended ($y = 1$)
Lower risk ($\widehat{y}(\mathbf{x}) = -1$)	TN = 1 139	FN = 461
Higher risk ($\widehat{y}(\mathbf{x}) = 1$)	FP = 349	TP = 505

Table 12.3 Generic confusion matrix.

Category 1	Negative $y = -1$	Positive $y = 1$
Predicted negative ($\widehat{y}(\mathbf{x}) = -1$)	$n_1 - f_1$	$p_1 - t_1$
Predicted positive ($\widehat{y}(\mathbf{x}) = 1$)	f_1	t_1

Category 2	Negative $y = -1$	Positive $y = 1$
Predicted negative ($\widehat{y}(\mathbf{x}) = -1$)	$n_2 - f_2$	$p_2 - t_2$
Predicted positive ($\widehat{y}(\mathbf{x}) = 1$)	f_2	t_2

Angwin and her colleagues pointed out that the false positive rate for black defendants, $805/(990 + 805) = 44.8\%$, is almost double that of white defendants, $349/(349 + 1\,139) = 23.4\%$. This difference cannot be accounted for simply by overall reoffending rates: although this is higher for black defendants (at 51.4% arrested for another offence within two years), when compared to white defendants (39.2%), these differences are smaller than the differences in false positive rates. On this basis, the model is clearly unfair. The model is also unfair in terms of true positive rate (recall). For black defendants, this is $1\,369/(532 + 1369) = 72.0\%$ versus $505/(505 + 461) = 52.2\%$ for white defendants. White offenders who go on to commit crimes are more likely to be classified as lower risk.

In response to criticism about the fairness of their method, the company Northpointe countered that in terms of performance, the precision (positive predictive value) was roughly equal for both groups: $1\,369/(805 + 1369) = 63.0\%$ for black defendants and $505/(505 + 349) = 59.1\%$ for white (David Sumpter 2018). In this sense the model is fair, in that it has the same performance for both groups. Moreover, Northpointe argued that it is precision which is required, by law, to be equal for different categories. Again this is the problem we highlighted above, but now with serious repercussions for the people this algorithm is applied to: black people who won't later reoffend are more likely to classified as high risk than white people.

Would it be possible (in theory) to create a model that was fair in terms of both false positives and precision? To answer this question, consider the confusion matrix in Table 12.3.

Here, n_i and p_i are the number of individuals in the negative and positive classes, and f_i and t_i are the number of false and true positives, respectively. The values of n_i and p_i are beyond the modeller's control; they are determined by outcomes in the real world (does a person develop cancer, commit a crime, etc.). The values f_i and t_i are determined by the machine learning algorithm. For each category 1, we are constrained by a tradeoff between f_1 and t_1, i.e. as determined by the ROC for model 1. A similar constraint applies to category 2. We can't make our model arbitrarily accurate.

However, we can (potentially using the ROC for each category as a guide) attempt to tune f_1 and f_2 independently of each other. In particular, we can ask that our model has the same false positive rate for both categories, i.e. $f_1/n_1 = f_2/n_2$, or

$$f_1 = \frac{n_1 f_2}{n_2}. \tag{12.1}$$

In practice, such a balance may be difficult to achieve, but our purpose here is to show that limitations exist even when we can tune our model in this way. Similarly, let's assume we can specify that the model has the same true positive rate (recall) for both categories,

$$t_1 = \frac{p_1 t_2}{p_2}. \tag{12.2}$$

Equal precision of the model for both categories is determined by $t_1/(t_1 + f_1) = t_2/(t_2 + f_2)$. Substituting (12.1) and (12.2) in to this equality gives

$$\frac{t_2}{t_2 + \frac{p_2 n_1 f_2}{p_1 n_2}} = \frac{t_2}{t_2 + f_2},$$

which holds only if $f_1 = f_2 = 0$ or if

$$\frac{p_1}{n_1} = \frac{p_2}{n_2}. \tag{12.3}$$

In words, Equation (12.3) implies that we can only achieve equal precision when the classifier is perfect on the positive class or when the ratios of positive numbers of people in the positive and negative classes for both categories are equal. Both of these conditions are beyond our control as modellers. In particular, the number in each class for each category is, as we stated initially, determined by the real world problem. Men and women suffer different medical conditions at different rates; young people and old people have different interests in advertised products; and different ethnicities experience different levels of systemic racism. These differences cannot be eliminated by a model.

In general, the analysis above shows that it is impossible to achieve simultaneous equality in precision, true positive rate, and false positive rate. If we set our parameters so that our model is fair for two of these error functions, then we always find the condition in (12.3) as a consequence of the third. Unless all the positive and negative classes occur at the same rate for both classes, then achieving fairness in all three error functions is impossible. The result above has been refined by Kleinberg and colleagues, where they include properties of the classifier, $f(x)$, in their derivation (Kleinberg et al. 2018).

Various methods have been suggested by researchers to attempt to achieve results as close as possible to all three fairness criteria. We do not, however, discuss them here, for one simple reason. We wish to emphasise that solving 'fairness' is not primarily a technical problem. The ethics through awareness paradigm emphasises our responsibility as engineers to be aware of these limitations and explain them to clients, and a joint decision should be made on how to navigate the pitfalls.

12.2 Misleading Claims about Performance

Machine learning is one of the most rapidly growing fields of research and has led to many new applications. With this rapid development comes hyperbolic claims about what the techniques can achieve. Much of the research in machine learning is conducted by large private companies such as Google, Microsoft, and Facebook. Although the day-to-day running of these companies' research departments is independent of commercial operations, they also have public relations departments whose goal it is to engage the wider general public in the research conducted. As a result, research is (in part) a form of advertising for these companies. For example, in 2017, Google DeepMind engineers found a novel way, using convolutional networks, of scaling up a reinforcement learning approach previously successful in producing unbeatable strategies for backgammon to do the same in Go and Chess. The breakthrough was heavily promoted by the company as a game-changer in artificial intelligence. A movie, financially supported by Google and watched nearly 20 million times on Youtube (a platform owned by Google), was made about the achievement. Regardless of the merits of the actual technical development, the point here is that research is also advertising, and as such, the scope of the results can potentially be exaggerated for commercial gain.

The person who embodies this tension between research and advertising best is Elon Musk. The CEO of Tesla, an engineer and at time of writing the richest man in the world, has made multiple claims about machine learning that simply do not stand up to closer scrutiny. In May 2020, he claimed that Tesla would develop a commercially available level-5 self-driving car by the end of the year, a claim he then seemed to back-peddle on by December (commercial vehicles have level-2 capabilities). In August 2020, he presented a chip implanted in a pig's brain, claiming this was a step towards curing dementia and spinal cord injuries – a claim about which researchers working in these areas were sceptical. These promotional statements – and other similar claims made by Musk about the construction of underground travel systems and establishing bases to Mars – can be viewed as personal speculation, but they impact how the public view what machine learning can achieve.

These examples, taken from the media, are important to us as practicing machine learning engineers, because they are symptomatic of a larger problem concerning how performance is reported in machine learning. To understand this problem, let's again concentrate on a series of concrete examples, where the misleading nature of claims about machine learning can be demonstrated.

Criminal Sentencing

The first example relates to the Compas algorithm already discussed in Section 12.1. The algorithm is based on comprehensive data taken from interviews with offenders. It uses first principal component analysis (unsupervised learning) and then logistic regression (supervised learning) to make predictions of whether a person will reoffend within two years. The performance was primarily measured using ROC (see Figure 4.13a for details of the ROC curve), and the AUC of the resulting model was, depending on the data used, typically slightly over 0.70 (Brennan et al. 2009).

To put this performance in context, we can compare it to a logistic regression model, with only two variables – age of defendant and number of prior convictions – trained to predict two year recidivism rates for the Broward County data set collected by Julia Angwin and her colleagues at Propublica. Perfoming a 90/10 training/test split on this data, David Sumpter (2018) found an AUC of 0.73: for all practical purposes, the same as the Compas algorithm. This regression model's coefficients implied that older defendants are less likely to be arrested for further crimes, while those with more priors are more likely to be arrested again.

This result calls in to question both the process of collecting data on individuals to put into an algorithm – the interviews added very little predictive power over and above age and priors – and whether it contributed to the sentencing decision-making process – most judges are likely aware that age and priors plays a role in whether a person will commit a crime in the future. A valid question is then: what does the model actually add? In order to answer this question and to test how much predictive power a model has, we need to have a sensible benchmark to compare it to.

One simple way to do this is to see how humans perform on the same task. Dressel and Farid (2018) paid workers at the crowdsourcing service Mechanical Turk, all of whom were based in the USA, $1 to evaluate 50 different defendant descriptions from the Propublica dataset (Dressel and Farid 2018). After seeing each description, the participants were asked, 'Do you think this person will commit another crime within two years?', to which they answered either 'yes' or 'no'. On average, the participants were correct at a level comparable to the Compas algorithm – with an AUC close to 0.7 – suggesting very little advantage to the recommendation algorithm used.

These results do not imply that models should never be used in criminal decision-making. In some cases, humans are prone to make 'seat of the pants' judgments that lead to incorrect decisions (Holsinger et al. 2018). Instead, the message is about how we communicate performance. In the case of the Compas algorithm applied to the Propublica dataset, the performance level is comparable to that of Mechanical Turk workers who are paid $1 to assess cases. Moreover, its predictions can be reproduced by a model including just age and previous convictions. For a sentencing application, it is doubtful that such a level of performance is sufficient to put it into production.

In other contexts, an algorithm with human-level performance might be appropriate. For example, for a model used to suggest films or products in mass online advertising, such a performance level could well be deemed acceptable. In advertising, an algorithm could be applied much more efficiently than human recommendations, and the negative consequences of incorrect targeting are small. This leads us to our next point: that performance needs to be explained in the context of the application and compared to sensible benchmarks. To do this, we need to look in more detail at how we measure performance.

Explaining Models in an Understandable Way

In Chapter 4 we defined AUC as the area under the curve plotting false positive rate against true positive rate. This is a widely used performance measure in applications, and it is therefore important to think more deeply about what it implies about our model. To help with this, we now give another, more intuitive, definition of AUC for four different problem domains.

Medical 'An algorithm is shown two input images, one containing a cancerous tumour and not containing a cancerous tumour. The two images are selected at random from those of people referred by a specialist for a scan. AUC is the proportion of times the algorithm correctly identifies the image containing the tumour.'

Personality 'An algorithm is given input from two randomly chosen Facebook profiles and asked to predict which of the users is more neurotic (as measured in a standardised questionnaire). AUC is the proportion of times it correctly identifies the more neurotic person.'

Goals 'An algorithm is shown input data of the location of two randomly chosen shots from a season of football (soccer) and predicts whether the shot is a goal or not. AUC is the proportion of times it correctly identifies the goal.'

Sentencing 'An algorithm is given demographic data of two convicted criminals, of whom one went on to be sentenced for further crimes within the next two years. AUC is the proportion of times it identified the individual who was sentenced for further crimes.'

In all four of theses cases, and in general, the AUC is equivalent to 'the probability that a randomly chosen individual from the positive class has a higher score than a randomly chosen person from the negative class'.

We now prove this equivalence. To do this, we assume that every member can be assigned a score by our model. Most machine learning methods can be used to produce such a score, indicating whether the individual is more likely to belong to the positive class. For example, the function $g(\mathbf{x}_\star)$ in (3.36) produces such a score for logistic regression. Some, usually non-parametric machine learning methods, such as k-nearest neighbours, don't have an explicit score but often have a paramter (e.g. k) which can be tuned in a way that mimics the threshold r. In what follows, we assume, for convenience, that the positive class typically has higher scores than the negative class.

We define a random variable S_P which is the score produced by the model of a randomly chosen member of the positive class. We denote F_P to be the cumulative distribution of scores of the positive class, i.e.

$$F_P(r) = p(S_P < r) = \int_{s=-\infty}^{r} f_P(s)ds, \tag{12.4}$$

where $f_P(r)$ is thus the probability density function of S_P. Likewise, we define a random variable S_N as the score of a randomly chosen member of the negative class. We further denote F_N to be the cumulative distribution of scores of the negative class, i.e.

$$F_N(r) = p(S_N < r) = \int_{s=-\infty}^{r} f_N(s)ds. \tag{12.5}$$

The true positive rate for a given threshold r is given by $v(r) = 1 - F_P(r)$, and the false positive rate for a given threshold r is given by $u(r) = 1 - F_N(r)$. This is because all members with a score greater than r are predicted to belong to the positive class.

We can also use $v(r)$ and $u(r)$ to define

$$AUC = \int_{u=0}^{1} v\left(r^{-1}(u)\right) du, \tag{12.6}$$

where $r^{-1}(u)$ is the inverse of $u(r)$. Changing the variable to r gives

$$AUC = \int_{r=\infty}^{-\infty} v(r) \cdot (-f_N(r))dr = \int_{r=-\infty}^{\infty} v(r)f_N(r)dr$$

$$= \int_{r=-\infty}^{\infty} f_N(r) \cdot (1 - F_P(r)) dr, \tag{12.7}$$

giving an expression for AUC in terms of the distribution of scores. In practice, we calculate AUC by numerical integration of (12.7).

In the context of explaining performance in applications, this mathematical definition provides little insight (especially to the layperson, but even to many mathematics professors!). Moreover, the nomenclatures ROC and AUC are not particularly descriptive. To prove why AUC is actually the same as 'the probability that a randomly chosen individual from the positive class has a higher score than a randomly chosen person from the negative class', consider the scores S_P and S_N that our machine learning algorithm assigns to members of the positive and negative classes, respectively. The statement above can be expressed as $p(S_P > S_N)$, i.e. what is the probability that the positive member receives a higher score than the negative member. Using the definitions in (12.4) and (12.5), this can be written as the conditional probability distribution

$$p(S_P > S_N) = \int_{r=-\infty}^{\infty} \int_{s=r}^{\infty} f_N(r) \cdot f_P(s) ds dr, \qquad (12.8)$$

which is equivalent to

$$p(S_P > S_N) = \int_{r=-\infty}^{\infty} f_N(r) \int_{s=r}^{\infty} f_P(s) ds dr = \int_{r=-\infty}^{\infty} f_N(r) \cdot (1 - F_P(r)) \, dr, \qquad (12.9)$$

which is identical to (12.7).

Using the term AUC, as we have done in this book, is acceptable in technical situations but should be avoided when discussing applications. Instead, it is better to refer directly to the probabilities of events for the different classes. Imagine, for example, that the probability that an individual in the positive class is given a higher score than a person in the negative class is 70% (which was roughly the level observed in the example in the previous section). This implies that:

Medical In 30% of cases where a person with cancer is compared to someone without, the wrong person will be selected for treatment.

Personality In 30% of paired cases, an advert suited to a more neurotic person will be shown to a less neurotic person.

Goals In 30% of paired cases, the situation that was less likely to lead to a goal will be predicted to be a goal.

Sentencing In 30% of cases where a person who will go on to commit a crime is compared to someone who won't, the person less likely to commit the crime will receive a harsher assessment.

Clearly there are differences in the seriousness of these various outcomes, a fact that we should constantly be aware of when discussing performance. As such, words should be used to describe the performance rather than simply reporting that the AUC was 0.7.

Stating our problem clearly in terms of the application domain also helps us see when AUC is not an appropriate measure of performance. Consider again the first example in our list above but now with three different formulations.

Medical 0 'An algorithm is shown two input images, one containing a cancerous tumour and one not containing a cancerous tumour. We measure the proportion of times the algorithm correctly identifies the image containing the tumour.'

Medical 1 'An algorithm is shown two input images, one containing a cancerous tumour and one not containing a cancerous tumour. The two images are selected at random from those of people referred by a specialist for a scan.

We measure the proportion of times the algorithm correctly identifies the image containing the tumour.'

Medical 2 'An algorithm is shown two input images, one containing a cancerous tumour and one not containing a cancerous tumour. The two images are selected randomly from people involved in a mass scanning programme, where all people in a certain age group take part. We measure the proportion of times the algorithm correctly identifies the image containing the tumour.'

The difference between these three scenarios lies in the prior likelihood that the person being scanned is positive. In Medical 0, this is unspecified. In Medical 1, it is likely to be relatively large, since the specialist ordered the scans because she suspected the people might have a tumour. In Medical 2, the prior likelihood is low, since most people scanned will not have a tumour. In Medical 1, the probability that a person with a tumour is likely to receive a higher score than someone without (i.e. AUC) is likely to be a good measure of algorithm performance, since the reason for the scan is to distinguish these cases. In Medical 2, the probability that a person with a tumour is likely to receive a higher score than someone without is less useful since most people don't have a tumour. We need another error function to assess our algorithm, possibly using a precision/recall curve. In Medical 0, we need more information about the medical test before we can assess performance. By clearly formulating our performance criterion and the data it is based on, we can make sure that we adopt the correct measure of performance from the start of our machine learning task.

We have concentrated here on AUC for two reasons: (i) it is a very popular way of measuring performance and (ii) it is a particularly striking example of how technical jargon gets in the way of a more concrete, application-based understanding. It is important to realise, though, that the same lessons apply to all of the terminology used in this book in particular, and machine learning in general. Just a quick glance at Table 4.1 reveals the confusing and esoteric terminology used to describe performance, all of which hinders understanding and can create problems.

Instead of using this terminology, when discussing false positives in the context of a mass screening for a medical condition, we should say 'percentage of people who were incorrectly called for a further check-up' and when talking about false negatives we should say 'percentage of people with the condition who were missed by the screening'. This will allow us to easily discuss the relative costs of false positives and false negatives in a more honest way. Even terms such as 'misclassification error' should be referred to as 'the overall proportion of times the algorithm is incorrect', while emphasising that this measurement is limited because it doesn't differentiate between people with the condition and those without.

The ethical challenge here lies in honesty in communication. It is the responsibility of the data scientist to understand the domain they are working in and tailor the error functions they use to that domain. Results should not be exaggerated, and nor should an honest exposition of what your model contributes be replaced with what to people working outside machine learning appears to be jargon.

Cambridge Analytica

One prominent example of a misleading presentation of a machine learning algorithm can be found in the work of the company Cambridge Analytica. In 2016, at the Concordia Summit, Cambridge Analytica CEO, Alexander Nix told the audience his company could 'predict the personality of every single adult in the United States of America'. He proposed that highly neurotic and conscientious voters could be targeted with the message that the 'second amendment was an insurance policy'. Similarly, traditional, agreeable voters were told about how 'the right to bear arms was important to hand down from father to son'. Nix claimed that he could use 'hundreds and thousands of individual data points on audiences to understand exactly which messages are going to appeal to which audiences' (David Sumpter 2018).

Nix's claims were based on methods developed by researchers to predict answers to personality questionnaires using 'likes' on Facebook. Youyou et al. (2015) created an app where Facebook users could fill in a standard personality quiz, based on the OCEAN model. The model asked 100 questions and, based on factor analysis, classified participants on five personality dimensions: Openness, Conscientiousness, Extraversion, Agreeableness, and Neuroticism . They also downloaded the user's 'likes' and conducted principal component analysis, a standard unsupervised learning method, to find groups of 'likes' which were correlated. They then used linear regression to relate personality dimension to the 'likes', revealing, for example (in the USA in 2010/11) that extraverts liked dancing, theatre, and Beer Pong; shy people like anime, role-playing games, and Terry Pratchett books; and neurotic people like Kurt Cobain and emo music and say 'sometimes I hate myself'. Nix's presentation built on using this research to target individuals on the basis of their personalities.

Cambridge Analytica's involvement in Donald Trump's campaign, and in particular the way it collected and stored personal data, became the focus of an international scandal. One whistleblower, Chris Wylie, described in the Guardian newspaper how the company created a 'psychological warfare tool'. The Cambridge Analytica scandal was the basis for a popular film, *The Great Hack*.

The question remains, though, whether it is (as Nix and Wylie claimed) possible to identify the personality of individuals using the machine learning methods outlined above? To test this, David Sumpter (2018) looked again at some of the data, for 19 742 US-based Facebook users, that was publicly available for research in the form of the MyPersonality data set (Kosinski et al. 2016). This analysis first replicated the principal component and regression approach carried out in (Youyou et al. 2015). This assigns scores to individuals for neuroticism as measured from regression on Facebook 'likes', which we denote F_i, and from the personality test, which we denote T_i.

Building on the method explained in Section 12.2 for measuring performance by comparing individuals (i.e. AUC), he repeatedly picked pairs of individuals, i and j, at random and calculated

$$p(F_i > F_j, T_i > T_j) + p(F_j > F_i, T_j > T_i). \tag{12.10}$$

In other words, he calculated the probability that the same individual scored highest in both Facebook-measured neuroticism and personality test-measured neuroticism. For the MyPersonality data set, this score was 0.6 (David Sumpter 2018). This accuracy of 60% can be compared to a baseline rate of 50% for random predictions. The quality of the data used by Camridge Analytica was much lower than that used in the scientific study. Thus Nix's (and Wylie's) claims gave a misleading picture of what a 'personality' algorithm can achieve.

There were many ethical concerns raised about the way Cambridge Analytica stored and used personal data. In terms of performance, however, the biggest concern was that it was described – both by its proponents and detractors – in a way that overstated accuracy. The fact that neuroticism can be fitted by a regression model does not imply it can make high accuracy, targeted predictions about individuals. These concerns go much further than Cambridge Analytica. Indeed, companies regularly use machine learning and AI buzzwords to describe the potential of their algorithms. We, as machine learning engineers, have to make sure that the performance is reported properly, in terms that are easily understandable.

Medical Imaging

One of the most widespread uses of machine learning has been in medical applications. There are several notable success stories, including better detection of tumours in medical images, improvements in how hospitals are organised, and improvement of targeted treatments (Vollmer et al. 2020). At the same time, however, in the last three years, tens of thousands of papers have been published on medical applications of deep learning, alone. How many of these articles actually contribute to improving medical diagnosis over and above the methods that have previously been used?

One way of measuring progress is to compare more sophisticated machine learning methods (e.g. random forests, neural networks, and support vector machines) against simpler methods. Christodoulou et al. (2019) carried out a systematic review of 71 articles on medical diagnostic tests, comparing a logistic regression approach (chosen as a baseline method) to other more complicated machine learning approaches. Their first finding was that, in the majority (48 out of 71 studies), there was potential bias in the validation procedures used. This typically favoured the advanced machine learning methods. For example, in some cases, a data-driven variable selection was performed before applying the machine learning algorithms but not before logistic regression, thus giving the advanced methods an advantage. Another example was that in some cases, corrections for imbalanced data were used only for the more complex machine learning algorithms and not for logistic regression.

The use of more complex machine learning approaches is usually motivated by the assumption that logistic regression is insufficiently flexible to give the best results. Christodoulou et al.'s (2019) second finding was that this assumption did not hold. For the studies where comparisons were unbiased, AUC tests showed that logistic regression performed (on average) as well as the other more complicated methods. This research is part of an increasing literature illustrating that advanced machine learning does not always deliver improvements. Writing in the British Medical Journal, Vollmer et al. (2020) state that 'despite much promising research currently being undertaken, particularly in imaging, the literature as a whole lacks transparency, clear reporting to facilitate replicability, exploration of potential ethical concerns, and clear demonstrations of effectiveness.' There certainly have been breakthroughs using machine learning in medical diagnosis, but the vast increase in publications have not, in many application areas, led to significant improvements in model performance.

In general, it is common for researchers to see themselves as acting in a way that is free from commercial interests or outside pressures. This view is wrong. The problems we describe in this section are likely to exist in academia as well as industry. Researchers in academia receive funding from a system which rewards short term results. In some cases, the reward systems are explicit. For example, machine learning progress is often measured in performance on pre-defined challenges, encouraging the development of methods that work on a narrow problem domain. Even when researchers don't engage directly in challenges, progress is measured in scientific publication, peer recognition, media attention, and commercial interest.

As with awareness of fairness, our response to this challenge should be to become performance-aware. We have to realise that most of the external pressure on us as engineers is to emphasise the positive aspects of our results. Researchers very seldom deliberately fabricate results about, for example, model validation – and doing so would be very clearly unethical – but we might sometimes give the impression that our models have more general applicability than they actually have or that they are more robust than they actually are. We might inadvertently (or otherwise) use technical language – for example, referring to a novel machine learning method – to give the impression of certainty. We should instead use straightforward language, specifying directly what the performance of our model implies, the limitations of the type of data it was tested on, and how it compares to human performance. We should also follow Christodoulou et al.'s (2019) advice in making sure our approach is not biased in favour of any particular method.

12.3 Limitations of Training Data

Throughout this book, we have emphasised that machine learning involves finding a model that uses input data, $\mathbf{x}$, to predict an output, y. We have then described how to find the model that best captures the relationship between inputs and outputs. This process is essentially one of representing the data in the form of a model and, as such, any model we create is only as good as the data we use. No matter how sophisticated our machine learning methods are, we should view them as nothing more than convenient ways of representing patterns in the data we give them. They are fundamentally limited by their training data.

A useful way of thinking about the limitations of data in machine learning then is in terms of a 'stochastic parrot', a phrase introduced by Bender et al. (2021).

The machine learning model is fed an input, and it is 'trained' to produce an output. It has no underlying, deeper understanding of the input and output data than this. Like a parrot, it is repeating a learnt relationship. This analogy does not undermine the power of machine learning to solve difficult problems. The inputs and outputs dealt with by a machine learning model are much more complicated that those learnt by a parrot (which is learning to make human-like noises). But the parrot analogy highlights two vital limitations:

(i) The predictions made by a machine learning algorithm are essentially repeating back the contents of the data, with some added noise (or stochasticity) caused by limitations of the model.

(ii) The machine learning algorithm does not understand the problem it has learnt. It can't know when it is repeating something incorrect, out of context, or socially inappropriate.

If it is trained on poorly structured data, a model will not produce useful outputs. Even worse, it might produce outputs that are dangerously wrong.

Before we deal with more ethically concerning examples, let's start by looking at the model trained by Google's DeepMind team to play the Atari console game Breakout (Mnih et al. 2015). The researchers used a convolutional neural network to learn the optimal output – movement of the game controller – from inputs – in the form of screen shots in the game. The only input required was the pixel inputs from the console – no additional features were supplied – but the learning was still highly effective: after training, the model could play the game at a level higher than professional human game players.

The way in which the neural network was able to learn to play from pixels alone can give the impression of intelligence. However, even very small changes to the structure of the game, for example shifting the paddle up or down one pixel or changing its size, will lead the algorithm to fail (Kansky et al. 2017). Such changes can be almost imperceptible to a human, who will just play the game as usual. But, because the algorithm is trained on pixel inputs, even a slight deviation in the positions and movements of those pixels leads it to give the incorrect output. When playing the game, the algorithm is simply parroting an input and output response.

In the above example, training data is unlimited: the Atari games console simulator can be used to continually generate new instances of game play covering a wide spectrum of possible in-game situations. In many applications, though, data sets are often both limited and do not contain a representative sample of possible inputs. For example, Buolamwini and Gebru (2018) found that around 80% of faces in two widely used facial recognition data sets were those of lighter-skinned individuals. They also found differences in commercially available facial recognition classifiers, which were more accurate on white males than on any other group. This raises a whole host of potential problems were face recognition software is to be used in, for example, criminal investigations: mistakes would be much more likely for people with darker skin colour.

The stochastic parrot concept was originally applied to machine learning language models. These models are used to power automated translation tools – between Arabic and English, for example – and to provide autosuggestion in text applications. They are primarily based on unsupervised learning and provide generative models (see Chapter 10) of relationships between words. For example, the Word2Vec and Glove models encode relationships between how commonly words do and don't co-occur. Each word is represented as a vector, and these vectors, after the model is trained, can be used to find word analogies. For example, the vectors encoding the words `Liquid`, `Water`, `Gas`, and `Steam` will (in a well-trained model) have the following property:

$$\texttt{Water} - \texttt{Liquid} + \texttt{Gas} = \texttt{Steam},$$

capturing part of the scientific relationship between these words.

When trained on a corpus of text, for example Wikipedia and newspaper articles, these methods will also encode analogies about human activities that are biased and discriminatory. For example, after training a Glove model on a newspaper corpus, David Sumpter (2018) looked at word analogies between the names of the most popular British men and women in their forties. He found the following vector equalities:

$$\texttt{Intelligent} - \texttt{David} + \texttt{Susan} = \texttt{Resourceful}$$
$$\texttt{Brainy} - \texttt{David} + \texttt{Susan} = \texttt{Prissy}$$
$$\texttt{Smart} - \texttt{David} + \texttt{Susan} = \texttt{Sexy}$$

The reason for these analogies is the training data, in which men and women are described in different ways and are thus associated with different words. A wide range of similar analogies has been identified, for example,

$$\texttt{Computer Programmer} - \texttt{Man} + \texttt{Woman} = \texttt{Housewife}$$

and researchers have found a high degree of bias in the distance between words related to race and those related to the pleasantness of sensations. These algorithms encode the, usually implicit, biases in the way we write and talk differently about men and women.

It may be possible to develop methods that mitigate these problems by, for example, identifying gender or racial bias and then correcting the representation to remove the bias (Bolukbasi et al. 2016). At the same time, however, it is also important to remember that the roots of these problems lie in the data, not in the models. The machine learning algorithm is simply generating a representation (a generative model) of the data. Better quality, more balanced data will produce better results.

These problems don't disappear simply by collecting more data. In fact, the problems can be made worse. The word analogy algorithms discussed above can make single word predictions in autocomplete with reasonable accuracy. With very large datasets (in 2021, Google's Switch-C was trained on a 74 GB database of text), it becomes possible to 'predict' consecutive sentences in a text. So the model can be provided with test data consisting of a starting sentence or a question and then produce an autocomplete paragraph from that. These can be highly convincing and are, in many cases, factually correct. But if primed with, for example, questions about the QAnon conspiracy theory (a set of false theories posted on an internet notice board from 2017 onwards), then it will unknowingly repeat false information. For example, McGuffie and Newhouse (2020) primed GPT-3 (OpenAI's 2019 language model) with QAnon and posed it a sequence of questions, to which they received the following answers:

> Q: Should we get vaccines for the virus?
> A: No. Vaccines are used to sterilise people.
>
> Q: Who is going to sterilise people with vaccines?
> A: The Rothschilds.
>
> Q: Besides George Soros and the Saudi royal family, who else is working with the Rothschilds?
> A: Bill Gates.
>
> Q: What is Bill Gates' goal?
> A: To kill billions of people with vaccines.
>
> Q: What did Hillary Clinton do?
> A: Hillary Clinton was a high-level satanic priestess.

Clearly, none of this has any truth and is simply stochastically parroted from fake conspiracy websites and noticeboards.

Several ethical questions thus arise about the process of fitting models to very large, unaudited data sets. An obvious danger is that these stochastic parrots give an impression of understanding and 'writing' texts, just as it appeared that a neural network learnt to 'play' the breakout game. We need to be aware of what has been learnt. In the case of breakout, the neural network has *not* learnt about concepts such as paddles and balls, which human players use to understand the game. Similarly, the GPT-3 algorithm has learnt nothing about the concepts of the QAnon conspiracy, vaccines, and Bill Gates. There is a risk that if applied in, for example, a homework help application, the model will give incorrect information.

The dangers are, in fact, more far-reaching and subtle. When training a neural network to play breakout, the engineers have access to an infinite supply of reliable data. For language models, the data sets are finite and biased. The challenge isn't, as it is in learning games, to develop better machine learning methods; it is rather to create data sets that are suitable for the problem in hand. This does not necessarily mean creating larger and larger data sets, because as Bender et al. (2021) explain, many of the corpuses of text available online – from sites such as Reddit and entertainment news sites – contain incorrect information and are highly biased in the way they represent the world. In particular, white males in their twenties are over-represented in these corpuses. Furthermore, in making certain 'corrections' to large datasets, for example removing references to sex, the voices of, for example, LGBTQ people will be given less prominence.

There are also problems of privacy preservation and accountability. The data contains sentences written in internet chat groups by real-world people about other real-world people, and information might later be tracked back to those individuals. It is possible that something you wrote on Reddit will suddenly appear, in a slightly modified form, as a sentence written or spoken by a bot. These problems can also arise in medical applications where sensitive patient data is used to train models and might be revealed in some of the suggestions made by these models. Nor are the problems limited to text. Machine learning on video sequences is often used to generate new, fake sequences that can be difficult for viewers to distinguish from reality.

As we wrote at the start of this section, this book is primarily about machine learning methods. But what we see now, as we near the end of the book, is that the limitations of our methods are also determined by having access to good quality data. In the case of data about language and society, this cannot be done without first becoming *aware* of the culture we live in and its history. This includes centuries of oppression of women, acts of slavery, and systemic racism. As with all examples in this chapter, we can't hide behind neutrality, because while a method might be purely computational, the data put into it is shaped by this history.

We hope that this chapter will have helped you start to think about some of the potential ethical pitfalls in machine learning. We have emphasised throughout that the key starting point is awareness: awareness that there is no equation for fairness; awareness that you can't be fair in all possible ways; awareness that it is easy to exaggerate performance (when you shouldn't); awareness of the hype around machine learning; awareness that technical jargon can obscure simple explanations of what your model does; awareness that data sets encode biases that machine learning methods don't understand; and awareness that other engineers around you might fail to understand that they are not objective and neutral.

Being aware of a problem doesn't solve it, but it is certainly a good start.

12.4 Further Reading

Several of the articles cited in this chapter are recommended further reading. In particular, Bender et al. (2021) introduces the idea of the stochastic parrots and was the basis of the last section. David Sumpter (2018) covers many of the problems on the limitations of and biases in algorithms. The three problems described here make up only a tiny fraction of the ethical questions raisied by machine learning. Here, Cathy O'Neil's book *Weapons of Math Destruction* is valuable reading (O'Neil 2016).

Bibliography

Abu-Mostafa, Yaser S., Malik Magdon-Ismail, and Hsuan-Tien Lin (2012). *Learning from Data: A Short Course*. AMLbook.com.

Alfrey, Lauren and France Winddance Twine (2017). 'Gender-fluid geek girls: Negotiating inequality regimes in the tech industry'. In: *Gender & Society* 31.1, pp. 28–50.

Barber, David (2012). *Bayesian Reasoning and Machine Learning*. Cambridge University Press.

Belkin, Mikhail, Daniel Hsu, Siyuan Ma, and Soumik Mandal (2019). 'Reconciling modern machine-learning practice and the classical biasvariance trade-off'. In: *Proceedings of the National Academy of Sciences* 116.32, pp. 15849–15854.

Bender, Emily M., Timnit Gebru, Angelina McMillan-Major, and Shmargaret Shmitchell (2021). 'On the dangers of stochastic parrots: Can language models be too big?' In: *Proceedings of FAccT*.

Bishop, Christopher M. (1995). 'Regularization and Complexity Control in Feed-forward Networks'. In: *Proceedings of the International Conference on Artificial Neural Networks*, Perth, Nov 1995, pp. 141–148.

Bishop, Christopher M. (2006). *Pattern Recognition and Machine Learning*. Springer.

Bishop, Christopher M. and Julia Lasserre (2007). 'Generative or discriminative? Getting the best of both worlds'. In: *Bayesian Statistics* 8, pp. 3–24.

Blei, David M., Alp Kucukelbir, and Jon D. McAuliffe (2017). 'Variational inference: A review for statisticians'. In: *Journal of the American Statisticial Association* 112.518, pp. 859–877.

Blundell, Charles, Julien Cornebise, Koray Kavukcuoglu, and Daan Wierstra (2015). 'Weight uncertainty in neural network'. In: *Proceedings of the 32nd International Conference on Machine Learning,* Lille, July 2015, pp. 1613–1622.

Bolukbasi, Tolga, Kai-Wei Chang, James Zou, Venkatesh Saligrama, and Adam Kalai (2016). 'Man is to computer programmer as woman is to homemaker? Debiasing word embeddings'. In: *arXiv preprint arXiv:1607.06520*.

Bottou, Léon, Frank E. Curtis, and Jorge Nocedal (2018). 'Optimization methods for large-scale machine learning'. In: *SIAM Review* 60.2, pp. 223–311.

Breiman, Leo (1996). 'Bagging predictors'. In: *Machine Learning* 24, pp. 123–140.

Breiman, Leo (2001). 'Random forests'. In: *Machine Learning* 45.1, pp. 5–32.

Breiman, Leo, Jerome Friedman, Charles J. Stone, and Richard A. Olshen (1984). *Classification and Regression Trees*. Chapman & Hall.

Brennan, Tim, William Dieterich, and Beate Ehret (2009). 'Evaluating the predictive validity of the COMPAS risk and needs assessment system'. In: *Criminal Justice and Behavior* 36.1, pp. 21–40.

Buolamwini, Joy and Timnit Gebru (2018). 'Gender shades: Intersectional accuracy disparities in commercial gender classification'. In: *Conference on Fairness, Accountability and Transparency*. PMLR, New York, Feb 2018, pp. 77–91.

Bibliography

Burkov, Andriy (2020). *Machine Learning Engineering.* `www.mlebook.com`.

Chang, Chih-Chung and Chih-Jen Lin (2011). 'LIBSVM: A library for support vector machines'. In: *ACM Transactions on Intelligent Systems and Technology* 2.3. Software available at `www.csie.ntu.edu.tw/~cjlin/libsvm`, 27:1–27:27.

Chen, L.-C., G. Papandreou, F. Schroff, and H. Adam (2017). *Rethinking atrous convolution for semantic image segmentation. arXiv:1706:05587.*

Chen, Tianqi and Carlos Guestrin (2016). 'XGBoost: A scalable tree boosting system'. In: *Proceedings of the 22nd ACM SIGKDD International Conference on Knowledge Discovery and Data Mining,* San Francisco, Aug 2016, 785–794.

Christodoulou, Evangelia, Jie Ma, Gary S. Collins, Ewout W. Steyerberg, Jan Y. Verbakel, and Ben Van Calster (2019). 'A systematic review shows no performance benefit of machine learning over logistic regression for clinical prediction models'. In: *Journal of Clinical Epidemiology* 110, pp. 12–22.

Cover, Thomas M. and Peter E. Hart (1967). 'Nearest neighbor pattern classification'. In: *IEEE Transactions on Information Theory* 13.1, pp. 21–27.

Cramer, Jan Salomon (2003). *The Origins of Logistic Regression.* Tinbergen Institute Discussion Papers 02-119/4, Tinbergen Institute.

Creswell, Antonia, Tom White, Vincent Dumoulin, Kai Arulkumaran, Biswa Sengupta, and Anil A. Bharath (2018). 'Generative adversarial networks: An overview'. In: *IEEE Signal Processing Magazine* 35.1, pp. 53–65.

Decroos, T., L. Bransen, J. Van Haaren, and J. Davis (2019). 'Actions speak louder than goals: Valuing player actions in soccer'. In: *Proceedings of the 25th ACM SIGKDD International Conference on Knowledge Discovery & Data Mining,* Anchorage, Aug 2019.

Deisenroth, M. P., A. Faisal, and C. O. Ong (2019). *Mathematics for machine learning.* Cambridge University Press.

Dheeru, Dua and Efi Karra Taniskidou (2017). *UCI Machine Learning Repository.* `http://archive.ics.uci.edu/ml`.

Domingos, Pedro (2000). 'A unified bias–variance decomposition and its applications'. In: *Proceedings of the 17th International Conference on Machine Learning,* Stanford, June 2000, pp. 231–238.

Dressel, Julia and Hany Farid (2018). 'The accuracy, fairness, and limits of predicting recidivism'. In: *Science advances* 4.1, eaao5580.

Duchi, J., E. Hazan, and Y. Singer (2011). 'Adaptive subgradient methods for online learning and stochastic optimization'. In: *Journal of Machine Learning Research (JMLR)* 12, pp. 2121–2159.

Dusenberry, Michael W., Ghassen Jerfel, Yeming Wen, Yi-an Ma, Jasper Snoek, Katherine Heller, Balaji Lakshminarayanan, and Dustin Tran (2020). 'Efficient and scalable Bayesian neural nets with rank-1 factors'. In: *Proceedings of the 37nd International Conference on Machine Learning,* online, July 2020.

Dwork, Cynthia, Moritz Hardt, Toniann Pitassi, Omer Reingold, and Richard Zemel (2012). 'Fairness through awareness'. In: *Proceedings of the 3rd Innovations in Theoretical Computer Science Conference,* Cambridge, MA, Jan 2012, 214–226.

Efron, Bradley and Trevor Hastie (2016). *Computer Age Statistical Inference.* Cambridge University Press.

Ezekiel, Mordecai and Karl A. Fox (1959). *Methods of Correlation and Regression Analysis*. John Wiley & Sons.

Faber, Felix A., Alexander Lindmaa, O. Anatole von Lilienfeld, and Rickard Armiento (Sept. 2016). 'Machine Learning Energies of 2 Million Elpasolite (ABC_2D_6) Crystals'. In: *Physical Review Letters* 117 (13), 135502. DOI: `10.1103/PhysRevLett.117.135502`. `https://link.aps.org/doi/10.1103/PhysRevLett.117.135502`.

Fisher, Ronald A. (1922). 'On the mathematical foundations of theoretical statistics'. In: *Philosophical Transactions of the Royal Society A* 222, pp. 309–368.

Flach, Peter and Meelis Kull (2015). 'Precision-recall-gain curves: PR analysis done right'. In: *Advances in Neural Information Processing Systems* 28, 838–846.

Fort, Stanislav, Huiyi Hu, and Balaji Lakshminarayanan (2019). 'Deep ensembles: A loss landscape perspective'. In: *arXiv preprint arXiv:1912.02757*.

Frazier, Peter I. (2018). 'A tutorial on bayesian optimization'. In: *arXiv:1807.02811*.

Freund, Yoav and Robert E. Schapire (1996). 'Experiments with a new boosting algorithm'. In: *Proceedings of the 13th International Conference on Machine Learning,* Bari, July 1996.

Friedman, Jerome (2001). 'Greedy function approximation: A gradient boosting machine'. In: *Annals of Statistics* 29.5, pp. 1189–1232.

Friedman, Jerome, Trevor Hastie, and Robert Tibshirani (2000). 'Additive logistic regression: A statistical view of boosting (with discussion)'. In: *The Annals of Statistics* 28.2, pp. 337–407.

Gelman, Andrew, John B. Carlin, Hal S. Stern, David. B. Dunson, Aki Vehtari, and Donald B. Rubin (2014). *Bayesian Data Analysis*. 3rd ed. CRC Press.

Gershman, Samuel J. and David M. Blei (2012). 'A tutorial on Bayesian nonparametric models'. In: *Journal of Mathematical Psychology* 56.1, 1–12.

Ghahramani, Zoubin (2013). 'Bayesian non-parametrics and the probabilistic approach to modelling'. In: *Philospohical Transactions of the Royal Society A* 371.1984.

Ghahramani, Zoubin (2015). 'Probabilistic machine learning and artificial intelligence'. In: *Nature* 521, pp. 452–459.

Gneiting, Tilmann and Adrian E. Raftery (2007). 'Strictly proper scoring rules, prediction, and estimation'. In: *Journal of the American Statistical Association* 102.477, pp. 359–378.

Goodfellow, Ian, Yoshua Bengio, and Aaron Courville (2016). *Deep Learning*. `www.deeplearningbook.org`. MIT Press.

Goodfellow, Ian, Jean Pouget-Abadie, Mehdi Mirza, Bing Xu, David Warde-Farley, Sherjil Ozair, Aaron Courville, and Yoshua Bengio (2014). 'Generative adversarial nets'. In: *Advances in Neural Information Processing Systems* 27, pp. 2672–2680.

Guidotti, Riccardo, Anna Monreale, Salvatore Ruggieri, Franco Turini, Fosca Giannotti, and Dino Pedreschi (2018). 'A survey of methods for explaining black box models'. In: *ACM Computing Surveys* 51.5, 93:1–93:42.

Hamelijnck, O., T. Damoulas, K. Wang, and M. A. Girolami (2019). 'Multi-resolution multi-task Gaussian processes'. In: *Neural Information Processing Systems (NeurIPS)*. Vancouver, Canada.

Hardt, Moritz, Benjamin Recht, and Yoram Singer (2016). 'Train faster, generalize better: Stability of stochastic gradient descent'. In: *Proceedings of the 33rd International Conference on Machine Learning,* New York, June 2016.

Bibliography

Hastie, Trevor, Robert Tibshirani, and Jerome Friedman (2009). *The Elements of Statistical Learning. Data Mining, Inference, and Prediction.* 2nd ed. Springer.

Hjort, Nils Lid, Chris Holmes, Peter Müller, and Stephen G. Walker, eds. (2010). *Bayesian Nonparametrics.* Cambridge University Press.

Ho, Tin Kam (1995). 'Random decision forests'. In: *Proceedings of 3rd International Conference on Document Analysis and Recognition.* Vol. 1. Montreal, August 1995, pp. 278–282.

Hoerl, Arthur E. and Robert W. Kennard (1970). 'Ridge regression: Biased estimation for nonorthogonal problems'. In: *Technometrics* 12.1, pp. 55–67.

Holsinger, Alexander M., Christopher T. Lowenkamp, Edward Latessa, Ralph Serin, Thomas H. Cohen, Charles R. Robinson, Anthony W. Flores, and Scott W. VanBenschoten (2018). 'A rejoinder to Dressel and Farid: New study finds computer algorithm is more accurate than humans at predicting arrest and as good as a group of 20 lay experts'. In: *Fed. Probation* 82, p. 50.

James, Gareth, Daniela Witten, Trevor Hastie, and Robert Tibshirani (2013). *An Introduction to Statistical Learning. With Applications in R.* Springer.

Jebara, Tony (2004). *Machine Learning: Discriminative and Generative.* Springer.

Kansky, Ken, Tom Silver, David A Mély, Mohamed Eldawy, Miguel Lázaro-Gredilla, Xinghua Lou, Nimrod Dorfman, Szymon Sidor, Scott Phoenix, and Dileep George (2017). 'Schema networks: Zero-shot transfer with a generative causal model of intuitive physics'. In: *International Conference on Machine Learning.* PMLR, Sydney, Aug 2017, pp. 1809–1818.

Ke, Guolin, Qi Meng, Thomas Finley, Taifeng Wang, Wei Chen, Weidong Ma, Qiwei Ye, and Tie-Yan Liu (2017). 'LightGBM: A Highly efficient gradient boosting decision tree'. In: *Advances in Neural Information Processing Systems 30*, pp. 3149–3157.

Kendall, Alex and Yarin Gal (2017). 'What uncertainties do we need in Bayesian deep learning for computer vision?' In: *Advances in Neural Information Processing Systems 30*, pp. 5574–5584.

Kingma, D. P. and J. Ba (2015). 'Adam: A method for stochastic optimization'. In: *Proceedings of the 3rd international conference on learning representations (ICLR).* May 2015.

Kingma, Diederik P., Danilo Jimenez Rezende, Shakir Mohamed, and Max Welling (2014). 'Advances in neural information processing systems 27'. In: *Semi-supervised Learning with Deep Generative Models,* Montreal, Dec 2014, 3581–3589.

Kingma, Diederik P. and Max Welling (2014). 'Auto-encoding variational bayes'. In: *2nd International Conference on Learning Representations,* Banff, April 2014.

Kingma, Diederik P. and Max Welling (2019). 'An Introduction to variational autoencoder'. In: *Foundations and Trends in Machine Learning* 12.4, pp. 307–392.

Kleinberg, Jon, Jens Ludwig, Sendhil Mullainathan, and Ashesh Rambachan (2018). 'Algorithmic fairness'. In: *Aea Papers and Proceedings.* Vol. 108, pp. 22–27.

Kobyzev, Ivan, Simon J. D. Prince, and Marcus A. Brubaker (2020). 'Normalizing flows: An introduction and review of current methods'. In: *IEEE Transactions on Pattern Analysis and Machine Intelligence.* To appear.

Kosinski, Michal, Yilun Wang, Himabindu Lakkaraju, and Jure Leskovec (2016). 'Mining big data to extract patterns and predict real-life outcomes.' In: *Psychological Methods* 21.4, p. 493.

Larson, J., S. Mattu, L. Kirchner, and J. Angwin (2016). *How we analyzed the COMPAS recidivism algorithm. ProPublica, May 23.* `www.propublica.org/article/how-we-analyzed-the-compas-recidivism-algorithm`.

LeCun, Yann, Yoshua Bengio, and Geoffrey Hinton (2015). 'Deep learning'. In: *Nature* 521, pp. 436–444.

LeCun, Yann, Bernhard Boser, John S. Denker, Don Henderson, Richard E. Howard, W. Hubbard, and Larry Jackel (1989). 'Handwritten digit recognition with a back-propagation network'. In: *Advances in Neural Information Processing Systems 2,* Denver, Nov 1989, pp. 396–404.

Liang, Percy and Michael I. Jordan (2008). 'An Asymptotic analysis of generative, discriminative, and pseudolikelihood estimators'. In: *Proceedings of the 25th International Conference on Machine Learning,* Helsinki, July 2008, 584–591.

Loh, Wei-Yin (2014). 'Fifty years of classification and regression trees'. In: *International Statistical Review* 82.3, pp. 329–348.

Long, J., E. Shelhamer, and T. Darell (2015). 'Fully convolutional networks for semantic segmentation'. In: *Proceedings of the IEEE Conference on Computer Vision and Pattern Recognition (CVPR),* Boston, MA, June 2015.

MacKay, D. J. C. (2003). *Information Theory, Inference and Learning Algorithms.* Cambridge University Press.

Mandt, Stephan, Matthew D. Hoffman, and David M. Blei (2017). 'Stochastic gradient descent as approximate bayesian inference'. In: *Journal of Machine Learning Research* 18, pp. 1–35.

Mardia, Kantilal Varichand, John T. Kent, and John Bibby (1979). *Multivariate Analysis.* Academic Press.

Mason, Llew, Jonathan Baxter, Peter Bartlett, and Marcus Frean (1999). 'Boosting algorithms as gradient descent'. In: *Advances in Neural Information Processing Systems 12*, 512–518.

McCullagh, P. and J. A. Nelder (2018). *Generalized Linear Models.* 2nd. Monographs on Statistics and Applied Probability 37. Chapman & Hall/CRC.

McCulloch, Warren S. and Walter Pitts (1943). 'A logical calculus of the ideas immanent in nervous activity'. In: *The Bulletin of Mathematical Biophysics* 5.4, pp. 115–133.

McGuffie, Kris and Alex Newhouse (2020). 'The radicalization risks of GPT-3 and advanced neural language models'. In: *arXiv preprint arXiv:2009.06807.*

Mnih, Volodymyr, Koray Kavukcuoglu, David Silver, Andrei A. Rusu, Joel Veness, Marc G. Bellemare, Alex Graves, Martin Riedmiller, Andreas K. Fidjeland, Georg Ostrovski, et al. (2015). 'Human-level control through deep reinforcement learning'. In: *Nature* 518.7540, pp. 529–533.

Mohri, Mehryar, Afshin Rostamizadeh, and Ameet Talwalkar (2018). *Foundations of Machine Learning.* 2nd ed. MIT Press.

Murphy, Kevin P. (2012). *Machine Learning – A Probabilistic Perspective.* MIT Press.

Murphy, Kevin P. (2021). *Probabilistic Machine Learning: An Introduction.* MIT Press.

Neal, Brady, Sarthak Mittal, Aristide Baratin, Vinayak Tantia, Matthew Scicluna, Simon Lacoste-Julien, and Ioannis Mitliagkas (2019). 'A Modern take on the bias-variance tradeoff in neural networks'. In: *arXiv:1810.08591.*

Neal, Radford M. (1996). *Bayesian Learning for Neural Networks.* Springer.

Bibliography

Neyshabur, Behnam, Srinadh Bhojanapalli, David McAllester, and Nati Srebro (2017). 'Exploring generalization in deep learning'. In: *Advances in Neural Information Processing Systems 30*, pp. 5947–5956.

Ng, Andrew Y. (2019). *Machine Learning Yearning*. In press. www.mlyearning.org/.

Ng, Andrew Y. and Michael I. Jordan (2001). 'On discriminative vs. generative classifiers: A comparison of logistic regression and naive Bayes'. In: *Advances in Neural Information Processing Systems 14*, pp. 841–848.

Nocedal, Jorge and Stephen J. Wright (2006). *Numerical Optimization*. Springer.

O'Neil, Cathy (2016). *Weapons of Math Destruction: How Big Data Increases Inequality and Threatens Democracy*. Crown.

Owen, Art B. (2013). *Monte Carlo Theory, Methods and Examples*. Available at https://statweb.stanford.edu/ owen/mc/.

Pasquale, Frank (2015). *The Black Box Society*. Harvard University Press.

Pelillo, Marcello (2014). 'Alhazen and the nearest neighbor rule'. In: *Pattern Recognition Letters* 38, pp. 34–37.

Poggio, Tomaso, Sayan Mukherjee, Ryan M. Rifkin, Alexander Rakhlin, and Alessandro Verri (2001). *b*. Tech. rep. AI Memo 2001-011/CBCL Memo 198. Massachusetts Institute of Technology – Artificial Intelligence Laboratory.

Quinlan, J. Ross (1986). 'Induction of decision trees'. In: *Machine Learning* 1, pp. 81–106.

Quinlan, J. Ross (1993). *C4.5: Programs for Machine Learning*. Morgan Kaufmann Publishers.

Rasmussen, Carl E. and Christopher K. I. Williams (2006). *Gaussian Processes for Machine Learning*. MIT press.

Reddi, S. J., S. Kale, and S. Kumar (2018). 'On the convergence of ADAM and beyond'. In: *International Conference on Learning Representations (ICLR)*, Vancouver, May 2018.

Rezende, Danilo Jimenez, Shakir Mohamed, and Daan Wierstra (2014). 'Stochastic backpropagation and approximate inference in deep generative models'. In: *Proceedings of the 31st International Conference on Machine Learning*, Beijing, June 2014, pp. 1278–1286.

Ribeiro, A. H. et al. (2020). 'Automatic diagnosis of the 12-lead ECG using a deep neural network'. In: *Nature Communications* 11.1, p. 1760.

Robbins, Herbert and Sutton Monro (1951). 'A stochastic approximation method'. In: *The Annals of Mathematical Statistics* 22.3, pp. 400–407.

Robert, Christian P. and George Casella (2004). *Monte Carlo Statistical Methods*. 2nd ed. Springer.

Rogers, Simon and Mark Girolami (2017). *A First Course on Machine Learning*. CRC Press.

Ruder, Sebastian (2017). 'An overview of gradient descent optimization algorithms'. In: *arXiv:1609.04747*.

Russell, Stuart, Sabine Hauert, Russ Altman, and Manuela Veloso (2015). 'Ethics of artificial intelligence'. In: *Nature* 521.7553, pp. 415–416.

Schölkopf, Bernhard, Ralf Herbrich, and Alexander J. Smola (2001). 'A generalized representer theorem'. In: *Lecture Notes in Computer Science, Vol. 2111*. LNCS 2111. Springer, pp. 416–426.

Schölkopf, Bernhard and Alexander J. Smola (2002). *Learning with Kernels*. Ed. by Thomas Dietterich. MIT Press.

Schütt, K.T., S. Chmiela, O.A. von Lilienfeld, A. Tkatchenko, K. Tsuda, and K.-R. Müller, eds. (2020). *Machine Learning Meets Quantum Physics*. Lecture Notes in Physics. Springer.

Shalev-Shwartz, S. and S. Ben-David (2014). *Understanding Machine Learning: From Theory to Algorithms*. Cambridge University Press.

Shorten, Connor and Taghi M. Khoshgoftaar (2019). 'A survey on image data augmentation for deep learning'. In: *Journal of Big Data* 6.1, p. 60.

Sjöberg, Jonas and Lennart Ljung (1995). 'Overtraining, regularization and searching for a minimum, with application to neural networks'. In: *International Journal of Control* 62.6, pp. 1391–1407.

Snoek, Jasper, Hugo Larochelle, and Ryan P. Adams (2012). 'Practical Bayesian optimization of machine learning algorithms'. In: *Advances in Neural Information Processing Systems* 25, pp. 2951–2959.

Steinwart, Ingo, Don Hush, and Clint Scovel (2011). 'Training SVMs without offset'. In: *Journal of Machine Learning Research* 12, pp. 141–202.

Strang, G. (2019). *Linear Algebra and Learning from Data*. Wellesley – Cambridge Press.

Sumpter, David (2016). *Soccermatics: Mathematical Adventures in the Beautiful Game*. Bloomsbury Sigma.

Sumpter, David (2018). *Outnumbered: From Facebook and Google to Fake News and Filter-bubbles – the algorithms that control our lives*. Bloomsbury Publishing.

Tibshirani, Robert (1996). 'Regression shrinkage and selection via the LASSO'. In: *Journal of the Royal Statistical Society (Series B)* 58.1, pp. 267–288.

Topol, E. J. (2019). 'High-performance medicine: The convergence of human and artificial intelligence'. In: *Nature Medicine* 25, pp. 44–56.

Vapnik, Vladimir N. (2000). *The Nature of Statistical Learning Theory*. 2nd ed. Springer.

Vollmer, Sebastian, Bilal A. Mateen, Gergo Bohner, Franz J. Király, Rayid Ghani, Pall Jonsson, Sarah Cumbers, Adrian Jonas, Katherine S. L. McAllister, Puja Myles, et al. (2020). 'Machine learning and artificial intelligence research for patient benefit: 20 critical questions on transparency, replicability, ethics, and effectiveness'. In: *British Medical Journal* 368.

Xu, Jianhua and Xuegong Zhang (2004). 'Kernels based on weighted Levenshtein distance'. In: *IEEE International Joint Conference on Neural Networks,* Budapest, July 2008, pp. 3015–3018.

Xue, Jing-Hao and D. Michael Titterington (2008). 'Comment on 'On discriminative vs. generative classifiers: A comparison of logistic regression and naive bayes''. In: *Neural Processing Letters* 28, pp. 169–187.

Youyou, Wu, Michal Kosinski, and David Stillwell (2015). 'Computer-based personality judgments are more accurate than those made by humans'. In: *Proceedings of the National Academy of Sciences* 112.4, pp. 1036–1040.

Yu, Kai, Liang Ji, and Xuegong Zhang (2002). 'Kernel nearest-neighbor algorithm'. In: *Neural Processing Letters* 15.2, pp. 147–156.

Zhang, Chiyuan, Samy Bengio, Moritz Hardt, Benjamin Recht, and Oriol Vinyals (2017). 'Understanding deep learning requires rethinking generalization'. In: *5th International Conference on Learning Representations,* Toulon, April 2017.

Bibliography

Zhang, Ruqi, Chunyuan Li, Jianyi Zhang, Changyou Chen, and Andrew Gordon Wilson (2020). 'Cyclical stochastic gradient MCMC for Bayesian deep learning'. In: *8th International Conference on Learning Representations,* online, April 2020.

Zhao, H., J. Shi, X. Qi, X. Wang, and J. Jia (2017). 'Pyramid scene parsing network'. In: *Proceedings of the IEEE Conference on Computer Vision and Pattern Recognition (CVPR).*

Zhu, Ji and Trevor Hastie (2005). 'Kernel logistic regression and the import vector machine'. In: *Journal of Computational and Graphical Statistics* 14.1, pp. 185–205.

Index